LIFTING MY VOICE

A MEMOIR

BARBARA HENDRICKS

CHICAGO
REVIEW
PRESS

An A Cappella Book

Copyright © 2014 by Barbara Hendricks
Foreword copyright © 2014 by Kofi A. Annan
All rights reserved
Published by Chicago Review Press, Incorporated
814 North Franklin Street
Chicago, Illinois 60610
ISBN 978-1-61374-852-7

Library of Congress Cataloging-in-Publication Data
Hendricks, Barbara.
  Lifting my voice : a memoir / Barbara Hendricks.
     pages cm
  Includes index.
  ISBN 978-1-61374-852-7 (cloth)
  1. Hendricks, Barbara. 2. Sopranos (Singers)—Biography. I. Title.

ML420.H3728A3 2014
782.1092—dc23
  [B]

                              2013037625

Interior design: PerfecType, Nashville, TN

Printed in the United States of America
5 4 3 2 1

To my parents
To Sebastian, Jennie, and Malcolm
To Ulf, the light in my life that illuminates my soul

"Negro National Anthem"
Lift every voice and sing, till earth and Heaven ring,
Ring with the harmonies of liberty;
Let our rejoicing rise, high as the listening skies,
Let it resound loud as the rolling sea.
—James Weldon Johnson

CONTENTS

FOREWORD

On November 20, 1948, when Barbara Hendricks's voice was heard for the first time on a rural farm in Stephens, Arkansas, her mother, Della, and her grandmother, Tumaie, could not have imagined the path that her life would take and where it would lead.

Her birth preceded by almost a month the proclamation by the United Nations General Assembly of the Universal Declaration of Human Rights, and she was born in a state in America where the Jim Crow laws, the model for the apartheid laws in South Africa, were the law of the land. As Barbara says, "for all intents and purposes I was born a refugee in my own country—born without the same protection under the law that the Constitution afforded every white girl born that day."

Barbara's voice has undoubtedly shaped her life. She began to sing in her father's church as soon as she could speak and her first repertoire was Negro spirituals, the music of the slaves with their roots in Africa and an expression of their suffering and hope for freedom.

Since then, Barbara has enjoyed a remarkable career that has taken her around the globe singing a repertoire that spans five centuries: opera roles, orchestral song, Negro spirituals, jazz, and blues. Today, Barbara claims to experience even more joy when singing than she did as a little girl singing a cappella in her father's rural church, because she is aware of the humility needed to serve her art whenever and wherever she sings.

Since I have known Barbara Hendricks, she has also used her voice to shape the lives of others and taken her responsibility as a citizen very seriously. For Barbara, her artistic engagement and her humanitarian engagement are one and the same; she believes that the place where "Art vibrates in us" is the same place from which the Universal Declaration of Human Rights has sprung.

I have been moved by Barbara's singing on a number of occasions; she seemed to have read my mind at the Nobel Peace Prize ceremony in 2001 when she sang, "Sometimes I feel like a motherless child," just before my acceptance speech, which began: "Today in Afghanistan, a girl will be born." And I will never forget her moving tribute after the deadly attack on the UN headquarters in Iraq that killed twenty-two of our most dedicated colleagues, including our close friend, Sergio Vieira de Mello, in August 2003.

She has sung for children in the ghettos of New York City, and over the twenty-six years that she has served as Goodwill Ambassador for the UN Refugee Agency (UNHCR), Barbara has comforted refugee children from Cambodia and Bosnia to Rwanda and Mali. Her commitment to the refugee cause and to the ideal of the United Nations working together for a better world is unwavering. Her dedication to the plight of millions of refugees by visiting camps, actively raising awareness, and providing the most passionate of voices for those who are forced to flee is an example to us all.

She has lifted her voice in song on the most prestigious stages of the world, in the cathedral of Dubrovnik under siege, and she lifts her voice in indignation against injustice and in defense of human rights. Her life has been fueled by an insatiable curiosity, a search for truth, and a willingness to serve. Through her work, Barbara has become a symbol of hope for millions.

KOFI A. ANNAN

Childhood 1

I learned that courage was not the absence of fear, but the triumph over it. The brave man is not he who does not feel afraid, but he who conquers that fear.

—Nelson Mandela

In 1948, Burma became a member of the UN, the Berlin Blockade started, and newly elected Prime Minister Daniel François Malan of South Africa began the apartheid era. In Montreux, Switzerland, the town where I would later live and raise my children, on September 20, Richard Strauss completed "September," the last song of his musical testament, *Vier letzte Lieder*; thirty years later this song cycle would become one of the mainstays of my orchestral repertoire. And in San Francisco, California, on December 10, the General Assembly of the United Nations proclaimed the Universal Declaration of Human Rights.

Also in 1948, in Stephens, Arkansas, on November 20, my mother, Della Mae, and my maternal grandparents, John and Tumaie Graham, heard my voice for the first time. None of them had ever heard of Richard Strauss or of the Universal Declaration of Human Rights, but they did know all about the Jim Crow laws that mandated racial segregation—America's apartheid.

"It must have been sometime after four o'clock," my mother said, when I asked her the exact time of my birth. She knew that it was shortly before my father, Malvin Leon, arrived home from

work around 5 PM. He had been a cook while in the army during
World War II and now, as a fledgling young pastor in the Colored
Methodist Episcopal (CME) Church, he was working in a restau-
rant kitchen to supplement his meager earnings.

I cannot presume that those first cries were in any way indica-
tive of how I would later use my voice. But I like to think that as
they penetrated the walls of that modest farmhouse and soared
freely into the countryside I had taken my first step on my way to
developing an instrument of service to art and justice.

In 1987 I started to work as a goodwill ambassador with the
United Nations High Commissioner for Refugees, the United
Nations refugee agency, and when I learned the official defini-
tion of refugee I realized that for all practical purposes I had been
born a refugee in my own country. My birth on American soil
entitled me to US citizenship but was not enough to afford me, a
Negro or colored child, the same rights and responsibilities of a
full-fledged citizen as provided by the Constitution of the United
States of America, a document that I would later learn to treasure.
Its Bill of Rights was ratified over 150 years before the Universal
Declaration of Human Rights. My parents and my grandparents
never told me that I had neither the same protection under the law
nor the same inalienable rights that every white male child born
on that same day and in that same place would have been able to
take for granted.

But for as far back as I can remember I had a feeling that confused me because I could not verbalize it. I know now that what
I felt was fear. It was as if an ominous, diffused cloud hung over
us, here and there, sometimes opaque and sometimes translucent,
ever present in the very air that we breathed. It was reflected in the
faces of the adults and nourished by the intense conversations that
took place when they thought that we were not listening. I wanted
to know more whenever I heard my mother speaking in hushed
tones to a neighbor or friend. I assumed that they were relating
tales too horrible to describe out loud. A story might begin with,
"Did you hear about what happened to poor Missus So-and-So's
son?" We children had to try to piece together the rest of the story
from the snippets of the conversation that we strained to hear
as their voices rose with indignation and anger and ebbed with

fear and pain. I picked up from their whispers and accompanying looks of sadness and inevitability a sense of an underlying shame in their own helplessness.

This ever-present fear seeped into our daily existence like fog rolling in from the sea. It lodged itself in the pit of my stomach. It never left us completely in peace. It seemed to come and go at its own whim. But a story, a word, or a glance could bring it back in an instant. Like most children who live mostly in the moment I could easily ignore it. But I was forced a little later in my life to learn what it was—and to defeat it. I have spent my entire life facing and trying to master this primordial fear, for to live without fear is true freedom.

Stephens is a small rural village in the southwest corner of Ouachita County, near Louisiana, whose population today is a bit more than a thousand people. During my first eight years I lived in similar communities in Arkansas where the great majority of the inhabitants, both Negroes and whites, were very poor and uneducated. Arkansas was usually classified in just about every positive category as number forty-nine of the fifty states, slightly ahead of Mississippi. "Thank God for Mississippi" was a kind of unofficial slogan. But I was unaware of life's trials and tribulations and did not know that my parents had difficulty making ends meet or that we were considered poor. My spirit was always free and I spent most of my time outdoors, in my own opulent and varied kingdom, discovering nature and letting my imagination run as fast as my legs could carry me. I climbed trees and communicated with every being in the real and imaginary kingdom of which I was the queen.

Ever since my first field trip to Namibian and Mozambican refugee camps in Zambia in 1987, I have been surprised to see how easily refugee children are able to laugh and play after being forced to flee their homes, having witnessed horrific scenes of violence and living with an uncertain future. The resilience of children is powerful; it gives me hope.

My grandfather Johnny and his wife were grandchildren of slaves and part Choctaw Indian. The Choctaw tribe came originally from Alabama, Mississippi, Florida, and Louisiana around the Mississippi River, and some members intermarried with freed slaves. Most likely my Native American ancestors were from nearby Louisiana.

I have no recollection of much in Stephens other than a gas station and a general store that sold everything from flour to heavy farm equipment. I loved to be on my maternal grandparents' farm and was proud that I had been born there. This subsistence farm barely provided for my grandparents' basic needs.

My parents were living near Stephens in Magnolia, some miles from the Louisiana border, not far from Emerson, where my father was raised and where his parents, Maggie and Clayton Hendricks, continued to live. I do not know if there was any particular reason that my mother chose to come home to her parents on that day but I am happy to have come into the world in the presence of my grandmother Tumaie, who herself had given birth to sixteen children. My mother was her eldest daughter.

I always looked forward to visiting them in Stephens, to going into the barn and climbing into the hayloft and lying there daydreaming. I would sit on the parked wagon, pulling at imaginary reins and pretending to give orders, "Giddy up" and "Whoa . . ." I tried to imitate exactly what I had seen my grandfather do when I rode with him in the wagon drawn by his two lethargic horses. He was a gentleman and never raised his voice to his animals or to us. He was always very caring to my grandmother, who for as long as I can remember was ill and mostly bedridden until her death. I do not know the cause of her infirmity but I would think that after sixteen pregnancies and births, one would be a bit worn out.

I don't have any photos of that farm or of my grandparents; unfortunately a camera was too much of a luxury item for our household. But I remember with tenderness and warmth the times that I spent there until my grandmother's death when I was about eight years old.

These memories are infused with myriad smells and sounds of the outdoors as well as the savory aromas of cooking that wafted from the kitchen out into the yard. I remember the feel and even the sight of the heat of the late summer days, the waves of humidity undulating in the air. When we came for Christmas the temperatures were much colder but we never had snow. Many of my uncles, aunts, and cousins would then gather around an abundant dinner table. We all brought our particular specialities and enjoyed them together with the dishes that my grandfather's farm provided: fried chicken, the Christmas ham, and a cornucopia of homegrown fruits and vegetables that had been preserved and canned in the fall. For breakfast we had bacon and sausage accompanied by delicious hot biscuits and gravy or cornbread that my mother made. I was especially proud that I had helped to churn the butter that melted on those mouthwatering biscuits. Today the smell of fresh fruits, especially oranges, and the sight of bowls of nuts remind me of Christmas because we never had them at any other time of the year.

My grandmother joined us in the dining room on the rare occasions when she had the strength to leave her bed. Whenever I took her something I would linger and sit with her for a little while. I loved her very much and cherished the moments that I could spend at her bedside. She was a picture of gentleness and serenity, propped upon pillows in her bed, her salt and pepper hair, more salt than pepper, braided and attached in a circle on the top of her head Indian style; to me she looked like a queen with a braided crown.

After her death, however, our family reunions ceased. My grandfather, unaware that his land had oil on it, sold it for a price well beneath its value, and the farm was torn down and oil rigs were put in its place. He later met and married a wonderful woman who, like my mother, was an elementary school teacher. Her first name was Ethel and my mother always called her Miss Ethel, so we did too.

I liked Miss Ethel very much. She was tall with a very noble bearing, articulate and cultivated. And she made the best hot-water cornbread I have ever eaten. Unfortunately my uncles and aunts were not as tolerant and supportive of my grandfather's new wife as my mother was. So my cherished family gatherings never resumed. We visited my grandfather and Miss Ethel whenever we were on our way to and from Emerson but less often than before. I missed the farm terribly as there was not so much to do in their new home. After my grandfather died I continued to have occasional contact with Miss Ethel; we corresponded regularly while

I was in college, and her sincere interest in me was an enormous encouragement.

Clayton and Maggie Hendricks were also poor subsistence farmers. They lived in a white wooden house outside of Emerson, very near the Louisiana border. My father, Malvin, was one of eleven children and his mother, Maggie, was a very authoritative woman. Her white skin and completely straight hair stood in stark contrast to the copper-toned and burnished complexion of Tumaie, whose warmth was also a contrast to the cooler ambience that I found on my father's side of the family. My father's brothers and sisters and their families often visited my grandparents and it was there that I met many cousins who came from as far away as Colorado as well as from nearby Louisiana. During my first ten or twelve years we attended the annual family reunion in the month of August and the revival at the country church where my father, the local boy, was often invited to be the guest pastor for the week.

During the revival entire days were dedicated to prayer, preaching, witnessing, and invoking the presence of the Holy Spirit. The wooden church was alone in the woods, with nothing but two outhouses nearby. Cars and pickup trucks arrived full of worshippers anxious to meet one another and to catch up on the news of those who lived far away. It was so hot that we had to roll down all the windows of our black Ford in hope that the warm breeze would cool us off a little. We arrived in our best Sunday clothes and hats covered with a thin layer of dust that had blown in from the dirt roads. We greeted each other with joy and enthusiasm. Parents rounded up children who were already running around and playing outside and we followed meekly behind them into the small white church that seemed to me at the time a towering cathedral. As soon as we were seated the church was inundated by the vigorous susurration of cardboard fans; the advertisement from the local funeral home printed on the back seemed to swoosh and swirl to the rhythm of the singing and praying. These fans were passed out to all, but it was mostly the women and some elderly men who used them. The fanning was a part of the ritual and it helped us all cope with the suffocating heat and humidity in the packed church. And those fans also came in handy to help revive some of the worshippers, mostly women, who were overwhelmed by their emotions and the fervor of the service. Sometimes they would shout and cry or run up and down the aisles and it would take several strong men to subdue them.

Men seldom gave vent to their emotions in such an open manner. It did happen—but it was extremely rare and probably not acceptable. Some of the ladies, the regulars, you could always count on to release their demons and sorrows this way during every service. When I was around nine or ten, we children would wait for these moments with great expectations, but we avoided sitting too close for fear of being hit with a stray handbag.

And of course we had to hold ourselves in check because if we were ever seen laughing or making fun of these pious souls we could expect to receive a severe punishment when we returned home. In *I Know Why the Caged Bird Sings*, Maya Angelou describes a similar scene so vividly that when I read it I laughed until I cried. She, however, could not hold back her laughter and was punished.

It was always very moving when the pastor gave the invitation to those who had decided to end their lives of sin and to give themselves to the Lord by becoming a member of the church. The entire congregation trembled with emotion and joy as the timid souls marched slowly to the altar accompanied by the congregation's choruses of "Amen" and "Praise the Lord." Even at a young age I could feel the fervor of their worship and see that their renewed faith comforted them and gave them strength to bear their suffering.

During these emotion-filled services, tears of sorrow and joy flowed freely and gave way spontaneously to songs of hope for a better life, if not here on earth then in the afterlife. Our voices rose and the sound filled the church and the surrounding fields and pastures. The congregation harmonized naturally, swept up in a collective catharsis.

The texts and music of these simple songs first taught me about our history of slavery and its inherent injustice. In Africa, song and literature were passed on orally, and this tradition came with the slaves to the New World. The Negro spiritual, America's richest musical heritage, was born of slavery. It combines a very simple expression of sorrow with Christian belief. Unfortunately, many of the spirituals that were sung in the early Negro churches of America were never notated and have been lost forever. Those that I heard and sang as a child constitute the backbone of my musical passion and inspiration.

When the service was finished the congregation streamed outside, hoping to catch a little cooler breeze. All the emotion had built up hardy appetites. In no time at all the entire field around the church was filled with tables set with homemade goods from the farm. The beds of pickup trucks were transformed into the most inviting tables. Those who had brought food shared their delicacies with those who had not. There was always enough to go around. There were many excellent cooks in the congregation, and eager visitors lined up at the tables of the ladies who were best known for one specialty or another. I was particularly interested in the cakes and pies. I liked my mother's cooking, but I also passed from table to table enjoying what I was offered. Since I was the pastor's daughter I was never refused. The good food nourished my body while the songs and the singing resonated in me, nourishing my soul.

As I grew older I became very interested in my own family's history, but unfortunately my parents never considered our past important enough to tell us about it. I tried once to make a family tree but I was not able to get very much farther than my paternal great-grandparents. My father sometimes spoke about his grandmother Harriet so I managed to gather some information about his family but little or nothing about my mother's. My parents did not have time to answer my questions. They were more occupied with making ends meet at the end of every month and preparing us for the future. They did not speak at length about slavery or even the segregation that we lived with daily.

I began at an early age to wonder why I was alive. I assumed that there must be some purpose and felt that the answer was somehow connected to the stories told in the spirituals that I sang because they touched me so deeply, so viscerally.

There were also some hidden, political connotations in the songs that the slave masters failed to detect. The singing of a certain song could be a coded message to those slaves who were planning to escape to a free state. "Steal Away" signaled that the time was approaching for those who were to be "stealing away" to freedom with the Underground Railroad. When I sang words such as "before I'll be a slave I'll be buried in my grave" it awakened my imagination about this time and brought me closer to the plight of the slaves and the dynamic power of the human urge to be free. The policies of the slave owners were particularly cruel. Immediately upon birth a slave baby could be separated from her mother, put on the auction block, and sold away from her family, her culture, her history, and all that could contribute to her identity—and thus her psychological, emotional, and social development. This was truly a process of dehumanization. A newborn slave was an object, not a human being. She had neither roots nor a past. Her future was the same as any other piece of property to be used at the whim of a cruel master who considered her of less value than the most common farm animal.

Nearly a hundred and fifty years after the abolition of slavery in 1865, American society still suffers from the side effects of its inhuman practices. In the segregated schools that I attended our teachers made a point to teach us about the slave trade, slavery, the Civil War, and segregation. This filled in the blanks and supplemented the emotional history that I had imagined from the spirituals. We learned about heroes and heroines such as Frederick Douglass, Dred Scott, and Harriet Tubman, as well as the many Negro inventors, artists, and scientists whose contributions still affect us in a very integral way. Our teachers taught us to be proud of our ancestors. Every year, the second week of February was observed as Negro History Week (Frederick Douglass and Abraham Lincoln were both born then). This helped us to understand our place in the cruel history of Western civilization, and complemented the American history that was taught to us from the hand-me-down books we received from the white schools after they had received their new editions. Not only did those books leave out the cost in lives and suffering of the slave trade, but they also ignored the importance of the contributions of slave labor to the building of the richness of our country. Of course, the white students in their separate but unequal schools did not celebrate Negro History Week and did not learn about Negro heroes and heroines.

After the civil rights movement, Negro History Week evolved into Black History Month. There should come a time when this month will not be necessary and my history will be incorporated into a history that all Americans can own. But the week was important for those of us growing up in the 1950s and '60s. And the word *Negro* holds a special place in my heart because I am so proud of the time when that is what we called ourselves. The many Negroes who fought and died for freedom and equality made it possible for me to be who I am today.

As my father advanced within the CME church we continually moved from rural communities to bigger towns. We lived in the parsonages, which were usually next door to the church. Thus my perimeters were rather small. Going to school was my first step outside them. With each passing year my space continually expanded to include new teachers and students. But most social and community events took place in and around the church. The slaves had been forced to convert to Christianity and found great solace in the life, teachings, suffering, and resurrection of Jesus Christ. They identified with the tribulations of the Jews in the Old Testament, and when they sang, "Didn't my Lord deliver Daniel, then why not every man," it gave them hope that they would also be delivered. Going to church and gathering together to worship was one of the only freedoms that the slaves were allowed. This freedom would later prove to be a very important pillar of the civil rights movement of the 1960s.

After abolition, Negro churches sprang up everywhere and in many different denominations. The Colored Methodist Episcopal Church began in 1870 in Jackson, Tennessee, and became the Christian Methodist Episcopal in the 1950s. The church was the center of the "official" society of the colored or Negro community and the pastors played a very important role because of the moral authority that position gave them. The pastors led, from within the church, the revolt of Negroes throughout the South from the beginning and throughout the civil rights movement.

My father was an electrifying preacher whose oratorical talent was more important than his theological knowledge. He intuitively conceived his sermons like a theatrical monologue and was known for converting many sinners from a life of transgression. His depictions of heaven and hell were so vivid that as a child I was often frightened by his sermons. The congregation hung on his every word, punctuating his phrases with their interjections of "Amen," "Praise the Lord," and the like. I was very proud of him and the admiration that he inspired in others.

These highly emotional church services and even stronger musical-spiritual experiences were my first contact with theater. They were in no way faked or make-believe, but they had all the elements of a theatrical experience. My father's first churches were in rural communities and the congregations were too poor to buy a piano or an organ. So the Negro spirituals and Methodist hymns were sung unaccompanied. The African tradition of spontaneous harmonizing made the sound colorful and rich. I can remember a song beginning with a single voice rising out of the silence, and after the first phrase the other members of the congregation, myself included, would intertwine the melody with harmony and fill every space with a joyful noise to the Lord.

Years later on Sunday morning, May 8, 1994, I arrived in Johannesburg, South Africa, from Paris to attend the inauguration of President Nelson Mandela as the representative of Federico Mayor, the director general of UNESCO. I held an unpaid post with the secretary general as consultant for intercultural relations, which involved giving my opinion and working on projects that would emphasize the importance of culture as a tool for conflict prevention and healing during reconciliation. We wanted to combat the more common use of culture as an excuse to incite war, barbarism, and destruction. The French ambassador met me at the plane upon my arrival and said that she planned to attend a mass in Soweto and added that if I wanted to come along we would have to go there directly from the airport, as the service was soon to begin. There was no time to go to the hotel to shower or change clothes. I was already overwhelmed that I could witness this historical event and I was not about to hesitate to visit Soweto, the scene of the brave student uprising in 1976. I still remembered the images of the brutality of the police against unarmed young students. Their struggle had finally triumphed after so many years of suffering. I felt that the new adventure facing the country would certainly present a very difficult task but in the long run would have repercussions not only for the neighboring countries in southern Africa, but also for the entire African continent.

We arrived at the Catholic church shortly after the service had begun and tried to slip surreptitiously into the seats that had been reserved for us. Soon after our arrival the choir began to sing unaccompanied and then the congregation joined in. I was stunned. I did not know the music but recognized immediately the way of singing and harmonizing that I'd heard so many times in my father's rural churches. Near the end of the mass, the French priest Emmanuel Lafont, who had served this parish for many years, introduced his guests to the congregation and shyly asked me if I would sing something for them. After a ten-hour flight and very little sleep I was certainly not in optimum shape, but I wanted to respond to the warmth and openness with which we had been received. I cleared my throat, stood before them with great humility, and sang two spirituals, "Sometimes I Feel Like a Motherless Child" and "Glory Hallelujah." They showed their appreciation by answering me with high-pitched sounds that resembled birdcalls whenever I sang in a higher register. In just a few moments, as the church filled up with the sound of my voice interspersed with those echoing birdcalls, I was able to make a trip that spanned two centuries and crisscrossed an ocean from Africa to America and back again. This deeply moving musical conversation I will never forget.

I had become interested in the struggle against apartheid while a university student in Nebraska. Then, in 1986, *Vogue Paris* asked me to be the guest editor of their December–January issue. Along with photos of myself in the world's major opera houses where I had sung and articles on musicians and artists such as Riccardo Muti and Maya Angelou, I insisted, against much resistance from *Vogue*'s editors, that they include a letter that was to be sent through Amnesty International, a letter I had written to South African prime minister Pieter Willem Botha asking him to liberate Sister Bernard Ncube, a prisoner of conscience. Back in Nebraska I never thought that I would live to see the end of apartheid, and certainly could never have imagined being in Soweto singing with these freed people.

But I have been singing about freedom since the first time I joined in with my parents at church. Both of my parents had good strong voices and often led the singing in church. As soon as I was able to make an intelligible sound I joined in with great enthusiasm. I cannot say now—because I did not I think about it then—if they had beautiful voices or not. They were so present in every service that it was like the sun rising in the east—a given.

My sister Geneice and my brothers Malvin Jr. and Michael joined in when their turn came to participate in the church services. When they were older we even sang as a quartet. But this did not last and I became the family soloist for church services, baptisms, weddings, and a lot of funerals.

Even though my talent was noticed in church at a very early age no one ever bestowed any special attention on me. That would have gone against the strict Protestant teachings of my parents. They believed that a child should be seen and not heard and was like virgin clay that they should shape according to the teachings of the Bible. To praise a child for a God-given talent would have been detrimental to her development, feeding one of the seven deadly sins, pride. This very narrow point of view didn't really keep me in line and most likely contributed to my natural rebelliousness over the years.

I was born curious and have always kept my eyes open, trying to learn as much as I can about the world and in turn about myself. I wanted to find my place. I did not know then that I was searching for freedom. My insatiable curiosity has never abated. I have always asked "What is the truth?" because I had learned in Sunday school that "the Truth shall set you free." I have always questioned the boundaries set for me by others and never allowed them to stifle my need to go further.

As early as age four it seemed to me that grown-ups had secrets about life that they were reluctant to share but that were written down in books. If I wanted to obtain the key to the chambers of knowledge, then I had to learn to read. My mother was an elementary school teacher who had not yet finished her university studies. It would take her many years of study by correspondence. She finally received a bachelor's degree in education in 1967 at age forty-four, the same year that Geneice graduated from college. I was impatient and benefited from the proximity of a private teacher whom I begged to teach me to read. When I entered my mother's first grade class in 1954 at the age of five I could already read, count, and write.

I read everything that I found printed at home and at school. I even read my parents' private papers and would play games with them to see if they had any idea that I was privy to information that I shouldn't have known.

School was a wonderful place. I rarely missed a day and had to be too sick to get out of bed to be convinced that I couldn't go. By the time I turned six that November my mother decided that I was too bored in her class. I was causing trouble for the other students, and it was good for neither me nor her that I remain. So I was placed in second grade with another teacher where I had a bit more of a challenge.

Aptitude tests were given to us in school on a regular basis to help determine our progress and in which direction we should be guided. I always scored very high in science and mathematics, so my teachers and my parents encouraged me to continue in that direction. I not only had an aptitude for mathematics, I also truly enjoyed it. I felt at home with the seeming certainty of numbers.

I always sang in church and became a member of the school choir at the age of twelve. Without ever considering a career in music, it was just a given that I would forever sing. But it was extracurricular.

I eventually learned that the certainty of mathematics was filled with grey areas and that constant searching often engendered a humbling doubt. I began to see the artistic aspect of science in my evolving quest for truth and meaning.

One day when I was in fourth grade, I was sitting quietly at my desk listening to my teacher explain something to the class and I had a revelation. It was as if a small voice inside me was warning me not to lose myself by allowing school to stifle my own questioning and reasoning. Education should help you to learn to reason and to think for yourself. I knew that my teacher wanted the best for all of us, but when one of us thought outside of the conventional box, nobody took it seriously. School was responsible for teaching children the rules and protocols of civil society. So I kept my little secret to myself. "I will follow the program as best I can and be the best student I can be, but I will always protect my freedom to question, analyze, and think for myself." This gave me a small sense of some responsibility for myself, knowing that I would not follow before trying to answer the question, "What do I feel in my heart and what is the truth?" To know myself and to be true to myself became my quest and credo.

At home my scholastic success certainly did not go unnoticed, but it was never the object of any overt praise; my achievements came to be expected. Only when I performed below expectations did my parents make comments, such as to question why I had received a B in one class and not all A's. Their attitude probably contributes to the fact that I am always a bit suspicious of too much overt praise or flattery. Not being easily flattered has been a real strength.

My father's position in the community led him to try to make his family a living model of what he preached from the pulpit every Sunday. He was authoritarian, strict, and at times severe and uncompromising. My mother believed that he was basically right, but during his absences she was much more tolerant of our failings.

For several years we lived in Magnolia, not far from my maternal and paternal grandparents, in a house that my father built himself; he was so proud of that house that he kept the plans for it many years after we left. We lived in a Negro community, but in many rural areas the Negro and white communities overlapped due to a shared poverty. Before I started school I played with white children who lived on the edge of our neighborhood, but these were the only white persons with whom I came in contact. We were oblivious about our racial differences, too young to care about the color of our skins. But the Jim Crow laws forced us onto separate paths. We were not even able to drink from the same water fountain. My parents protected me quite well from the ugliness, pain, and humiliation of segregation until I was nearly nine. But after September 4, 1957, it would have been impossible for me to remain ignorant of the terrible reality of segregation in Arkansas, as well as the existence of racial inequality in the rest of the country. My innocent and protected childhood came to an end on that day.

Birth of a Rebel 2

No one has yet realized the wealth of sympathy, the kindness
and generosity hidden in the soul of a child. The effort of every
true education should be to unlock that treasure.

—Emma Goldman

In November 1956 my father was assigned to the Miles Chapel CME Church in North Little Rock, across the Arkansas
River from Little Rock. My mother had already begun working in the Jefferson County School District the previous school
year and we lived in Pine Bluff, not far away. We traveled in our
little black Ford to go to church on the weekends until the end of
that school year. Our family had expanded by this time to include
my younger brothers, five-year-old Malvin Jr. and four-year-old
Michael. We spent the summer in North Little Rock, and I made
friends and sang in the church choir. Then we began preparing
for our return to Pine Bluff with my mother. I was eight years old
and was to start fifth grade at the same rural school where my
mother taught.

I do not know why we were still in North Little Rock on September 4, 1957. It could be that the Jefferson County schools
started their 1957–58 school year later than the Pulaski County
schools. But what happened at Central High School, Little Rock,
on that day would become a milestone in our country's history.

In 1955 the Little Rock School Board had decided to imple-
ment the 1954 Supreme Court ruling of *Brown v. Board of
Education of Topeka* that declared racial segregation of schools
unconstitutional. They chose to do so in the 1957–58 school
term. Desegregation was to be done progressively in order to
avoid problems. The Little Rock School Board chose Central
High School as the first candidate. This choice was not made by
chance: Arkansas was considered to be the most progressive of
the southern states and it was thought that desegregation would
most likely succeed there. Even though many segregation laws
were still in place, Arkansas was not known for racial extremism
and was gradually changing some of those laws, such as seating
arrangements on the buses.

My parents would have known about the plans of the local
NAACP (National Association for the Advancement of Colored
People) because nothing was a secret within the Negro community. They certainly knew Mrs. Daisy Bates, the president of the
Arkansas chapter who, together with her husband L. C. Bates,
owned the *Arkansas State Press*, a black newspaper. Before the end
of the previous school year, all of the Negro students who were
about to go into the tenth, eleventh, and twelfth grades were given
the opportunity to volunteer to enroll in Central High School for
the coming school year. Many students applied but only ten among
the most brilliant and emotionally solid were selected. Mrs. Bates
was responsible for guiding and advising them through their long
and difficult ordeal. They could not have imagined they were
about to be immortalized in American history alongside Rosa
Parks and Martin Luther King Jr.

One of the students was fourteen-year-old Gloria Ray. She
later told me:

> My father was born in 1899 and his father was born a slave.
> All of the children in my family except me graduated from
> Tuskegee University in Alabama, the oldest Negro univer-
> sity in America. He studied there under Booker T. Washing-
> ton and was the laboratory assistant to George Washington
> Carver, the great Negro scientist. I was in ninth grade and
> was about to finish junior high school when a paper was sent
> to us in the spring stating that Central High School had been

ordered to desegregate the schools starting the following school year 1957-58. We had to sign up to enroll in Central High School or the all-Negro school, Horace Mann High. I did not hesitate for a second. I signed up for Central High because it was considered to be one of the best schools not only in Arkansas but also in the nation. I, like the other nine, wanted to go to Central not because I wanted to desegregate the schools but to get the best education possible.

Central High School was in a beautiful five-story building with a pond at the entrance and marble staircases. It covered two blocks and, most important, had the latest textbooks and laboratory equipment.

Gloria is a remarkable woman. After leaving Little Rock she was a brilliant student at the Illinois Institute for Technology in Chicago where, like me, she received a bachelor of science in chemistry and mathematics. She was in a class with the first women and Negroes to be admitted to the school. While there she was confronted with another kind of discrimination than what she had dealt with in Little Rock: sexual discrimination against women, which forced her to confront the obstacles facing both Negro and white women who wanted to pursue a higher education. She also met her future husband, Christer Karlmark from Sweden, there.

When I was remembering and researching information about the Little Rock students I recalled that my Swedish mother-in-law, Margareta, had given me an article in a Swedish newspaper about Gloria turning sixty. She lived in Stockholm. I read the article with great interest and thought, I hope to meet this great lady sometime. I contacted Gloria and invited her and her husband to a concert that I was singing in Stockholm's Konserthus. We met briefly after the concert and I was so moved. We sat face to face, just two little girls from Little Rock. I told her that I was writing this book and asked if they would like to come for lunch and tell me about her experiences in 1957. She agreed and they arrived on a mild winter's day, their arms full of clippings and a scrapbook of the events. She and I sat around the table reminiscing about our similar childhood experiences. I felt like I had found a lost sister, and my husband, Ulf, discovered facts about life under Jim Crow that he couldn't have previously imagined had occurred so recently. Gloria and I shared similar memories and fears about traveling through Mississippi and playing with white children with whom we could not go to school or sit next to at a coffee counter. Suddenly I was transported back more than fifty years and the past came back to me so vividly. I saw the same faces twisted with hatred and the terrifying cries from the mob as Gloria told me her story:

> I was the youngest in my family and was very protected by my parents. Carlotta Walls and I had already registered for the school in August and that had not been a problem so we were looking forward to our first day in school.
>
> The principal was against the desegregation of his school and when it became clear that some Negro students seriously intended to come, segregationists from all over the South decided to organize against it. They felt they had to stop this from happening because it would signal the end of their "way of life." The media sent out fearmongering messages about desegregation such as, "Do you want your daughter to marry a Negro?" Governor Orval Faubus, who was a moderate and who had not been against desegregating the schools, saw the writing on the electoral wall. In a televised address made the night before the first day of school he declared that integration was impossible and ordered the Arkansas National Guard to surround the school and to keep all Negroes out. He was up for reelection.
>
> This move surprised everyone at the NAACP, especially Mrs. Daisy Bates, who would have never imagined that Faubus would defy the Supreme Court ruling to "desegregate schools with all deliberate speed." The first day of school should have been September 3 but we did not go to Central High because it was completely surrounded by the soldiers of the Arkansas National Guard. That evening Mrs. Daisy Bates was very concerned about our safety; she called a white minister, Rev. Dunbar Ogden, a supporter of integration, to help to devise a plan for the next day, September 4, that we hoped would be our first day of school. It was decided that we would go to the school but that all ten of us

should go together. So we—Ernest Green, Jane Hall, Jefferson Thomas, Terrence Roberts, Carlotta Walls, Minnijean Brown, Thelma Mothershed, and I, accompanied by Reverend Ogden, his son who was also a minister, two Negro ministers, Reverend Driver and Reverend Bass, and Mrs. Bates—arrived together at the school. Melba Pattillo and her mother did not make it to our meeting place because they were accosted by some white men and chased back to their car, barely escaping with their lives.

During the summer and especially after registering for school I had everything to look forward to because of the quality of the education that I would receive. My head was full of the dreams that I would have a life like the white girls that I had seen in television series. But it was not to be so.

When we arrived the soldiers blocked our path to the entrance, but when a white student came to the entrance they would open the way and let them enter. Ernest, who was the oldest asked, "Does this mean that you aren't going to let us go to school today?" And the answer was a simple yes. The image of the Arkansas National Guard blocking us at the entrance and the mob of angry whites that surrounded us was seen around the world.

But Elizabeth Eckford was living a worse nightmare: she arrived alone at the school on the corner that was nearest her home. Mrs. Bates and Reverend Ogden had spent many hours trying to convince several white and Negro clergymen to accompany us but without success. In the wee hours of the morning Mrs. Bates called all of our parents to explain the plan to meet the next morning. Elizabeth's family did not have a telephone and it was too late to go to her home so Mrs. Bates had planned to go there before the meeting to inform her. She was in her car on the way to the meeting when she heard the news on the radio that one of the Negro students was completely surrounded by a mob screaming "lynch her, lynch her." She had forgotten to inform Elizabeth.

Elizabeth said, "They moved closer and closer. . . . Somebody started yelling. . . . I tried to see a friendly face somewhere in the crowd—someone who maybe could help.

I looked into the face of an old woman and it seemed a kind face, but when I looked at her again, she spat on me."

Fortunately another white woman ushered Elizabeth into a bus, which probably saved her life. The images of poor Elizabeth Eckford being threatened by the white mob shocked the nation and the world. After the confrontations that day the parents of Jane Hall, who had registered in my class, pulled her out under pressure and enrolled her in Horace Mann High. Thus we became the Little Rock Nine.

Word spread quickly throughout the Negro community that the nine Negro students who had tried to enter Central High School that morning had been turned away by the Arkansas National Guard. We did not have a television at home and I found myself that evening seated in front of our next-door neighbor's television watching the news with my parents. I had previously been allowed to watch children's programs on Saturday mornings with their children. I do not know why I was permitted to come along; maybe in the fear and confusion my parents had not noticed that I had followed them. I don't think that they had expected the scenes that we saw. We sat in North Little Rock, watching the unbelievable black-and-white images that were so compelling it felt as if everything were happening in that very room. The proximity of the events made it all even more chilling.

I could never forget what I saw and heard, the visceral hatred and the overall menace of ugly violence. I had always enjoyed being in school: even before the end of the summer vacation I began to be eager for the new school year to begin and looked forward to the first day. It was a place of peace and security for me. But what I saw on that day turned my world upside down.

The following days and weeks we listened to the radio and watched the television, following with fear those courageous teenagers whom I did not know but with whom I identified so strongly.

Gloria recalls:

We did not return to the school, and while the National Guard stayed posted around it, NAACP lawyers led by Thurgood Marshall, who had argued the case of *Brown v. Board of Education* before the Supreme Court and would later become the first Negro Supreme Court justice, led the court battles. They were finally granted an injunction that prevented Governor Faubus from using the Arkansas National Guard to block the entrance to the school. He took them away and replaced them with the Little Rock City Police.

We had been waiting nearly three weeks not knowing when or if we would go to school. We gathered together to study so as not to get too far behind. On the twenty-third of September, three days before my fifteenth birthday, we went into the school for the first time, but by a side door. When we arrived in our first classes some white students left the building. There was a horrible mob outside composed of segregationists from all over the South, many from Alabama and Mississippi. I could hear the noise of the crowd and, as I was curious, I went to sharpen my pencil—the sharpener was near the window. I saw the mob below and I was petrified to see their angry faces and to read the hateful messages. It was the most frightening day of my life.

When the mob heard that we had entered the school they went mad. The city police was not going to be able to contain them. We went to our classes but after two or three hours we were all called from our respective classes to the principal's office and the police told us that we were to go down to the basement of the school where cars were waiting to take us out of the building. We could not hear the noise down there. The police told us to stay on the floor of the car and not raise our heads. I did not see anything but as the car advanced through the mob the sound of their voices drowned out my own heart beating. Gradually the sound died down and we were well away from the mob.

The mob wanted blood. Four Negro journalists were attacked and one photographer, a veteran of World War II who refused to run when the crowd chased him, was beaten to death.

My father sent a telegram to President Eisenhower and the mayor of Little Rock also asked him for help; Eisenhower sent an airborne division of the US Army to escort and protect us. Finally, on September 25 we began our school year. From that day on we were picked up every morning, rode to school in army jeeps, and were escorted to the door of the school by parachute troopers. They escorted us to the entrance of the school and to each of our classes but did not accompany us into our classroom and thus could not protect us from the taunts and abuses of the students and teachers who spat on us, threw things at us, and tore our clothing with sharp objects. Every day there was something. I never left my books in my locker because I was afraid to find them destroyed. I remember one day I sat down in my seat and felt a sharp pain in my thigh. Someone had put a nail on my seat. Even though I was in pain I did not react. I went home after school and my mother took me to the doctor to get a tetanus shot. That was how it was all year. We had to accept lots of injustice and humiliation in stoic silence. None of us ever cried inside Central High School. One day in the cafeteria a boy spit in Minnijean's bowl of chili and she poured it out over his head. She was suspended from school but he received no punishment at all. There were two white girls who spoke to me; one was the daughter of a journalist at the *Arkansas Gazette*. She always spoke to all of us and she eventually received the same treatment that we received. The other white girl was in my class and we communicated by passing notes in secret to one another. Once I asked her in a note if I could speak to her outside of class; she passed me a note that I still have: "Please, Gloria do not speak to me, I am afraid of what they might do to my parents, the white citizens councils have eyes all over the place." My mother lost her job because she refused to take me out of the school. Daisy Bates and her husband L. C. Bates were able to get the national press to cover our story and this brought the shocking images directly into the living rooms of Americans all over the country and to the rest of the world and even moved President Eisenhower to act to uphold the ruling of the Supreme Court.

From then on, although nothing in my personal life had changed, everything was different. It was as if I had lived in a silent movie in black and white that had become in an instant a talkie in technicolor. The sound of angry and menacing voices filled my ears as their twisted faces surged toward me in blinding colors, magnified by their hatred and ignorance. Some of the missing pieces of the puzzle of our lives started to fall into place. I began to understand what that ominous cloud was about, what the adults were sometimes whispering about. Yet I understood nothing at all. The cloud had descended and enveloped me and its damp chill permeated my bones. All that I could see was the thick, grey fog. But there was a smoldering fire in the pit of my stomach that mirrored my desire to burn away the fog, to emerge from the obscurity of fear, to see the light and to be free. At the age of eight, I saw the faces and heard the voices of the ignorance and cruelty that was waiting for me in the bigger world, outside of the safety of my family and community.

Particularly troubling was that I could not fathom *why* they hated us. What had the Little Rock Nine done to deserve such hatred? What horrible deed had Elizabeth committed for which the mother of a white girl Elizabeth's age could even entertain the idea of threatening to murder her, and all other children like her, just for wanting to go to school and get an education?

My parents tried to assure me that I was safe and all would be fine. But they could not help me understand what this new intrusion into my life meant. They too were trying to come to terms with what was happening and to maintain for us the sense that they had some control over their lives and ours.

Now there would be no going back for those men and women, Negroes and whites, who were fired up to continue the struggle for civil rights in America. There was certainly no going back for me. I learned that I lived in a land where I was to be segregated from other citizens and that I had to live under different and sometimes arbitrary rules and laws that were all unconstitutional.

Now I had a focus for my overactive curiosity that had too often gotten me into trouble with my parents and teachers. I began to notice the other outward signs of this separation that I had seen but had not understood. After 1957 I saw so many WHITE ONLY signs in the toilets of service stations, in bus and train stations, and at water fountains and lunch counters all over the South. The sight of a WHITE ONLY sign that had not yet been taken away from above the door of a restaurant in Johannesburg jolted me back from 1994 to 1957 in a fraction of a second and I felt a chill go down my spine.

My mother could buy me an ice cream cone at the Dairy Queen but I could not sit down there with my family and friends and eat it. Before 1957 if I had asked my mother to sit down she would have found some excuse for why we had to leave and could not stay. Now she could tell me the truth: "You know Negroes cannot sit here and eat in the same places as whites." We could buy goods, hand over our hard-earned money, but we would receive only a portion of the services that the same purchase would normally have provided to a white customer. These inequalities would soon become the target of the famous sit-ins, started by a group of well-dressed Negro students in 1960 in Greensboro, North Carolina, at the lunch counter of a Woolworth store.

I had to learn to navigate these rules and to understand that not knowing "my place" could have serious and dangerous consequences, even for a child. From snippets of conversations I had overheard and articles that I had read in black publications such as *Ebony* and *Jet* I began to understand and piece together the tragic story of Emmett Till. Emmett lived in Chicago with his mother who had emigrated there from Money, Mississippi, where she had been born. In the summer of 1955, she sent him back there to visit her uncle, Reverend Moses Wright, a minister and sharecropper. Money had a population of fifty-five, a cotton gin, a service station, and three stores. Before seeing him off, Emmett's mother admonished him to behave himself because she knew about the dangers for Negroes down there in Mississippi. Negro men and young boys had to be especially careful and to watch their every step whenever they were in the presence of southern whites. We southern Negroes knew the written rules, the Jim Crow laws, but we also had to intuit the more arbitrary and unwritten rules of engagement in order to stay out of jail—or even to stay alive. We were supposed to know our place and always behave in a subservient manner in the presence of whites, no matter how ignorant, crude, or incompetent they were or whether they were adults or children. A misstep could be dangerous and life threatening.

Just over a month after his fourteenth birthday Emmett, who stuttered heavily, was brutally tortured and murdered. Roy

Bryant, the husband of Carolyn Bryant, and his half-brother J. W. Milam abducted Emmett from his great-uncle's home around midnight and forced him into their car where Carolyn was waiting. Some days later, his badly mutilated and swollen body, with one gouged-out eye, was pulled out of the Talla-hatchie River. It had been weighted down with a seventy-pound cotton gin fan so that it would sink to the bottom of the river. His murderers assumed that there was little chance that they would be arrested for the crime but they knew that if they were they would never be convicted. Justice was a one-way street in Mississippi when the crime involved Negroes and whites. No white man had ever been convicted for the murder of a Negro, whether man, woman, or child. However, I take note that they still went to great lengths to dispense with the body and to cover up their crime. But what was Emmett's crime? It was being born a Negro male who did not know his place and did not keep to his place. Emmett had been bragging to his cousins about his white friends back in Chicago and boasted that he was not afraid to talk to white people. On a dare he went into the store and said something to the cashier that would be his death sentence. The white woman in Bryant's Grocery and Meat Market was Caro-lyn Bryant, age twenty-one. It is not exactly known what he said, but it was said that upon leaving the store with his cousins and friends looking on through the window from outside, he turned and let out a wolf whistle.

This story has haunted me since I first heard it and I always think of him when I sing "Strange Fruit." He has received many tributes; one that moves me deeply is Langston Hughes's poem "Mississippi—1955 (To the Memory of Emmett Till)," which begins,

Oh what sorrow!
Oh, what pity!
Oh, what pain
That tears and blood
Should mix like rain
And terror come again
To Mississippi.

Rosa Parks is known as the mother of the civil rights movement. She was a seamstress at a Montgomery department store and secretary of the Montgomery branch of the NAACP. She said that she too was thinking about the young Emmett Till on the first day in December 1955 when she got on the bus at the front and paid her fare. Tired in her body from a day's work and tired in her soul from the affronts of the unjust Jim Crow system, she did not get off to enter the bus at the back but sat in the nearest empty seat. When the bus driver ordered her to go to the back of the bus she refused. He then called the police and had her arrested.

This sparked a citywide boycott of the bus system, organized by the Montgomery Improvement Association, who elected a young pastor new to Montgomery to lead the boycott. He was the Rev. Martin Luther King Jr. The boycott began on the day of her trial and lasted more than a year. During that year the buses stood idle and the bus company nearly had a financial collapse. The more than forty thousand members of the Negro population of Montgomery walked, hitchhiked, rode in carpools, or took taxis owned by Negro drivers who charged the same price as the bus fare. The boycotters received support from black communities all over the country who sent money and even shoes for those who wore out their own walking to and from work. Some brave local whites helped by driving their Negro workers to and from their workplace and they were threatened and ostracized. Help even came from abroad. Local insurers refused to insure the cars of those driving the carpools and taxis, so the British company Lloyds of London agreed to sell them insurance policies.

The segregationists then responded with terrorism. Negro churches were burned and bombed; the home of MLK was bombed. Many were threatened, beaten, fired from their jobs, arrested. Martin Luther King Jr. was among those arrested and he stayed in jail for two weeks. On June 4, 1956, the Supreme Court ruled that segregation on public transportation was unconstitutional. This great victory of the boycotters in Montgomery, Alabama, was a milestone in the march toward equality and would launch Martin Luther King Jr. to the forefront as a leader of the civil rights movement.

Of course I was not able to put all of this into a perspective that could help me understand where my small, heretofore rural life fit in the big pictures of these events. But fear now had many faces: that of the angry mob spitting out their own fear at Elizabeth Eckford, and the mutilated face of Emmett Till. But the fearlessness that I would strive to obtain also had several courageous faces: Rosa Parks and the Little Rock Nine.

We returned to Pine Bluff and I started fifth grade at the rural school where my mother taught. I returned to the protected environment of school knowing that my mother was never far away.

In 1958 Governor Faubus continued to defy the law to desegregate Central High School by closing all of the schools in Pulaski County for the entire year. Those white students whose families had money entered private schools and those with the opportunity went away to school elsewhere. The other students, mostly Negroes and poor whites, received no education that year.

This decision did not affect the schools in the rest of state. My sister and I began the new school year in the Pine Bluff city school system. In September 1958, I started sixth grade at the Townsend Street Elementary School. My brothers returned with my mother to the rural school that I had attended the year before. My teacher, Mrs. Whitfield, was also the music teacher. I immediately loved her and strived to be one of her best students. I discovered a love for the English language and its grammar in her class and I could sit and diagram sentences all day. I had a rather obnoxious habit that the other students did not at all appreciate of correcting them when they spoke in class. It made my skin crawl to hear bad grammar.

I had a very unpleasant experience with one of the other teachers. She took the opportunity to criticize me every time she met me outside of my class when Mrs. Whitfield was not around. It was so bad that I did not want to go to school, and when I was there I did not venture outside the classroom during recess. But in order to eat lunch I had to go out of my classroom to get to the cafeteria. I could not avoid her and she always managed to find me. I finally had to tell my mother about my problem and to my great surprise she defended me. She spoke to Mrs. Whitfield and then called the other teacher directly. The bullying stopped as abruptly and inexplicably as it had begun and I again looked forward to coming to my beloved Mrs. Whitfield's class. This episode was a real surprise to me because adults, even one's own parents, never took a child's side in a dispute with another adult. So I assumed that there was some bad history between that teacher and my mother.

That year the school play was to be a musical, *Sleeping Beauty*, and each student in the sixth grade music class sang a song that was a kind of audition. I sang a spiritual that I had often sung in church and to my surprise I was chosen to sing the lead role. The son of the principal of the school played Prince Charming. This was the first time outside of the comforting, familiar setting of my father's church that my talent was acknowledged and that I sang for an audience. The performance was a big success with both the students and the parents. I was most happy that Mrs. Whitfield was proud of me.

The civil rights movement was gaining momentum and its major events and activities en route to the passage of the Civil Rights Bill in 1964 would punctuate my entire journey toward adulthood. The violent crimes against Negroes and those whites who marched and sat-in with them would continue to appall the world. I was lucky not to have experienced any violent acts, but I knew that something bad could occur if I happened to be in the wrong place at the wrong time.

I began seventh grade at Merrill Junior and High School. The junior high school did not have a choir. I was supposed to wait to join one until I entered high school in the tenth grade. But Mrs. Whitfield had written a little note about me to the high school choir director, Mr. Wilford Glenn, asking if I could sing for him. Since he lacked a strong soprano section, he allowed me to audition, even though I was only ten years old. Without knowing or thinking about what I was doing I sang naturally as he played a few scales on the piano and I sang a song, most likely the same Negro spiritual that I had auditioned with in the sixth grade. I was able to sing over a large range with a solid and easily sung high C. He did not have enough sopranos who had that range so I was accepted.

Junior high school presented me with a new situation. I was to have a different teacher for every course instead of my doting Mrs.

Whitfield and I was a little nervous about it. But being accepted into the choir helped me make a smooth and painless transition.

Principal Cheney was notorious for his strict rules about the students' appearance. No sloppy dressing or unkempt hair was allowed. We had to be on our best behavior and respect our teachers like all adults expected in those days. Most important, he set the bar very high for scholastic achievement. He obviously inspired the teachers, who religiously invested themselves in their students, especially the gifted ones. If a student was absent from class the teacher would call her parents and ask why. They held the parents responsible and the entire tight-knit Negro community participated in the upbringing and education of the youth. If a neighbor or a church member saw one of us out of school on a school day, our parents and the school knew about it before we got back there. The teachers seemed to want to make up for the inferiority of our books and equipment with their dedication to the highest standards of education. When the schools were integrated, however, the best Negro teachers went on to the white schools, and in 1963, when we moved to Little Rock, both of my brothers went to the integrated Central High School where their white teachers basically ignored them.

My father was transferred about every two years, and in November 1959 he was to leave North Little Rock to start his new job in a much bigger church in Chattanooga, Tennessee—leaving, for the first time, Arkansas, his family, and his friends. My maternal grandmother had died two years before and I did not want to move to a strange faraway place. I had also just begun to make new friends at my new school.

I could hardly contain my joy when my mother told us that we would be staying in Pine Bluff at least until the end of the school year. It would be impossible for her to go to Chattanooga in November and get another teaching job. My mother would also have to make sure that her certification for teaching in Arkansas would meet the requirements for teaching in Tennessee, and then hope for an opening in the Chattanooga school district. So I got to stay in the choir at Merrill. My father moved into the parsonage in Chattanooga, and in order to be together for the Christmas holidays he drove back to Pine Bluff to fetch us.

When I learned that we would have to travel through both Alabama and Mississippi I was horrified. My overactive imagination conjured up the pictures of the mutilated body of Emmett Till, who was about the age of my sister when he was murdered. I knew that we did not have to be guilty of any crime to be stopped and pulled over just because of the color of our skin. I was praying all the time that we would arrive safely and that we might by some magical power travel along the roads invisible to anyone who might want to cause us harm.

It was a long trip and we packed enough food to make the drive because the restaurants and hotels that we would pass on the way were for whites only. We could never afford to eat out in restaurants in any case so we did not miss that. We did not plan any stops since we did not have any family or friends along the route. My father could have inquired about a CME church along the way but I assume that he did not want to stop either. The toilets in the gas stations where my father had to fill the car had signs outside saying WHITES ONLY. The facilities for whites were not great, but when they did exist for Negroes they were usually rundown and dirty outhouses. I prayed that my young brothers who sat huddled near me, totally oblivious to the danger that lurked outside our vehicle, would not need to stop to pee in the woods somewhere, especially after dark. I was praying the whole way that we would not have to stop at all.

We arrived safe and sound and without incident, but I was exhausted from the long trip and my efforts to mentally ward off the real and imaginary dangers that menaced us along the route.

We made this trip a few more times during 1958 and 1959 before my mother was able to find a teaching job in Chattanooga. Every time we made this trip I fell asleep when we entered Mississippi and only awoke when we had arrived in Alabama. This was evidence of the force of my will to not see anything of Mississippi. Maybe I felt better in Alabama because of Rosa Parks.

I had a clear, even soprano voice and sounded more like a boy soprano than the sixteen-, seventeen-, and eighteen-year-old full-breasted sopranos. My voice always carried well over the ensemble and my easy high register was an asset to the choir. The older singers did find it a bit strange to have a singer so young in their midst but I never felt that it was a big problem. Any resistance that they may have had disappeared after the first time I sang a solo in the school assembly, when I managed, without any strain, the high C at the end of Victor Herbert's "Italian Street Song." I had passed the test. Mr. Glenn had high ambitions for his choir and taught us a varied and rich repertoire. We sang, of course, my beloved Negro spirituals in wonderful arrangements for full chorus that were completely new to me. The repertoire ranged from extracts from Handel's *Messiah* at Christmas time and Bach cantatas at Easter to Broadway musicals and American operas such as *Porgy and Bess*.

Because of my young age Mr. Glenn was very protective of me. He never gave me anything to sing that would have caused me to force my voice. He was paying more attention to me and my singing than anyone had ever before. He listened to me, corrected me, and encouraged me. I was now a member of a real trained chorus and I loved every minute of it. The rehearsals were moments of pure joy for me. I did not feel the slightest need to stand out from the others.

Neither my parents nor my other teachers showed much interest in my vocal talents and my passion for music. I agreed that academic studies, especially mathematics and science, were more realistic keys to unlocking the door that would lead to a productive professional life. Since I sincerely liked these courses too I was in no way conflicted. I am certain that singing in the choir every day for two years enhanced my intellectual abilities.

In any case the opportunity to become a professional classical singer was not offered me. The idea was totally unknown to my parents and even Mr. Glenn never mentioned it. They must have thought it an unobtainable dream for a little Negro girl from Arkansas. We had read and heard about the great Paul Robeson and Marian Anderson in our studies of Negro history. Marian Anderson was the first Negro to sing at the Metropolitan Opera in 1955, albeit at the end of her career. I did not know that the young Leontyne Price, a young woman from Laurel, Mississippi, was about to be launched on to the world stage and would be preparing the way for my generation of black singers to follow in her footsteps. But at that time neither I nor those around me dared dream about my becoming a professional singer. When I see parents who push their young children to pursue careers on stage long before they or their children have any inkling of what such a career might entail, I am most grateful that I was not being pushed in any way. Instead I was learning valuable music lessons in a nonpressured environment. I have been able to retain the joy that singing has given me from the first notes that I sang as a child up to now.

Soon after my twelfth birthday I sang my first opera role: Amahl, the boy soprano in Menotti's *Amahl and the Night Visitors.* We began rehearsals in September for our Christmas production. It was a big role for me, but I didn't feel that at the time. I just had fun in the rehearsals and performances. I could have never imagined that years later I would meet and work with the composer. Early in my career I was often invited to the Festival dei Due Mondi in Spoleto, Italy, as well as its counterpart the Spoleto Festival USA in Charleston, South Carolina, both founded by Menotti. The first time that I met him it felt unreal. We worked together in the 1980s at the Paris Opera when he directed one of my favorite roles, Mélisande, in Claude Debussy's *Pelléas et Mélisande.*

I was able to maintain a good balance between my schoolwork, household chores, choir rehearsals, and performances. Because I did well in my academic subjects my parents let me enjoy my passion of singing in the choir. My mother sometimes worried that my older friends in the choir might have a negative influence on me, but the only problem that came up concerned my first pair of high-heeled shoes. All of the girls had to have the same shoes with their choir robes, so a very simple black pump had been chosen and reserved for us in a downtown store. But my mother thought that I was too young for them. This was a big crisis for me—not because I wanted to wear high heels but because I wanted to be like the others and not have it pointed out that I was still just a child. I thought that the problem was solved when my mother agreed to pay for the shoes. I was so happy. But when I returned home my mother took them to have them "adjusted"; our local shoe repairman had the heels cut down. The toes of the shoes now stuck up and I had a funny walk, but I was so happy to be almost like the others that I swallowed my pride, bit my tongue, and walked away on my toes in silence.

My father was away in Tennessee so he was not able to closely follow our daily lives and routines. Those years in Pine Bluff were easy and relaxed because my mother was more laid-back when he was not around. She laughed and joked with us. She made all of the decisions about our daily lives, although she consulted him about the big decisions for she knew that he would hold her totally responsible if something bad happened to one of us. I have always wondered if she would have been the same person if she had not married a preacher and had not chosen to take on the role of the pious preacher's wife. She believed in what she was doing and followed the rules of the church strictly, but I felt that she was harder on herself than was necessary. She was smarter, more educated, and more flexible than my father, but she always deferred to him when he was home. They both finished their college education by correspondence, studying late at night and on weekends. She not only studied for her own courses, but she also helped my father; if she hadn't, he would not have finished. We all shared in her joy when she finally received her college degree. Her perseverance was a great incentive for me to study hard.

She always encouraged my sisters and me to get the best education we could so that we would be able to get a job and take care of ourselves. She often said, "Never ever be dependent on anyone else for your livelihood." During those early years she was never financially dependent on my father because she always earned more than he did. When we moved back to Little Rock his salary was almost the same as hers, but both together were barely enough to support the family.

My life in junior high school still revolved around my home, school, and church. We attended a CME church in Pine Bluff on Sundays, but since my father was not the pastor there we were less involved. I had to do my homework for school but I also had my chores at home, helping my mother clean the house, doing the laundry and ironing. We washed the laundry in a large tub of hot water in the backyard and I scrubbed every piece with my small hands on a washboard before rinsing, wringing out, and hanging them out on a line outside. I had to hang them in a certain order so that they looked good on the clothesline. It was a big day for me when we were finally able to afford a wringer washing machine. I had to iron everything including my brothers' shirts and stiff jeans and the bed linens. I shared with my mother and siblings a small two-bedroom shotgun house with a small front porch and a backyard. You entered the living room directly from the front porch and then continued into a bedroom with two beds: I shared one with my sister and my brothers shared the other. The next room was divided into a small bathroom and my parent's bedroom. We ate all the meals that my mother cooked in the kitchen, the last room of the house. The back door led to a small yard where we played and where I did the laundry.

I had used the school libraries since I was able to read but I was now allowed to go myself to the local public library and spend hours reading and taking in the ambience of knowledge that permeated it. I spent most of my free time there and whenever we moved to a new town, the first place I wanted to seek out was the public library. That first library was in my neighborhood and was segregated. When we moved to Tennessee I went to integrated libraries for the first time.

My father followed closely the progress of the civil rights movement and met often with ministers from other churches to discuss the news from all over the country. Martin Luther King's nonviolent ideas, inspired by Gandhi, were a motto for them and the strength of the movement. Like King they kept their eyes on the goal of peacefully winning rights for all Americans, putting an end to injustice, and not seeking revenge for past injustices. The Negro and colored churches were largely independent of the white establishment since their financial support came from their members. But those members were dependent on the white community for their jobs. The ministers had to walk a fine line between activism and the protection of their congregations. They managed to find ways to support student activists without exposing themselves to too much danger. When my father participated in marches and sit-ins we were never allowed to come along because we were too young—and because of the potential danger. My parents spoke about whites with frustration, anger, and sometimes fear in their voices, but they never taught me to me hate the white race. Before moving to Pine Bluff I had lived very near white families and even played with their children. I did not fear them nor did we care about the difference in the color of our skin. Not all whites in the South were racists. Many were courageous and actively supported and participated in the civil rights movement. They too envisioned an America for Americans of all races and religions. I am grateful that my parents taught me to differentiate between the act of a person and the group to which that person belongs. I have learned that fear and hatred are like tangled knots that grow and grow inside oneself and can easily take over one's soul, suffocating the very energy that gives meaning to life. Once they are installed it requires a strong will to unravel them and to free one's soul from their embrace.

We moved to Chattanooga in May 1960. I had been living in Pine Bluff for nearly five years, a long time for a child. We had been moving since I was born but this time was harder than ever. From then on each new move and separation would prove to be more difficult than the previous one.

When we arrived my father was in the midst of overseeing the construction of the new building of the Phillips Temple CME Church. It had been forced to relocate from its old address in 1959 because of an urban renewal project. This happens to poor people all over the world—they are forced to move from their land because some developer who has the authorities on his side or in his pocket wants to have it. The parsonage was a big two-story house on Vine Street that seemed like a mansion to me. Geneice and I would no longer have to share a room with my brothers. There were three bedrooms; one was for my sister and me, and we would each have our own bed.

During the past three years my mother had been the authority in the home. Now my father would be the head of the household. I was twelve going on thirteen and I was not about to accept the new rules without some resistance. My father most likely felt that he had missed out on a part of our lives during those two years that we were in Pine Bluff without him and wanted to make up for this lost time. He did not explain it to us in that way but it was clear that he was now the boss. Maybe the bigger church and the fine house situated at the edge of the University of Tennessee campus made him want to live up to the image of the man that he thought he had now become.

I found many of his rules arbitrary. I was hurt that he did not see me as Barbara, with my own attributes and my own faults. I felt that I was generically "girl-child number two." I defied him and questioned him when I found him unjust. When I was seven or eight years old, I loved to ask him silly religious questions that children ask such as, "Can God make a rock so heavy that even he can't pick it up?" Or more seriously, "Would God condemn a child to hell who was born and lived in another county far away and did not have the benefit to have a pastor as a father and to know about Jesus and the teachings of Christianity?" Even the silly questions were asked in earnest and I wanted a serious, honest answer. He tried to answer me, all the while showing little patience for the latent insolence behind my questioning. But now he often met my resistance to his newly reclaimed authority with corporal punishment and more work to do at home.

My mother fell ill after our arrival in Chattanooga and spent most of the summer in bed, reminding me a little of my grandmother Tumaie. I never knew the cause of her illness but I assumed that it might be contagious since my father rarely went in to her. My sister said that it was tuberculosis. Mom never told us and Dad never talked about it at all. He was very afraid to be ill. He had quite a fear of death. We were not allowed to go away from home nor did he drive the car on holidays such as the Fourth of July because of the high rate of car accidents on those days. I wondered to myself, "Why is he so afraid to die? Isn't he anxious to get to heaven and meet Jesus?" Sometimes it seemed that he doubted his own beliefs, although you would never know that when he preached a sermon. I began to be bolder about pointing out the hypocrisy that I sometimes saw in some of the pious and judgmental churchgoers. I sang at a funeral of a woman whose husband had mistreated her during their entire marriage, but during the funeral service he was howling with grief and even tried to throw himself into the grave with her casket at her burial. When I remarked to my father afterward, "Wasn't that something? He never had a kind word to say to her when she was alive and now when it is too late he is grieving and putting on a ridiculous show, for all of us," my father said severely, "This is none of your business and I do not want to hear any more remarks like that from you."

I spent that summer getting to know my new neighborhood and the young people at my church, some of whom would be going to school with me in the fall. Since my mother was bedridden, she was unable to do any housework, so my summer vacation was filled with chores that I shared with my sister. My brothers were too young to help with much. When we lived in Pine Bluff I was eager to show my mother how well I could take care of the laundry. I was especially good at ironing. Whenever Geneice had ironed a shirt it was more wrinkled than it had been when it was still hanging on the clothesline. Maybe she was just very clever about getting out of doing this chore. So my mother said, "Barbara, you iron so well, you continue to do that." I did not have to iron my father's white shirts in Pine Bluff, but now all of his white shirts and his handkerchiefs were added to my ironing pile. He wore a white shirt, either with short or long sleeves, every day of the year, with a tie and a white handkerchief in the breast pocket of his suit jacket. I never saw him wear a T-shirt or jeans. I took care of the cleaning and laundry and my sister did the shopping and cooking. My father was a good cook and had prepared meals for the family when we lived in Magnolia when my mother was working everyday. But now he only came into the kitchen to lecture us about cleanliness and our lack of order. This fit in with the new role that he had designed for himself in our lives, and the fact that my mother was confined to her bed made it difficult for us to run to her to complain or seek sympathy.

My mother recovered in time to start teaching in September in the school where she had found a job. I was so glad when she was well enough to return to the kitchen to prepare our meals. I had really missed her cooking.

On the first day of school at East Fifth Street Junior High, the first thing that I did was to ask about a choir, but there was none. The high school for Negroes in Chattanooga, Howard High

School, had a very renowned choir, but I would have to wait one year to go there. There was no daily choir practice so I was able to concentrate on my academic studies. I added French to my curriculum. I was starting in my fifth school so I had learned over the years to make new friends easily and to adjust to new surroundings as I let the longing for the old ones gently slip away. I managed to keep in contact by mail with a few of my girl friends, but eventually that tapered off.

I settled in quickly and was involved in many after-school activities including a theater project and the debate club. As captain of my debate team I was very absorbed in their efforts and, being a little bit of a control freak, I not only prepared my argument but also those of some of the weaker members. The teacher in charge realized this when in the heat of a debate one of my team members had to ask me what a word was that I had written for her. We could have won the debate on points but my stunt got us graded down. At the end of the year the theater group prepared a show with excerpts from the musical *My Fair Lady* so I did get to sing a little.

Chattanooga was the biggest city that I had ever lived in, and I was allowed to go downtown to the public library. I was so grateful that my father, in his zealousness to establish his own rules and boundaries for us, did not take away this permission. I also discovered the movies in Chattanooga. On the rare Saturday afternoons that my father would concede that all of my chores had indeed been completed I went with friends to a matinee performance. This meant rising before five in the morning so that I could go down into the basement, a part of which had been turned into a laundry room. The rest was dark and I imagined that unknown small beasts and maybe even ghosts lurked in the shadows there. But by getting up early I could wash all the clothes, hang them out to dry, clean the house while they were drying, and then iron them. I had to make sure that my father's white shirts were done and that he had an abundance of white starched and ironed handkerchiefs for wiping his brow during his sermon the next day. Ironing or any other housework was absolutely forbidden on Sundays. The matinee performance, the only one that I was allowed to attend, began at 2 PM so I had to finish my chores by one o'clock in order to have time to get dressed and walk downtown to the cinema. Sometimes my father found other chores that would have taken too much time for me to finish so I would have to call my friends at the last moment to say, "Today I can't come with you, maybe next week." I think that he wanted to protect me by keeping me at home but could not justify himself intellectually to me so he came up with extra chores that sometimes were not even mine to do. I felt that he was just being inconsistent and mean. When I did manage to meet my friends at the cinema we had to buy our tickets and popcorn at the entrance to the cinema, then go around to the back and climb the stairs to the balcony reserved for Negroes only. We refused to be belittled by this. We were convinced that the balcony seats were the very best seats in the house.

The majestic Smoky Mountains were one of the unexpected gifts of our move to Chattanooga and I fell in love with them immediately. I remember that on a clear day I would look at them in awe and I felt as if I could reach out and touch them. We went on excursions with our class to Lookout Mountain and Ruby Falls. Jim Crow laws meant that we could not benefit fully from the extraordinary natural beauty surrounding Chattanooga since some places and parks were for whites only. However, the view that I had of the mountains everyday, no one, including my father, could keep me from enjoying. I have loved the mountains since then and it is no wonder that I ended up living in Switzerland.

At the church, my parents encouraged us to be involved and I enjoyed meeting the other children my age and singing in the church choir. We went on hayrides and picnics, where the older teenagers would pair off in couples and find clever ways to avoid the eyes of the vigilant adults as they held hands or managed to steal a kiss or two.

I always welcomed the change in temperature from the torrid summer as the sun gradually retreated over the horizon. I love to feel the cool air on my cheeks during the first days of autumn, my favorite season. I can never forget the yearly display of fiery colors playing out against the magnificent backdrop of the majestic Smoky Mountains.

I enrolled in Howard High School in September and auditioned for the choir and to be a cheerleader. I could not walk to school as I had done since sixth grade; I had to take the bus or ride with my mother. Being a cheerleader meant going to all of the games, and there was a game every weekend. My father absolutely refused to allow me to take the bus with other students to and from the football games on Friday evenings, but instead of just saying that I could not be a cheerleader my father insisted that my mother would have to accompany me to every game. If she could not, then I had to stay at home. Sometimes I did not know whether I could go to a game until it was time for me to leave for the stadium. After missing too many games I was dropped from the squad. I resented more his lack of backbone and honesty to just say no to me than his actual strictness. We were too often in a tortuous conflict and I never knew how the dice would fall. The more he insisted on his new rules, the more confidence I lost in him. The more stubborn he was, the more stubborn I became.

Although many of the graduates from East Fifth Street Middle School went to Howard High they were dispersed into different homerooms and classes. I managed to settle in quite well and was starting to get noticed by the choir director. But just two months after I started, the CME Church's General Conference decided that my father should move again to an even bigger church in Memphis, Tennessee.

I had a hard time understanding this since the construction of the new church had just been finished; it was officially inaugurated in the presence of all of the biggest officials of the church in the spring of 1962.

As it happened, some of the money that had been raised for the building fund was unaccounted for in the books. I noticed during the summer that my mother often seemed to be very annoyed with my father and I could not guess what it was. She told me after we had moved that unbeknownst to her, he had "borrowed" money temporarily from the fund for some investment that backfired. She had had to help him pay it back. This news devastated me. In spite of his erratic and unjustified strictness I held him in the highest esteem and I expected and needed him to live up to my image of him. He had fallen far from that high pedestal near to Jesus Christ. His word and wishes no longer carried the same weight with me.

Memphis was a musical town: its famous Beale Street blues clubs, the "Home of the Blues," the home of Elvis Presley, and, since 1906, a stop on the Metropolitan Opera's yearly tour. We moved to the parsonage on Park Avenue, just across the street from Mt. Pisgah CME Church. Just after my fourteenth birthday in November 1962, I enrolled in Melrose High School, home to the Wildcats football team. The curriculum did not include French so I enrolled in Spanish. I immediately auditioned for the choir and was accepted. I also wanted to try again to be a cheerleader but all of the cheerleaders had been chosen at the beginning of the school year, so I settled for being in the pep club, a backup group. Nonetheless, during the games I screamed and gesticulated as enthusiastically as if I had actually been one of the selected cheer-leaders. The school was only a fifteen-minute walk from my new home so my father could no longer use transportation as an excuse to keep me from going to the football games. However, being in the pep club presented me with a more serious problem. After the games I often lost my voice due to screaming for our losing team and my choir director gave me a choice: the pep club or the choir. The choir did not meet every day so she said to me, "If you go to a football game on the weekend and scream your brains out, then you will be hoarse for several days which means that you will have to cancel the choir rehearsals until the end of the week, and then you start the same cycle all over again. What do you want?" Of course, I chose the choir although I was a little sad. My older classmates were a little condescending to me because I was two years younger than they were and my parents never allowed me to go out to parties with them. I felt a bit left out so I continued to go to the football games in order to have some social life, but I kept my mouth shut.

My father's financial transgression in Chattanooga had made it more and more difficult for me to accept his authority, and I continued to question and defy my parents. In spite of the impending punishment I dared to openly voice my opinions and my objections to their decisions. I refused to obey them when they ordered me to stop associating with a friend from school because her mother was single and had several children with different fathers. I had been going to Sunday school since I was four or five and my more tolerant and forgiving interpretation of the lessons of Christ and the meaning of Christianity seemed to differ from my parents' words and actions, even in the church. I questioned them constantly: "What would Jesus do?" "What would Jesus think?" I tried to use the teachings of the Bible that I had learned to justify my own arguments. I wanted them to convince me, and maybe unconsciously I still needed my father to earn back his authority with me. That would have made the unknowns in life less frightening.

We were not allowed to do housework on Sundays but I did have to help prepare for the Sunday meal after church. I developed a habit of arriving late for the service. I would actually arrive on time but I would hang around outside and not go into the church until just before my father's sermon. I did not dare to miss that. One day after the service one of the elders called me over to complain. He said, "Young lady, you are the pastor's daughter and you are supposed to be a good example to all of the young people in the church." My response to him was, "My father is indeed pastor of this church and he says that he has heard the word from God but I have not heard anything so I feel no responsibility at all to do the job of the parents of the young people in this church." I felt good that I had asserted myself and spoken the truth, but when this conversation was related to my father the price for my insolence was a severe physical punishment and I was grounded for several weeks. No more football games. The immediate punishment hurt my body and pride and the long-term punishment hurt my social life, but I remained defiant and more determined to think for myself—even if I had to hold my tongue and not always say exactly what I was thinking. I related this story to my teenage son, Sebastian, when I had to go to speak to his teacher about his disruptive behavior. He tried to justify his need to speak his mind by saying, "Mom, you always said that I should always speak the truth and what I said to the teacher was the truth. I said that she was a hypocrite." "You are right," I answered, "but sometimes it is better to choose your time so that you are able to make a positive difference with what you feel that you must say. The most important thing is to define your goal and seek the best way to obtain it, and sometimes that takes time and diplomacy."

Years later when I was studying in New York I began to better understand my parents and the many difficulties that they had been confronted with. Although I still did not agree with them about many things, being a witness to the struggle for civil rights made me more aware of our recent history and I grew to honor them for the many sacrifices they made and the difficult decisions that they were forced to take. I marveled at their ability to retain their dignity while cleverly maneuvering around the Jim Crow laws.

The movement had been constantly gaining strength during the seven years since the Montgomery bus boycott. Activists all over the country were working for the cause. I was soon to meet one in none other than the person of my half sister, Ruthie Buffington.

Ruthie was my mother's only child from a previous marriage. They divorced when Ruthie was only two years old. After the divorce Ruthie went to live in Pine Bluff with Mr. and Mrs. Ira Brown, her father's aunt and her husband. They lived in a big white house next to the grocery store that the Browns owned. Mrs. Brown was a tall, light-skinned, very strict God-fearing woman, a pillar in her local AME (African Methodist Episcopal) church. Mr. Brown was a tall, thin, mild-mannered man with the kindest eyes. Whenever we visited Ruthie he always offered me and my sister and brothers something from the store. We just had to say what we wished for. I always thought that Ruthie was like a princess and their big white house looked like a castle to me. Occasionally some of her other paternal cousins would be sent down from Saint Louis to spend the summer with their great-aunt to get a little discipline, but most of the time Ruthie lived there alone with them. I never knew why Ruthie did not live with us because my father always seemed to have been kind to her whenever we visited her or whenever we met in Stephens at our grandparents' farm for Christmas. During the years that we lived in Pine Bluff we saw her often.

She was attending the Arkansas Agricultural Mechanical and Normal College in Pine Bluff. The Merrill High School and AM&N had some collaboration for certain courses for high school students. Since I was in junior high school when we lived in Pine Bluff I did not have any classes there, but I enjoyed walking around the wooded campus, daydreaming about being in college one day. Ruthie was five years older than I was and in the spring of 1963 she was already in her third year of college. She was a member of SNCC, the Student Non-Violent Coordinating Committee, which had been founded in 1960 after the sit-ins in Greensboro, North Carolina. Some white students, who came mostly from the North, gradually joined SNCC. Ruthie had met a young white student from Ohio, William Hansen, who had come to Pine Bluff to participate in sit-ins. She called him by his nickname, Bill. They fell in love and in the spring of 1963 they were married in Cincinnati, Ohio, since it was unlawful for Negroes and whites to marry in the state of Arkansas. In April, when they returned, there was so much of an uproar in the press that Ruthie decided to come to Memphis to hide out for a while.

On April 16, 1963, Martin Luther King wrote his famous "Letter from Birmingham City Jail," while he was confined after being arrested during a nonviolent protest, as a response to a statement made by six white Alabama clergymen who argued that the fight against racial injustice and segregation should be fought in the courts, not in the streets. I have read it so many times and for me it is a must-read for anyone who wants to understand the civil rights movement in America. It included these immortal words:

> We know through painful experience that freedom is never voluntarily given by the oppressor; it must be demanded by the oppressed. . . . For years now I have heard the word "Wait!" It rings in the ear of every Negro with piercing familiarity. This "Wait!" has almost always meant "Never." . . . We have waited for more than 340 years for our constitutional and God given rights. . . . Perhaps it is easy for those who have never felt the stinging darts of segregation to say, "Wait." But when you have seen vicious mobs lynch your mothers and fathers at will and drown your sisters and brothers at whim; when you have seen hate filled policemen curse, kick and even kill your black brothers and sisters; when you see the vast majority of your twenty million Negro brothers smothering in an airtight cage of poverty in the midst of an

affluent society; when you suddenly find your tongue twisted and your speech stammering as you seek to explain to your six year old daughter why she can't go to the public amusement park that has just been advertised on television, and see tears welling up in her eyes when she is told that Funtown is closed to colored children, and see ominous clouds of inferiority beginning to form in her little mental sky, and see her beginning to distort her personality by developing an unconscious bitterness toward white people . . . when you are humiliated day in and day out by nagging signs reading "white" and "colored"; when your first name becomes "nigger," your middle name becomes "boy" (however old you are) and your last name becomes "John," and your wife and mother are never given the respected title "Mrs."; when you are harried by day and haunted by night by the fact that you are a Negro, living constantly at tiptoe stance, never quite knowing what to expect next, and are plagued with inner fears and outer resentments; when you are forever fighting a degenerating sense of "nobodiness"—then you will understand why we find it difficult to wait.

When my mother told me that Ruthie was coming to visit I was very excited. My mother had told us that she was married but nothing more. When Ruthie arrived my mother was unusually nervous, irritable, and short-tempered. Before falling asleep at night, I would crawl into Ruthie's bed and we would talk. I asked all sorts of questions about her life and about things that I never felt free to speak about with my sister Geneice, who certainly would have related the entire conversation verbatim to my parents. Ruthie was just shy of twenty but she seemed to be so grown up to me. She was in love and she was an activist. She told me all about Bill, that they both were members of SNCC, and the activities that they had participated in together. I sat and listened in complete admiration. I could hardly believe that she was old enough to be a real political activist. She wanted to help solve the core social problems of her time; SNCC was in the process of expanding its causes to include resistance to the Vietnam War and support for equal rights for women. It was a treat to lie in bed talking with her about boys and dating. This idyllic time was short-lived, however. In just a few days a journalist from Arkansas tracked my sister to Memphis and wrote an article in the Pine Bluff paper stating that she was staying with her mother's family there, that my mother was teaching in the Memphis school district, and that my father was the pastor of the Mt. Pisgah CME Church. The local Memphis paper picked this up and there was enough information about us, including our exact address, that we inevitably received a lot of hate mail, phone calls, and threats.

For some strange reason, when I read the first letters and threats that we received I was not afraid but completely fascinated. I wanted to read every hateful line of every letter. I noted the bad handwriting and even worse grammar and spelling. After a while my mother, who was understandably upset and afraid, tried to get to the mailbox before I could so that she could destroy the letters. This hateful mail came from whites from all over the South. They described in graphic terms exactly what they wanted to do to Ruthie, Bill, and us, her family. We expected to have crosses burned on the lawn and were afraid that someone would set the parsonage afire or throw a bomb into the house or church. Luckily this did not happen. I tried to keep all of the mail but my mother took it and destroyed it.

The reaction within the Negro community in Memphis was mixed. Many feared that actions aimed at us might spill over into a larger tragedy. Some also thought that it was an act of treason for a Negro woman to marry a white man. My parents were very afraid for our physical and mental well-being. My mother could have lost her job and the church could also have had problems with the city authorities. I know that there were discussions between my parents and the members of my father's congregation. I do not recall there being any call for him to leave the church. But something else was worrying my parents. I am not sure if there was an official rule of the CME Church forbidding pastors' divorcing or marrying divorcees but it was not known within the church that my mother had been previously married and divorced. I do not know how this information was received. This was never a secret for us. We knew that Ruthie had a different father and I had never given any thought to the details of my mother's previous marriage.

My parents and Ruthie decided that for everyone's safety it would be better for her to leave Memphis immediately. Ruthie went to Ohio, and only then did my mother agree to talk to the local press.

I remember my shock when I read the small article stating that Mrs. Della M. Hendricks was indeed related to Ruthie Buffington Hansen, but was not her mother! She had denied that Ruthie was her own child. This was completely inconceivable. My mother had been my ally against the overbearing strictness of my father but now she had also become a villain to me by not standing up for her daughter and being brave enough to suffer the consequences. What and who put enough pressure on her to make her do such a thing? She always refused to talk to me about it and as she got older she seemed to not even remember it. She and my sister reconciled their differences after many years when my nephew William Hansen III was killed in 1985 in a military plane crash over Gander, Newfoundland. This tragedy helped them to heal the painful wound that Ruthie suffered and the horrible guilt from a less-than-ten-line newspaper article. I decided that if Ruthie could forgive my mother, then I should too.

Once Ruthie was no longer in Memphis things calmed down, the storm blew over, and on the surface my daily life gradually returned to how it had been before she arrived. I never knew how the officials of the church and the school board had reacted; my parents never talked about that to me again. But this had been a horrifying experience. I knew now that racial violence was not a thing that happened elsewhere to others but could be around the corner for me, my family, and members of our church. The ominous cloud of fear that had stalked me since my birth had descended closer to me. The possibilities of our becoming another tragic statistic in the struggle for our civil rights had been very real.

The NAACP activist Medgar Evers was murdered in Jackson, Mississippi in June of 1963. In August we were uplifted and hopeful as we watched MLK give his "I Have a Dream" speech on television from Washington, DC. But again, horror struck on Sunday, September 16. A bomb that had been planted by members of the Ku Klux Klan near the basement of the Sixteenth Street Baptist Church in Birmingham, Alabama, blew up at 10:22

AM, just before Sunday school as the children were entering the basement, injuring many and killing four young girls. One was only eleven years old and the other three were my age, fourteen. I began to realize how real the danger had been for my parents and for us. They had had to deal with a very tricky situation on many levels and I am sure that they kept from us the most frightening details of this nightmarish episode.

When the new school year began in 1963 I entered the eleventh grade at Melrose High School. Geneice had left home to go to Lane College, an all-black CME college in Jackson, Tennessee. This meant that I would finally have my own room. I was looking forward to being in the choir and with my new group of friends. I was happy with my life. My parents gave me permission to have my very first birthday party ever. They had accepted that I could have my friends at home. I had been planning it all summer so that it would be just right.

I could not believe my ears when my parents informed me that my father was to be promoted back to Arkansas. I was devastated and had to cancel all of my plans. This time, he was to become the presiding elder of the district of churches around Little Rock, overseeing their pastors. I don't know if the episode with my sister Ruthie had anything to do with this move. I was not used to being told the reasons for most of my parents' decisions and this case was no different. We started to pack up everything immediately and the move took place on the weekend before my birthday, on the exact day that I should have had my canceled party. I could forget having a party upon arrival in my Little Rock as I did not know one single person living there. I was depressed and in a very foul mood during the packing and moving. Instead of preparing games, decorations, and a cake for my party I fought back the bitter tears as I sat in the middle of endless boxes.

Even though Little Rock was the capital of Arkansas I felt it was a demotion for me to be moving back to a city that was smaller than Memphis. The church calendar, beginning and ending in November, was very disruptive for families; children had to change school after the school year had begun and in the case of teachers like my mother there was an added economical and emotional hardship if they had to give up their job and search for a new one. The church eventually changed their General Conference to take place during one of the summer months, but too late to affect my scholastic and social life. My mother did manage to keep her post in Memphis and decided to stay there to work until the end of the 1963–64 school year, coming to Little Rock on the weekends and for the holidays. This was the sixth move for us in ten years and was of course the most painful for me. I was devastated to leave new friends from both school and church. As they are for most teenagers, my friends were more important to me than my parents and siblings. Leaving them meant leaving behind all that mattered.

I started school on November 18, two days before my fifteenth birthday. My parents had debated about which school I should attend. There were three choices: the infamous Central High School on Fourteenth Street that was desegregated and was walking distance from our house on West Twenty-Second Street; Horace Mann High School, the segregated high school for Negro students that was on the other side of town; or Hall High School that was located in a well-to-do white suburb even further away from my home. I had also looked at all of the possibilities and had selected Hall High School. It had opened its doors in 1957, been recently desegregated, and had an excellent reputation for high standards. In spite of my wishes, my parents chose Horace Mann. Maybe they had had enough excitement and danger in Memphis and preferred to put me in what they thought would be a safer and less controversial environment. I would have to take two buses to get to and from school. Since there were no special school buses we had to take the city buses and there was not even a special student fare.

We moved into the parsonage provided for the presiding elder. My father was to run the show alone, and I can't say that I was looking forward to it. With Geneice away at college and Malvin and Michael too young to help out I was going to have to accept more responsibility in the house. I was already used to cleaning and doing the laundry but now I would have to start to do the shopping and cook most of the meals. I also had to get my brothers up, prepare their breakfast, and get them off to the nearby elementary school. I then had to get the bus to school myself. After school I prepared dinner and helped my brothers with their homework. Since it was easier for me I often just did their homework for them. I realized later that I really handicapped them by doing this, and they were a bit lost when I went off to college and left them on their own. I was too young to know that and wanted to do what was most expedient since I had also to do my own homework after putting them to bed. At the beginning my father got up with us in the mornings to make sure that everything was in order but as I managed well enough he gradually let me take care of everything on my own.

I was a little nervous about starting over again in a new school with new teachers, new students and their social rules, and new protocol to follow. I can't imagine that I made such a good first impression that first day of school. I had such a long face and I felt as if I had arrived at the end of the earth. I knew no one at all, was regretting my canceled birthday party, terribly missed my friends back in Memphis, and was five hundred miles away from my mother. I also had a bit of a chip on my shoulder because I considered myself a city girl who had been forced to move to a smaller town and go to school with the hicks in Arkansas.

I signed up for the choir and was sent off to the choir room immediately on my arrival at school. I would have to pass an audition; if I was accepted I would start every day with choir practice. Choir and band members began their school day earlier than the other students because the daily practice began before the other classes.

The choir was preparing to sing in the Thanksgiving program at the school assembly the following Wednesday, the day before the holiday. One of the songs had a solo part for soprano and the choir director, Arthur Porter, asked all of the sopranos who wanted to audition for the part to sing it. When the last of them had sung, he turned to me and asked me if I would like to try the solo. I thought to myself, Is this my audition, in front of the entire choir? I had listened while the others sang the part so I knew the tune. I swallowed hard and said, "Yes, of course." I was younger than the four sopranos who were obviously the stars of the choir and who were used to sharing all of the solos. But I assumed that I was auditioning just to become a member of the choir, not for the solo part. Not only did I pass my audition but Mr. Porter also gave me the solo, which I sang a week later in front of the entire school. I do not remember what the piece was but what an introduction to the choir and to my new school! I received congratulations from other members of the choir, but mostly from the alto section. And certainly in that first year my closest friends in the choir were senior altos. I found my smile again and the choir immediately became my home at Horace Mann.

I had been in my new school only a few days when tragedy struck. Horace Mann was not a traditional closed building. It was built with breezeways and the entrance to classrooms were from outside. I do not remember how or where the announcement was made. Were we told in the classes to go back to our homerooms or to assembly? Maybe we were all in the cafeteria for lunch. The only clear memory I have is of wandering around in a daze, speechless, from one breezeway to another. It was November 22, and we had just learned that the thirty-fifth president of the United States of America, John Fitzgerald Kennedy, had been shot in a motorcade in Dallas, Texas, around 12:30. We waited, frightened and anxious, to hear the news about his condition, and when he was declared dead everything and everyone froze. Everyone, students and teachers, was in a state of shock. "What does it mean?" "Was this an attack from the Russians?" we asked. "Maybe a nuclear bomb is already on its way to attack Washington, DC, and other cities in the United States." The sirens that went off in the weekly drills that were supposed to warn us to take shelter in case of a real attack were silent.

On June 11, 1963, JFK had given a civil rights speech in which he asked Congress for legislation that would become the Civil Rights Act. Although he had been reluctant to meet Dr. King he did call him when he was in jail in Birmingham and met with him and other leaders of the movement in the White House on August 28. These timid acts gave some hope that the president would work for justice and equality for the Negro race. Maybe the assassin was some racist who was opposed to the president's civil rights agenda. Could that happen in America?

We left school early and all along the way the faces of everyone that I saw, white and black, mirrored the shock and fear that I felt. My father was home when I came in and he was also shocked and at a loss to explain to us what it all meant. My mother was in Memphis and my brothers were too young to understand what had happened. We watched the images that were played over and over of the motorcade, the shot to the head, and the First Lady, Jackie Kennedy, climbing onto the trunk of the car; we listened to Walter Cronkite, his voice breaking as he confirmed that the president had indeed died at Parkland Hospital in Dallas, Texas, at 1:00 PM.

After the benign calm of the postwar years the country had now crossed a threshold. With the luxury of hindsight we can see that this assassination marked the end of an era of innocence for so many of us and the beginning of one marked by violence: the assassinations of Robert Kennedy and Martin Luther King, the massacre perpetrated by Charles Whitman at the University of Texas, and the countless mass killings since then. In spite of the difficulty to live as a Negro in a segregated, cruel society, most Americans still believed that America stood for justice, and there was hope that justice would prevail. But those beliefs died with JFK.

I had so many questions. What would happen now, in the world, in America, in Little Rock, and at Horace Mann High School? The civil rights movement had awakened my interest in the politics of the struggle for our equality but I had not been at all interested in electoral politics. This assassination awakened that in me and it became imperative for me not only to know more about how our political system actually worked but also to begin to participate. I had not followed the election in 1960 closely and had no clear opinion about Kennedy. But I needed and wanted to know more. I had just turned fifteen and was coping with my feelings of personal despair during this moment of global grief and shock. The words that he addressed at the end of his inaugural speech to all Americans came back to me to give me strength and inspiration. "Ask not what your country can do for you—ask what you can do for your country." I wanted to be able to serve, not only my country, but also the cause for justice for all.

On school days I rose early and rushed through my chores so that I would not miss my bus. I was so eager to start off the day singing in the choir. But between home and school we had to get through the racial obstacle course where we were always reminded about our "place." Little Rock had not changed so much since 1957. Central and other schools were integrated and we did not have to sit in the back of the bus, but we were not in any way treated as equals. I remember vividly one day we had taken shelter from the rain under the awning of a shop near our bus stop. When the white shop owner saw us huddled together, she pulled the awning in and we were soaked. She would have had more consideration for a dog. Gratuitous and mean acts like this were painful but we learned to shrug our shoulders and go on our way. Away from the safety of my neighborhood and my parents and neighbors I had to manage my anger and hurt, to take in the blows and let them run off me, so that by the time I started to sing the first notes of our vocal warm-up I had already forgotten the incident. Living in the present did not mean that the incident had been erased. I had always used my sense of humor to cover up my sadness, fear, and shame, especially when I was in a position of weakness and could not fight back. So I made a joke or found something comical about our situation. Had we sought revenge and retaliated with some kind of vandalism we would have been no better than the shopkeeper.

I was always the youngest in my class and an honor student and my sense of humor helped me to be accepted by my older peers. I think that the other students often found me different, but I could make them laugh easily, albeit sometimes at their own expense.

We were always cautioned by our parents and teachers, "Whenever you are in the presence of whites, even white children, behave and do not draw attention to yourself." Since I was prone to say what I thought they added, "Barbara, just keep your mouth shut." My thoughts of poor Emmett Till were not far away. I longed to have magical powers to somehow wish myself invisible on the bus or in the streets whenever we were in town. Whenever we were outside our own neighborhoods we knew that we did not need to be doing something wrong to have a problem. How can one avoid being in the wrong place at the wrong time? Any place could have been the wrong place. Even our own neighborhood could become the wrong place if they decided to come into our safety zone. Like the narrator of Ralph Ellison's *Invisible Man* I too wanted to become invisible and to hide from the burning humiliation and fear whenever I felt in danger. Since the age of four I had had an imaginary friend, my good fairy or angel to whom I told all of my secrets. I asked her to make me invisible whenever I needed to be protected. Every day in class we opened the worn, secondhand books that had been handed down to us when the white schools had received the latest editions. Even our schoolbooks were constant reminders that we were considered inferior. Our science laboratories were an insult to scientific research. As we were not expected to excel there was no need to provide us with adequate facilities. Our parents and teachers repeated the same mantra to us over and over again: "You must work twice as hard and be twice as qualified as a white child in order to succeed in life." Even then we knew not to expect the same job as a white person with the same or even lesser qualifications, and certainly not the same pay. And of course we girls knew that we had also to study twice as hard as the boys.

At Horace Mann I had an excellent math and physics teacher and our English and literature professor was a legend in the school and among the alumni. Mrs. Harper was a handsome woman with a streak of white hair that separated her long black hair right down the middle. She widened my literary horizons with books by Negro writers such as Ralph Ellison, Richard Wright, and James Baldwin. In my senior year I had to write an essay on Joseph Conrad's *Lord Jim*, and this book also made an enormous impression on me. In it, Jim, petrified during a storm, abandons his ship, leaving the passengers on their way to Mecca to perish. Although the boat did not sink, for the rest of his life he runs from place to place trying to overcome his shame. He dies as a hero, accepting himself. I wanted my essay to be on the same level as the novel but my teacher was not so impressed. She found it too sentimental.

No one had guided my selection of books. When I was thirteen and fourteen I adored detective novels by Raymond Chandler and had a particular weakness for Perry Mason novels because of the popular television series. It was a mathematical challenge for me to find the solution to a crime myself before coming to the end of the novel. Mrs. Harper suggested that I join an interracial book club during the summer at the desegregated public library. One of the books that we read and discussed was Fitzgerald's *The Great Gatsby*. I understood little of this novel: it could have taken place on the moon as far as my life experiences were concerned. I could not in any way relate to the characters and I was not very good at analyzing it. I do not know what the other white students in the group thought about being in a mixed group, but I was surprised that my first experience in an integrated group of people was not only interesting but also unthreatening. We discussed things freely with one another but of course at the end none of us made any contact outside of the library.

Every Saturday morning on my way to the library I walked past the synagogue and was curious about the people who went to church on Saturday instead of Sundays. I had always lumped all white people together and never looked at them as having a multitude of origins. I remembered my history lessons about the horrors of World War II, and the sight of the synagogue inspired me to take out a few books from the library on the history of the Jews. Maybe that curiosity was a kind of premonition, considering the influence that Jews and their culture would have in my life.

My mother moved home from Memphis for good in the summer of 1964: she had found a job in the Pulaski County school district and I was happy to have her back. We moved to West Sixteenth Street in a house belonging to the church and later my father built a house in the lot next door. My parents had become accustomed to having me do the housework so I continued even after my mother returned. I found it hard to balance so many chores at home with my schoolwork but I managed. I became a very good cook because I had to learn how to prepare a tasty meal on a very meager budget.

In 1964 Ruthie, her husband, Bill, and a new addition to their family, baby Billy, moved to Little Rock about ten minutes from our house. She came by with her son to show him to my mother, whose only remark was that he looked very white. My parents did not want us to see Ruthie. I can imagine that they wanted to avoid the danger that had come so close to us in Memphis, but I felt that their treatment of her was unjust. I defied them and visited her at her apartment as often as I could during the time that they lived in Little Rock. I had to find an excuse that my parents would accept whenever I wanted to visit them or babysit my little nephew. One day when I stopped by, Ruthie was preparing dinner for a visiting guest from Atlanta who was to arrive shortly. I could hardly hide my astonishment and admiration when Bill walked in through the door with Julian Bond, one of the founders of SNCC. I wanted to stay for dinner and to listen to their conversation. So against any realistic hope I called home and asked my mother if I could babysit for Ruthie, but she refused. Ruthie was a true example of courage for me and was living her life in Arkansas in spite of the danger. She could have fled with her family to Ohio but there was still much to be done and the struggle was far from over. In 1965 Julian Bond was elected to Georgia's House of Representatives and Ruthie moved with her little family to Atlanta. She inspired me to learn more and I started to read everything that I could about the politics of the day and the civil rights movement. I had studied the Declaration of Independence and the Constitution and at the time of their conception neither the slaves nor freemen nor women were included. George Washington and Thomas Jefferson were slave owners. Nevertheless, these documents along with the Emancipation Proclamation of 1863 that led to the Thirteenth Amendment to the Constitution abolishing and prohibiting slavery in 1865 were an inspiration to me; I found that within these cornerstones of our nation lay the solutions to equality in America for all of its citizens.

Arthur Porter, our high school choir director, was also one of the most successful and sought after jazz pianists in the state. The Art Porter Trio performed every weekend in clubs and hotels. As Mrs. Porter was often with him, they needed a babysitter for their four children. I got the job. I have always been a "baby person" so I loved to take care of children—and I could earn a little pocket money at the same time. This little job became another learning experience for me. Mr. Porter had an extensive record collection and once the children were asleep, I would out of curiosity play some of the records while I sat studying or reading and waiting for the Porters to come home. My passion for jazz began in his living room. I discovered Count Basie, Oscar Peterson, John Coltrane, Charlie Parker, Nancy Wilson, Ella Fitzgerald, Duke Ellington,

Sarah Vaughan, Dinah Washington, Billie Holiday. He had everything and everyone. I would have loved to have been able to sing
with his trio but I was underage. I would never have been allowed
into an establishment that served alcohol, and whenever I timidly
asked to sing with him he said that it might ruin my voice. Even
though he never tried to persuade me to give up my science studies to concentrate solely on my voice, he was always very protective. He said to me, "I don't want you to sing too often in the
school assembly programs; when it is announced that you will
sing, the students and teachers should consider it a special event,
something rare." It was obvious that he considered my talent to be
special and I never knew why he did not push me toward a musical career. Was it that I would be only sixteen when I left high
school and was so committed to my studies? He certainly knew
what a nearly impossible task it would be for a young Negro girl to
have a career in America as a classical musician.

We had learned about great artists like Paul Robeson and
Marian Anderson and their difficulties. We were unaware of
the generation that followed, which included Camilla Williams,
Grace Bumbry, Betty Allen, George Shirley, and Shirley Verrett,
all of whom were making advances onto the international stages
of the world. But Leontyne Price's 1961 debut at the Metropolitan Opera in Verdi's *Trovatore* marked a point of no return. She
received a forty-minute standing ovation for her performance—
and for the history that she was making. This took place far, far
away from Little Rock. There was a movement in the opera world
of which I certainly was unaware; if Arthur Porter knew about it,
he never mentioned it to me.

The Fourth of July, 1964, was my first Independence Day and
confirmed my belief in the ideals of democracy and its process.
President Johnson had had to conduct his presidency in the
shadow of an international tragedy as well as in the void left by the
personality of his late predecessor. He continued the legislative
agenda of the fallen president and pushed against the odds that
the majority of all legislators from the South would work with all

of their energy and power against the passage of the Civil Rights Act. Two days before the annual celebrations of Independence Day the bill passed and became law: one hundred years after the Emancipation Proclamation ended slavery and nearly 350 years after the arrival of the first slaves in 1619. Freedom was more than a word. It was now something tangible because I had been acknowledged by the law of the land to be a citizen in the eyes of the power of the land. I considered these rights a gift to be cherished but I would also have the responsibilities of citizenship. Taking them seriously would be the best insurance that I could have against losing my own rights and for protecting and promoting the rights of all for generations to come. Racial discrimination did not suddenly come to an end. The struggle would continue as long as there were two human beings on this earth; the defense and promotion of human rights would be a present and necessary struggle for me from that moment on.

In September 1964 I began my last year of high school. I was a member of the honor society and had been elected my class representative to the student council. One day I was looking at the school bulletin board and saw the announcement that the school had decided to change the rules for choosing the homecoming queen. The teachers and students always looked forward to that special weekend. Many alumni returned to the school; parents and students lined the downtown streets to watch the parade with the marching bands, the colorful floats, the new queen waving to all, and finally the big football game. Heretofore the queen had always been chosen by the members of the football team and was usually one of the girlfriends of one of the players and one of the most popular girls in school. But now it was decided that there should be a pageant, similar to the Miss America pageant, with different categories, including swimsuit, talent, and intelligence. As I was a budding feminist I disdained the whole idea. One of the girls from my class had often commented snidely about my wardrobe. "Is that skirt a hand-me-down from your sister?" she would ask; my mother had recycled it from one of her own dresses and had used the fabric to sew a skirt for me. Most of my clothes had been sewn by my mother and were not store-bought. When this girl saw me looking at the bulletin, she said, "Of course you are not thinking about entering." Indeed, I had not been, but I said, "Oh no? Just watch me." I signed up without giving very much thought to it.

I was not at all the type of girl to enter this kind of competition. It seemed silly to compete with other girls for the attention of teenage boys for whom I had little patience. I found the majority of them such a waste of time. I often thought to myself, Is there anything on earth more stupid than a teenage boy, especially when he is talking to a girl? However, I did have two very good friends who were boys, Frank and Stuart; Frank lived not far from me and we often spoke on the way home from school, and Stuart studied physics with me. Stuart and I made a pact to go to the graduation prom together so that we could both avoid the pressure put on everyone to be in couples. I had not gone to the junior year prom; my father had offered to take me because I refused to have a date, but I turned him down. It did not help my social life that my parents were overly strict, and even more aggravating, they were indecisive. Neither wanted to assume the responsibility of having given me permission to go out in case something happened to me. I spent most of my weekends babysitting for Mr. Porter's children, not going on dates.

When it was time for the pageant, I had never been swimming, so I had no swimsuit. I borrowed one from the sister of a friend. It was much too big but I managed to tuck it in here and there so that it worked for me. I had always been skinny: my mother used to call me "string bean" when I was little. I knew that I had little chance to win the swimsuit competition. When I stood next to the other voluptuous and curvy contestants I looked like I had not yet reached puberty.

I looked in the back of our closet and found my sister's prom dress that she had worn in Memphis three years before. I knew that there would certainly be prettier dresses, so maybe I would not get the highest marks for the evening gown competition either. There were two more categories, talent and intellect, where I figured that I might get high points, so I had a chance. Although I found this kind of pageant degrading for women, I was in it to win. In the talent part I was up against baton twirlers and many "dramatic readings." One of the judges was a music teacher from the local Negro college, Philander Smith, and she was obviously impressed with my a cappella singing of a spiritual and a semi-classical song, "Love Is Where You Find It," that displayed my solid high voice. In the last part of the competition the contestants were asked questions about what we wanted to do in the future, what was important in our lives, what is the meaning of life, etc. I do not remember the question and certainly not the answer but I assume that my answer took me over the top. When the results were announced there was a gasp from the crowd of students who expected that one of the more glamorous, voluptuous, and popular girls would win. An even louder gasp came from my mother. I had not told my parents that I was entering the competition but on the night of the event I had missed my ride to school and pleaded with my mother to drive me there. She did not have time to change her clothes or to put on any makeup. When we arrived, she asked me what the event was and I had to tell her. I told her not to stay because I would surely not win. She decided to stay anyway and when I did win she realized how she was dressed and looked and was a little put out with me although she was extremely proud at the same time. I only glanced briefly at my tormenters as they crowned me Homecoming Queen of Horace Mann High School, Little Rock, Arkansas, 1964–65.

My friends in the choir were truly happy for me and the group of "in" kids thought it would be great to include me in their inner clique, even suggesting a boyfriend for me. But that did not work. I was flattered for about five minutes. During the homecoming parade that went through downtown Little Rock I sat on the float waving to the crowd on Main Street, secretly enjoying the bet that I had won. That evening I was escorted onto the football field on the arm of the football captain at halftime of the homecoming game. My little friend—my silent companion—and I relished the moment; and then on Monday I was again just Barbara.

Some of the teachers and the little in crowd in my class expected me to change my way of dressing—worn gym shoes with holes in them—and my hair, which I wore in a bad Beatle cut with bangs down over my eyes. My mother had gotten a job that year that was near Horace Mann so I was able to get a ride with her to school, but she refused to drive me when she disapproved of my hair and clothes and I sometimes had to take the bus. Some of the other contestants were not pleased that I did not play or dress the part of homecoming queen. I answered them that I was on the honor society and a member of the student government where I could represent all of the students' more serious problems and deal with important needs like better facilities in the classrooms. They soon gave up on me, and I did not have to try the new boyfriend that they had chosen for me.

I graduated in May 1965 with honors. I was voted wittiest in my class and at first I was disappointed because I would have preferred to have been voted the most likely to succeed. But I thought, I can succeed just as well without that title and I will always have my wit.

During the Easter holidays in 1993 I visited my parents in Little Rock with my family—my first husband, Martin, daughter Jennie, and son Sebastian. We attended the Easter Sunday church services in the rural church outside Little Rock where my father was then the pastor. Even though he was past retirement age, he refused to stop working and he had not lost any of his fire when he preached a sermon. During the service Jennie looked around and noticed that there was only one white person in the congregation. She tugged on Martin's sleeve and whispered, "Papa, there are hardly any other white people here, are you feeling OK?"

So many of my cherished professors were no longer living or had moved away. But the first person that I wanted to visit was Arthur Porter. He and I had kept in touch while I was studying at Juilliard but it had been many years since we had met or spoken.

After a big lunch at the church that was reminiscent of the meals during the revivals of my childhood we went back to town. Mr. and Mrs. Porter invited us to their home for a gathering with some of the old members of the choir from Horace Mann High. I arrived an hour before the other guests, and it was immediately apparent that Mr. Porter was not well. His wife, Pauline, informed me that he was suffering from late stages of lung cancer. But he was so happy to see me and to meet my family. He took me aside and said, "You know that I have been following you ever since you left school and am so proud of your achievements, but even more proud of the young woman that you are, in spite of the success that you have had. I am so happy to meet again the same person I saw on your first day of school at Horace Mann—the sparkle in your eyes that revealed the rascal that you are has thankfully not diminished." I gave him a big long hug, something that I would never have dared do when I was his student, because like so many of the girls in the choir I had had a little crush on him. He had arranged a gathering with some of the old choir members, many mezzos, of course, and we reminisced about our times together in the choir. We shared news of the other members who were no longer in Arkansas or alive. Mr. Porter discussed how frustrating it was that we had missed one another in Washington, DC, in January 1993 during the inaugural festivities of President Bill Clinton, where he had played for the Arkansas Ball and I had sung during the inaugural gala. We had both found this out the next day.

I proudly informed him that I was finally going to do a jazz concert after all these years. I was sitting with him in the same room where my initiation into jazz had taken place. I told him that I was preparing a tribute to Duke Ellington, my first real jazz performance, at the legendary Montreux jazz festival the following summer of 1994, and that I wanted to invite him and Mrs. Porter to come and be my guests. Until the end of the year I thought that this would be possible, but when I called him at home later that year he was in the hospital. Not knowing that his condition had worsened I held out hope that we might meet at my home in Montreux, but it was clear from his voice that he was much too weak to travel, although he expressed his hope and desire to come hear me there. We were never able to speak again and he died shortly afterward. Although he never made the trip he was with me in that first concert that inspired me to add jazz to my repertoire, and I feel his presence today more than ever.

University 3

The truth isn't always beauty, but the hunger for it is.

—Nadine Gordimer

I left home for college in September 1965 at the age of sixteen. I had little to say about the choice of school. My parents had decided that I was to go to Lane College, which was founded in 1882 as a CME high school to provide education for former slaves; Geneice had been attending it since 1963. I received a full scholarship because of my good grades in high school and my scores on the college entrance exams. The scholarship was obviously a decisive factor in my parents' decision because I would have not been able to go to college at all without it. They also felt assured that the strict moral education that they had tried to give me at home would continue there. I wished that they had also looked more closely at the school's curriculum, but I must admit that I was looking forward to going back to Tennessee because I had wonderful memories of my time in Chattanooga and Memphis.

My first disappointment was that Jackson was a smaller town than I had expected; the second was that the school did not offer all the subjects that I had hoped to study. I wanted to major in mathematics and minor in physics, but there was no physics department. I had to minor in chemistry. Legally I could have enrolled in a white Christian college that would have satisfied my scholastic needs but the majority of them in the South were still segregated and again my parents chose to avoid controversy. They wanted me to attend a CME school and that was the end of the discussion.

The Vietnam War was starting to get more and more attention, inchoate dissent was mounting on many campuses in the country, and the hippie subculture's mixture of music, alternate lifestyle, and psychedelic experimentation was beginning in San Francisco. I was closely following the student movement at Berkeley. My limited experiences at Central High and my sister's activism had aroused my interest in politics and law and I had very much hoped to take some political science courses, but there were none in the curriculum. Unlike at Ruthie's college, there was no SNCC chapter at Lane College. The school was aware of its responsibility to prepare us for an uncertain future in a fast-changing world, but it also assumed that our parents had sent us there for a safe, noncontroversial, and thus nonpolitical environment.

At the beginning of my first year I was unhappy and complained, but I gave up after a while. I was still a minor and could not change schools without my parent's permission. In spite of my frustrations I was pleased that my math professors were devoted and inspiring. The head of the department encouraged me to become a tutor, and the salary enhanced my ten-dollar monthly allowance, which was hardly enough to cover my personal needs such as toothpaste and soap, not to mention an occasional movie or book. I also found a job in the school cafeteria. I was allowed to take as much milk as I wanted and during the winter months the outside windowsill of my room was always filled with milk cartons. I wonder if a sensitivity that I have developed to milk products has anything to do with the fact that I drank so much milk during that time to supplement my diet.

I shared a room with three other girls. We had two bunk beds and I had one of the top beds. I have always been very much a morning person so when I would jump from my bed early with a chirpy "Good morning" I was usually pelted with pillows and whatever else they could get their hands on as my roommates buried themselves deeper under their covers. The house rules were very strict. We had to be in by ten at night when the library closed, and of course no boys were ever allowed in the girls' rooms or vice versa. We also could not leave the campus without permission.

One of the first things that I did was audition for the choir. My acceptance was not a given since I was not a music student. Being in choir or band was a requirement for music majors, who were accepted first. I was the only non–music major in the choir. The fourth-year students were at least twenty-one, and I was immediately aware that my voice lacked their maturity. But being a choir member was my greatest joy and inspiration at Lane College. The director, Robert Owens, was considered one of the best in the country and was very demanding, but he never pressured me to sound like the older sopranos or to force my voice. Negro spirituals were, of course, a big part of our repertoire, but he also challenged us with the pillars of the classical choral repertoire. During that first year I had to learn the entire *Messiah* of Handel. Luckily I already knew the few excerpts that I had sung in high school.

The first thing that I did upon returning to Little Rock for summer vacation in 1966 was to look for a summer job, and I ended up working with the Head Start program aimed at helping poor children be better prepared to start elementary school. My father had become involved in the campaign of Winthrop Rockefeller, who was running for governor of Arkansas in his second attempt to unseat the infamous Orval Faubus and his notorious political machine. I got a part-time job working for his campaign, manning the phones, canvassing, and spreading the message to Negroes and whites alike that it was time to have a new face in the capital. The following November, Winthrop Rockefeller was elected, the first Republican governor in a state that had voted Democrat since Reconstruction. In order to disenfranchise Negroes and poor whites who were in the majority and who had banded together in interracial coalitions, the Democratic Party in the South had been instrumental in enacting Jim Crow laws, literacy tests, and poll taxes. The Voting Rights Act of 1965 changed this and it felt good to participate in a small way in the first election in which all could register to vote.

Because of the black power movement we started to call ourselves blacks instead of Negroes and coloreds, terms that young blacks who wanted to move on associated with our painful past. I still have a great affection for the term Negro because I am so proud of the Negroes who taught me and inspired me to be who I am today and grateful for those dignified and courageous Negroes who fought and died for the cause of equality and liberty.

Although I had made some good new friends during my first year at Lane College, was happy with my own schoolwork, and was even happier to sing in such a good choir, I complained bitterly during that summer vacation. I asked my parents to let me transfer to another school that could offer me the subjects that I wanted to study. "Why not Fisk University in Nashville?" Fisk was one of the most renowned of the Negro Colleges and Universities and boasted alumni such as Booker T. Washington, James Weldon Johnson, and of course the Fisk Jubilee Singers.

My entreaties fell on deaf ears. I was given the choice to continue to study at Lane College or stay in Little Rock, live at home, and go to the local college, Philander Smith. I packed my bags and returned to Jackson.

In the beginning of my second year I decided to do something about my frustration with the school program and to work within the system to make some improvements. I ran for student government and was elected as one of the representatives of my class. I set out to revolutionize the campus with the fervor of a true believer. I was very naïve and came up against a majority of my fellow student government members who did not share my opinion about the curriculum and an administration that refused to take the few of us who pushed for these demands seriously. The student government's most important issue was the selection of and budget for the band for the big dance at the end of the year. I was frustrated and was constantly taking my ideas and complaints to the dean of the school. I made such a nuisance of myself that my father was informed. The assistant dean called me in to say that they had no intention of making the changes that I wanted and that if I was so unhappy with the conditions at the school then I should consider going elsewhere. Higher education comes at great cost to students in America. Private institutions like Lane depend solely on private donations from outside to supplement the tuition charges paid by the students; that support came mainly from the

CME church whose members had very modest incomes. I am sure that the administration strived to give us the best education that their means could provide. Most likely there was not enough money to pay for the professors needed to add other subjects to the curriculum. I had to admit that I was benefiting from a scholarship that paid my full tuition costs.

In my first year I had made a valiant try to accept the situation and to concentrate on what was fun and positive, but by the end of my second year I decided to heed the dean's advice and to search for a college that could correspond to my academic wishes. I was eighteen, the same age as the young boys going off to fight and die in Vietnam. I became very interested in the Free Speech Movement at the University of California at Berkeley, started by students who had participated in Freedom Summer, a voter registration campaign organized in large part by SNCC, which brought together thousands of Negro activists from Mississippi and a thousand or more state volunteers, 90 percent white and Jewish, who came there during the summer of 1964. Mississippi had the lowest percentage of Negroes registered to vote in the entire country. The local authorities, the police, and especially the White Citizens' Council and the Ku Klux Klan responded immediately with violence, intimidation, firings, drive-by shootings in the Negro neighborhoods, Molotov cocktails, and all forms of harassment. On June 21, I, along with the nation, was shocked by one of the first acts of violence; it received international attention. James Chaney, a Negro activist from Mississippi, Michael Schwerner and Andrew Goodman, two Jews from New York City, were reported missing after being arrested in Philadelphia, Mississippi, by the deputy sheriff, a member of the KKK. During the entire summer I held my breath and hoped and prayed for the best while fearing the worst. Finally after much foot dragging by the local police, including accusations of the whole thing being a publicity stunt, Robert Kennedy, the attorney general, ordered the FBI to take over the investigation. On August 4, our worst fears were confirmed: their buried bodies were found; Goodman and Schwerner had been shot dead but Chaney had been tortured before being shot three times. These murders had as much an effect on me as the killing of Emmett Till.

The students who returned to Berkeley from Mississippi had seen the injustice with their own eyes and had feared for their lives and the lives of the Negroes who had befriended them. When they attempted to continue their political activities in support of the civil rights movement they came up against university laws prohibiting political activity on campus. They held protests, insisting that the administration acknowledge their right to free speech and academic freedom and that they lift their ban on on-campus political activities. These words taken from Mario Savio's speech inspired me then and still do today:

> There's a time when the operation of the machine becomes so odious—makes you so sick at heart—that you can't take part. You can't even passively take part. And you've got to put your bodies upon the gears and upon the wheels, upon the levers, upon all the apparatus, and you've got to make it stop. And you've got to indicate to the people who run it, to the people who own it, that unless you're free, the machine will be prevented from working at all.

I longed to follow in the footsteps of my sister Ruthie and my new hero, Mario, to become an activist for change.

I don't know where I got the political literature about the movement, but it was probably during my many visits to the public library or from Ruthie. Although Geneice was also at the same college, I saw little of her and spent my free time with my own friends. She never expressed any interest at all in politics and tended to treat me as her little baby sister, which annoyed me. I wanted to assert my independence from my family and could not tolerate her treating me like a baby.

By 1965 SNCC had extended its activities from student sit-ins to the more dangerous voter registration drives. In 1966 it also came out against the Vietnam War. None of this activity was present in the protective cocoon of Lane College, nor did the lifestyle of the white, middle-class hippie movement hold any attraction for Negro students in places like Jackson. Negro activists were fighting to catch up with the white society in terms of opportunities and fundamental rights. Their goal was not to bring down the entire white establishment but to be accepted by American society. I was asked some years later why so few blacks were "dropping out" and I responded, "Because we've been fighting for so long to drop into American society that it is a little premature to think about dropping out."

That year the choir's biggest project was Beethoven's *Missa Solemnis*, a very complicated piece. The choir had a very good reputation and was invited to perform concerts all over the country, touring in our own Lane College bus. My first tour would take us to Wisconsin and Nebraska. One of our concerts was at the small, private, progressive Beloit College. When I found out that we would be going there, I wrote to them of my interest in enrolling and asked for an interview for admission to the mathematics department for the following year. Of course I hoped to receive a full scholarship, for in order to defy my parents and leave Lane College I had to be financially independent. I waited impatiently for their reply during the summer break.

That summer of 1967 I met some young, white law students from New York who had come to work in the office of a black civil rights lawyer in Little Rock, a friend of my parents. They were looking into the practices in the state prisons. I was fascinated by the work that they were doing there and begged them to take me along on one of their visits. We visited the Cummins State Farm and I watched and listened while they interviewed some black prisoners under the distrustful and sometimes hateful glare of the prison officials and guards. It was depressing to see the conditions in which the prisoners had to live and it was frightening to imagine what life must be like for them when we were not around. Some were no older than I was and their stories broke my heart. Governor Rockefeller had been elected on a platform for prison reform, and one of his first tasks was to dismantle one of the most horrible legacies of the Orval Faubus era, the cruel penitentiary system where prisoners were routinely tortured. Rockefeller greatly improved the conditions in the state farms and prisons in Arkansas, providing better food and medical care as well as educational possibilities, and most important of all, he replaced the cruel trustees (designated inmates given authority over their fellow inmates, resulting in egregious physical abuse) with professional prison guards. I had not informed my parents that I would be going to visit a prison with death row inmates. I wrote a letter about it to a classmate from Lane and my mother read the unfinished letter. She told my father and they forbade me to continue with the visits and even forbade me to see the two young lawyers again. I was eighteen and needed parental approval to visit the prison, so I had to submit. I had become quite fond of one of the lawyers, John, and I continued to meet him in secret until the end of the summer. We spoke about the race riots that had taken place in many American urban centers that summer; we rejoiced at the confirmation of the first black Supreme Court justice, Thurgood Marshall; and we agonized over Muhammad Ali's conviction for draft evasion. John and I remained friends for many years.

During the previous school year I sang a concert with the choir in a state prison in Tennessee. This was a big enclosed facility with high walls and was completely segregated. I met an eighteen-year-old boy who was the chaplain's assistant and had been in prison on a life sentence since the age of fifteen for the murder of a white boy during a gang fight. I corresponded with him for a while and tried to encourage him to study and to learn as much as he could. I discussed his case with my lawyer friend, but there was little that he could do for him. When my mother found out about my pen pal she was not happy about that either, but I continued to write to him throughout the summer.

Every day I was looking for a letter to arrive from Beloit. I had been accepted as a student but I was waiting to find out if I would receive a scholarship. I knew that I might have to supplement it with a student loan, and I would certainly need to find a job on campus in order to make a little money for my personal needs. However I received another letter first, from the dean at Lane College, inviting me to participate in an exchange program that the presidents of Lane College and Nebraska Wesleyan University in Lincoln (a mostly white university of the United Methodist Church which the choir had visited on our tour) had started the previous year. In spite of my reputation for being a bit of a nuisance, I was chosen to represent Lane. A student exchange program was a very progressive endeavor in 1966 for an administration that I considered anything but progressive. Four students and a professor from Wesleyan came to Lane for the first semester of studies and four students and a professor from Lane went to Lincoln at the same time. The first year had its difficulties, but how could it have been otherwise given the different worlds blacks and whites lived in? I had not had any contact with the black or white exchange students from the year before; they were juniors and seniors and not in any of my classes. I had heard that the white students had not been happy with the semester that they had spent at Lane. But I found the idea fascinating and jumped at the chance. I do not remember why I decided to accept this offer as I was already mentally preparing myself for the hard winters of Wisconsin.

My parents were proud that I was one of the students to be selected but were wary of my getting further away from their influence. But that September five of us traveled to Lincoln from Jackson in a Cessna. The plane had arrived with the students and a professor from Wesleyan and returned to Nebraska with us on board. I assumed that it belonged to someone with connections to NWU. It was the first time that I had ever been in an airplane and I was excited—and petrified. It seemed that everyone at Wesleyan had been looking forward to our arrival: the students and the teachers truly made every effort to make us feel welcome.

The subjects that I had wanted to study and many others that were not affordable for Lane College were available at NWU. I signed up immediately to study physics. I could not believe my eyes when I walked into the chemistry laboratory for the first time. I had never seen so much lab equipment in my life. The abundance and variety in both the chemistry and physics laboratories were overwhelming. I was like a child in a toy store.

I had only one roommate, a girl from Colorado with a Swedish surname, Hedberg, who played the guitar and sang Bob Dylan songs all the time. I made friends easily in my dormitory and in my classes; I am still in contact with some of them today. The other girl that had come with me from Lane, whom I hardly knew, was in another dormitory and I did not see her often outside of the one math course that we had in common. The other black students on campus were mostly from Nebraska, and every day they would all sit together at the same table in the cafeteria. I would sometimes eat lunch with them but I also ate lunch with friends from my classes or my dormitory. I always refused to be in any one clique in school and I did not want to isolate myself with the few black students like some of the other exchange students. I wanted to meet as many different kinds of people as possible.

I now had the opportunity to take private voice lessons for the first time in my life. (I had not been allowed to take voice lessons at Lane College because they were exclusively for music majors.) I had been privileged to work with wonderful choir directors since I was ten, but none of them had been trained as voice teachers. After an audition I was accepted by the head of the voice department, a kind, elderly gentlemen whom all of the students affectionately called Pop Bennett. I auditioned for the choir, but the director felt that my voice didn't blend with the other sopranos. However I was invited to sing solos with them on special occasions.

Pop Bennett suggested songs and arias that we worked on in my voice lessons and was very kind and rather indulgent with me; since I was not a music student he did not have to prepare me for exams for a degree. The lessons were fun and I learned a lot. Some of his students were preparing for the Nebraska state auditions for the Metropolitan Opera and one of them convinced me to enter just for fun. I had not entered a competition since becoming Miss Horace Mann in 1965. I had purchased two recordings on sale, one with Joan Sutherland, of whom I had never heard, and one with Leontyne Price, whom I had heard and seen perform on TV. I found that the coloratura repertoire on the Joan Sutherland record had just too many notes and was too difficult for me. I thought then that one must be born with feathers to sing like that because the music was written for birds. Dame Joan, a very laid-back and humorous lady, was later my neighbor in Switzerland until her death in 2010. I told her this story at dinner one evening and she laughed and agreed that maybe she did have some feathers somewhere.

I felt vocally and emotionally more at home singing the lyric arias that I had heard on the Leontyne Price recording so I learned four of them for the competition. I chose two arias from Puccini's *Turandot*, "Signore, ascolta!" and "Tu che di gel sei cinta"; "Un bel di vedremo" from *Madame Butterfly*; and "Depuis le jour" from Charpentier's *Louise*. (The latter became my standard audition and competition piece for many years to come; whenever I sang it in a competition I won first prize.) I learned the arias by listening to her record and even though I have a good ear, the language was certainly approximate. I arrived at the competition very relaxed because I had nothing at stake and expected to be eliminated in the first round; but I advanced to the semifinals and then to the finals. And no one was more surprised than I when I was awarded the first prize. Winning meant that I would be going in the spring to the regional competition in Minneapolis, Minnesota. There was of course much ado made about me being the winner—not because I was black but mainly because I was a math and chemistry student with little formal vocal training and I had been chosen over voice majors from all over the state.

But there was a dilemma. I was supposed to return to Jackson after the Christmas holidays with the other exchange students and professors. I would not be able to prepare for the competition there, and I certainly did not have the means to travel all the way to Minnesota from Tennessee. The rules of the exchange program stated clearly that neither school would accept any exchange student as a permanent student. I knew that I would need more serious preparation for the next stage of the competition if I wanted to advance to the finals in New York City.

Being the state winner brought me many new friends and supporters, including the ladies of the Met Opera auditions committees in Lincoln and Omaha, as well as the president of NWU, Dr. Vance Rogers. He asked his friend President Kirkendoll at Lane for special permission for me to stay in Lincoln until the end of the school year so that I could prepare for the regional Metropolitan Opera auditions and represent Nebraska. Permission was granted. I expected to return to Lane the following semester.

In January 1968 I moved into my own room in Centennial Hall to begin the spring semester. I was so thrilled to be able to continue studying physics and singing. I threw myself into my studies and the preparation for the competition in April.

I had a lot more freedom than I had ever had at home or at Lane. I went out on weekends with my friends to the movies, roller-skating rinks, bowling alleys, restaurants, and other public places, and my presence didn't raise an eyebrow. I took these changes in my life in stride. I was born with such a strong lust for life that I didn't stop to analyze what was happening but tried to live every new experience as fully as I could.

After my last class around 7:00 PM on the fourth of April, I walked back to the dorm; the housemother was waiting for me at the entrance with a very grave face. She asked me to come to her office. I thought, What have I done now? I wondered if she had found out that we had been slipping out at night to go to buy food at an all-night truck stop off-campus where we bought the best Texas fries to satisfy our late-night cravings. Or that I had continued to see my former lab partner in physics, David, who had been suspended from school for refusing to lie about whether he had ever smoked marijuana. I did not approve of smoking of any kind, even cigarettes, but the others who had been called in with him had lied and were allowed to stay in school. It was forbidden for him to come on campus during the semester and for any students in the school to socialize with him. I defied the rules and occasionally met him at an off-campus coffee shop. When the new semester began he returned to school. David was my first boyfriend and we were together until the beginning of the summer.

I took a deep breath and went into her office. She took my hand and said, "I have some very sad news to tell you. Martin Luther King has just been assassinated tonight in Memphis, Tennessee." I could not believe what I was hearing. Her face seemed to fade away and I heard her voice as if it came from another room. I was in a state of total shock. I sat quietly and rose to go to my room. I felt so completely alone. Later she came up to my room and asked me if there was something that she or the school could do for me. I appreciated the sincerity of her gesture, thanked her for her kindness, and replied, "I do not want anything special for me. What I really want is to be treated like any other student, nothing more and nothing less than any other of the girls under your charge, just the simple respect that every human being should be given." She hugged me and left me to ponder what this new tragedy would mean for all of us in America.

The night before his assassination King had ended his speech to the crowd at Mason Temple in Memphis, Tennessee, thusly:

Well, I don't know what will happen now. We've got some difficult days ahead. But it really doesn't matter with me now, because I've been to the mountaintop.

And I don't mind.

Like anybody, I would like to live a long life. Longevity has its place. But I'm not concerned about that now. I just want to do God's will. And He's allowed me to go up to the mountain. And I've looked over. And I've seen the Promised Land. I may not get there with you. But I want you to know tonight that we, as a people, will get to the promised land!

And so I'm happy, tonight.

I'm not worried about anything.

I'm not fearing any man!

Mine eyes have seen the glory of the coming of the Lord!!

I cannot to this day read nor hear these words without tears welling up in my eyes. But that night in Lincoln I could not yet cry. Stunned, I watched the news with my friends Laurel, Jane, and Barbara. Robert F. Kennedy, who was on a campaign stop in Indianapolis had to announce the assassination to an unknowing, mostly black crowd. Without preparation, standing on a flatbed truck; he looked directly into their faces and said, "For those of you who are black and are tempted to be filled with hatred and mistrust of the injustice of such an act, against all white people, I would say that I can also feel in my own heart the same feeling. I had a member of my family killed, but he was killed by a white man." There were riots in many American cities that night but none in Indianapolis. His words comforted me and I began to look forward to his coming visit to Nebraska.

I arrived at Minneapolis for the Met auditions feeling much more pressure than during the Nebraska competition, but I had the whole Nebraska committee, headed by Mrs. Sidles, behind me. As I listened to some of the singers in the first round it was clear that I would hold my own, but if I did not win the first prize it would be a blessing for me. I was clearly, in my mind, not ready to compete on the stage of the Met. I made it to the finals but thankfully I did not win the right to go on to New York City as the winner of the region. All of my supporters were convinced that I should have won. I received a copy of the judges' remarks many years later. They were very favorable but considered me too young and inexperienced to go further that year. By the way, the winner in Minneapolis did go on to have a modest career at the New York City Opera. I returned to Lincoln enriched by my experience and anxious to make up the time that I had spent preparing for the competition and neglecting my organic chemistry, physics, and quantitative analysis classes.

When the theater group decided to put on Johann Strauss's *Die Fledermaus*, I was given the lead role, Rosalinda. This took up a lot of my time, and because I was in rehearsals every evening I was still neglecting my academic subjects. After the performances ended I had one month to prepare for final exams. I practically moved into the library at the agriculture campus because it was usually empty and spent every hour trying to catch up.

Near the end of the school year I knew that I would have to return to Lane to finish my last year of college. NWU was not allowed to accept me for my senior year. I was also trying to figure out what to do over the summer. My organic chemistry teacher offered me the opportunity to come to Vermillion, South Dakota, to do ion complex substitution research with her. I thought that that could be interesting and was about to say yes when fate sent me around another corner.

I had been singing in the choir of the Saint Paul United Methodist Church in Lincoln during that semester to earn a little more pocket money. One of the few black members of the congregation had been pursuing me for months. She wanted me to sing for a meeting that she was organizing for university officials. The more persistent she became the more I resisted because the meeting was to take place the evening before my big final exam in physics. I was already far behind in my preparations and had no time to lose singing a concert. Finally her persistence prevailed. I agreed, but only on my conditions. I insisted on singing at the very beginning of the meeting and leaving immediately. I came, sang, and went away without giving any more thought to it. Present at that meeting was a lawyer, Mr. Richard Smith, who was a member of the board of trustees of the University of Nebraska as well as the Aspen Music Festival and School. He wrote a letter some days later to Pop Bennett offering me a full scholarship to attend the music school for the entire nine weeks of the Aspen Festival and proposed that I study with Jennie Tourel. I had heard of Aspen and its Rocky Mountains but the name Jennie Tourel meant absolutely nothing to me. Nevertheless, complex ion substitution was beginning to sound much less exciting. Pop Bennett and I spoke about the offer and he encouraged me to accept it without delay.

Robert Kennedy came to Lincoln and gave a rousing speech that inspired many of us who had volunteered to work for his campaign. He usually ended his campaign speech by paraphrasing George Bernard Shaw: "There are those who look at things the way they are, and ask why? I dream of things that never were and ask, why not?" This was also a signal to the Secret Service that the speech had come to an end. I remember that it was pouring rain and he spoke longer than planned and at the end he said, "As George Bernard Shaw said, 'Run for the buses.'" He won the Nebraska primary on May 14.

Now my summer was planned. To prepare myself to go to Aspen at the beginning of July, I was staying in the apartment of a friend who had gone home for the summer. I never watched television in the mornings but I awoke with a very strange feeling on June 5 and I turned it on. I saw the images of Robert Kennedy, who been shot some hours before in the ballroom of the Ambassador Hotel in Los Angeles. I waited with friends all day to hear any news, hoping and praying that he would survive. We sat in silence and in total disbelief that this man, who had just been here in Lincoln speaking to us, was now at death's door. He was pronounced dead nearly twenty-four hours later. I truly had believed in him. He was the first politician for whom I had actively campaigned based on my beliefs, not as a summer job as I had done for Rockefeller. I, like so many others at school, had supported his campaign because of his opposition to the Vietnam War and had hoped to build together a better world with him as the president in the White House. I was crushed and devastated. I wondered if politics in America wasn't becoming too violent and too cruel for the angels that we had lost.

Aspen 4

You have to be completely dedicated, put blinders on your eyes and go to your chosen goal and reach as high as you can. The road to perfection is as intangible as the road to the stars.... The stars are far away no matter how high you reach.

—Jennie Tourel

I arrived in Denver and took a bus up the winding mountain route. Mr. Smith had written to me that his good friend Courtland Barnes could pick me up at the bus station in Glenwood Springs, forty miles from Aspen. In the car, Mr. Barnes warned me, "You are coming from sea level; please take it easy the first days in Aspen because you need to give yourself time to adjust to the altitude." The small ex-mining town was nestled in a valley of breathtaking beauty in the Rocky Mountains, eight thousand feet above sea level. I thanked him and said goodbye, but with my usual enthusiasm and impatience, I bounded up the stairs to my room, taking two or three steps at a time, and nearly passed out before I could get through the door. I had already forgotten his warning. I was impatient to get started. But I was going to have to slow down.

The school had provided housing in hotels designed for skiers who stayed only a week or a weekend during the ski season; it was a far cry from Centennial Hall back at NWU. There were two bunk beds in my room but I only had one roommate, a Chinese

American from Phoenix, Arizona, who was a percussion student. My first question to her was, "Do you practice in the room?" She said, "Oh no, don't worry, I have these padded wooden boards that I use for practice when I am in the room, the real drums are in the practice rooms on campus." I was relieved.

I was awakened the next morning by birds singing outside of my window, accompanied by an orchestra of many different instruments—strings, woodwinds, brass, everything except percussion. Throughout the hotel students were warming up and practicing for their lessons, and as the morning progressed voice students joined in, singing scales and bits of arias and songs. This wonderful cacophony was the overture heralding my entrance into a new and uncharted world. Every day of the nine weeks that I was in Aspen the exhilarating combination of the majesty of the Rocky Mountains, the sounds of music that surrounded me from morning to night, and the embellishment of crisp mountain air intoxicated all of my senses. Images of the far-away Smoky Mountains outside of Chattanooga, whose distant peaks had inspired my imagination and fed my daydreams, came vividly back to me. But in Aspen I was actually in the mountains' grandeur and I felt right at home; I was exactly at the place I should be, doing exactly what I should be doing. It was not only the thin air that made me dizzy. I was filled with the expectation of something that I could not even begin to imagine.

The Aspen Music Festival had been taking place for nearly sixty years and had become one of the most important summer music festivals, where the best international classical music artists performed and taught enthusiastic students in the idyllic setting of the Rocky Mountains. The dean of the Aspen School, Mr. Gordon Hardy, was also one of the deans at the Juilliard School and many of the teachers who came to Aspen for the summer were from Juilliard as well. Dean Hardy was also a very close friend of Mr. and Mrs. Richard Smith from Lincoln and of Jennie Tourel, the voice teacher Mr. Smith had chosen for me.

I visited Aspen again in January 2000 to sing a recital in the newly built Harris Concert Hall. When I arrived I could not believe my eyes. I had not been back since 1970, the second summer that I studied there. I could hardly recognize the town—it had become a very glitzy and expensive backdrop for the American jet set and Hollywood stars.

But in the summer of 1968 Aspen was a sleepy village whose main streets were not even paved. I was taken aback by a sign in the main drugstore that read, WE RESERVE THE RIGHT TO REFUSE SERVICE TO CUSTOMERS WITHOUT SHIRTS OR SHOES. Many hippies were living in Aspen and the surrounding areas. The only stars in town were the old miners and, during the festival, some of the great artists who came there to perform. But everyone was very low key and relaxed; the immense grandeur of the Rockies put even the most capacious ego in its place.

I went to nearly all of the concerts during the weekends, and my favorites were the Friday night chamber music concerts with the Juilliard Quartet. They were in residence that year, playing and teaching master classes. My love affair with chamber music began then in the chilly Aspen evenings. It was often raining, so I would wrap myself in a blanket, sit in the back of the hall, and enjoy the music as if it was being played just for me. The large tent was especially designed for the needs of classical music but nothing could be done about the pitter-patter of the rain on the roof; I thought that it added a cozy element. I loved the intimacy of the format and when I watched those four musicians interact every weekend I too wanted to have that experience.

From the first time that I worked together with other musicians in this way I knew that the process of rehearsing and performing chamber music was how I wanted to approach all the music that I would sing, whether it was a concert with a big symphony orchestra, an opera with many different partners, or a simple recital with piano. To this day my greatest pleasure in the musical process is taking part in the dialogue that takes place when I am able to balance singing and listening, trying to match colors, textures, and dynamics in a natural way with my partners.

On Saturdays and Sundays there were symphonic and solo concerts. Teachers and students comprised the festival orchestra and chorus, and they had the privilege to play and sing with well-known soloists such as Itzhak Perlman and Jennie Tourel. I was able to listen to many great artists rehearsing and performing right under my nose.

So many of my fellow students had been studying their instruments since a very early age and were accustomed to going to concerts, but this was entirely new for me; I felt as if the world that I had known in Arkansas, Tennessee, and Nebraska was far, far away. I could have been spending my summer on the moon. I would not want to exchange this for any chemistry laboratory anywhere in the world.

The concerts and the nature in and surrounding Aspen were overwhelming, but they were only the backdrop to the most important event of my summer, my encounter with Jennie Tourel. I had a private lesson with her once a week in her apartment. I arrived a little early for my first lesson and rang the doorbell. Her secretary, Gina, opened the door and just as I stepped into her living room I saw an object fly past the head of the student who was standing at the piano. She ducked and no harm was done. I could not believe what I had just seen and whispered to Gina, "Umm, if she is not feeling well today, I can come back another time." "No, dear," she said, "She is just fine, come on in. You can start in a few minutes." I swallowed hard and sat down to wait for my turn, thinking, Oh my, this is not going to be like my lessons with sweet old Pop Bennett.

Jennie Tourel was a little more than five feet tall, slightly round, dressed very colorfully, and always wore lots of jewelry, especially bracelets. She looked like an elegant bohemian. Once the previous student had left, practically bowing out of the door backward, she turned to me, smiled and asked, "Soooooooo, how are you, dear?" I answered, "*I* am fine. And you?" She assured me that she too was fine and the lesson began.

She had not heard me sing yet so this was in effect an audition. I sang the aria "Ah! Non credea mirarti" from Bellini's *La sonnambula*. She listened with bowed head as if deep in thought, a pose that I came to recognize when she did not want to show what she was thinking. I can say now that I had in no way prepared the music well enough for a lesson with such a demanding teacher. Pop Bennett had let me sing whatever amused me and however I could. He had taught me what I was unable to learn on my own. Jennie Tourel was, however, very patient with me and corrected my musical mistakes without scolding me. It was clear to me that she was impressed with my voice though it was in a raw state. She said, "You have a very natural instrument and I would be happy to accept you as my student." She then gave me explicit instructions about how to prepare for the following week's lesson and asked the pianist to work with me. However, I took as a warning the episode with the flying object, and even though I had no idea what had been the cause of such a reaction, I decided then to never come to my lessons unprepared. I got to know the student who was the target of Miss Tourel's shotputting effort and, given her obsequious stupidity, I understood the urge to throw something at her head since it was devoid of any substantial brain matter.

I was not able to analyze the meaning of what was taking place in my life. I did not understand then, nor do I know if Miss Tourel understood, the mutual importance of this first meeting. During nine weeks my life revolved around the lessons in her apartment and from each one I took away a small piece of the puzzle of my life, which I did not yet even know that I was trying to solve.

I also enrolled in a French diction and repertoire class and in an acting and opera class. My French and acting teacher was none other than Madeleine Milhaud, the wife of the composer Darius Milhaud, who was on the faculty of Mills College in California. I was less interested in the choir than I had been before coming to Aspen because I was concentrating on my lessons, but I looked forward to singing in an unforgettable performance of the Second Symphony of Gustav Mahler with Jennie Tourel as soloist. It would be the only time that we would sing together on the same stage. I also sang in the chorus of Puccini's *La bohème* and fell in love with this touching opera and the character of Mimì. I said to myself then, *I want to be able to sing this beautiful, moving music and to play the role of Mimì someday.*

I heard my first *liederabend*, Schumann's *Dichterliebe*, sung by a tenor whose name I no longer remember. The songs were very beautiful and Heinrich Heine's poetry so touched me that I kept my copy of the translations; I read them so many times that it gradually fell apart. I longed to be able to sing such beautiful and moving poetry. I also heard a lovely soprano, Benita Valente, singing Schumann songs; she inspired me as well.

I made many friends during those nine weeks. One was an excellent black mezzo-soprano, Cynthia Bedford from Mills College, who was a student of Mme. Milhaud. She was the first black singing student whom I had met who was seriously pursuing her classical-music studies. A very young conducting student, James Conlon, would later conduct my first Mimì in *La bohème* at the Juilliard School as well as the soundtrack for the film of the same opera many years later in Paris, directed by Luigi Comencini. Lorraine Nubar, who was a singing student from Juilliard and was also Jennie Tourel's assistant, and I started a friendship in Aspen that has lasted to this day—she is my son's godmother. A teenage boy, Fred Webster Jr. from Lincoln, Nebraska, attached himself to me from the first days of the summer because I too was from Lincoln.

Nearly every afternoon came a short burst of rain; these showers were refreshing and enhanced the smell of the rich earth. Whenever I smell that mixture of earth and summer rain I always think of Aspen. Those nine weeks seemed to pass by in a flash and I had absorbed everything that came my way. It was time to return home.

But where, I asked myself, *is my home now?* I had actually been "at home" during these last nine weeks, not only because of the spectacular mountain setting, but because I had discovered that the language of music was my mother tongue.

At the end of my last lesson of the summer, Miss Tourel said to me, "You have a lot of talent and even though you have never studied singing, you have made a great deal of progress during this summer. If you want to continue to pursue music seriously I would be happy to accept you as my student at the Juilliard School of Music in New York City."

I replied, "I also want to continue to study with you. I must go back to school and finish my degree, but I will apply to the Juilliard School and I will prepare myself for the audition next spring."

It was clear to me that my life's path was not only about to change but that it had in fact already made a 180-degree turn when I got off that Cessna plane in Lincoln in September 1967. I had only to accept the new direction and the challenges that it was going to present to me. It offered no guarantees of success, but I did not know or care about what success would be or look like. This would be the first great leap of faith in my life.

Being practical by nature, I didn't want to throw away all my years of study since the age of five by running off without a plan. The question was not if I would eventually go to New York, but how. I should have been preparing to return home to Little Rock to visit my parents during the few weeks that remained of my vacation before returning to Lane College in Jackson. Both prospects were out of the question for me now. Going home meant that I would have to withstand the pressure from my parents to maintain the status quo and to return to Lane College. Going back there would mean turning my back on the new path that had opened before me. I couldn't return to Nebraska Wesleyan because they had an agreement with Lane College that forbade them to allow me to stay even though they wanted to keep me. (They made up for this by giving me a doctorate degree in music in 1988.)

I called Dale Ganz, the choir director at the Saint Paul Methodist church where I had sung the previous year, and asked for his advice and help. He was one of the voice teachers at the other larger university in town, the University of Nebraska, known for its excellent football team, the Cornhuskers. He was very pleased that my summer in Aspen with Jennie Tourel had gone so well and was convinced that I would be accepted at the Juilliard School if I were able to prepare a good audition. He offered to help me with my application to the University of Nebraska. The university accepted my application immediately and also gave me a full scholarship that covered my studies but not my living accommodations. Dr. Ganz offered me a scholarship as a member of the church choir that gave me a little more money, but it was insufficient to cover the cost of even the most modest living quarters. I was able to take voice lessons as an elective course and he accepted me as his voice student and would help me prepare for my audition, which would require much more preparation than what had gone into the Metropolitan auditions. Everything was falling into place, but where was I going to live?

Fred Webster Jr. was only seventeen but had a most persuasive charm, especially with his mother. I told him about my plans to go back to Lincoln because I was most likely going to be accepted as a student at UN and that I was still looking for a solution for housing. Without telling me, he called his mother and later came to me and announced, "I have just spoken with my mom and suggested you come to live with us during the next school year." His older sister, Nan, who was my age, had decided to go to live on campus in the sorority house and his older brother, Larry, was away in medical school. The rest of his family consisted of his little brother, Doug, and his parents, Wanda and Dr. Fred Sr., a well-known orthopedic surgeon. Of course I didn't take him seriously and was dumbfounded when he came to me the next day to say that all was settled. His parents thought that it was a great idea.

Now I had to call my parents to tell them of my decision. My father, of course, acted as if I had completely lost my mind and insisted that I come home immediately to discuss the matter. I told him as gently as I could but with some satisfaction that I had solved my problems about school for the coming year without him. "I have been accepted at UN with a full scholarship and have found housing for myself." I was finally independent. "There is nothing more to discuss. I have made up my mind and my plans are clear. I will soon be twenty years old and, as a matter of fact, I did not call to discuss this with you but to inform you of my plans."

What a year 1968 had already been for me!

My passion for numbers and logic led me to a bachelor's of science from the University of Nebraska. Mathematics would be a foundation of my thought and reasoning for the rest of my life even though at the end of the summer of 1968 it was relegated to a secondary role in my ongoing quest. I left my mathematics studies in 1969 but I have never regretted those years of study. From the first time that I open a score and play through the music and throughout the never-ending process of learning and performing it, my mathematical mind unconsciously analyzes the piece. It helps me to decipher the score and to translate it from the two dimensions of the page to multidimensional sound and emotion. It enables me to see the musical architecture of the piece, which sometimes even appears to me as a kind of mathematical formula. This ability to analyze is an enormous aid for memorization as well as a first step to understanding more deeply the sense of the piece. I build first on the cerebral perspective in order to gradually let the essential emotional and spiritual facets of the artistic process take over.

Now I understand the correlation of music, with its components of harmony, melody, and rhythm, to mathematical formulas, and even hear the mathematical phenomena within music. From Jennie Tourel I learned that the artist's primary task is to be at the complete service of the music and to become the optimal instrument on which the music can be played and thus revealed. All of the preparation that leads to a performance—vocal technique, language studies, research, and life's own personal lessons—allows the artist to arrive at that goal and those privileged moments of grace.

———

Freddy came to pick me up when I came back to Lincoln and drove me to his home on a beautiful tree-lined avenue, Sheridan Boulevard. I met the entire family. I moved into my attic room upstairs and was very pleased because I had lots of space and was a little off to myself. To find myself living in the middle of a white family was like awakening in some distant exotic land many light years away. It was a possibility that had never crossed my mind as a child and would have seemed absurd if it had. However, ever since the episode concerning Ruthie's marriage to Bill I had been curious to know more about the "others" in my world. Until I came to Nebraska, Bill had been the only white person with whom I had ever had close contact. At NWU I had made friends very easily and had been living naturally among the white students in the dormitory. But life within a family in the confines of a house was something quite different. My only ideas about life in white families came from the sitcoms that I had seen on TV like *The Donna Reed Show* or *Leave It to Beaver*, with a perfect couple who slept in separate twin beds, the understanding father and husband who went to work, and the ever-smiling, perfect homemaker and mother of mischievous yet rather well-behaved children. Of course this picture did not correspond to any family in America.

Yet many families tore themselves apart trying to fit into a mold that was pure fantasy.

I wondered what the discussions had been in the family about my coming to live with them. In any case Dr. Webster and his wife welcomed me into their home in the most natural way. I gradually allowed myself to accept being a member of their family. Their youngest, Douglas, was only six and I sometimes babysat him, but they did not demand anything of me except to behave normally. So I helped around the house when it was needed, but much less than I had done when I was home. They had a housekeeper but I cleaned my own room and bathroom. Wanda Webster was a petite, energetic, and enthusiastic woman. She had studied dance and had wanted to work in the theater but her mother had refused to consider it and had cut her desires short. She was very supportive and excited that I might get to go to New York City to pursue a dream that she had been forbidden to realize. She was also an exemplary hostess and I learned a lot about cooking and preparing fine meals from her. Of course it is easier to cook good meals when you could afford the best ingredients, as they were able to do.

Dr. Webster was a very well-respected orthopedic surgeon; he was also a connoisseur of good wines, studied German with a group of friends, and often traveled with his family to Europe during the summer vacation. They belonged to the Lincoln Country Club, which was not far from our house, and it was their Sunday evening ritual to have the family dinner there, so of course I was included. I do believe that I was the first black person to dine there, and I seemed to have integrated the country club without any apparent fuss being made. If there was any resistance to my being there I never felt it. Dr. Webster was highly respected in Lincoln and, given the position that his family had in the community, they managed this with grace. Interestingly, they were not firebrand liberals. They were typical conservatives, like most people in the Midwest. Having me in the family was probably a little like having a exchange student. They had to be aware of the anger and the riots that occurred after the assassination of Martin Luther King, which had cost almost fifty lives, but we never discussed politics much. I felt that their kindness and generosity was genuine and I saved my politics for my discussions with my friends on campus.

I had to accept that I had come with many of my own preconceived ideas about white people. I am sure that having me in their home was equally an education to them, and after a very short time I had truly become a real member of the family. We had a late night ritual that I loved. When I had finished studying for the evening Freddy and I gathered in their bedroom and installed ourselves there together with his parents on their very large bed watching Johnny Carson, who was from Nebraska, and eating popcorn that Dr. Webster had made.

My classes began at 7:00 AM and I took a bus or got a ride to campus with one of the professors, Dr. Goebel, who was the father of my friend Sue. They lived across the street from us. I was very grateful for those rides because during the winter the wind chill felt like −50 degrees outside. I studied hard and started to prepare for my audition.

The University of Nebraska had a student body of more than twenty thousand students and many different disciplines and interests. I did miss the smaller, more intimate campus of Nebraska Wesleyan University across town, but I had more opportunities to meet many interesting students and professors at UN. The University of Nebraska was a far cry from the hotbed of activism of the University of California–Berkeley, but we were very much engaged in the growing dissent against the Vietnam War and, of course, the budding struggle for equal rights for women. Each department seemed to have carved out its own territory on campus, especially the meeting places for lunch and after school. If I wanted to meet with actors and other drama students or philosophy, music, or architectural students, I simply chose to have lunch in their respective hangouts. I circulated between the various locations, changing almost daily. I often met my friends David Meyer and David Lattrell for lunch at a bar that served the best roast beef sandwiches in town and was the hangout for the architectural students on campus.

Most of my chemistry and mathematics professors were aware that I was not spending my last year at the university just to obtain my bachelors of science degree in preparation for further studies and a career in science but that I was also preparing for my entrance exams to the Juilliard School to start new undergraduate studies from scratch. I lacked too many credits in mathematics to be able to finish with a math major but I had enough credits in chemistry. I made the switch to chemistry major and a math minor and thus was going to be able to finish all requirements for my degree in time to start at the Juilliard School the following year, if I were accepted. My advisor turned out to be the head of the chemistry department, Dr. Norman Caldwell, who was interested in music and was among my supporters. I was his only undergraduate advisee and he helped me devise a curriculum that would allow me to graduate in time. I had to spend most of my time in the chemistry lab and was so fascinated by my physical chemistry course that I entertained some pangs of regret that I would not be continuing with quantum mechanics.

My elective classes were archery and voice lessons with Dr. Ganz and I was accepted into the University Singers but was not allowed to sing any solos because I was not a student in the music department. Only once was I asked to learn a solo for a concert, in order to replace a tenor who was ill. When he heard that I had been given his solo to sing he miraculously recovered.

While I was having lunch at the café that was the preferred hangout of the theater students I heard that they were looking for extras for their next production and I was persuaded by my friends to audition. I was chosen for a small role and also volunteered to be an all-purpose stagehand for a production of Peter Shaffer's epic play, *The Royal Hunt of the Sun,* about the Spanish general Pizarro's capture of the Incan Sun King, Atahualpa; the experience made me a theater enthusiast. The head of the drama department, Dallas Williams, was an authoritarian and demanding director. I played a nonspeaking role, the wife of the Sun King who gets tortured by the Spanish conquistadors. I took my acting and my work in the theater very seriously. Dr. Williams had very strict rules about theater protocol and I learned from him that the contribution of each person involved in the creative process, no matter how small, is equally important and must be respected by all in order to make the production a successful artistic endeavor. He constantly reminded the actors that without the work of the people behind the scene they were nothing and that their supposed genius was useless. For him the beauty and richness of the process is to be found in the collective effort. This idea would become an important building block in my own inchoate ethics of artistic collaboration.

There were more black students at the University of Nebraska at Lincoln than at Nebraska Wesleyan University, but they were more spread out. In 1968, programs and departments for Black Studies were being created in schools and universities all over the country as a result of a demand for them. Some black students had formed an organization to deal with their concerns and problems on campus. One of them invited me to attend one of the meetings. I explained that the evenings that they had their meetings coincided with the after-school rehearsals for the play that I was in. My interlocutor said that he understood but just wanted to check out "how black" I was. I asked him, with a strong southern accent, "Where are you from?" and he answered, "I am from Omaha, Nebraska." "Well," I said, "I come from Little Rock, Arkansas. You have heard of Little Rock? Well, I really don't feel that I need to prove to anyone how black I am. My entire childhood has made it impossible for me to negate who I am or to forget where I come from. My Negro heritage is a source of strength that I wear with pride like a badge of honor."

Many years later I read an interview that I had given in the French newspaper, *Le Figaro*, which stated that I had overcome the handicaps of being female, poor, and black. This was the journalist's preconceived idea. I have never said nor felt that these were handicaps in my life, but rather that they were empowering tools that have moved me forward, made me strong inside, and, in spite of the pain and difficulty, have greatly enriched my life. The difficulties I have faced have made me more curious and have engendered empathy for others. Are these not the tools that every artist needs? They have certainly helped me to relate to an imaginary character in a play, an opera, or a two-minute song, and to interpret her emotions.

On Sunday mornings Dr. Ganz would pick me up at nine o'clock for choir rehearsal before the church service at eleven. The previous spring I had found a very good friend in an unlikely place: the pulpit of the church. Dr. Clarence Forsberg was the pastor at the Saint Paul Methodist Church. When I accepted the job at the church it was for the extra money that I could earn, and I used to put my chemistry book in my choral folder and study during the sermon. One day I had no patience to study and began to listen to the sermon and was very moved by his words. I began to look forward to his sermons as he looked forward to my singing. He became a close friend and counselor to me.

Finally the spring came and I was going to New York for my audition. Dr. Ganz helped me to fill out the application, get references, and, of course, prepare my audition program. I had chosen the same Puccini and Charpentier arias that I had performed for the Met competition and we added some German and French songs that I had studied with the French coach in Aspen, Madeleine Milhaud. I continued to meet my friends from NWU: Jane, Laurel, Barbara. Karin Eisen had included me in a group of her Jewish friends on campus and one of them invited me to stay with his parents in Long Island while I was in New York. He said that they would be delighted to have me and they even had an upright piano at home so that I could practice.

Juilliard had not yet moved to Lincoln Center and I went to the old building on 116th Street. I sang my audition in front of the voice faculty without problem and I could see that Miss Tourel was pleased; but there was no time for us to speak at length. I also had to take an exam in piano and solfège, or ear training, so that I could be placed in the right class. I had never taken piano lessons and could not play the piano at all. I informed the person who was to give the exam that this was a waste of her time. She insisted that I try. First she asked me to play a scale on the piano in the key of G. I answered her, "I have no idea where G is on the piano." I was placed in beginning piano and solfège courses. Some weeks after my return to Lincoln I received my letter of acceptance to the Juilliard School of Music in the bachelor of music program in voice and opera, with a full scholarship for all of my studies. I would have to take care of my housing, food, and transportation myself.

I did not finish all of my requirements for graduation until the end of the summer, although I was included in the list of graduates for the ceremony in May 1969. My parents wanted to come for the ceremonies but I told them that I was in a class of thousands and that they would not even get to see me receive my diploma. Instead of hanging around for graduation, I went to Atlanta to visit my sister, Ruthie. She had sent me a ticket as a graduation present. I was very happy to spend some time with her again and to see little Billy, who had been a toddler the last time that I had seen him in 1965. Billy was about five years old and as cute as a button with a big head of flaming red hair and freckles. He was also very mischievous; I awoke one morning to find him and three friends standing around my bed. He wanted to show them his aunt who had come to visit. I spoke a lot with Ruthie and Bill about how my life had changed during the past years and they were very supportive and encouraging. They were still very involved in the work with SNCC and this time I was able to join in the conversation with their close friend Julian Bond.

I returned from Atlanta to start the summer semester at the University of Nebraska so that I could finish the few remaining courses that I needed to complete in order to receive my diploma. I was making the last preparations to go to New York but I had the time to add an elective course in music. I auditioned and was chosen to sing the role of Amelia in Verdi's *Un ballo in maschera*, the university's music department's summer semester opera production. Of course my voice was more suited to the lighter soprano role of Oscar but the singer who was chosen for that role had a voice so much lighter than mine that in comparison the music director's choice made some sense. Dr. Ganz reluctantly agreed and he was watching closely over me to insure that I did not force my voice and that the orchestra did not play too loudly. We both considered it to be a good experience for me to perform a major role in an opera production. I knew that as a non–music major I would never have been allowed to sing a leading role during the school year. During these rehearsals I gained a little more experience about how to learn and interpret a role. My performance was warmly applauded by friends and family and I had learned how to navigate the difficulties of the role without causing any damage to my voice. I never sang the role again.

Although my parents were disappointed not to come to the big graduation ceremony in May, they and my brothers, Malvin and Michael, came to visit when I finished my studies in August. I sang a farewell recital at the home of Pat and Dick Smith with both of my families present—my own family and the Websters. Mrs. Sidles and the other ladies from the Metropolitan Opera auditions committee, Reverend Forsberg and members of the St. Paul Methodist Church, my chemistry, math, and voice professors, friends from the choir and church, and other supporters were also present. There was a big reception given for me at the Lincoln Country Club. My parents did not know what to think when we arrived there for dinner. This could never have happened in Little Rock even in 1969. My close friend Percy, president of the student council at Horace Mann High, had worked as a busboy at the country club in Little Rock and told me about the young black boy who worked with him who tripped and fell into the swimming pool. They immediately drained the pool and cleaned it out because none of the guests would have swum in the same water.

I continued to visit the Websters during my school holidays from Juilliard. I often went with them to their chalet in Breckenridge, Colorado, where a Norwegian, Olaf Pederson, taught me to ski. They never missed my important debuts in New York and came to my concerts whenever I was performing within five hundred miles of where they were. After Wanda's death I saw less of Dr. Webster, who had retired and moved from Nebraska to Colorado. I met him again in 2000 in Aspen; he came over from Breckenridge for my concert. We met the day after for lunch. It was the last time that we would meet; I was so grateful that I was able to say to him, "I can never find the words to thank you and Wanda for the support and the love that you gave me. It has been a true privilege to be a member of your family." Little Dougie, who at age six was a bit of nuisance, later became a professional singer and says that it was listening to me practice while hiding under the piano that had inspired him to want to sing too. Doug still keeps me updated about how things are with his family and in his professional life.

New York 5

Music expresses that which cannot be said and on which it is impossible to be silent.

— Victor Hugo

When the summer of 1969 came to an end I packed all of my earthly belongings into an old trunk I had bought at the army-navy store. My favorite books filled most of it: my art history book, my physical chemistry book about quantum mechanics, a complete collection of Hermann Hesse that my friend Sue Goebel had lent me, and a book on the history of the international cinema. I put my few clothes and toiletries into the rest of the space.

As I was making the final preparations to leave I began to have mixed feelings. I was uncertain what to expect or what to wish for, yet it was all so exciting. I have always relished the "so what now?" moments in my life that occur after the end of an episode or relationship and before a new one has started, the small windows of opportunity that one can so easily fail to seize. Somehow by looking at my fears straight on I have been able to cross those thresholds, forging through them on my path to freedom.

Dr. and Mrs. Webster accompanied me to the train station. We gave each other long, tearful hugs and Mrs. Webster gave me final words of encouragement. "You are going to love being at Juilliard and studying singing; I know that you are going to be just fine. We are proud of you and love you." I boarded the train and we waved to each other as it pulled away from the platform. Mrs. Webster and I were crying like babies and Dr. Webster wiped away a few tears from his cheeks.

I installed myself in my couchette on that night train to Chicago. Had I taken the train some years earlier from Arkansas I would have been seated in the part of the train reserved for "Colored Only." The last of my tears dried on my cheeks, and I took out the meal that Mrs. Webster had so lovingly prepared for me. I ate in silence and looked out the window at the passing landscape, my thoughts rushing at the same pace as the changing images. I was trying to imagine what was lying ahead. Nothing came to me. I had just an empty screen. Tired from all of the emotion, I allowed the sound of the train wheels rolling into the night to lull me into a deep sleep as the plains of Nebraska disappeared.

I awoke in time to see the approaching enormity of Chicago. Memphis, the largest city that I had ever known, was a quiet sleepy town in comparison. I had several hours to kill before continuing on the night train to New York. I walked out of Union Station and searched for a place where I could eat some breakfast. I sat down at a table in a nearby café, watched the bustling flow of people to and fro, and listened to the subway overhead empty out its passengers and then fill up again. I wondered how I should fill the day before returning to catch my next train. I had put my belongings in a locker, so after breakfast I decided to walk around. I was afraid to go too far from the station and get lost; I could not miss my train. After some time walking around I passed a cinema and I decided to watch a few films to pass the time. (Going to the cinema during the day when it was nearly empty with my lunch in a bag became one of my favorite pastimes later on when I lived in New York.) I bought some sandwiches and sat through two films. I do not remember the first film but the last was *Midnight Cowboy* with a very young Dustin Hoffman. I was a little shaken by the violent and merciless picture that it presented of New York City. It should have frightened me enough to make me take the return train back to the safety of Lincoln, but an hour before the departure time I walked slowly back to Union Station to take my place on the train to Pennsylvania Station.

I had wanted to learn to play the piano since I was about ten years old and had often asked my parents if I could take lessons, but there was never any money left over in the family's budget. And now as the train edged me closer to the opportunity to not only learn to play the piano but also to study singing I knew that there was going to be so much more that I was going to be able to learn. I was feeling a little numb; my imagination was still unable to conjure up a plausible scenario of what my life was going to be like. Most of the music students that I had met had been studying their instruments since a very young age; I would have to work very hard to catch up on fundamental and rudimentary musical knowledge.

I believe that, in general, our purpose in life is to learn; I define my success by the quality of that process and it is a source of true joy for me. I decided there on the train that I would become a human sponge to soak up all the knowledge that my studies at Juilliard, the city, and its inhabitants could offer me. Since I had no cherished outcomes I expected nothing. I was not about to fulfill a childhood dream since this was not a dream afforded to a little Negro girl from Arkansas. I certainly had never dreamed about becoming a rich and famous diva. I was just continuing on my journey.

When I was a little girl running through the fields, conversing with my imaginary friend, I dreamed about being able to fly far beyond the boundaries of that existence in search of my purpose. Now I was on my first great leap of faith. Throughout my life, I have met angels who have inspired me, guided me, and protected me on my way and I knew that I would not be alone. When I turned sixty I wanted to be able to say to myself and to my children, "I dared to grab the reins of opportunity and run with the wild horses and that is why I am who I am today." I did not want to bitterly say, "I could have been something else, had a different life, but I did not dare." Had I not succeeded as a musician, I would have preferred to say, "I tried something really crazy when I was twenty. It was fun but did not lead to a career and I am completely happy and fulfilled with my life as it is."

Dr. Victor and Mrs. Margaret Young picked me up at Penn Station. Margaret Young was the cousin of my adviser, Dr.

Cromwell, head of the chemistry department at UN. Dr. Young was a physics professor at a local college on Long Island and Mrs. Young was a housewife. I stayed with them in Port Washington on Long Island until I could find housing. I had received a full scholarship for my studies, but as Juilliard had no dormitories at that time all students had to find and provide for their own housing, transportation, and food, as well as all other personal expenses. After a few weeks Mr. Smith called me to say that his former pastor in Lincoln, Reverend Stewart, was now at the Presbyterian Church on Park Avenue on the East Side. He was willing to rent me the maid's room in his apartment. I could use the kitchen and I would have my own bathroom. I would have preferred to be on the West Side nearer school, but I felt safe to be within a family yet still independent. During my first year Mr. Smith sent me forty dollars for my rent every month, which he had collected from my group of Nebraska supporters.

I visited Dr. and Mrs. Young regularly on weekends whenever I wanted to get away from the city. I sometimes sang in their church on Sundays. They became very loyal friends and ardent supporters, never missing any of my concerts in the New York area; whenever Mrs. Young came into the city, she always brought me some homemade cakes and cookies.

I immediately sought work through the school, so already on the first day I was working at the registration desk to welcome new and returning students to their new building at Lincoln Center. I met my future boyfriend, Norman, that day when he came to get his registration card— I noticed that he was from North Little Rock.

After everyone had finished with registration we all gathered in the new Juilliard Theater for the first student assembly in the new building. I was very humbled and a little frightened by a phrase in the welcoming speech that President Peter Mennin gave to the student body and faculty that day. When he referred to us as the "La crème de la crème," I thought, Not so fast—I am just raw milk, please allow me the time to become cream.

Juilliard had been on 116th Street near Columbia University, where I sang my audition, since 1920. Because the 1969–70 school year was the inaugural year for the new building, events were organized every weekend to present the facilities to sponsors, alumni, and so on. I was able to find work as a guide showing the new school to these special visitors, and I served champagne and hors d'oeuvres during the many receptions. I became well acquainted with Dr. and Mrs. Peter Mennin because I met them often during those many functions. Lorraine Nubar, student and assistant to Jennie Tourel, whom I had met in Aspen, helped me to find work on the weekends in an upscale shoe store, Pappagallo's on Fifty-Fourth Street between Fifth Avenue and Madison Avenue. Nearly all of the young girls who worked there were aspiring artists, dancers, singers, or actresses. The shop was owned by a benevolent soul, Mr. Seligman, who loved music and enjoyed offering the opportunity to his talented salesgirls to give a recital before a live audience in the small concert hall located in the basement floor of the shop. I worked there two years, but he sold the shop before I was ready to give a recital. The new owner changed the name of the shop and the concerts and other artistic activities ended.

I also found work at an insurance company that was just across the street from Juilliard on the corner of Sixty-Sixth and Broadway, so whenever I had more than two hours free I could go down and work. My bachelor's degree in chemistry and mathematics left me overeducated for any job that they might offer me, but completely underskilled. My typing was disgraceful. So I was given a job filing away or searching for cards among the endless walls of filing cabinets. I found this work tedious but convenient. I always had sore and bloody cuticles because I did not know that I could buy a small rubber protector for my fingers.

The Stewarts were very kind, but I never became a member of the family as I had with the Websters. And politically, they were extremely conservative. I began attending the mostly white Presbyterian church with them on Sundays, but it was not at all the warm atmosphere that I had grown fond of in the Saint Paul United Methodist Church in Lincoln with Dr. Forsberg. Reverend Stewart was an assistant pastor in this big city, Upper East Side church whose members were as wealthy as they were conservative. His superior was very clear about his political point of view, especially in his support for the Vietnam War and President

Nixon. So I excused myself from Sunday services, saying that I had so much work to do. I slept in a little later than on week-days and ate a late breakfast in the kitchen with their teenage son, Bob, who was grateful to have someone young to speak with and was also happy to avoid the services as well. I most often met my friends at their apartments; we spent the day walking around in Central Park whenever the weather permitted. The park was my injection of nature in the concrete city.

The school was closed on Sundays so I could not go there to work. During the week and even sometimes on Saturdays after work I spent most of my time there, often staying late after my classes to practice and to learn new repertoire. I did not have a piano in the apartment, nor my own record player—I had to listen to records in the school library. I again found my home away from home in the libraries at Juilliard and later at the one in Lincoln Center, just as I had done as a little girl in Arkansas and Tennes-see. I was often in school until the building closed at ten at night.

Just being on the streets of New York was a varied and col-orful adventure. The "pastor's daughter" had been my identity in my community in Arkansas, so I had enjoyed being one stu-dent among thousands at NWU and U of N. The anonymity of New York City was perfect for me; I was happy to melt into this mixture of different cultures and backgrounds. I was constantly watching people and listening to the many sounds of the city. It was like being on a movie set. I often walked through the park from the east side to the west side and then took the bus or subway downtown to Lincoln Center; my head was full of the impressions of my crosstown commute. But when I walked through the doors of the school I sensed that I was entering a sanctuary because I was there to study with Jennie Tourel. After my musical baptism in Aspen it was as if I had been chosen to enter an order, and I was at the first stage, a postulant. It would be determined at a later date whether I would become a novice and earn the right to serve the high and noble cause of Art.

My life revolved around my lessons with Miss Tourel. They inspired and fueled me. I had other classes that were also impor-tant—piano, solfège, music theory, and three foreign languages—but none as inspirational. In our voice curriculum, each year was devoted to one language's diction and its repertoire. The first year was Italian, and then came German, French, and English. Yes, English. Although the English-language repertoire is small, English is a difficult language to sing well so that it is intelligible, even or maybe especially for one whose mother tongue is English. I was taking a bachelor of music program and so I had some other courses such as civilization and history in my schedule. Because I already had a BS from the U of N I was given credit for those humanities courses that I had already taken. I was in the vocal and opera department, so I also took lessons in dance, mime, and acting. My dance teacher was José Limón, one of the pioneers of American modern dance, and my mime and acting teacher was Moni Yakim.

Of course, my top priorities were my weekly private lesson with Miss Tourel and her Tuesday afternoon master class. Already in Aspen we had begun to bond, and from the beginning we spoke the same language and understood one another. We shared the same passion for learning the music and we both treasured traveling along the track from the written score to a living performance. The starting point, the score, is a map; vocal technique, diction, rhythm, and dynamics are rails on which black dots on white lined paper travel and are transformed into emotions and vibrations and, if we have earned it, moments of grace.

When I arrived at my appointed time to her studio, her first question was, "Have you warmed up?" I answered, "Just a little bit." She said, "All right, let's do a few scales." We both found vocalizing for the sake of vocalizing a bit boring. As she played the scales I sang them as she indicated; she would make comments, and then when we had finished and my voice was warmed up she asked with curiosity in her voice, "What do you have to sing for me today?" Then the lesson and the fun would begin in earnest. We were both impatient to get to the piece of music that I had chosen and to sink our teeth into it. She accepted that I arrived without warming up my voice, but she expected that I had worked enough on the music and the diction to be able to sing it almost from memory. I could use the score but not sight-read from it. She sometimes asked me to speak the text and even to translate the poem into English before beginning to sing. She was multilingual so she was able to correct German, French, Italian, and Russian diction. I was prepared to read the poem in the original language, and although I could not yet speak any of these languages, I had to know the meanings of each word that I was singing. I often chose the songs that I sang in my lessons. When I came to a passage in the score that was difficult or that I just could not sing as indicated, Miss Tourel would stop and we would work technically on that problem.

During those first lessons Miss Tourel was trying to classify my voice; she asked me to learn songs and arias in different styles and different tessituras. She was trying not only to determine what my repertoire should be for my lessons but more important to foresee the direction in which it might evolve as I grew vocally and artistically. I had a very pure, boyish sound with an extended top up to a comfortable high E, which might have indicated that I was a coloratura and would sing roles such as Blonde in Mozart's *Die Entführung aus dem Serail* or Zerbinetta in Strauss's *Ariadne auf Naxos*. To my relief she determined immediately that I was not a coloratura. The first time I heard the term "coloratura" when I was in the choir in Merrill Junior High, I thought it meant "colored" soprano. Lorraine thought that maybe my voice was more suited for the soubrette roles like Despina, Zerlina, or Marcellina, the "ina" roles. But Miss Tourel said no. She based her decision on my timbre. She said, "Your voice is light and slim but when I hear the color and intensity in your sound, and especially your timbre and temperament, I hear a lyric soprano, not a soubrette, and certainly not a coloratura." I was happy not to be a coloratura, as I was not at all attracted to the repertoire. She also said that my voice already could expand easily in the higher range like a full lyric soprano in a way that soubrette voices could never do, as they tend to become thinner as they ascend in range. She asked me to prepare "Sola, perduta, abbandonata" from Puccini's *Manon Lescaut*. As soon as I finished, she said, "This is not something that you can sing now: the top is no problem but you do not have the medium yet for these roles. Puccini can wait for a while but you can start with roles such as Mozart's Susanna and Pamina and when the medium catches up with the top of the voice you will leave these behind and go into the French roles such as Massenet's Manon and Offenbach's Antonia. You must be patient; you have time, and for now we will concentrate on song repertoire and some Mozart arias. But I can hear that your voice will be perfect for a Mimì or Liu in some years and maybe even Madame Butterfly." This made me very happy because I had longed to sing Mimì since my first encounter with Puccini's *La bohème* in Aspen in 1968. I would get my wish in my third year at Juilliard and sang Mimì and Lauretta in *Gianni Schicchi* the same year with the Met Studio. I was content to begin slowly and to take my time.

The Italian language and diction class was taught by Miss Evelina Colorni; I improved my Italian, learned some simple Italian songs, and then gradually added a few Mozart arias in Italian, of course.

Every Tuesday afternoon Miss Tourel gave her master class. The class had a different title every year, like "Russian Songs and Arias" or "French Mélodies," but we could really sing whatever we wanted. For her students this was a perfect complement to our weekly private lesson, almost a continuation, although in front of a very critical and sometimes jealous audience of other singing students. Her master class was very popular with her own voice students as well as the students of other teachers at Juilliard; many pianists offered to play for it and others came just to listen, along with some instrumental and conducting students.

I was slowly building a repertoire of songs and arias that I had heard in concert, but Miss Tourel's Tuesday afternoon master class was one of my richest sources of new songs. Whenever I heard a song or an aria that touched me I wanted to learn it and sing it right away. I added Schubert lieder, Mozart concert arias, and even Russian songs to my repertoire. I also listened to many of her recordings during my late evening visits to the school library. In addition to the new Italian repertoire that I was learning Miss Tourel also introduced me to the French mélodie.

When I listened to a recording of Miss Tourel singing Debussy's *Cinq poèmes de Baudelaire* I could not resist them. I decided to prepare them for my lesson. I wanted to make sure that I would perform them well so I learned them completely from her recording because she had the most impeccable diction—but I also copied how she sang, including every one of her mannerisms.

Even though I had heard her admonish other singers during the master classes for having listened to and tried to imitate some well-known singers, like Maria Callas or Birgit Nilsson, I thought that she would not mind and maybe would be flattered that I had listened to her. I arrived quite pleased with myself, thinking that I knew exactly how she would like to hear me sing the songs. When I had finished, she said with horror, "Where did you pick up those tasteless habits of scooping into the notes like that? It is awful." I swallowed hard and said, sheepishly, "Oh, I just felt it that way." I did not dare admit that I had been listening to her recording and had just copied her. So I had to start all over again and sing only what was written in the score, cleaning away all of her mannerisms. I looked at the score in a different way, searching for what Debussy wanted, and I tried to do that to the best of my abilities. The result was that I sang Debussy's music with my own voice and sensitivity while taking the lead directly from him, not some other interpreter. Needless to say, I never listened to another recording as part of my preparation to learn my music.

I was very happy that she had been so strict with me because I was chosen to sing these songs in a master class with a Swiss tenor, Hugues Cuénod, and I was very well prepared. I sang my European opera debut with him in Cavalli's *La Calisto* at the Glyndebourne Festival Opera in 1974. When I moved from Paris to Switzerland, Hugues, who lived to be over one hundred years old, became my neighbor. Of course I sometimes listen to recordings of others when I am searching for repertoire, but once I decide to learn a piece, I will only listen to it again after having performed it at least once myself.

This also taught me another very important lesson: not to seek shortcuts to get to the interpretation of the score. I had to give the time necessary, like a good detective trying to solve a crime, to follow the clues that the score indicated so that I would arrive closer to the interpretation inherent in it. It took many years for me to master my impatience, to tame my frustration, and to accept that there is no substitution for the time that it takes to do anything well. When the interpretation is true and genuine, it comes of itself, naturally, and that is sheer grace.

Learning this has certainly helped me in other aspects of my life. A journalist once asked me, "Do you ever get so discouraged that the peace and reconciliation that you believe in and work so hard to obtain in so many parts of the world has not been achieved that you want to give up?" I answered, "Oh, of course I get discouraged, but I have accepted that I may not live to see the fruits of my activism for human rights. I do feel deeply that I have a responsibility to participate by making the small steps necessary while maintaining constant vigilance, without expecting medals or honors for it."

Miss Tourel was extremely demanding and had no tolerance at all for superficial singers who only wanted to show off their voices. She made it clear that we should strive to express true emotions and at all costs avoid self-indulgence by resorting to cheap sentimentality. She considered that the beauty of the voice was indeed an important asset, but a wasted one without dedication and hard work. She was more supportive of and interested in working with students who were serious about their music even if they had not been endowed with the most beautiful instrument.

She was not a "technical" teacher—she could work on small problems but she was not the right teacher for those with severe technical problems. I don't think that the technique of singing was so interesting to her; it was only a tool to facilitate an artistic end, not an end in itself. In any case she would certainly not fit into what I call the "car mechanic school" of voice teaching that became the rage after her generation of teachers had disappeared. If the voice is broken, they can probably fix it, resulting in perfectly tuned, standardized, all-purpose singers who are impressive while you listen to them but instantly forgotten as soon as the music ends.

I am not sure that singing can be taught in the same way that piano or violin playing can be taught. The teacher-student relationship is a very complex one and no one teacher is good for every student. At best a good voice teacher can inspire a student to search for the best that she has in herself and to help with small problems on the way. The impetus for singing must come from within.

I did have a natural voice and sang with ease; I was like a rough stone and she was the ideal person to polish the edges. She said, "You will just need to let your voice evolve into what it wants to be, not what you want it to be, and you will be fine." Many singing students seemed to be obsessed with technique. I never knew what to say during these conversations. I did not think about how to produce a sound; I thought about how to sing the phrase. I would often think to myself, You don't have any technique; you just sing naturally and when she tells you to do something you just do it.

When I left every lesson I could not wait to get to a practice room so that I could try alone what I had managed to do with her guidance. But I was also still trying to figure out how what I was doing would help me decipher the many questions that I had about my life. I began to find some answers. Miss Tourel showed me by example the path to take. She always warned me about listening to what ignorant critics of all kinds—including other students, family members, and eventually agents, record company heads, etc.—might say about my voice or performance. "Don't listen too much to what is being said around you: most of it is complete rubbish anyway. Put on blinders like the ones that are put on horses," she would say, placing her hands on the sides of her face, "and stay true to your own path." That is what I continue to do. I do not bother with the *noise*. "Never mind if they say that the voice is small or that the voice is big or whatever, never force your voice and respect what it can and cannot do."

I had no preconceived ideas about what success should look like. I had known since I was in sixth grade that I had a better than average talent and would have certainly been happy to continue as an amateur, singing solos in the church or in an amateur choir. But the meeting with Jennie Tourel put me on another path. I was still in flight, but I had a parachute and I was savoring the glide.

In 1969 Jennie Tourel was sixty-nine years old and belonged to a privileged generation of European artists and teachers that was slowly beginning to disappear. She was an important connection to a tradition and time that would soon be gone. Her generation had traveled and toured by boat and train, not by plane—and certainly not on the Concorde. The slower, more deliberate rhythm of their voyages and tours certainly reflected the deliberation with which they developed into great artists. She passed on to me an invaluable and rare legacy. This came not only from my lessons with her, where we searched together like two obsessed explorers to find the way to breathe life and meaning into a score, but also in my observations of Jennie Tourel, the performing artist. An artist, I concluded, is one who has accepted the call to serve and is always at the service of her art. Once I had diligently studied the score and vocally adhered to its demands my goal was to become a master at communicating the true emotions of the music, to add flesh to the skeletal form of the score as it breathes emotional life into the music.

I was beginning to develop a relationship with my own talent. I saw it as a gift to be nurtured and felt that I should never exploit it to feed my ego or even my financial prosperity. I relished the knowledge that my talent, my birthright, could be called to a higher purpose than just a tool for obtaining employment. This gave me a strong sense of purpose and an enormous responsibility. I saw that the way of true service would require musical preparation as well as important work on myself. I had to put myself into question at all times. The task seemed daunting, but when I thought about it I felt so light and free. This was the same equation that I discovered in 1965 when the Voting Act was passed: civic responsibility equals freedom. Being a true artist would free me from the need to seek love or acceptance from outside of myself, from critics, and even from future audiences. I had to be true to the score, be responsible, and serve it with humility.

Miss Tourel was and still is my greatest inspiration. I observed her in class, in rehearsal, and on stage. She often performed with friends like Leonard Bernstein or Pablo Casals who admired her artistry and professionalism. She was "a musician's musician," and that is what I wanted to become. So I realized that I too must always push outward from my limits, never to be content with present or past achievements. This meant always trying new repertoire, not just singing what was considered my *Fach*.*[1]

I do not believe in idols. As a matter of fact, one of the reasons our relationship was successful is because it was based on mutual admiration and respect. She was so impressed that I had received a university degree in mathematics and chemistry because she said that she had problems balancing her checkbook.

When I began my studies in New York, I was very happy and excited, but I had doubts that were a residue of my strict Protestant upbringing. I was preparing myself for a profession that my parents did not consider necessary for the enhancement of society, like being a teacher or a doctor would have been. In addition, I so enjoyed singing that I felt a bit egotistic, and therefore ashamed. Miss Tourel was the living counterargument to this line of thought. After many years working to become a true artist it was clear to me that art is as necessary for human existence as the air that we breathe and the water that we drink because it comes from our collective consciousness and has the power to remind us of the original unity of humanity. I felt that striving to become an artist like her was indeed a noble cause that could give profound meaning to my life and my quest, even as undefined as it was at that time. Until I turned fifty I never dared to speak of myself as an "artist," but called myself a musician seeking to become an artist. When I did speak of myself as an artist it was in a whisper.

---

*The German *Fach*, pl. *Fächer*—literally "compartment" or also "subject (of study)," here in the sense of "(vocal) specialization"—system is a method of classifying singers, primarily opera singers, according to the range, weight, and color of their voices. It is used worldwide, but primarily in Europe, especially in German-speaking countries and by repertory opera houses. The *Fach* system is a convenience for singers and opera houses. A singer who is identified as being of a certain *Fach* or voice type will usually be asked to sing only roles that belong to that *Fach*. This prevents a singer from being asked to sing roles which he or she is incapable of performing. Opera companies keep lists of available singers by *Fach* so that when they are casting roles for an upcoming production, they do not inadvertently contact performers who would be inappropriate for the part.

Miss Tourel was a bit of a mystery for us; we knew very little of her private life. There was much confusion about where she was born and her birth date. I was told that she was born in Russia and that her family had lived in St. Petersburg when she was a child. She fled with her family after the revolution to Latvia, then to Germany, and finally ended up in France. She played the flute and later the piano and because of her talent was the star of the family. She was planning a career as a pianist but started to take voice lessons and decided instead to become a singer. I found out after her death that she was born in Russia, in Vitebsk, in what is now Belarus, in June 1900, but she always said that she was ten years younger. Born Jennie Davidovitch or Davidson—I have seen both names—she composed the name Tourel from the name of her voice teacher in Paris, Anna El Tour. She also studied with the composer Reynaldo Hahn. She made her career at the Opéra-Comique and was one of the mezzo-sopranos responsible for reversing the tradition of light coloratura sopranos singing the original mezzo Rossini roles such as Rosina from *Il barbiere di Siviglia*, *La Cenerentola*, and *Il turco in Italia* solely as vehicles to show off their technical prowess. She was able to give a depth and dramatic aspect to the roles that was often sorely missing when sung by lighter voices. She was also devoted to the French repertoire: Thomas's *Mignon*, Bizet's *Carmen*, and Charlotte in Massenet's *Werther* were among her signature roles at the Opéra-Comique. It is not clear if she ever married her longtime companion, Yakob Michaelson, a Russian painter whom she had met in Paris. According to her good friend Joseph Machlis:

> This chapter in Tourel's life was brought to an abrupt end by the German invasion. With her longtime companion, the gifted painter Yakob Michaelson, she escaped just a week before the Germans entered Paris. Along with other desperate refugees, they set out on a hair-raising journey, part of it by foot, that brought them to Portugal. An epidemic of typhoid was raging in Lisbon, and Tourel became very ill. She had the good fortune to be admitted to a nunnery, where she was taken care of until she recovered. After many difficulties, Tourel and Michaelson obtained the necessary visas

for Havana, from which they made their way to Canada and finally reached New York.

America did not have an open door policy toward those fleeing Nazi Germany and was not even in the war when Jennie Tourel fled from Paris. The immigration laws were complicated: one could enter on a tourist visa but then had to leave the United States for another country and then return with a different kind of visa. And knowing what I do about the resourcefulness of refugees this could have been what she had to do. In any case, she was already singing lead roles at the Metropolitan Opera in 1943.

She had such a strong connection to Russian culture, its art, its music, and its literature that she infected me with her passion. I had already read some Dostoyevsky and Tolstoy novels and never missed an opportunity to see the Juilliard theater school productions of Chekov and Gorky plays. The book *Chaliapin: An Autobiography as told to Maxim Gorky,* told by the great Russian bass Fyodor Chaliapin, was a gift from Miss Tourel that I immediately treasured. Chaliapin states:

> My life has as its leitmotif the struggle against:
> The sham glitter that eclipses the inner light
> The complexities that kill simplicity
> The vulgar externals that diminishes true grandeur.

I memorized the passage from the book and adopted it as my own leitmotif.

After my discovery of German lieder in Aspen in 1968, I wanted to sing this repertoire and I began with Schubert. At the end of my first year I prepared Schubert's "Gretchen am Spinnrade" from Goethe's *Faust*. I had also just broken up with my boyfriend, Norman; rather, he had broken up with me without giving me a reason. I was very sad and confused when I walked into Miss Tourel's studio to sing Gretchen's sorrowful song about her broken heart and the impossibility of finding inner peace. I projected all of my pain and confusion into the song, started to cry, and could not finish. Miss Tourel gave me a tissue to dry my eyes, sent the pianist out, and sat me down. I told her what had happened. She said, "I know that you are hurting so you should not try to sing this song any more today. You must be able to use your experiences for your art but never substitute your life for the life of the character that you want to portray. Gretchen's story is not yours and you owe the audience Gretchen's story." So I made a rule for myself: "Even if someone in your family dies and you decide to go on stage to sing, the audience must not be aware that you have a problem. If you can't do this then you should cancel."

When I was not in school or working, I walked through the streets of the city, soaking up all that the Big Apple had to offer me. I never felt quite at home in my wealthy upper class neighborhood between Madison and Park Avenues, but living very close to the Metropolitan Museum and the Guggenheim was one of the advantages. The Museum of Modern Art was not far from where I worked on Saturdays and I went there whenever I could. I found ways to get student tickets to see dance performances, the theater, orchestral concerts, jazz, lots of chamber music, and some opera. I had made friends with some dancers at school and I went with them to see the Martha Graham, Alvin Ailey, and José Limón dance companies. Sometimes the tickets were much cheaper at the Brooklyn Academy than they were in the city so I would get on the subway and go there. I had friends who worked in Carnegie Hall as ushers and I would go and hang around in the lobby and then manage to slip into a seat just as the doors were closing. I heard many recitals with the greatest musicians in the world. Since latecomers were not allowed into the hall once the concert had begun I knew that I was safe in my seat at least until intermission and then I could wait around for another empty seat if someone had shown up to take "my" seat.

When I read that Rudolf Nureyev and Margot Fonteyn were going to perform Prokofiev's *Romeo and Juliet* with Covent Garden's Royal Ballet at the Metropolitan Opera I did not want to take a chance. I saved enough to buy an orchestra seat down front and center. I took the money that I had saved for my weekly food allowance and spent it all on my ticket. It was to be the first time that I would even enter this part of the theater. Before that I had only sat up in the very top of the house where there were a few student seats with no visibility. I felt that I had given myself a luxurious treat as I walked down the center aisle. The unforgettable performance was worth a week of living on peanut butter sandwiches. I could not take my eyes from Nureyev; even when he was in a crowd with his back to the audience his energy was so strong that he filled the entire stage with his vibrant presence. Margot Fonteyn, already at an age when most ballerinas had long been retired, was the most youthful ballerina there. To this day she is the most touching Juliet that I have ever seen. I left the performance inspired by both of them. I wanted to be able to master my own energy like Nureyev and acquire Margot Fonteyn's ability to imbue every fiber of her being with the essence of her character. She was a model for me when I sang Juliet at the Paris Opera years later.

On May 4, 1970, near the end of my first school year in New York, four students were killed and nine others wounded by members of the Ohio National Guard at Kent State University. Some of them were protesting the American invasion of Cambodia. Others were merely passing by or watching from a distance. All over the country millions of students from junior and senior high schools, colleges, and universities responded to this horrible massacre with a national strike on Friday, May 8.

I was among the students and faculty members at Juilliard who wanted to join in the strike. This was more difficult than I had imagined because most of the music students had little or no interest in politics and some even asked questions such as, "Does being on strike mean that I cannot practice?" or "Will I be able to do my final jury next week?" After three days of trying to agree on the meaning of the word "strike" we decided to do a partial strike; the school did not close down like hundreds throughout the country had. But we managed to do a successful silent march at lunchtime in Lincoln Center Plaza, wearing black armbands, and we were joined by others who worked there. (The professors who had participated in the silent march in Lincoln Center were all fired, as we found out when we returned in September.) After the silent march I went to work a few hours at the insurance company where my black armband was not at all well received. I decided to quit my job there that day. A small group of us joined with students from Yale to charter a bus to go to Washington, DC, for the big march over the weekend.

We were a merry crowd on the bus to and from Washington singing protest songs; the Yale students had put a big banner on the side of the bus: "Get our Dick out of Vietnam." On Saturday, May 9, I marched with one hundred thousand people from all over America at the same place where Martin Luther King gave his "I Have a Dream" speech. I stood at the Lincoln Memorial and pictured the brave Marian Anderson singing there in 1939 and was moved and humbled. Of course, I had come in solidarity with the fallen students but even more to protest a war that I did not believe in. I could not forget the horrifying images of the My Lai massacre that were published on the cover of many national magazines on my birthday, November 20, 1969.

I applied for a full scholarship from the Aspen Music School to study with Miss Tourel over the summer and I was happy that I received it. School concluded at the end of May and I had one month free before classes in Aspen began. I returned to Lincoln to visit the Webster family and to sing at the wedding of my friend Lynn Purvis. Larry, Nan, and Freddy were also home to meet me. I met many of my friends from NWU and the U of N. After the wedding I went to Little Rock to prepare for my first recital there, with Arthur Porter playing the piano. My mother did not at all like my new hairdo, a large Afro that demanded a lot of upkeep.

I returned to Aspen for the summer of 1970 as a "Jennie Tourel student." I had a new direction in mind and was able to benefit from this time with her in a way that I had not been able to do in 1968. It felt good to be back in the Rocky Mountains, to slow down to an entirely different rhythm than I had in New York City. This setting allowed Miss Tourel and I to be more concentrated and to intensify our work together. I had fewer classes and much less distraction than at Juilliard. I again studied French diction and acting with Madeleine Milhaud. She had been an actress and I looked forward to working in more depth in her acting class. She greatly appreciated the fact that I worked hard and loved to sing French mélodies. After the death of her husband Darius in 1974 she moved back to her apartment in Pigalle in Paris and I visited her there often.

I knew my way around Aspen and was not just the fascinated observer that I had been in 1968. After a year in New York attending many concerts I actually listened to them differently. I spent a lot of time reading about theater, Stanislavski, Antonin Artaud, and Jerzy Grotowski. Mr. and Mrs. Smith came from Lincoln to visit and stayed with their close friends Mr. and Mrs. Courtland Barnes, who had a beautiful ranch. I had met them already in 1968 and they invited me often to their home. At the end of the summer course I went to visit the Websters and my parents briefly before returning to New York. My parents were still not at all convinced that I had not totally lost my mind.

I had to get back to New York before school began so that I could get installed for the new school year. I needed to find an apartment and had decided that I wanted to live alone. I knew how difficult it was to find an apartment in the city, especially on a student budget, but I did not expect the horrible experience that awaited me. The first time that I would have to personally deal directly with racial discrimination was to be in cosmopolitan New York City, not in Mississippi or Arkansas.

Before the end of the previous school year I had entered a few competitions, the Liederkranz and the Marcella Sembrich at the Kosciuszko Foundation in New York City (the competition honors the great Polish soprano who won an international reputation and established the voice faculties at both the Juilliard School and the Curtis Institute). I won the first prize in both of the competitions—one thousand dollars each. I had used some of the money to get to Aspen and had put the rest of it away for the apartment. I had hoped that after paying the agent's fee and the two months rent as a guarantee I would still have a few months' rent left.

The blatant racism of the unscrupulous real estate agents who I met was overwhelming. I had been staying with different friends and when their roommates showed up for the school year I would have to move to another friend. I would get up early to get the *NY Times* or stay up late the night before to get one of the first copies. The big Sunday edition of the paper had the bulk of the ads and came out just before midnight on Saturdays. I went to Times

Square to buy it and return to my friend's apartment in the wee hours of Sunday morning. On Sunday I combed the ads looking for apartments that I could afford and that were not too far from school. As soon as I awoke on Monday morning I started to call and let the phone ring until someone answered, knowing that I was the first person to call that day. I would say, "I am interested in the apartment in the ad, is it still free?" and they would say, "It is still free, you can come and look at it this morning." When I arrived, the agent would look at me and say straight to my face, without missing a beat, "Oh, I am so sorry but the apartment is no longer free, the person who saw it last night just called and has decided to take it." This happened to me so many times that I knew the response as soon as I saw by the look in her eyes that she had not realized that I was black. I tried not to let this deter me or get me down, because I still had two more weeks to find something. I met one agent who seemed to want to help me but she only offered me apartments in very dangerous neighborhoods far from school; the only apartment that she sent me to visit was on the first floor above a liquor store. I would have been afraid to leave or come home after dark. She would never have sent her own daughter to these places.

I had been longing for an apartment near school so that I could walk and save money on transportation. I found one apartment that was just a ten-minute walk from school and had even given my money to the agent to reserve it. When he called and said that I could not have it I did not even listen to the reason because I panicked when he refused to give me my money back. But I was lucky; a friend of mine who was a lawyer threatened to go to the police.

Time was running out and I did not know what to do. School was going to start in a few days and I was still living out of a suitcase on the kindness of friends who themselves had very small living quarters. I put my money back in the bank, grateful that I had not lost it all. The next day I went back to the office of the lady who had sent me to the dangerous neighborhood. She was just signing over an apartment in my price range to a white law student at Fordham University. It was on the other side of the Metropolitan Opera building, a five-minute walk from the

Juilliard School. This guy had come to her that very day for the first time and I had been groveling in front of her for the last three weeks. As I sat watching this transaction before my eyes I could not contain myself and became hysterical. She tried to calm me down and said, "I have something for you, a little more expensive than you wanted, but I am sure that you can have it." I went to see a very small one-room studio in a rundown building on 102nd Street between Broadway and Riverside Drive. I did not have the time to be difficult. I took it. To add insult to injury, when I paid her commission, she asked for a little more because she had to pay for the tip that she had gotten from the handyman who took care of the building. She only accepted cash for everything. I went to the bank and took out two months rent, her commission, and the kickback. I only had about fifty dollars left from my prize money. I had to live on this for a month and get a job to earn the next month's rent. I handed over the money to her.

After some weeks in the new apartment I asked my new neighbor, Chuck Cahn, if he knew how to contact the handyman since I had something that needed to be repaired. He laughed and said, "Handyman? There is no handyman for this building. Nothing is ever repaired by the landlord. If you want something fixed you will have to do it yourself. Our landlord, Stanley, is a slumlord."

This agent had actually stolen money from a poor student. This was the first time that I can say that I actually hated someone. She had her office on Seventy-Second Street between Broadway and Columbus Avenue. During the years that I lived in New York City I always walked on the other side of the street so as not to walk near it. When I did look up there I wished that she would someday have to pay for cruelty and dishonesty. I am sure that I was not her only victim.

I installed myself in my tiny apartment in my new home, a brownstone full of a variety of interesting characters. I am still in close contact with my next-door neighbor, Chuck Cahn, who shared the apartment next to mine with two roommates. In the apartment above mine lived a very nice gay couple who actually saved my life one night when someone followed me into the building. I rang their bell frantically and when they both ran down the stairs to open for me, the intruder left. I often helped Chuck get

over a bruised ego after an unsuccessful date by preparing homemade pancake suppers for him.

I had quit my job at the insurance company; when I returned
to New York I had to find a new one, so I signed up to participate in the Lincoln Center Student Program. It was a comprehensive program in the performing arts for senior high schools
selected by the New York City Board of Education and located
in federally designated poverty areas in mostly black and Latino
neighborhoods. The program was intended to provide a concentrated instructional program that would relate the performing
arts to literature, media, language growth, and general learning
improvement.

I had already participated during the previous year as a member of the Met Studio, the Metropolitan Opera's young singers
program. Four singers—a soprano, mezzo-soprano, tenor, and
bass—sang a concert of opera arias, duos, and ensembles. In that
first year the mezzo was Florence Quivar, who would later record
Serena in *Porgy and Bess* with me. We had a very good program
with beautiful music but the presenter was totally unsuited to the
task. He spoke as if he were talking to a group of middle-aged
ladies at teatime. He came from Alabama or Kentucky and had
a very strong southern accent that reminded me of Orval Faubus. With his condescending tone and manner this was a disaster
waiting to happen. The singers in the Met Studio program were
among the best in New York City and our program was interesting, but he could not hold it together. Even we found him unin-
spiring. Our usual scenario was that we would get about one-third
of the way through the program and somewhere in the middle of
the exquisite trio from Mozart's *Cosi fan tutte* the noise and boo-
ing of our captive audience just forced us to stop, leave the stage,
and get back to Manhattan. On some rare occasions when we had
another presenter we did manage to sing the program's finale, the
quartet from Verdi's *Rigoletto*.

So in 1970 I applied to perform my own recital with piano
with the Lincoln Center Student Program and was accepted. I
put together a forty-five-minute recital that included songs by
Schubert, Debussy, and Rachmaninoff as well as some Negro
spirituals. My first incentive was to earn the fifty-five dollars per

concert. From my experiences with the Met Studio I knew that it could be very unpleasant, but I was still excited to be able to sing in front of a live audience. I was doing in one way what I had come to New York City to learn.

I was not at all sure if we would be able to achieve the noble objectives of the program for the high school students, but it certainly turned out to be a most valuable education for me. I was given the address of the school, the nearest subway station, and the name of the teacher who was responsible. My pianist and I on most occasions traveled together but sometimes I arrived alone. When I came out from the subway station I was sometimes horrified to see the conditions of the neighborhood of the schools where I was to go. Some neighborhoods in the South Bronx and in Brooklyn resembled war-torn countries that I would later see on my travels for the UN refugee agency. As I made my way to the addresses that I had been given I wondered how my young audience could get up in the mornings, walk through those demoralizing streets to and from school, and yet maintain the desire and the energy to learn, let alone have the patience to listen to an embryonic musician sing and speak of her passion for music.

Confronted with a captive and sometimes hostile audience I usually started out by stating the obvious; that I was a young black woman from the South and I had come to sing a concert of classical music. I proposed enthusiastically to sing for them a program of music composed by dead, mostly European white men with names that were difficult to pronounce. I began by acknowledging this as God's little joke and explained that if I had the voice of Aretha Franklin or Mahalia Jackson I would be thrilled to sing their repertoire. "My voice is suited to the music that I have chosen to sing for you today—Mozart, Debussy, and Schubert—and I feel a deep connection to this music, unexplainable even to myself. I love all of the songs that I have chosen and I feel that I can express something important about life today through these songs that speak of human emotions that we all have felt. This mini recital is an example of the concert that I might sing later in Lincoln Center if I have a career as a singer." I told them that I was aware that I was pursuing something that was not at all an evident choice for me and that I was totally unsure of the outcome of my endeavors. My parents thought that I had lost my mind to come to New York City to pursue something that they were totally unable to grasp instead of using my diploma from university to get a job or to continue to study for a master's and even a doctorate degree. I wanted them to see that I was listening to my own voice and following my own path and that I knew they could too.

My approach seemed to work because I gained a successful reputation in the program. I was able to finish all of my concerts without any incidents. Sometimes a few students would come and talk to me, accompany us back to the subway station, or even go as far as Manhattan with us. I arrived at one technical high school for boys in Brooklyn earlier than my pianist, who was a fair-headed blond. When I came out from the station I saw an all-black neighborhood, for which the word *tough* would be an understatement. Even though I was black, I felt that I was in foreign territory. I was a bit worried for my pianist but he arrived safely and had no problems at all. The teacher who was in charge greeted us and astutely assigned two well-known troublemakers the task of helping us backstage. We told them what we needed and they were eager to help us prepare for the concert. The concert went well and later our two helpers and a few of their friends accompanied us to the subway; although they should have been in class, they rode a while with us toward Manhattan. When they left the subway I asked them, "What is your neighborhood called?" and they answered, "Bed-Stuy." "Bedford-Stuyvesant," I said and smiled meekly. Bedford-Stuyvesant had been in the news. In 1964, a white police lieutenant shot and killed fifteen-year-old James Powell and a race riot followed, breaking out first in Harlem before spreading to Bedford-Stuyvesant, resulting in looting and destruction of neighborhood businesses. Additional riots took place again in 1967 and 1968 and of course I had seen reports on the news.

The following year I continued with my recitals and participated in other programs as well; I had a duo recital program with Sir Willard White and an improvisation program with a group of musicians that included Guillermo Figueroa, an early member of the Emerson String Quartet and a founding member of Orpheus Chamber Orchestra, and dancers including Janet Eilber, who became the protégé and muse of Martha Graham and is now, after an illustrious career, the artistic director of the Martha Graham Center of Contemporary Dance. The Lincoln Center Student Program was discontinued after the 1972–73 school year due to lack of funds from the Nixon administration.

I do not know if I inspired anyone in my audience to go to hear a concert of classical music, let alone a recital of lieder and mélodies, but I do hope that I inspired a few of those students to dare be true to themselves even if it did not fit the preconceived and accepted ideas that their family, friends, and society may have had of them. Maybe they resisted the pressure to conform. One of the most important lessons I've ever learned was from those students in the ghettos of New York: the sincerity and depth of my relationship with the music that I sing plays an enormous role in establishing a connection between the music and the audience and has the power to engender their attention and openness. They taught me that I must sing without artifice or condescension to my audience no matter who they are or from where they come.

Once I had found an apartment and a job, I was looking forward to going to more concerts and sometimes took some risks to make that happen. One day a friend, Charles Bornstein, and I got caught trying to slip in to a concert performance of Beethoven's *Fidelio* at what was then the Philharmonic Hall; the Juilliard Orchestra was being conducted by Leonard Bernstein. Charles had studied conducting with him. Hoping to hear the sold-out concert he and I had hidden for several hours under a stairwell in the backstage area waiting for the right opportunity to slip into the hall. Just as we were going through the door a hand grabbed both of us by the neck and a voice asked, "What do you two think you are doing?" Mr. Carlos Moseley, the general manager of the New York Philharmonic, was throwing us out. Bernstein saw us, recognized Charles, and invited us to sit in the viewing loge at the edge of the stage where we could see and hear but not be seen by the audience. This was my first meeting with Leonard Bernstein. While we waited to be taken to the loge, we tried to make ourselves invisible to all around us but could not help witnessing the ritual of his friends kissing his cufflinks to wish him good luck. I would see this again many years later when we worked together.

I never participated in this ritual. The cuff links had belonged to his teacher Serge Koussevitzky, who had been the conductor of the Boston Symphony from 1924 to 1949, and Bernstein always wore them when he conducted. After one of the many renovations that attempted to improve the disastrous acoustics, this loge was taken away and the hall was named Avery Fisher Hall after the man who financed the renovation. In 1977, I sang my debut there with the New York Philharmonic with Erich Leinsdorf conducting the New York premiere of David Del Tredici's *Final Alice*. When I met Mr. Moseley during the rehearsals, he had thankfully forgotten all about this painful episode.

My love and fascination for the theater started very early when I played my first role, Sleeping Beauty, in the sixth grade, and had grown with working backstage and playing small roles at the University of Nebraska. The first boy that I dated in New York was an acting student, Norman Snow from North Little Rock, and on most of our dates we went to the theater and the movies. As a matter of fact I continued to date actors because I thought that they might share some secret with me that would bring me closer to what attracted me most about the theater: the process of putting together a work of art. Thankfully I grew out of that.

In 1968 the Juilliard School of Music added a drama department and was renamed simply the Juilliard School. President Mennin had called on the French theater director, actor, and drama theorist Michel Saint-Denis and producer, director, and actor John Houseman to develop the new department. Mr. Saint-Denis was in ill health and died in 1971, so Houseman ran the department alone. Houseman was born in 1902 in Romania, received his education in England, and immigrated to America in 1925. Beginning in 1934 he collaborated with Orson Welles in many Federal Theater projects, including the Negro Unit's "Voodoo *Macbeth*" directed by Welles with incidental music by Virgil Thomson, and the censored production of *The Cradle Will Rock*. They founded the Mercury Theatre, whose infamous airing on the radio of H. G. Wells's *The War of the Worlds* caused panic all over America. Their collaboration ended after a stormy relationship during the filming of *Citizen Kane*. During my third year at Juilliard he directed the world premiere of the opera *Lord Byron* by Virgil Thomson and I sang Lady Charlotte. In 1934 he had directed the very successful production of the world premiere of Thomson's *Four Saints in Three Acts* with a libretto by Gertrude Stein and an all-Negro cast. Alvin Ailey was the choreographer for *Lord Byron* and I could barely contain my joy not only because I was to meet one of my favorite artists but also because I was able to watch him work up close with the dancers during the rehearsals.

I actually went to the theater more often than to the two opera houses. I saw nearly all of the major productions that were performed by the new drama department at Juilliard with Norman and other young acting students such as Kevin Kline and Patti LuPone and teachers such as Marian Seldes and the director Michael Kahn, whose performances I saw on Broadway. Later Robin Williams and Christopher Reeve were also enrolled there. I was always on the lookout for student discounts for Broadway shows, but it was easier to find affordable tickets for the off-Broadway and off-off-Broadway shows, and their productions were often even more interesting. One time I got so busy with my schoolwork that I forgot to get tickets for David Storey's *Home* with the great Sir John Gielgud and Sir Ralph Richardson. I suddenly realized that there was only one more performance left before the show would close for good and I called to see if there were any seats available. To my surprise there were still two or three ten–dollar tickets left but I could not reserve one over the phone. I had two five-dollar bills and two subway tokens, one to go the theater and one to get back home. I dashed out to the subway, but when I arrived the ten-dollar seats were sold out. Only twenty-five-dollar seats remained. I was crushed so I ran to a pay phone and called my neighbor, Chuck, and asked if he could lend me the fifteen dollars and another subway token. He agreed and I returned to 102nd Street to fetch the money and ran back to the theater just before the curtain went up. The man at the ticket office was so impressed that I had gone all the way back uptown to borrow the money from a friend that he sold me the ticket for ten dollars. I was in heaven to be able to see those two extraordinary actors together in that historical performance.

I rented a piano from Juilliard that took up almost half of my room. When my fold-out sofa bed was open there was not an inch of empty space. I was still nursing a broken heart and during the weekends it was more difficult to keep occupied on a limited budget. I devised a program of activities. I began baking bread every Friday evening and my neighbors appreciated the smell wafting out into the hallways to greet them when they came home from work. I loved to go to the cinema during the week but during the weekends I found it hard to stand in line with so many amorous couples. I would scour the *Village Voice* when it came out every week and look for lectures, workshops, or small off-off-Broadway productions that were cheap or even free. I went regularly to the Brooklyn Academy, which presented a wide range of interesting concerts and theater productions, the La MaMa Theatre where Peter Brook often came with his group, and Joseph Papp's Public Theater on Lafayette Street down on the Lower East Side. Peter Brook and his troupe had just returned from an African tour and had performed Shakespeare for tribes out in the bush. I was particularly interested to hear his lecture about this tour. He said that he decided to do an experiment with the audience who had never heard of Shakespeare and did not even speak English. They would perform the play once giving one hundred percent of themselves, and then do another performance where they were not at all concentrating nor playing with any purpose in their acting. In the first case they were able to hold the attention of the audience and in the latter the audience grew restive, began to talk, and even got up and left. This confirmed my experience with the students who were my audience in the Lincoln Center Student Program about the importance of singing with intention.

Miss Tourel also encouraged me to go to museums and concerts. She informed me when someone interesting was coming to town whom she thought that I might enjoy, such as Régine Crespin, Jean-Louis Barrault, or Maurice Béjart. She said, "You must live your life fully because your knowledge and experience will form the reservoir which you will draw upon for true expression of the emotions of the characters that you will interpret whether in an opera role or a one-minute song."

Once I ended up at a free lecture in the East Village by the Polish director Jerzy Grotowski. I had been reading a lot about theater during the summer in Aspen and had read a book about his work. When he was finished I went to speak to him and asked if I could study with him during one of his courses outside Poland. We communicated through an interpreter; he spoke French, Polish, and Russian, while I, of course, only spoke English and the rudimentary French I needed to sing the few French mélodies and arias that were a part of my repertoire. He said that he was giving a course in Marseille the coming summer and that I could apply. I decided that it would do me good to leave the Upper West Side sometimes, and so I enrolled in a French course at the New School in Greenwich Village. However, when it was time for me to enroll in the class in Marseille it was clear to me that my French was in no way good enough. So I asked John Houseman for his advice. "I do not want to be a dilettante and to take the place of some serious actor or actress who might benefit from being in his class," I said. He replied, "Perhaps this is not the moment for you to do this, because if your French is not good enough you will not be able to learn from him and that would be a great pity."

———

Maria Callas's first attempt at teaching was in the spring of 1971 and ended in total disaster. She was to give a two-week master class at the Curtis Institute of Music in Philadelphia but left after three days and never returned. Callas began her career in 1949 at age twenty-six and had retired from the stage in 1965. After losing quite a bit of weight in 1954 and living a jet-set life with Aristotle Onassis her vocal decline began. "It's all tension, you know," she said. She had been taking her voice down, so to speak, trying to build it up from nothing again, like a conservatory student. In the process, she was apparently forced to articulate for herself, precisely and formally, the concept and techniques upon which her art rested; therefore, when Peter Mennin, president of the Juilliard School, invited her to work with a select group of twenty-five young professional singers in a series of master classes in "The Lyric Tradition," she accepted. The classes ran from October 1971 to March 1972, during which period she presided "like a Delphic Oracle," as one commentator put it, before sold-out audiences of students, fans, the press, and such distinguished colleagues as Elisabeth Schwarzkopf, Tito Gobbi, Bidu Sayao, and Franco Zeffirelli. In John Ardoin's words, "Not only were Callas's comments extraordinary insights into her training and thinking, but they were a virtual summing-up of a grand-line operatic tradition reaching back to Donizetti, Verdi, and beyond which she had learned and practiced under such conducting giants as Tullio Serafin and Victor de Sabata. It is a tradition of which Callas was not only a principal exponent but one of the last of the breed."

Of course all of the teachers encouraged their students to audition for Callas but even then I felt that Miss Tourel did not find the whole thing such a great idea. And of course once the entire circus around the class was apparent she stated her displeasure more openly. She often made us laugh when she tried to use English idioms and I could hardly keep a straight face when she said that "Callas is just a was-one," meaning "a has-been."

I auditioned nonetheless and was among the students chosen. We were then invited to have a little interview with her in the presence of Dr. Mennin. I knew very little about her, as she had already stopped singing before I discovered opera and arrived in New York. Through all of the noise made about her in the media I did learn about the scandals, but I had never listened to her recordings.

We were called in alphabetical order for our five to ten minutes with her. When I entered the room, which was Jennie Tourel's studio where I always had my lessons, I felt at home and very relaxed and greeted the president, whom I had met on many occasions in school. "Hello Dr. Mennin, how are you?" I said then "Hi," to Maria Callas and shook her hand. She said, "I have accepted you for my class," and I nodded shyly and waited for her to continue, but after an awkward moment she said that I should get some vocalizing books, Concone and Vaccai, and work on them during the summer. She did say something about my being overweight but since I weighed a bit more than one hundred pounds I did not understand what she meant and replied with something vague like, "Well I haven't been skiing this season so I could be a little bit out of shape." My interview lasted less than five minutes—it was perhaps the shortest one.

Just before the end of the school year I was summoned by the dean of the school in charge of this project. I thought that he would tell me what my assignment for the class would be, but instead he informed me that Maria Callas had put me on probation because I had greeted her with "hi." She felt that I had been disrespectful. I later understood that many of the students entered the room on their knees, professing their admiration and gratitude to Madame Callas. I was sure that I had been respectful, as this was my upbringing, but I had certainly not been obsequious. So I said, "With all due respect, I refuse to be put on probation. I am either in the class or out of the class, but I am not on probation. If I am going to have to adjust my behavior based on our cultural differences, me a girl from Little Rock and she a Greek lady born in Brooklyn, then this class will be a big waste of time for me. When I come back in October, let me know." I was not in any way panicked by the prospect of being out of the class since my classes with Miss Tourel were always inspiring and fulfilling. I did not give a thought to it during the summer and I did not even mention it to Miss Tourel.

Although I had decided not to enroll in the acting class in Marseille, I was still going to Europe that summer. Jennie Tourel had decided not to return to Aspen but to accept invitations to give master classes in Zurich and Graz and a concert in Spoleto. She invited me to come with her. I saved my money for the trip and when I arrived in Reykjavik I witnessed for the first time the long days of summer in the north. The sun rose around 3:00 AM through my hotel window. I had found a very cheap ticket to Europe with Icelandic Airlines that was only valid if I left New York City before May 31. Two years later I would have to miss my graduation from Juilliard in order to take advantage of this fare. I walked around Reykjavik and saw what I could of the city before boarding my flight to Luxembourg. I bought a Eurail pass for the whole summer and was on my way to Paris. On the train I met some American students and we went to a youth hostel for a few days. After I had stayed the maximum time in the youth hostel I had to find a cheap hotel. I went with two American students that I had met in the hostel to a small hotel in the fifteenth arrondisement, but when they left Paris I decided to go to the

Latin Quarter. Miss Tourel was taking a direct flight from New York to Paris and I had just one more week alone to discover the city. I finally ended up in a hotel in the fifth arrondisement that cost ten dollars a night and had a toilet and shower in the hallway.

I wandered around discovering Paris on my own with other students that I met. I was overwhelmed by the majesty and the history of the cathedral in Chartres and spent an entire day in Versailles. I traced the steps of Hemingway in the back streets of the fifth arrondissement. I walked the streets all day, absorbing the atmosphere and taking in the city's beauty. I spent a day at the Louvre and was underwhelmed by the *Mona Lisa*. Miss Tourel arrived and installed herself at her hotel on the rue Saint-Honoré. I did not want her to see my hotel because I knew that she would have taken me right away to hers. I would have stayed in a *chambre de bonne*, which would have been a much nicer room, the amenities would have been much improved, and she would have certainly invited me for all of my meals. But I wanted to keep my independence, and so whenever she wanted to take a taxi with me to my hotel I asked the taxi to stop at the corner, saying that it was in the courtyard of a one-way street. I spent some time with Miss Tourel discovering the Paris that she had known. She took me to her favorite museum, the Galerie Nationale du Jeu de Paume, which had been home to the impressionists who had not been accepted in the Louvre. It became a must-stop for me whenever I came to Paris until the collection was moved to the Musée d'Orsay. She invited me to eat lunch at the famous La Coupole with some of her old Russian friends, musicians and singers from the Opéra-Comique, and of course with Mr. Michaelson, who had fled with her to America but had moved back to Paris. Whenever Miss Tourel and I were in Paris we always met Mr. Michaelson for lunch at La Coupole. I ate my lunch listening to them speak animatedly in Russian the entire time. I assumed that they were reminiscing about the times that they had spent together in Paris before the war. I own a portrait that Mr. Michaelson painted of her that I bought from her family when she died. I think that she was still in love with him even in 1971.

I did not understand enough French, and no Russian at all, so I did not participate in the conversation, but she spoiled me with white asparagus and real hollandaise sauce and *fraises du bois* with crème fraiche. I soaked up the atmosphere as I watched all of the interesting people go by. Everything was very new to me: the sights, the sounds, the food, and the different cadences of the multiple languages that I heard in the streets. Everything was different from America and yet it did not feel at all foreign to me.

I was sad to leave but it was soon time to go to Switzerland to work. I used my Eurail pass and met Miss Tourel on the morning of the first of her European master classes, a two-week course in Zurich. I had a scholarship and had been given a room with a nice Swiss family. A few of her private students from New York had enrolled in the class but I knew that I had to earn my scholarship and was expected to sing everyday. Every morning I took the tram to the class, which was in Das Muraltengut, a beautiful eighteenth-century Baroque estate surrounded by a big park. I warmed up because she often asked me to sing first. She sometimes invited me to lunch at the Mövenpick at Paradeplatz and then dessert at Sprüngli, a chocolatier. The quiet beauty of Switzerland and the discovery of real chocolate added to this learning experience. I was a chocolate lover before but became a true chocoholic once I had eaten the real dark chocolate truffles. After lunch I tried to see a bit of the city but I usually had to practice and learn new songs. The other students came with the repertoire that they had accumulated over the year. I had been singing my entire repertoire in my private lessons and in her weekly class and she expected me to have prepared new songs for this class. I sang mostly lieder and French mélodies and a Swiss-German singer approached after one class and said, "You sing German lieder very well for an American." I thanked him and smiled and did not say what I was thinking: *You sing it very badly for someone whose mother tongue is German.* Miss Tourel told me that he did not have a clue about what he was doing.

At the end of the two weeks we went on to another class in Freiburg, Germany, and we took the train together. It was the first time that she had been back in Germany since the war and it was difficult for her to relate to me the frightening experience of her last train voyage there. She had been in a compartment filled with other passengers who looked away while she sat quietly in fear as young German soldiers walked through the train harassing Jews. Her voice trembled when she told me how afraid she had been when they called her a "dirty Jew." I recognized immediately the fear, as if I had been there with her. I told her about growing up under the segregation laws in the South. We formed a closer although silent bond that deepened our relationship. It was the first time that I felt truly close to her. She fled to America as a refugee and I, born a refugee in America, was to become an activist for refugee rights. Our relationship had always been mutually respectful; I was able to avoid anything too invasive. I rarely spoke about my own personal life or even my money worries. After the episode with the Schubert lied, "Gretchen am Spinnrade," we had never discussed my private life until now.

The master class in Freiburg lasted only a few days and I did not have to sing as much as in Zurich. Our next stop was the Festival dei Due Mondi where she was to perform, not give classes, so I could relax a bit. She traveled by plane from Zurich and I used my Eurail pass to get to Rome. I was fetched by someone from the festival. Her flight was delayed so I traveled alone with a driver who drove so fast that I spent the better part of the journey crouched behind the back seat. This was long before seat belts were ubiquitous. When the winding of the road calmed and I felt safe to lift my head I discovered the immense beauty of the Umbrian countryside. The entrance into the main piazza in front of the Duomo of Spoleto was breathtaking. Jennie Tourel sang in the chamber music series in the old theater.

I had a few days free after Tourel's concert and I left with friends to discover Florence and Bologna. I checked out all of the museums and architectural wonders that I had read about in my art history class back in Lincoln. Miss Tourel and I met up again for just one short week of master classes in Graz, Austria. Then she went to Israel and I had a few more weeks left before taking my flight back to New York. I spent a week visiting my sister Ruthie, who had moved to Spain and was in Frankfurt because she had found work at an American military base, where she later worked as a psychologist, specializing in alcoholism and substance abuse. I managed to even get a cheaper return ticket on Pan Am from Frankfurt.

In October when I returned to school I was informed that I was not on probation for the Callas class, whatever that was supposed to have meant anyway—I would be a full member. I had not worked on one line of those vocalizes during the summer; I found this tedious. I had other things to think about than singing scales.

Miss Tourel was very proud that I had been chosen to be in the class but still was a bit jealous that Maria Callas was getting what she considered to be undue attention from the school and the media. On the days of the class Callas's enthusiastic fans and curious opera buffs formed long lines all around the school for many hours before the doors opened. We had classes twice a week with her during three weeks in October 1971 and in March 1972. Each of us was to have the opportunity to sing in the class at least twice each semester. She had some favorites in the class, not necessarily the most talented ones, and with me she was correct but distant.

Jennie Tourel was well known for her Rossini, but I was never attracted to it and never worked with her on the bel canto repertoire. In preparation for the Callas class, I tried to learn more about Maria Callas the musician. When I was in high school I had a recording of opera arias with Joan Sutherland and I had briefly looked at some Bellini arias from *La sonnambula* and *I puritani*. Maria Callas had also sung these roles so I chose to sing the aria "Qui la voce" from *I puritani* instead of one of my usual audition and competition arias. I decided not to sing the same repertoire for Maria Callas that I sang for my lessons with Miss Tourel so as to avoid any tensions during my lessons. I must admit that I found Miss Tourel's attitude a bit disappointing, even though I did agree with her that the Callas class could never begin to compare to her Tuesday afternoon classes. I still felt that such a great artist as she should be above this.

I thought that the master class should above all be for the benefit of the students, so after the first three weeks I returned to the dean and asked if we could have one of the two classes in the week during the next semester in private with just Maria Callas and the students and no audience. We all were under such pressure because of the media circus around the class. It was very disturbing and was a far cry from the sanctuary that the building on Sixty-Sixth Street had provided us. We were all playing a role. Even though she gave sincere opinions to her young students Maria Callas spoke with a very European accent, sometimes forgetting English words and having to ask, "How do you say it in English?" Granted, she did return to Greece as a child and lived with her husband in Italy, but we found it a bit pretentious. I also had heard the rumor that when she called the pianist to speak to him she spoke English with a true Brooklyn accent. We mostly sang arias that we knew that we could sing well because we did not want to take risks in front of famous singers like Elisabeth Schwarzkopf, Marilyn Horne, Rudolf Bing, or any of the other famous singers and musicians passing through New York City who showed up to watch the class. But my request was denied.

What I learned was invaluable, but it had little to do with what she taught me about how to sing the arias that I presented. She had asked me to prepare the first act aria, "Sempre libera," and the duet with Germont from Verdi's *La traviata* for my last lesson but I was sick and never performed it. It is hard to say if she was a good teacher. I do know that the public conditions of the class made it more difficult for us to profit from her knowledge and even harder for her to be herself, to relax and enjoy the experience of teaching.

This class lacked the intimacy and profound searching that I had been accustomed to. We never got past a superficial layer of work and we should have been able to do more since we were given so much time with her. I listened attentively to her advice to all the singers but I found myself more interested in observing her very closely.

And little by little, this woman that I had found at the beginning arrogant and a little silly began to touch me. Her vulnerability was so apparent and she seemed not to have any confidence in the over-the-top masquerade of the sycophants around her who never stopped reminding her about how great she "had been."

I felt a great empathy for her and thought that if loneliness and mistrust was the price to pay for a spectacular—albeit in her case, short—career (she started to have vocal problems at the age of thirty-one and her career was essentially over at age forty), I did not want it. I decided then that my personal quest to become a fulfilled woman would always take precedence over whatever career I might have. Little Barbara from Arkansas would always guide La Hendricks, the singer.

I performed in many opera productions, including two world premieres, while I was at Juilliard. One was about a motorcycle gang and appropriately entitled *The Losers*, and was composed by Harold Farberman, a friend of Dr. Mennin. I have never heard of it since. The other was Virgil Thomson's opera *Lord Byron*, directed by John Houseman. In the spring of 1972, after the end of the Callas classes, I auditioned for the role of Mimì in Puccini's *La bohème* for Maria Callas; Thomas Schippers, the conductor; and the director Michael Cacoyannis, the prominent Greek Cypriot filmmaker who received three Oscars for *Zorba the Greek*. Maria Callas was to be a kind of consultant to the production and most likely had something to do with the choice of Cacoyannis, with whom she had worked. I was thrilled to be selected to sing Mimì. There was a double cast for the roles of Mimì and Rodolfo. The other soprano was a beautiful Korean singer, very timid and demure with a beautiful voice to match. It was clear to me in the first rehearsal that she was the choice of the director and that I was the choice of the conductor. Typically for a film director, he had chosen her because her timid demeanor corresponded to his physical idea of the consumptive Mimì. I on the other hand was a 1968 feminist who walked with a determined gait around the set not willing to die without a fight. And I expressed a lust for life from my first entrance. Unfortunately Thomas Schippers fell ill and had to cancel on short notice. He was replaced by James Conlon, a young promising student who would definitely be following more orders than he would be giving. During the rehearsals Cacoyannis spent all of his time with the other cast and once they had worked on a scene, my Rodolfo and I rehearsed when the other members of the cast were taking a break. Every move that I made was criticized: my arms were too long, my gait too wide. I felt quite alone, since Miss Tourel was away on tour and I no longer had the support of Schippers.

I kept my unhappiness to myself and tried to give 110 percent in the rehearsals. I really tried to do whatever the director asked because I was singing one of the most beautiful roles that I had ever heard and I wanted to be a good Mimì. Two weeks before the opening we had a production meeting to discuss the final weeks' rehearsal schedule. The two casts were to start to alternate the orchestra and dress rehearsals. But since the set would not be completed on time Cacoyannis wanted me to do my final dress rehearsal five days before the opening, giving the other cast their last dress rehearsal in a completed set. That was the last straw. I said to him, "If I manage to do this role at all it will be in spite of you not because of you." He responded as I was leaving the stage, "You do not have to sing." To which I responded holding back my tears, "I know." I left the theater and went straight to President Mennin's office. He had already gone home and his secretary saw how upset I was so she called him at home. I spoke to Mrs. Mennin who said that he should arrive any minute. His secretary offered me a glass of water and I sat in his office trying to hold back my tears and trying to control my anger. After a few minutes he called back and asked to speak to me, and informed me that he had just spoken to Dean Waldrop, who was still in the building. I was to go back to the theater and the dean would meet me there. I went reluctantly back and when I arrived he was waiting for me in the hall. I went to sit next to him. Dean Gideon Waldrop was a very close friend of Jennie Tourel and had been very helpful and supportive to me since my arrival at Juilliard. I told him about how I felt that I had been treated during the rehearsals and that I managed to still do my work but that the schedule for the dress rehearsals with the orchestra was the last straw and totally unfair. I said, "Dean Waldrop, you know more than anyone here at Juilliard except maybe Miss Tourel how much it means for me to be able to study, to sing, and all I want is to be able to give the best of myself but if I must kiss his ass, or anyone else's for that matter, in order to sing this or any other role I would rather work at the subway selling tokens for a living. He is supposed to be here at Juilliard for us, the students, not the other way around." He managed to calm me down and spoke to Cacoyannis. We decided that I would continue and that he would give me more rehearsal time but I would still have to give up my dress rehearsal to the other cast.

The big night came and I was hoping to give a good performance. He had been so concentrated on his first cast that he only saw my performance in the set on my opening night. During the performance he finally looked at me and saw my Mimì for the first time. I was acting the role of Mimì and not just playing myself. But I played a Mimì that loved life and wanted to live and love and die on her own terms.

He came backstage afterward with Dr. and Mrs. Mennin and Maria Callas. All of them congratulated me enthusiastically. Mrs. Mennin gave a warm hug and a wink when Michael Cacoyannis hugged me spontaneously and said, "You are fantastic, where have you been hiding this?" He liked my performance so much that he tried to get more performances added to extend the run, but the hall was not free.

In the 1990s I met him after a recital at the Odeon of Herodes Atticus in Athens. We were having dinner in a restaurant on a terrace under a starry sky with a view of the Acropolis and he proclaimed to all in the restaurant that he had never forgotten my performance and that I was the Mimì of his dreams. So it goes. Jennie Tourel heard about the episode before she returned and halfheartedly scolded me for walking out of the rehearsal. I said to her, "Under the same circumstances, you would have done the same thing." She smiled slyly and said, "Yes, maybe, but I don't want you to start behaving badly when you work." I felt that I knew the difference between bad behavior and standing up for what was right and just.

We went back to Europe in the summer of 1972 and started over the same scenario as the year before. I arrived earlier than Miss Tourel and enrolled at the Alliance Française to take a few French classes and continued to discover Paris and its surroundings.

I had entered the Paris Competition and won the First Prize and the Mozart Prize. Miss Tourel had not yet arrived in Paris and was so proud of me. She began to see that I could go out on my own and maybe actually have a career. She once told me after a lesson, "Barbara, you will have a much bigger career than I had. You have intelligence and musicality and a more beautiful voice than I." I did not know what to say.

When she arrived in Paris we went to La Coupole to celebrate: *fraise du bois* with crème fraiche. We visited museums, had lunch with Mr. Michaelson, and I tagged along when she met her old friends until it was time to get the train to Zurich.

Easter Sunday, in front of our house in Arkansas—six years old (on the far left) with my brothers Michael and Malvin Jr. and my sister Geneice. We did not own a camera and this is the only photo that I have from my early childhood.

My parents, Della Mae and Malvin Leon Hendricks. Mama was the eldest of sixteen children. She received her college degree by correspondence. Papa was one of eleven children and was a pastor in the Colored Methodist Church.

I sang my first solos in Papa's churches in rural Arkansas. I was often called upon to sing—sometimes for weddings but mostly for funerals.

Miss Horace Mann's 1964 homecoming queen. As a budding feminist I was very much against beauty contests and entered on a dare from a classmate. No one was more surprised than I when I won.

During the last year of my studies in chemistry and mathematics at the University of Nebraska in Lincoln I lived as a member of the Fred Webster family in their home on Sheridan Boulevard.

Mr. Richard Smith, a lawyer in Lincoln, heard me sing at a meeting and offered me a scholarship to study with Jennie Tourel at the Aspen Music School during the summer of 1968. Here I am with him and his wife, Pat.

With my parents, brothers, and Reverend Clarence Forsberg in Lincoln, Nebraska, in 1969 after my graduation from Universty of Nebraska.

From then on the focus in my life changed from science to music.

My debut as Juliette at the Paris Opera in 1982 in Gounod's *Romeo et Juliette* with Neil Shicoff and Gino Quilico.

Liu, the little slave in Puccini's *Turandot* who sacrifices her life for love. I made a part of Herbert von Karajan's dream come true when I sang Liu in the Forbidden City in Bejing in the 1998 production of Teatro Communale directed by Zhang Yimou and conducted by Zubin Mehta.

Antonia in Offenbach's *Les Contes d'Hoffmann* is one of my favorite roles. Here in the 1998 production for the opening of the renovated Lyon Opera with José van Dam and Natalie Dessay.

Adina in Donizetti's *L'Elisir d'amore* with Gino Quilico, the most beautiful baritone voice of his generation.

In 2004, Peter Eötvös's opera *Angels in America*, based on Tony Kushner's epic play, had its world premier in Theâtre du Chatelet in Paris. I sang the role Angel and spent most of the opera suspended over the stage.

In 2000 at the Opèra de Nice, as Tatiana in Tchaikovsky's *Eugene Onegin* with Vladimir Chernov. It seemed that all of the roles that I had played until then had been leading to Tatiana.

With José van Dam at a concert in Brussels in 2008. José showed me what it meant to be a supportive colleague when I sang my first Susanna with him in Berlin in 1975.

Leonard Bernstein was a beloved friend of Jennie Tourel. His knowledge, energy, and political engagement were a great inspiration to me.

To sing with Herbert von Karajan was one of my most precious experiences. He had a way to support the voice on a cushion of glorious orchestral sound.

With the composer David del Tredici and Sir Georg Solti in front of the enormous score of *Final Alice*. Sir Georg and I performed the world premier with the Chicago Symphony in 1976.

Carlo Maria Giulini was like a monk; he always brought a spiritual element to all of his work. We shared the same belief about the necessity to be totally faithful to the score and our demands for proper rehearsal time.

Chamber music gave me my first musical
family. I have always chosen to sing with the
best pianists as real musical partners. From
left to right: Radu Lupu; Michel Béroff (first
row). Dmitri Alexeev; Maria Joao Pires and
Michel Dalberto at home in Montreux
(second row). Swedes Love Derwinger;
Roland Pöntinen (third row)

I arrived in Johannesburg in May 1994 to attend the inauguration of Nelson Mandela as the first Black president of a free South Africa and was invited to attend mass at parois Moletsane in Soweto. Father Emmanuel asked me to sing, and I sang a Negro spiritual and the congregation joined in. It was a magical moment.

I had been so stressed in 1971 with the daily preparations for the class in Zurich. I decided to be smart for the classes in 1972 and had been preparing in secret all spring. I worked on *Vier letzte Lieder* of Richard Strauss. I thought that we could spend at least one week working on them. From the first time I heard the cycle I felt that it had been written for me. The first day of the class I pulled out "Frühling" and sang my heart out. Miss Tourel was surprised that I had done all the work on my own and said with some admiration that it was fine work—but that it would be some years before I would be able to sing them with an orchestra. So I should put them to rest until then. Then with a slight grin she asked, "What else do you have?" I was back to square one. I had to prepare new repertoire every afternoon for the following morning. It was indeed a very good discipline for me although I did not feel so at the time. I would have rather spent my afternoons wandering around the old town in Zurich.

As I said, I tried hard to keep a distance between what I did with Miss Tourel and what I performed in the Callas classes but I was not to get away without her getting the last word. Jennie Tourel never attended the Callas classes but she knew exactly what had happened to the minutest detail. We never discussed the class during our lessons, but by the time we arrived in Zurich in the summer of 1972 for her master class it was too much for her. She insisted that I sing the aria "Io son l'umile ancella" from Cilea's *Adrianna Lecouvreur* that I had sung in the last semester for Callas. I reluctantly walked toward the piano knowing that this was a very bad idea.

Jennie Tourel was a very demanding teacher and could be very cruel with some stupid students. I had never had a problem with her but as soon as I opened my mouth she stopped me and started to lecture the class about the dangers of the teaching of Maria Callas. I realized that there was nothing I could do. My instinct was to fight back and I saw myself walking out and tearing the score into small pieces. But I could not do that to her in front of students who did not really know her, so for once I kept my mouth shut. Everything that she did not like about my performance she said was the fault of Maria Callas. This was not true and not fair. I was very disappointed that she was not above this. When it was all over, I left the hall silently and went back to my room. She called me later and invited me to dinner at her hotel. She seemed a little ashamed and tried to justify herself by saying that it was not my fault but that a woman who had destroyed her own voice after a too-short career should not be able to do the same with talented and vulnerable students like me.

We had a great meal, well above the standards that I was used to, so I quickly forgot her bad humor. The rest of the summer was without a single cloud, as if nothing had happened. When the classes in Zurich were finished I joined Miss Tourel in Graz and then we went on to Jerusalem for classes that she gave at the Rubin Academy. Jerusalem was a wonderful discovery, a magic place, and on our days off Miss Tourel and I visited the Dead Sea, Ein Gedi, Bethlehem, and other tourist attractions.

The summer passed quickly and I began the school year with enthusiasm. After the Juilliard classes Maria Callas decided to prepare her comeback; after all, she was only fifty years old, but she had not performed since 1965. She had decided to go on tour in 1973 with the tenor Giuseppe di Stefano, a tour that was eventually aborted in 1974 due to vocal shortcomings of both singers. After Onassis had left her for Jacqueline Kennedy she stayed alone in her Paris apartment with her chagrin.

When the concerts in New York were announced I had no interest in going because the rumor was that she was in bad condition. I was invited on a blind double date with a girlfriend and her boyfriend for dinner and a surprise concert. The surprise was tickets for the Long Island recital of Maria Callas and di Stefano.

The date started out badly: there was a snowstorm and I was afraid that I would have to spend the night in the car. Finally we arrived and the excitement in the room was that of a corrida. Her audience was made up mostly of young fans who only knew her from her recordings and a few older fans who had actually seen and heard her in her prime and were carrying a memory of her from fifteen or twenty years before. Imagine my horror when I was ushered to that very first row right in front of her. My blind date had decided to really try to impress me since the tickets were nearly impossible to obtain.

I remembered that Callas was incredibly myopic and hoped that she would not recognize me. I did not want to cause her any pain or discomfort or have her think that I had chosen to sit right in front of her because I wished to judge her performance as she had done with us. I kept my head down whenever she seemed to look in my direction. But I did not see a flicker of recognition in her eyes so I relaxed a bit.

The rest of the evening was almost unbearably painful. There was fright in her eyes and at the same instant a determination to sing out notes that her vocal chords could no longer produce. After each aria the crowd screamed for more. I felt that they wanted to witness her death on stage so that they could say "I was there when she died." I really think that had she started to cough up blood, they would have cheered. Tears slowly ran down my cheeks and I wanted to run away from this spectacle. But I was stuck in a snowstorm on Long Island with no idea how to get back to Manhattan so I had to endure it until the end. Some pieces were better and di Stefano tried to be supportive but he was not in much better shape. Luckily the weather conditions forced us to get back to Manhattan as soon as it was over. I could not wait to get away.

I happened to be in New York in November 1995 for the premiere on Broadway of Terrence McNally's play *Master Class* about Callas. I went with my friend Allison, who worked for Deutsche Grammophon and who had been in the audience at Juilliard. In the intermission I told her that I did not remember Maria Callas being so unpleasant. She said, "Oh yes, she was." I suppose that I had been more interested in Maria Callas the woman and artist but we were served Maria Callas the star, a sort of extraordinary "was one."

I do regret that I did not meet the true Maria Callas; maybe she did not know this person either. I moved to Paris in 1976 and thought about visiting her but I was not sure that she would want to see me. She died in 1977, alone in her apartment on the rue Mandel. Afterward I bought several of her recordings and listened to them while reading the score. I realized what a true and honest artist she had been. Like Jennie Tourel, she placed her voice at the service of the music and the texts. Maybe she became sidetracked by her desire to be the woman that Onassis wanted, thus letting music take a secondary place. It is so hard to find and maintain a balance between the different aspects of one's life. It is particularly difficult for a woman who wants to have both a meaningful career and a fulfilled personal and family life.

She did not betray her art. She thought that she had found in Aristotle Onassis a soul mate, and in my humble opinion he never understood or appreciated the artist that she was. Her art and greatness only added to her value as another acquisition to his trophy room.

During my fourth year at Juilliard I auditioned for one of the opera productions. Mozart's *Die Zauberflöte* was directed by the bass-baritone George London, whose career had been cut short because of a strange throat ailment. I had initially been chosen to sing the part of Pamina. Then there was a change of conductor and so it was decided that I should sing the role of "Die Erste Dame." So after having learned Pamina I had to learn a new role. Some weeks before the premiere, George London called and said, "Barbara, you are doing a great job with the role of the First Lady, but we have a very serious problem. The girl who sings the First Boy has such severe intonation problems and we have been trying together with the conductor and her teacher to correct this but there is nothing to do. This ensemble role is so important but as it is now this could be disastrous. Would you please learn this role? It is much easier to find a replacement for the First Lady but finding a singer that has your perfect intonation is not so easy." My heart sank. I had started out thinking that I would sing Pamina and now they were asking me to sing the smallest of the female roles, one that is usually sung by a boy soprano in most professional productions. I could have refused but I decided to accept—and the First Lady role had not been so much fun for me anyway. I had to learn the new role and memorize it in just a few days and had to go to fittings for a new costume. Nevertheless I sang and acted the role as best as I could. I would have to wait until 1981 to sing Pamina at the Chorégies d'Orange. I was certainly more ready to do it then.

I was disappointed about all of the changes but it was my performance of this role that attracted the attention of an agent, Thomas Thompson from Columbia Artists Management, the biggest agency for classical music in America. After the performance he called Miss Tourel and had a long conversation with her. When I graduated at the end of the year I already had an agent.

Göran Gentele, the Swedish actor and director, had been named to succeed Rudolf Bing as head of the Metropolitan Opera in 1972. He had been the director of the Royal Swedish Opera in Stockholm since 1963. During that summer he, along with his two daughters, were tragically killed in a head-on collision with a truck in Sardinia. When I heard how they had died I remembered my experience the first time that I was driven to Spoleto. He had made plans to have a "Piccolo Opera," which was to be called the "Mini-Met at the Forum" (the Forum was one of the theaters at Lincoln Center). He was to direct the inaugural production of *Four Saints in Three Acts* with Alvin Ailey as the choreographer and I had been chosen by Virgil Thomson to sing the role of Saint Settlement. His widow, Mrs. Marit Gentele, wanted her husband's Mini-Met project to continue even after his death and she was very much involved in that first season. It was decided that Ailey should direct the opera himself, and so I found myself working directly with him. It was a wonderful, inspiring experience. I ran into Mrs. Gentele many times during the first years of my career. Whenever she came to any of my performances she was always encouraging and seemed proud of the fact that I had been involved in that production.

That summer of 1973 Miss Tourel and I went back to Paris and Zurich and on to Jerusalem for her classes at the Rubin Academy. She was often tired but never said a word to me about being seriously ill. I could not see what was unthinkable for me—that I would soon lose her. I had just finished my studies at Juilliard, receiving my second bachelor's degree. I had taken a full degree program, unlike many at Juilliard who only took the music diploma because there are no college degree requirements. I had an agent at Columbia Artists and I still had a scholarship to continue my private lessons with Jennie Tourel. I was looking forward to passing the stage from student to young professional with her guidance.

When I returned to New York after the summer of 1973, I finally left behind my friends on 102nd Street and moved a little further downtown to Ninety-Fifth and Riverside Drive. When I told the father of my friend Rona, Mr. Abraham Klinghoffer, about my ordeal finding my first apartment, he and his wife helped me get a new one. It was in a building owned by a big company and he called them directly when I went to apply for the apartment, so I was spared the pain and humiliation that I had had to accept three years before.

I was impatient for Miss Tourel's return and for my first lesson after the summer. I was listening to Berlioz's *Les nuits d'été* and during the song "Sur les lagunes" her secretary, Gina, rang to say that she was back. But I could hear in her voice that something was wrong. She then told me that she was not well at all—that the cancer had come back, this time to the lungs.

Miss Tourel must have known the previous spring, but in spite of her illness she decided to finish her performance for the film as La Dame de Piques in Tchaikovsky's *Pique Dame* for PBS. I later remembered that she had been ill during the filming and I understood her determination to get it finished. She even performed the speaking role of the Duchess of Krakenthorp in a production of Donizetti's *La fille du regiment* with Joan Sutherland, conducted by Richard Bonynge in the beginning of September of 1973.

I was terrifically shocked by the events of September 11, 1973, when the democratically elected government of Salvador Allende was overthrown by the Chilean military supported by the United States. But I was so preoccupied with my thoughts and fears about Miss Tourel that it was only months later that I was able to take in the tragic consequences of this illegal coup.

She was admitted to the hospital in October but none of her students could really accept that it was so serious that she would never return to her studio, look up with her head tilted to one side, and ask with genuine anticipation, "So what have you prepared for today's lesson?" I went to visit her often but was never left alone with her. There was always someone from her family, close friends, or other students. Her two sisters lived in New York and she had a brother in Tel Aviv. Her sisters were already wearing her clothing and jewelry when they came to visit in the hospital!

The night of Thanksgiving 1973 I went to see her; her family wanted to go for dinner and I agreed to stay. I was left alone with her for the first since she had been admitted. They told me that there was no more hope; the doctors were draining her lungs constantly, but soon there would be nothing more to do. However no one had informed her of this. When I came in she looked at me and her face broke out into a wide sad, smile. I could see that she was very tired and spoke with difficulty. I took her hand and asked how she felt. After a silence she looked me directly in the eyes and said, "I do not want to die." Her family had not told her that she was terminally ill; Lorraine Nubar and I were the only students who knew but we had been sworn to secrecy. But this night it was only the two of us and I could not be evasive. Besides, she was a smart woman and not easily fooled. I answered, "You will not really die: you have given so much to so many throughout your life. You will live on forever through your art. What you have given to me is immeasurable and I promise you that I will not let it die. What you have passed on to me I will keep alive and pass it on wherever I go." I squeezed her hand and told her for the first time that I loved her. A nurse came in and gave her a cup of tea in a styrofoam cup; the tea was too hot and had the look that she gave the nurse been daggers the nurse would have died on the spot. Until her last moment she reacted with her usual energy, character, and disdain for sloppiness and unprofessional behavior. She asked for something to help her sleep. I sat with her until she fell into a peaceful sleep. I kissed her forehead and said goodbye. I left the hospital. It was Thanksgiving night and the tenth anniversary of the assassination of JFK. She never awoke.

As I walked along Riverside Drive the next day I felt so terribly alone. No one so close and so important to me had ever died. I listened to the wind blowing in the trees and saw that life was continuing; the leaves that had turned orange and then brown had been swept to the ground by the rustling wind. How could everything else in the world continue like it did yesterday? She was no longer alive. I was numb. But the wind blowing in the trees seemed to say to me that life had to go on for me too. Moreover I had made a promise to her the night before that I was determined to keep. Again I stood before an empty slate but this time equipped with the guidance and inspiration that I had received from Jennie Tourel. In spite of my terrible grief, as I walked I began to give thanks for the very precious gift that I had received.

Leonard Bernstein had not come to the hospital in those last days because he was devastated when he heard the news that she was not going to recover. We were all disappointed but we knew that he was capable of losing his composure in front of her, and none of us wanted that. However her sisters asked him to give her eulogy in the small funeral home on Columbus Avenue. I was afraid that he would not be able to do it with the dignity that I wanted for her. I knew that she would not have liked that at all. I had refused to sing Rachmaninoff's "Ne poy, krasavitsa, pri mne" that she had taught in my first year at Juilliard because I knew that I would not be able to do it without crying and she would not have approved. A string quartet played the slow movement of Debussy's String Quartet. Lenny stood and nervously pushed at his yarmulke that kept sliding off his head. He finally took it off and held it in his hand as he began to speak.

He spoke poetically with great sincerity and love. The entire eulogy was beautiful but the part that remained etched in my memory is this anecdote: In the Jewish religion there is one day, one place, and one word that are the holiest of the holy. The day is Yom Kippur, the place is the Temple, and the word is the name of God. Whenever Jennie sang it was a sacred moment, where she stood was holy ground, and what came out of her mouth was the name of God.

Lorraine Nubar and I went with the family to her burial and said a last farewell. In spite of my immense grief and sense of loss I had to organize myself. I still had my scholarship for lessons at Juilliard but with whom could I continue to study? I appealed to Lorraine Nubar to teach me because she had been Miss Tourel's assistant, but she refused. She said, "I don't dare take that responsibility. If I harm your voice, she will come back to haunt me every night."

She suggested one of the new teachers at Juilliard who was in vogue at the time. There always seemed to be one teacher or another who was the teacher of the moment with whom everyone went to work in secret. I remember going out to New Jersey to hear a piano concert played by a friend who had discovered some elderly Russian lady from whom all of the pianists were secretly taking lessons without their official teachers being aware. This continued until the next new miracle teacher came along. In 1973 Daniel Ferro was the "in" voice teacher. Since I still had my scholarship for lessons and had not had lessons for some time I was eager to get back to work with some supervision. He was indeed a respectable teacher and had many famous and about-to-be-famous students, but I left his lessons feeling so empty. It was not only that I was missing Miss Tourel terribly, but that his lessons were only about technique. The music seemed to be secondary. After my lessons I walked from his apartment on Central Park West to West End Avenue to Lorraine's apartment, my tears flowing silently down my cheeks. What was wrong? I felt no inspiration, no shared passion for the music. In one lesson we worked on an exercise for what seemed like an eternity to me and afterward he said, "With this exercise, a famous singer [whom he named] developed her pianissimo." And I answered, "But since God gave me a perfect pianissimo why do I need to do these exercises? I have other problems that we could spend our time working on." I continued with him until the end of the school year and never had another voice lesson with him or any other voice teacher after that.

Jennie Tourel, one of my angels, had had breast cancer and a mastectomy in 1963. She lived for another ten years and I believe that the last five were dedicated to passing on the rich tradition that she had inherited as well as her knowledge, her experience, and her passion to me. I have strived every day to earn the privilege to carry this torch with humility and to fuel its flame so that it will burn forever.

Debut 6

In September 1973 I went to meet with my agents, Tommy Thompson and Michael Ries, at CAMI (Columbia Artists Management Inc.). Both were kind, elegant middle-aged gentlemen who seemed genuinely enthusiastic about working with me. I was anxious to get started even though I had no idea how things should proceed. I had met Tommy the previous spring and Jennie Tourel had discussed the terms of my contract with him. I accepted on faith that it was a good deal for me. It would have been useful if the Juilliard School had offered a course or even a seminar about the business side of a professional career. Then I would have known more about the relationship between an agent and an artist as well as their respective rights and duties. I had never even filled out a simple tax declaration form and certainly did not know how to decipher a contract. I left the conservatory full of enthusiasm and landed in a business world where my priorities were above all artistic. I was not in any way abused or badly treated but I was very naïve and there were some surprises. Many of today's young "stars" have lawyers who control every clause of their first contracts and press agents that invent news about them before they have performed a concert and certainly long before they have anything of interest to say or have earned the right to be taken seriously. I knew nothing about my rights as an artist and did not give this any thought. My first questions were about the repertoire that I should perform, the persons or ensembles with whom I would work, and the working conditions, especially the number of rehearsals. I needed and wanted to be able to have sufficient rehearsal time. Lastly, I took note of the financial conditions. I assumed that my agent would always be working on my behalf to get concert engagements while also protecting my rights. I expected them to not only know more about the business but also to know quite a lot more about music than I did. Sadly, the latter proved not to be at all true. I had also been expecting Jennie Tourel to be there to guide me through my initiation into the professional world and to help me make the transition from being a student to becoming a professional artist. She had prepared me for the artistic side but as for the rest I was going to have to rely on my new agents and my own common sense.

The relationship between an artist and her agent must be one of trust and I gradually learned that I needed my agent to be more than just a booking agent. I needed someone who shared with me a mutual vision about music and its place in society, someone who saw who I was artistically and who was willing to allow and encourage me to stay true to myself while helping me to build a career. Michael and Tommy's ambitions for me were more business oriented, and I was more often the voice of reason in artistic matters.

The CEO of CAMI, Ronald Wilford, took an interest in me right away and had an open door policy for me whenever I wanted to speak to him. So I felt like I was in experienced hands and would be well looked after. I took advantage of this privilege to speak my mind to him, Tommy, and Michael about how I wished to work. Being outspoken earned me a reputation for being a little difficult, too demanding, and someone who did not just follow orders. I insisted on complete transparency in my business. I developed a very good relationship with my agents because they appreciated my talent, my sense of humor, and the fact that I was down to earth. They realized immediately that I was very serious and professional about my work and I was able to stand up for myself without resorting to tantrums or capricious behavior.

When I received my first monthly statement from CAMI I asked them to explain some of the costs attributed to me. They were a little taken aback that I asked them to justify the expenses that they had paid out on my behalf for photos, posters, etc. These were perfectly justifiable expenses, but I had never been informed about them beforehand and felt that I had a right to know. I had not expected that so much money would come out of my first fee, leaving me less than I had left over from the odd jobs that I had as a student. During the entire four years that I studied at Juilliard I was always anxious around the twentieth of every month because I did not know if I would have enough money to pay my rent. I was never sure where the $200 would come from until a few days before, but most often a few days after it was due. I was now a professional and was determined to control my expenses and not to get in debt.

I worked more with Michael than Tommy and he liked me, although he did find that I was different from most other singers and maybe a wee bit radical; but we never discussed politics. Michael revealed their plan for me. During those first months I was to audition as much as possible for festivals, orchestra managers, or opera house directors, but mostly for conductors.

A New York City concert was a must for all the major conductors of European and American orchestras when they were touring the United States. This meant that there were many opportunities to audition for great conductors when they were in town. CAMI and other agencies organized big cattle calls of the most talented young musicians in town, and there were many of us who wanted a chance. In my first year I auditioned for Herbert von Karajan, Daniel Barenboim, Claudio Abbado and Sir Georg Solti, each of whom engaged me for an orchestral concert. I also auditioned for opera directors from Europe such as Bernard Lefort who engaged me to sing Susanna in 1976 in Aix-en-Provence and for Kurt Herbert Adler from the San Francisco Opera.

Mozart's concert aria "Vorrei spiegarvi, oh Dio!" had been one of the standards of my repertoire since my first year at Juilliard. I always sang it for the many singing competitions I won. My experience singing in competitions helped me to stay calm and to audition well. This Mozart aria was little known and was a welcome change from the ubiquitous arias that were so often sung by several different sopranos at every audition. Mozart's music demands a pure legato line, a wide vocal range, and a deep emotional involvement. Singing this aria was a very efficient way to show the most demanding of judges and conductors what I could do. When the conductor was a CAMI artist these auditions sometimes took place in CAMI Hall, a small recital hall in the CAMI building on West Fifty-Seventh Street just across the street from Carnegie Hall. It almost seemed that one might go into the CAMI building for an audition and then come out and go directly across the street to Carnegie Hall to perform. However for me this short distance took much longer and for some the journey never occurred.

Kurt Herbert Adler, the music director of the San Francisco Opera, engaged me immediately after my audition for him. He invited me to sing the role of Erisbe in Francesco Cavalli's *L'Ormindo* in the 1974 "Spring Opera" season. We were a cast of young singers, a young conductor and director, and we had a great time working together on the production and discovering the wonderful city. I wanted to visit the places associated with the student movement of the 1960s, such as Berkeley and the Haight-Ashbury district. I fell in love with the city and spent most of my free time walking around it. In the Haight-Ashbury district we met musicians and others who still maintained the hippie lifestyle that had originated there. I also went to the university in Berkeley and imagined myself in the crowd listening to Mario Savio. A group of us were staying in a hotel that was not very good but was so cheap that we had a reasonable sum left over from our per diem to try some of the many good restaurants in town. This was the beginning of a most important tradition for me of making good music and sharing good, healthy food with my friends and colleagues.

When I returned to New York after my performance at the San Francisco Opera, Michael was curious to know if Kurt Adler had liked me. I did not really understand the question. I would have expected that he would ask me about my performance, if I had arrived well prepared, if I had been professional in the rehearsals, or even if the audience had liked my performance. I replied, a bit disappointed and quite a bit annoyed, "I do not know, but as I did not go there to be voted Miss Congeniality, I really do not care whether he 'liked' me or not. I hope that he appreciated my work." It was clear that they were not going to be the ones to pull me up and to demand more of me than I was asking of myself. Without Miss Tourel I was going to have become my own taskmaster until I could find someone else who would set the bar high for me and make the demands on me that would inspire me to keep evolving as an artist. When I left their office that day on Fifty-Seventh Street I walked back uptown to my apartment on Ninety-Fourth Street. I decided to spend the afternoon in my neighborhood cinema, Thalia, watching a film. I felt very alone and missed Miss Tourel more than ever.

Some weeks later I received a request to sing the role of La Calisto in another Cavalli opera, *La Calisto,* at the Glyndebourne Festival in England. Word of my debut in San Francisco had traveled across the Atlantic, and the English conductor Raymond Leppard wanted me to come replace the ailing Rumanian soprano Ileana Cotrubas. In 1974 he was an important champion of baroque music and played an instrumental role in its rebirth, although at that time no first class baroque orchestras existed. He conducted orchestras that played on modern instruments with a higher tuning than baroque orchestras, but he can certainly be credited with getting the baroque ball rolling. I returned to San Francisco in the fall of 1975 to sing two smaller roles, Amore and La Damigella in Monteverdi's *Poppea* conducted by Raymond Leppard and directed by the German director Günther Rennert with Tatiana Troyanas, Eric Tappy, Maureen Forrester, and Beverly Wolff. During that following summer I made my debut at the Holland Festival as Amore in Gluck's *Orfeo ed Euridice.* While still a student I had sought out Albert Fuller, the harpsichord professor at Juilliard and a foremost baroque music specialist, to learn about correct baroque performance practices. He was happy to advise me and when he founded the Aston Magna Festival in Great Barrington, Massachusetts, he invited me to perform in the opening season of his new festival in 1972. I made both my American and European opera debuts in 1974 in two baroque operas by Cavalli, so it may have looked at that point as if I was on my way to becoming a baroque singer.

Sir Georg Solti, the principal conductor of the Chicago Symphony Orchestra, offered me a concert with the CSO during the fall 1975–76 season. The program was two concert arias by Mozart, one of which was, of course, "Vorrei spiegarvi, oh Dio," and the American premiere of the contemporary French composer Gilbert Amy's *Un espace déployé*.

I had sung some contemporary music at Juilliard, including two operas, but did not consider myself in any way to be a contemporary music specialist. When I saw the score, composed for two orchestras, two conductors, two pianos, and soprano, I was petrified. I found it quite daunting. I spent the entire summer learning it. Finally, I just hoped that I would be able to find my starting pitch in the middle of all the sound that would fill the stage of Orchestra Hall. Sir Georg conducted the larger orchestra and Amy conducted the smaller one; I was placed somewhere in the middle of the stage between the two pianos. The first rehearsal was only with the composer conducting. This was back in the days when we had the luxury to have orchestra rehearsals that began on Monday or Tuesday for a Thursday night concert. The norm today is a rehearsal on Wednesday and a Thursday morning dress rehearsal. Amy lifted his baton and I took a deep breath and started hoping that my work over the summer would pay off. After we finished the rehearsal Amy called me over and pointed to one place in the score and said, "This note you sang a quarter tone too high." I chuckled, breathed a sigh of relief, and said, "A quarter tone? You be can happy that I showed up—I was so afraid not to be able to learn it well enough to sing this at all, especially with you conducting." When Solti came for the following rehearsal he was more interested in working with me on the Mozart than the Amy piece and when I told him how nervous I was about getting the Amy piece right he said to me with a very reassuring voice, "Don't worry my dear, let's just try to end together." This concert was my orchestral debut with one of the "big five" American orchestras, and it was the beginning of a long relationship with Sir Georg and the CSO.

I returned to Chicago in October 1976 to sing the world premiere of *Final Alice* by David Del Tredici. This piece was commissioned by the CSO for the US bicentennial celebrations. Each of the "big five" plus one, the Los Angeles Philharmonic, commissioned a piece that then made the rounds to the other five orchestras. *Final Alice* was a sixty-five-minute-long virtuoso piece composed for amplified soprano/narrator, bullhorn, folk group, and orchestra from the last two chapters of Lewis Carroll's *Alice in Wonderland*. During the next year and a half I sang it with the Boston Symphony Orchestra conducted by Seiji Ozawa, the Philadelphia Orchestra conducted by Eugene Ormandy, the Cleveland Orchestra conducted by Lorin Maazel, the Los Angeles Philharmonic conducted by Zubin Mehta, and the New York Philharmonic conducted by Erich Leinsdorf. The Minnesota Orchestra, although not a part of the original commission, also immediately engaged me for a performance.

I do not have perfect pitch, but I have very good relative pitch and a very good pitch memory—that is to say, if I have sung a song many times I can usually start on the right pitch without thinking about it. I must pay special attention to contemporary compositions because I need to spend a lot of time methodically learning the music. This is slow and tedious work but it has been vocally beneficial because it gives my voice the necessary time to adjust to the demands of the score. Like a dancer learning a new choreography I need time to adjust to the stretches, jumps, and leaps that I do not usually encounter in the sixteenth- through nineteenth-century classical repertoire (although singing Bach is good training for singing contemporary music). By the time I have learned the music and memorized the score, my voice has learned how to maneuver around its pitfalls and I can sing it with the same ease and in the same way that I sing a Mozart aria. Singers who specialize only in contemporary music need to have even better singing techniques than singers who sing the bel canto repertoire. They usually have the ability to sing perfectly the score *prima vista* but must take care that their voices are not damaged by the acrobatics as they follow the notes on the page.

As soon as I looked into David Del Tredici's two enormous scores I thought to myself, "I have just begun my career in Chicago but if I sing this piece it might well end in Chicago." I had no one to ask for advice. I listened to some of Del Tredici's earlier *Alice* compositions but there was no indication of the demands of this new piece. Neither Solti nor Del Tredici knew how singing it would affect my voice, so I was on my own, and began to learn the music slowly. The score indicated that I scream most of the spoken texts, shouting them in a bullhorn. I had to find a way to do this without getting hoarse because the singing lines were very high and demanded a Straussian sound and purity. I spent the entire summer working on it. I had moved to Los Angeles to be with Gary, an actor whom I had met in New York City the previous summer. I found a good pianist that could play from the orchestra scores and I transported the two big scores in the trunk of my car to and from the rehearsals with him. I arrived in Chicago well prepared, but I was still concerned that I would not have the vocal and physical stamina to sing three days of rehearsals, Thursday morning's dress rehearsal, Thursday evening's concert, Friday's matinee, Saturday evening in Chicago, and Tuesday evening in Milwaukee, Wisconsin. No one was more surprised than I was that I survived with my voice intact. I was learning more and more about how my instrument functioned in the actual situations of rehearsals and concerts. I was not nearly as fragile as I had imagined myself. It had not been more taxing than Mozart or Strauss.

The performance and the piece were a great success. The conductor, Leonard Slatkin, wrote,

October 7, 1976. America was nearing the conclusion of the bicentennial celebration of its Revolution. But in Chicago on that night, another revolution was born. John Edwards, the executive director of the Chicago Symphony Orchestra, called to tell me something extraordinary was taking place and to suggest I hop on a plane for the premiere of David Del Tredici's *Final Alice*. The general impression was that the musicians had a duty to perform something new and the audience had a corresponding duty to tolerate something unfamiliar. But what came was one of the most significant events to grace a concert hall in the second half of the 20th century, and its dimensions were large in every respect. On stage, with Sir Georg Solti conducting, was a Mahler-sized orchestra, with sirens, a Theremin, and other unexpected instruments. In a semi-circle around the conductor were two saxophones, a mandolin, a banjo, and an accordion. And the soprano Barbara Hendricks would jump into the national spotlight with a performance of a solo part unlike anything I had heard before. At the end the audience leapt to its feet and gave an ovation usually reserved for the greatest of soloists in the revered treasures of Western music. And people came out of Orchestra Hall whistling, humming, and actually singing the melodies of the preceding 65 minutes. Overnight, the musical world changed.

I performed *Final Alice* with the all of the major orchestras and conductors in America and barely three years after leaving Juilliard these performances established me as a serious concert artist. I might have risked being classified as a baroque and contemporary music specialist. But all of the five orchestras invited me back to perform standard repertoire. Zubin Mehta and the Los Angeles Philharmonic engaged me to sing Mahler's second and fourth symphonies and Penderecki's *Dies Irae*. Gradually my repertoire with orchestra grew and included masses and requiems (Bach, Haydn, Mozart, Fauré, and Brahms), choral symphonies (Mahler and Beethoven), solo repertoire (Barber, Berlioz, Ravel, Britten, Strauss), and, of course, Mozart concert arias.

Since 1970 I had sported a big afro. That was the norm on the streets for young black women, but it was rarely seen on the stages of concert halls. Most black female opera singers wore wigs made of straight Caucasian hair. I arrived in Philadelphia for my first orchestra rehearsal of Brahms's Requiem with Claudio Abbado conducting dressed in jeans—also not commonplace attire for opera singers. The first violinist asked me, "Are you sure that you are old enough to sing with us?" I smiled and answered, simply, "I think so." After the first performance he came over to me and said, "You are indeed old enough and good enough to sing with us; it has been a real pleasure." But my big hairdo was high-maintenance. A slight change in the wind or leaning my head against the back of a chair would result in a search for the nearest ladies room so that I could comb my hair back into shape. I went to a dress rehearsal at the Metropolitan Opera once and just as I sat down I heard a moaning voice behind saying, "Oh no." I turned around to see Irving Kolodin, one of my professors from

Juilliard. I apologized for the obstruction to his view and moved over to a seat with no one directly behind me. Occasionally my agents did try to give me advice about how I should dress—they once suggested that I buy a fur coat so that I would look more like an opera diva. They thought that I should immediately engage a press agent. I politely declined. "I am finally able to pay my rent on time. I just cannot afford the added expense of a publicity agent. I do not want to live above my means, and besides I do not have anything much to publicize just yet." In fact I only had a concert about every two months and spent the time in between learning new repertoire. To learn the music, perfect the diction, and then memorize the entire piece or role was a slow process. I was no longer in school where I could spend a whole year on one language and its repertoire. I had to continue to try to master many languages—not only German, French, and Italian, which comprised the vast majority of my repertoire, but also English, Russian, and Spanish. It was not unusual for me to sing in four different languages in one recital.

In the 1920s Americans had access to radio, recordings, and film and developed a taste for the performing arts with professional artists. Even though the appetite for live performances grew, they were only available to those who lived in large cities. A revolutionary idea that began as a humble experiment in some Eastern states and in the Great Lakes regions was an ingenious solution to the problem: Community Concerts. Instead of taking a financial risk before a concert and then trying to make up deficits after the fact, the CC associations raised the money first and then hired the artists. People who would have never paid to hear a classical concert were willing to pay a modest sum for an entire series of three or four varied concerts. These concerts flourished in spite of the financial crisis of 1929 and grew into a large, enduring network of performing arts presenters, with artists and audiences alike benefiting from "a Carnegie Hall in every town." They were more than entertainment—they were food for the soul during very difficult times. At the time of the crash there were forty-two associations in America. In the 1930s the newly formed artist agency Columbia Artists Management adopted Community Concerts and by 1950 there were 1,008 associations, not only in the United States but also in Canada, Mexico, the Caribbean, and briefly in South Africa. The combination of the CAMI roster and the association ensured an enormous success and brought concerts to people who would never have had the chance to hear some of the greatest artists of their time. CAMI and Community Concerts dissolved their relationship in the 1990s.

For my first program with Community Concerts I was asked to add a few opera arias and I agreed, but as soon as we started to perform on tour it became very clear to me that this was not at all the kind of program that I wanted to sing. After that tour I refused to include opera arias on a recital with piano. I wanted to become a true recitalist. Once, I made an exception in the 1980s when I was engaged for a recital tour in Japan, Korea, and Taiwan. The local promoter of the recital in Seoul insisted that he would not be able to sell a full house with the program that I was doing on the tour without at least one opera aria. After much pressure from my agent I compromised by substituting two Mozart concert arias for one of the group of songs. My pianist Staffan Scheja and I were not happy about it, but I tried to be accommodating since I did not know the actual situation in Seoul. The concert went well but the affirmation that I should not have given in came from some singing students who came to see me after the concert. One of them said to me, "Thank you for tonight's recital, it was a great concert. Your artistry is a reference for us here in Korea, but we had hoped to hear you sing tonight some of the French mélodies that you do so well." The group of songs that I had taken away just for the Seoul concert were by Claude Debussy. The students in Bedford Stuyvesant had already taught me about the importance of a musician's relationship to the music that she has chosen to sing and the students in Seoul taught me to stick to my convictions.

Community Concerts was to be a very important training ground for me as a recitalist. But Michael and Tommy wanted me to concentrate more on opera. They often said, "No one can make a career singing recitals." To which I replied, "I enjoy singing opera but I love and want to sing recitals as well." I did not consider if this was a good career strategy or not but I had to speak my own truth. I kept asking myself, What would Miss Tourel say?

How would she handle this? A little voice would answer me, "You have to decide what you want to do."

After my first season in the Community Concerts I had a discussion with Ronald Wilford and told him that I would not be singing any opera arias in my program. He knew absolutely nothing about music or what was suitable or not for recital so he asked me to make an effort with my program for the next year by including something more accessible, like Negro spirituals. Once a year there was a big convention in New York City of all the Community Concerts Associations from around the country. Every day there was a series of show-and-tell concerts in CAMI Hall where newcomers like myself, as well as some veteran musicians who needed a boost to their careers, performed mini concerts of about thirty minutes. I presented a little sample of the recital program that I was preparing for the following season. After my performance Ronald came to congratulate me and I said proudly, "You see I sang some Negro spirituals in my program today." "Yes," he said, "but not very well known ones." And I replied, "Not well known to someone who was brought up in the Greek Orthodox Church."

The following year I submitted my new program that included the great American song cycle *The Hermit Songs* of Samuel Barber. The director of Community Concerts sent the following message: "Even Leontyne Price could not make these songs work so please change your program." Leontyne Price had borne with the greatest grace the mantle of being "a credit to her race." Her courage and perseverance made it possible for me and subsequent generations of black singers to be free to just be themselves and strive to be a credit to their art. I wrote back, "I have the greatest admiration for Leontyne Price but I am not Leontyne Price and please do not forget it. The program that I will sing will include *The Hermit Songs*. You choose another program and you can sing it." This did not endear me to them but since I had the backing of Wilford I sang my program. The tour went well and the entire program was received with enthusiasm even in the smallest towns. I remember one elderly gentleman who came to me after one of my recitals and said, "Thank you so much for coming to us with such a good and interesting program. So many artists think that because they come to a little town that they must present a program for the 'country people.' Just because we have chosen not to live in a big city does not mean that we are uncultivated. We truly appreciate it that you do not attempt to sing down to us." I found out later that he had been a professional musician. Later when I proposed the *Poèmes pour Mi* by Messiaen I did not hear a word of dissent from the head of the CC division.

Today my programs are based on my desire to sing a particular song, a song cycle, or the poems of a particular poet. When a song speaks to me then I feel that I can relate that to the audience. I sang my first recital in Lincoln, Nebraska, in 1969. I was nurtured in the recitals of so many wonderful recitalists: Jennie Tourel of course, Victoria de los Angeles, Benita Valente, Elly Ameling, Imgard Seefried, Christa Ludwig, Brigitte Fassbaender, Gundula Janowitz, Jan DeGaetani, and many more. It is the tradition in which they excelled that I have tried to continue. Today very few opera singers sing even an occasional recital, and then it is usually a mixed repertoire of songs and opera arias. Only a small group of singers devote themselves to recitals and chamber music. When I came to Europe, the recital was still a very important part of the classical musical scene. But I have watched that importance gradually diminish. Most of the singers of my generation who could have filled major concert halls singing this repertoire abandoned the art form. Some chose to sing in "events" or stadium concerts. Instead of enlarging the classical music audience and inspiring an interest in true classical music repertoire these events might just have contributed to its decline. Luckily I am still to this day able to sing my recital program to full concert halls all over the world. Therefore I have been able to gently impose the programs that I believe in on my willing audience. Many come to a concert just because it is me, but they know that I will always offer an interesting program with no compromises even though it most likely will be composed of songs that are completely unknown to them. I am sad to see that very few younger singers, and almost no female singers, actually devote a major part of their efforts to the recital repertoire in addition to their opera roles. Maybe the art of the recital must die out for a while before it can enjoy a renaissance like the one that has brought baroque music back. It is rare to find a promoter or concert hall manager who has sufficient knowledge of the repertoire to make an intelligent judgment about whether a program will be a success or not, but that ignorance does not seem to deter them from trying to impose their will on artists. In the 1990s my agent at IMG, Edna Landau, informed me that unless I was willing to conform to the promoters' demands concerning my recital program—opera arias and songs that they considered to be popular—or could come up with some gimmick in my programming, then there was no market for my recitals in the United States. I told her what I was singing in the rest of the world, and she acknowledged that the market had entirely changed in America since I was a student at the Juilliard School and could enjoy several high quality recitals several times a year. To prove her point she passed on to me a letter from a promoter in Toronto, where I had just sung. The promoter essentially said that she had no interest in "Herz and Schmerz" programs no matter how famous the singer is. I replied to her after receiving this shocking letter, "Well, Herz and Schmerz is what I do and I am not about to change that now." I have never returned to the United States for a recital since then. I am quite happy to sing many different kinds of programs that include more popular repertoire, such as jazz, or opera and operetta arias with orchestra, but each in its own context.

I can say that from the beginning of my relationship with CAMI I received a great deal of support from Michael, Tommy, and Ronald. They were aware of my potential and registered the positive feedback from my concerts. Even though my endless questions sometimes irritated them they respected me for standing up for my own values. Having a good sense of humor came in handy for turning around any disagreement and ending it with good-natured laughter. However, they were above all else businessmen who looked at the bottom line, not at the artistic line, so it was clear to me that I was not going to find my new mentor on Fifty-Seventh Street. I was always honest, direct, and assertive without being aggressive with them. When Michael died after a long illness, Ronald chose my new agent, Doug Sheldon. Doug grew to appreciate my frankness and professionalism; he later informed me that when I had been assigned to him his task was to change my reputation in the office because I was considered too demanding.

When I was a student I thought the critics were an important part of the musical life of a performer. I recalled the scenes from films about an opening night of a show with everyone in the production sitting around a table in a fashionable restaurant, wining and dining while waiting for the reviews that would mean life or instant death for the show. I too thought that the reviews were an inevitable part of the process. One of my first concerts made it very clear to me that this was not and should not be the case.

I auditioned for Claudio Abbado in 1974 and he invited me to sing the soprano solo in Brahms's German Requiem with the Philadelphia Orchestra in 1975. The main character of the Requiem is definitely the chorus because the baritone has only two arias and the soprano has one very beautiful aria.

I sat in the rehearsals and absorbed every note of the music from the beginning to the end. I had memorized my solo as I would with the vast majority of my orchestral repertoire. I feel that the physical score is a barrier between the music and the audience.

At the end of the first concert I felt so completely uplifted by the entire musical experience that I realized something special had happened. I left the hall exalted and with a sense of having accomplished something close to what Brahms wanted. I felt no urge to run out the next morning to buy the newspapers because I did not need to read a review to reinforce or to explain it to me. When I arrived for the second performance the orchestra manager was raving about the reviews and wanted to show them to me, but I was totally uninterested. I felt that I had done my best and the actual musical experience was more than sufficient. A bad review would not have taken anything away from my experience nor would a good one have enhanced it. I was on the path that I had chosen, following in the footsteps of the great artists upon whose shoulders I was trying to stand, especially Jennie Tourel. She had pointed out the direction of that path and given me a torch with which to light it. In Philadelphia I had glimpsed my far-off goal. I just had to be patient and stay true on my way.

Terry McEwen, the director of London Records, the American branch of Decca, was one of Jennie Tourel's closest friends. We had met a few times at the hospital during Miss Tourel's last days. I spoke to him at her funeral and he told me, "Jennie and I have spoken a lot about you lately and she said to me in the hospital, 'Terry, if anything happens to me I have one student that I want you to look out for. Please take care of Barbara.' And I promised her to do so." He called me some months later and said, "In the summer of 1976 Decca is planning a recording of Gershwin's *Porgy and Bess* with Lorin Maazel conducting the Cleveland Orchestra and I want you to sing the role of Clara." Needless to say, I was thrilled to be asked to do a recording so soon. Decca assembled a cast of the best black singers that they could find. Leona Mitchell, who sang Bess, had one of the most beautiful voices I had ever heard; my friend Florence Quivar, with whom I had worked often at the Met Studio, sang Serena; and my duo partner from the Lincoln Center Student Program and member of the Maria Callas class, Sir Williard White, was Porgy. Terry had convinced Lorin Maazel to accept me without an audition. I already had a previous engagement that summer at the Santa Fe Opera, singing the Vixen in Janáček's *Cunning Little Vixen,* and the last performance there overlapped with the first rehearsals for *Porgy and Bess,* but Maazel had accepted my late arrival. We were to start to record immediately after an open-air concert at the Blossom Music Center, the orchestra's summer home in Ohio. The day after my last performance I flew to Cleveland, arriving late Friday afternoon a few hours before my first rehearsal. I found no instructions in my hotel upon arrival so I called the office number on my schedule that I had received from my agent, Michael. The lady who answered the phone said that I should take the bus from the hotel at the time indicated on the schedule I had received. All of the other singers would be waiting in the hotel lobby and would take the same bus to the Blossom Music Center. I asked if there was a musical coach with whom I might speak who could perhaps give me some indication of the maestro's wishes and she said, "I can't help you, you should just go to the rehearsal." I greeted my colleagues on the bus, happy to see Williard and Florence again. Upon my arrival I warmed up a little bit and went to take my place on stage. Lorin Maazel arrived about thirty seconds before the beginning of the rehearsal, greeted everyone, welcomed me, and went straight to the podium. Clara's role is not very big: it consists of the aria "Summertime," which she sings twice, and a few short lines here and there. I had been a little unsure about a few of the entrances of the shorter passages, but I did not have any problems with them during the orchestra rehearsal. After the rehearsals many of the soloists went to speak to Maazel, but I felt that my small role had not posed any difficulties and I felt a little silly to bother him about it. I was happy to know that I had not made a fool of myself in front of everyone. I returned to the hotel feeling that I had things under control and that all would go well.

The next morning I arrived for the dress rehearsal feeling confident, but as soon as I opened my mouth to sing Maazel made a very nasty remark, and this continued throughout the rehearsal. It was obvious to everyone that he was not at all pleased with me. I could not begin to fathom what the problem was. Florence said to me, "Girl, what did you do? You had better go to talk to him." I replied, "He should come to talk to me, because I have not done anything wrong." After the rehearsal I went to speak to the record producer from Decca, James, a very correct Englishman, and I said to him, "I will sing the concert tomorrow because it is too late to find someone in the next twenty-four hours to sing, but I have no intention of recording on Monday unless he apologizes to me."

The next day when we arrived with the bus to the parking lot backstage, I saw Maazel pacing up and down outside of the stage door entrance, so I decided to wait a little before going in. But he did not go away and I was obliged to go in in order to warm up and get dressed for the concert. "Summertime" is the first song after the overture. I approached the entrance timidly and just as I was about to pass him he said, "Miss Hendricks, it seems that you would like to speak to me." I swallowed hard and said, "Hello, Maestro, yes, that's true." I followed him to his dressing room and he asked me, "What is the problem?" And I said, "I should ask you what the problem is after the way that you treated me in yesterday's rehearsal. I do not know what I did to get such a response from you." He said, "You were late for rehearsals and you did not come to speak to me before the rehearsal upon arrival." I replied, "You were informed of my late arrival since the beginning of negotiations and my contract states that my arrival date was yesterday." I then said, "I called the orchestra's office when I arrived and the lady that I spoke to was neither very helpful nor very pleasant: she just said that I should just show up at the rehearsal."

"Oh, that was my secretary who is being replaced next month," he said, and seemed to calm down. I continued, "I did have some questions before the first rehearsal on Friday night but after the rehearsal seemed to go well I felt comfortable and you also seemed pleased. I assumed that with an orchestra, a chorus, and eleven soloists, you did not need to have me bothering you about Clara. I thought that I was being professional." He nodded and said, "OK, that is clear." I then asked, "Is there something that I am doing with the role that you would like me to do differently?" He thought a moment and then said, "Yes, when you begin 'Summertime,' the second time, take more time and sing the first two notes a little slower." I looked at the score and said, "Yes, you mean here where it is written *poco ritardando*? OK, I would be happy to do that."

I went on to sing the concert and to record the role of Clara, my first recording.

Since this very difficult first encounter we have worked together very often. A year after *Porgy and Bess* he invited me to sing Marzelline in a concert version of Beethoven's *Fidelio*. He was brilliant in the rehearsals with the singers but just awful to the orchestra and it was a terrible atmosphere. During one of the performances I made a mistake, entering a bit too soon, and he held his hand in my face during the rest of the performance so as to show everyone that I was dependent on him for every entrance. It was his way at getting back at me. So we were even. Still he invited me to come back and when it was the turn of the Cleveland Orchestra to do the very difficult *Final Alice* I could not wait to see how he would handle this very complex score. I had already performed it with four other orchestras and knew it inside out. Although I had the score before me, I was singing it by heart. Needless to say he was very impressed. This was for me by far the best performance by any orchestra of all of the *Final Alice* performances that I did.

Normally I avoid people who are difficult and unkind to others. But I had seen a photo of Lorin Maazel in short pants when he about six years old playing the violin, and that child touched me. When he is in the zone he is a brilliant musician and conductor. Perhaps the child in the photo did not want to perform or to practice, who knows. He respected my humanitarian engagement as well as my talent. We met in the 1980s at the Cannes Festival for an evening dedicated to opera. I made a little speech, and when I returned to my seat, Lorin, who had been seated next to me, reached over and said, "You carry your success with a lot of grace." We continued to work together for many years when he was in Munich at the Bayerischer Rundfunk Orchestra. He conducted the world premiere of Tobias Picker's *Rain in the Trees* in Pittsburgh in 1996. Our last concert together was in Tokyo with the World Symphony just after September 11, 2001. We dedicated our performance of Richard Strauss's *Vier letzte Lieder* to the victims.

The night that Miss Tourel died, after saying farewell, I went from the Lenox Hill Hospital to a Thanksgiving dinner with some friends. Staffan Scheja was there and we talked about our teachers. His piano teacher, Ilona Kabos, had just died during the summer of 1973, and he sympathized with my grief. Staffan had been a child prodigy and a star in Sweden since he was twelve. After finishing his studies he went back to Sweden and spoke to his agent about me. They then invited me to come to Stockholm to perform a recital with him in the Grunewald Salen of the Konserthus. I arrived in December 1974. Stockholm was completely white and enchanting with snow on the rooftops, the frozen sea, and glimmering candlelight from every window.

My flight from New York was more than six hours late. Staffan had a concert that evening and was not able to meet me at the airport. He sent one of best friends, Martin Engström, to fetch me and take me to get something to eat. Martin was barely twenty-one, charming, and had an unbridled passion for music. He had studied the piano but had decided that a professional career was not for him. The legendary Swedish agent Henrik Lodding, who later became my agent in Sweden, lived in Göteborg and hated to come to Stockholm. When Martin was just a teenager Lodding hired him to be a kind of surrogate for him in Stockholm. He met the artists at the airport with a taxi, took them to and from their hotels to rehearsals, concerts, and meals, and translated for them whenever necessary. He spoke fluent English and German. Since most Swedish people were shy and assumed that artists did not want to be bothered after the concert Martin was often the only person who came to greet them. Martha Argerich, Zubin Mehta, Daniel Barenboim, and many more were happy to open the door to their dressing room after a concert and find this enthusiastic young man who congratulated them on their performance, talked to them about music, and offered to take them to dinner on the strict expense account that Lodding had given him. By the time he had found a job in Paris in 1975 at the agency Opera et Concert he could count many of the very important artists whom he had taken care of in Stockholm among his friends.

Martin's father was a painter and sculptor and his mother, Inge, had fled the Nazis from her native Nuremberg a day after her family home was vandalized during Kristallnacht. She never lost her love for classical music, especially German lieder. She eventually worked as a producer of programs with and for children for the Swedish Radio. Many of Martin's artists were also regular visitors in his family's home along with other family friends, including Dietrich Fischer-Dieskau, the Amadeus Quartet, and Antal Doráti.

Martin turned pages for my European debut recital in Stockholm. I felt then that the Swedes appreciated me for who I was artistically, and this was especially important for me in those early years.

After the concert Martin and I kept in contact via letters and a few postcards. I found him charming but I thought that he was too young for me. At the end of the summer of 1975 I met Gary, yet another actor, on the bus on the way to a ballet class. I was running a little late and I had debated whether to take the bus or spend the money for a taxi. We romantically assumed that my decision was fate and that we were meant to be together. After nearly a year Gary decided that trying to get a break in New York City was too difficult—too many auditions where he was never called back and too many disappointments. In the spring of 1976 he decided to move to Los Angeles to pursue his career in the hopes of having better luck there. At the beginning of the summer, against the wishes of my agents, I moved for what I call "a short but unpleasant time" to Los Angeles to be with him. I really missed the street life and entertainment of Manhattan. After the recording of *Porgy and Bess* I came back to Los Angeles and it did not take me long to come to the same conclusion as Woody Allen in *Annie Hall*: "The only cultural advantage that Los Angeles has over New York City is that you can turn right on red." I hated to have to take the car everywhere. Although L.A. had better weather than San Francisco it had none of its beauty and enchantment. I had gotten my driver's license while I was in Santa Fe but I actually learned to drive on the freeways of L.A. The relationship with Gary started to go sour as the summer came to an end, and I was very happy to return to New York in September. I needed to finish the preparations for the premiere of *Final Alice* in Chicago. We had decided to give each other a little breathing room. We spoke regularly on the phone, but he had forgotten to mention that he had found someone else since I left and had moved in with her while I was away. He tried to justify himself in our last conversation, but the last thing that I said to him before hanging up was, "You know, Gary, I should have taken a cab."

I also had to prepare myself for the biggest event yet for me, my New York City recital debut. I wanted to give my recital debut not in the new Alice Tully Hall in Lincoln Center but in the legendary Town Hall, where all of the greatest recitalists had sung. Marian Anderson had made her debut there in 1935 and Jennie Tourel on November 13, 1943. Forty-three years later, almost to the day, I made my debut on the same stage, the 14th of November, 1976. This concert helped establish me as a serious recitalist in a great tradition.

Martin began working in Paris in 1975 for the agency Opera et Concert, handling instrumentalists and conductors. In one of my letters to him I said that I would let him work for me in Europe if he wanted to since I did not have any European agents. He answered that he did not know anything about the vocal repertoire but his boss, Germinal Hilbert, agreed to add me to his roster of singers. Doug Sheldon accepted that Opera et Concert would become my European agency. The first thing that Germinal wanted me to do was come to do an audition tour in the German opera houses. I had to refuse because I did not have enough money to pay for the trip and expenses.

In January 1977 Martin rang and asked if I was free to replace a sick singer who had just canceled a concert with the Radio Orchestra in Paris. He asked if I could learn Pergolesi's *Stabat Mater* and a work of Benedetto Marcello in a week's time. This was long before fax machines existed so I went to the public library at Lincoln Center to search for the Marcello score. I found a hand-written manuscript that I copied and learned on the plane. This was the first time that I had flown directly to Paris. I was excited to make my official French debut there. I had sung a recital, a part of my first prize of the Concours de Paris, the previous year. I had spent a month in Paris studying French and preparing the recital at the Salle Gaveau in June 1973 before starting on my summer master-class tour with Jennie Tourel. Unfortunately the concert was so badly organized that there was only a very small albeit enthusiastic audience and it went completely unnoticed.

The orchestra concert was in a series of concerts at Radio France produced by Yvon Kapp. It was then that I fell in love with Pergolesi's *Stabat Mater*, although it would be more than thirty years before I would sing it again. Immediately after this concert Yvon engaged me to perform in the same series for the following season that took place in some of Paris's most beautiful churches. He invited me often to perform concerts with the Radio Orchestra and was one of my faithful supporters until his untimely death.

After the concert I had earned enough money to make the German opera house audition tour and because Martin spoke fluent German he was sent with me. By the end of the tour we had fallen in love and decided that we wanted to continue to see one another. Martin had just begun a new job in Paris, and since it would not have been easy for him to find a job or get a work permit in the United States we decided that I would move to Paris. I already had a very full schedule and I needed a reliable airport from which to fly in and out. I returned to New York City, packed up my belongings, and installed myself in Martin's studio apartment on the rue Richelieu just in front of the statue of Molière. I did not receive any invitations to become a member of the ensemble in the opera houses where I had auditioned but I did not mind so much because I knew how the *Fach* system worked in the German opera houses and I was a little afraid to get stuck in it.

To be a member of one of the repertoire theaters in Germany was attractive during the slower pace of the 1950s and '60s when the system truly nurtured young talents and helped them to evolve. At the Vienna State Opera was the Wiener Mozart-Ensemble directed by Josef Krips, who developed the lighter "Viennese sound" for Mozart singing and playing. Among the illustrious sopranos that were on the roster were Irmgard See-fried, Lisa Della Casa, Sena Jurinac, Christa Ludwig, and Elisa-beth Schwarzkopf. These singers were given the chance to start with small roles and grow into larger ones as their voices and art-istry evolved. They sang opera, operetta, and, of course, lieder. I had hoped to follow in this tradition in terms of the repertoire and the Viennese sound but by the end of the 1970s this kind of nur-turing was no longer the rule. I felt that I was much better off as a freelancer, independent and able to develop my repertoire myself based on my needs as an artist, not on the needs of an administra-tor to fill a certain role in his yearly program.

Martin and I revisited the places where I had been with Miss Tourel and the friends that I had made there, and I was so happy to be back in my magical Paris. I walked all over the city and it was really light years, not just nine hours, away from Los Ange-les. I went to La Coupole for the first time without Miss Tourel. I passed by the hotel that was ten francs a night. And I introduced Martin to Galerie Nationale du Jeu de Paume.

Martin and I went to a concert at the Théâtre des Champs-Élysées with Birgit Nilsson in 1977. I accompanied Martin back to her dressing room after the concert and congratulated her on a fantastic performance. Martin had to leave to fetch her fee from the promoter and said to her in Swedish, "Birgit, I will be right back but if you need anything Barbara will help you." She looked at me quizzically and said to me in English, "Sweetheart, just sit down back there, I must sign some autographs." She sat at a table that had been placed at the entrance to her dressing room with a small bag beside her on the floor. Whenever one of her admirers mustered up enough courage to ask for a signed photo she looked back at me, sighed, stuck her hand deep into her bag, and pulled out one photo. After signing it she said to me, indicating her stack of photos, "They are very expensive, you know." She was one of a kind and irreplaceable.

Martin and I married in July 1978, shortly after his twenty-fifth birthday, in Menton, France, and we invited our families and closest friends from both sides of the ocean. I had sung at the Menton Festival the summer before and André Böröcz, the founder and director , a friend to many artists, arranged the entire wedding with the city. We were married in the chapel designed by Cocteau and had our reception at the Villa Maria Serena.

From the point of view of CAMI I had again chosen my heart over my career. The first time was when I left to live in Los Angeles, and they humored me a little. But now I had not just left them and New York, I had left to go live in another country. For Ronald and Doug the classical music world revolved around their few blocks on Fifty-Seventh Street. Doug had even said to me when I told him that I had a concert in Stockholm, "Those small Scandinavian countries are so unimportant, you don't need to go there to sing." After moving to France, Martin started to work for me and I decided that he should become my world agent, coordinating my other agents, including CAMI, because I still wanted to have them as my American agent. Doug was basically a salesman; he worked mostly on orchestra tours and knew nothing about vocal repertoire or singing. He told me that he had received an enquiry about an orchestra concert with me and he actually looked into the Schwann record catalogue to see who had recorded the piece in order to determine whether I should sing it or not! Before I moved to Paris, Ronald Wilford had decided to put me on his roster of artists. He had first suggested that I work with their star agent for opera singers, Matthew Epstein, so we met for dinner one evening to discuss the possibility of working together. As we were walking from the restaurant along Seventy-Second Street down to Broadway he saw a dress in a shop window that he thought would be a great concert dress for me. He said that he often picked out dresses for his favorite soprano. Since I knew how she dressed, I thought to myself, This is not going to work. So Ronald took me onto his roster. He was very supportive, but he never really understood that my artistic and personal values were intertwined and that I wanted to evolve as an artist and human being, not as a star. Ronald was used to calling the shots, and the biggest conductors and orchestra managers trembled when he spoke. We had an open and respectful relationship. He was in therapy and we often had heated discussions about Freudian theories. I did not agree with them because I much preferred the new age therapies of self-help and was very much into the Tao and Zen Buddhism. These discussions were always animated but were never in any way unpleasant. I think he rather enjoyed the fact that I stood up to him. I had begun to have a very well-established career in the United States so I was very surprised when requests for me started to dry up. It was clear that there had been a breakdown somewhere. Ronald did not have the same enthusiasm for working for me as he had had before. On more than one occasion I was puzzled to hear from conductors whom I met in Europe, "So sorry that you were not free for a concert with me on that date with that orchestra." I would be surprised and think, What? I had never received that offer. When I found out the singers who had sung the concerts were other CAMI artists, it was clear that Wilford had changed his priorities as far as I was concerned. So I wrote to him:

Dear Ronald,

Firstly, since my arrival at CAMI you have supported me and shown a true belief in me and for that I want to sincerely thank you. And secondly, something has gone wrong because this is no longer working for me. I know what an astute businessman you are so you must appreciate that from a business point of view it is just bad business for me to stay with you.

I changed to another agent in America, Alan Green, and my career in the United States continued as before. But two years later he and his partner were recruited to work for CAMI. I followed them, but with a heavy heart. I asked them if they could work for me without placing my name on the official artist list but this was not accepted. Even though I liked them I always felt ill at ease being back at CAMI, and I never went into the building on Fifty-Seventh Street while I was with them. After a year or so I decided to leave. I wrote to them and said, "Staying with a company whose values do not in any way coincide with mine is a bit like sleeping with the enemy and I have felt a malaise ever since I had returned so in spite of the fact that we have had a good collaboration I cannot stay."

In Paris I searched for a singing teacher to replace Jennie Tourel, but I had no more luck there than I had had in New York City. When I sang my opera debut in Aix-en-Provence in 1978 I met a wonderful coach, Irène Aïtoff, who was working on the *Figaro* production. I worked with her in Paris until 1985 when we moved to Montreux, Switzerland. Mme Aïtoff was in no way a replacement for Miss Tourel. However, we both spoke the same musical language and we enjoyed so much getting to the essence of the music. I always worked on my scores myself before arriving and she did not treat me like an idiot who needed to be taught how to sing a phrase. She would come up with her special recipes for helping me to memorize difficult passages in the score. When she was younger she had worked many years with the famous French *diseuse* Yvette Guilbert and was as interested in emphasizing the importance of the words and the diction as I was.

Susanna in Mozart's *Le nozze di Figaro* was an important role for me and was my debut role in Berlin, Munich, Hamburg, Aix-en-Provence, France, La Scala Milano, and the Vienna State Opera on tour in Japan. I had auditioned for Daniel Barenboim in New York when he was the principal conductor of the Orchestre de

Paris and he invited me to Paris to perform concerts and later record Debussy's *La damoiselle élue*. I performed many concerts with the orchestra and some chamber music (Messiaen) with him at the piano. He wanted me to be his Susanna in his first production of *Figaro* at Die Deutsche Oper in Berlin. I went to London to sing for the director, Götz Friedrich, and when I had finished my concert aria "Vorrei spiegarvi, oh Dio!," he asked Barenboim if I could sing Susanna's aria "Deh, vieni, non tardar." I learned the aria and went to Berlin to sing it for him. I was stupefied that he did not have enough musical imagination to determine that in my audition. This was not an exception for opera directors, who most often were not musicians, but more the rule. Anyway I sang Susanna's aria and he accepted me in the cast. Again, as with *La bohème* at Juilliard, it was clear that I was more the conductor's choice than the stage director's choice.

I arrived in an overcast Berlin enclosed in the infamous wall. I marveled every time I escaped to Paris that the sun was indeed shining above Berlin because when I was commuting back and forth from the room that I rented to the Deutsche Oper on the Richard Wagner Strasse, it was rarely in evidence. The role of Susanna is immense. She is on stage nearly four hours and has to sing her famous aria with perfect intonation and legato line just before the end. The cast for my first *Figaro* was impressive: Dietrich Fischer-Dieskau, the Count, celebrating his thirtieth anniversary since his debut at the Deutsche Oper; Julia Varady, his wife, singing the Countess; José van Dam, my Figaro, a singer with whom I would sing and record often over the years; Hanna Schwartz, the Cherubino, also one of Götz Friedrich's previous girlfriends. I had been very interested in working with Friedrich because he had been the assistant in East Germany of the famous opera director Walter Felsenstein. He had a strange relationship with his ex-girlfriend Hanna's reactions and was even more afraid of Fischer-Dieskau. I still have a picture in my mind of him kneeling beside a seated Fischer-Dieskau pleading with him to accept some staging that the latter had refused to do. Friedrich wanted the Countess to masturbate during the orchestral entrance to her second act aria, "Porgi, amor," but Fischer-Dieskau and Varady did not come back to rehearsal until this was eliminated.

During the first rehearsal Götz was quite rude to me and made a snide remark about Juilliard students. I did not understand why. The assistant director, a very nice young man from Argentina, warned me that Götz had a very bad reputation with his female singers, who often left the rehearsals in tears and even sometimes pulled out of the production altogether. I told him not to worry. "I am not easily bullied and if there will be a big blow up between us, when the smoke clears I will still be standing." I had seen too many cowboy films.

I watched him in his obsequious relationship with the Fischer-Dieskau couple and with Hanna Schwartz, who refused to do anything the way he asked. If he said, "Please, Hanna, jump off the chair to the left" she did the exact opposite. We spent an entire three-hour rehearsal just on her first act aria when I was fighting off a cold. It was torture for me. He continued with his mean remarks to me but I could see through him. He wanted a fight and for me to be unpleasant to him. I ignored him while trying my best to do what he asked me with the staging.

José van Dam was incredibly supportive and helpful. He offered to rehearse the many recitatives that we had together outside of the rehearsal times so that I would become comfortable with them. I needed to speak the recitatives as if they were my native language and that took some time.

I am still very grateful to him. I vowed that were I to become an experienced artist like José I would be as supportive and generous with my younger colleagues as he had been with me. I had been the victim of fear and jealousy from some older sopranos, and I did not want to become like them. I found it difficult then and even more now to think of my work in terms of comparisons with others. I am who I am, with my strengths and weaknesses, just like everyone else. I saw my older colleagues as examples from whom I could learn, but sometimes they saw me as a threat. I had assumed that all great artists were also generous in spirit. José van Dam did not disappoint me. The others were very professional but not so generous. Fischer-Dieskau said to me as we were waiting for an entrance during a rehearsal, "You have a lot of nerve to sing your first Susanna under these circumstances and with this cast." I answered, simply, "I am trying to do my best." His wife

Julia Varady thought that the Countess and Susanna should not be too close, and once when I placed my hand on her shoulder in act 2 she reacted, "My dear, Susanna should not touch the Countess." So I stayed away from her. As we approached the final rehearsals she must have realized that I was not going to be so bad and maybe might even have a big success, because suddenly I could not get away from her. She was, as we say back home, "like white on rice."

Friedrich did not let up on me. Once he screamed to me from the hall, "Why didn't you do that like I told you?" And I answered, "Because you obviously told it to someone else but you have not said that to me." During a meeting about the costumes and makeup he turned to speak to the makeup lady about how my makeup should be as if I was not there. So I interrupted him and said that I would be doing my own makeup and if he had any special requests he had to talk to me. He ignored me and continued to talk to her. I said, "In any case I am not making myself look whiter since this is the voice and the color of skin that God has given me." I developed then an unconscious rule that I have always kept in opera productions: once the orchestra rehearsals begin I will not tolerate nonsense and people who make me waste my time. This was the last straw. So I left the stage and went directly to the office of the intendant, Siegfried Palm. I told him about my problems with Friedrich since the beginning of the rehearsals. Of course he was not surprised since I was not the first to complain about him.

He tried to calm me down and said that he was aware that Friedrich was sometimes very difficult but that he was a great director. I said, "If you think that he has so much talent then send him to see a good psychiatrist and then he can come back when he knows how to treat people." At that moment Friedrich burst into the room and wanted to know what I had said. I was speaking in English since my German was not good enough for me to express my hurt and anger—but it was good enough to know that the intendant did not translate my words. I insisted, "Tell him exactly what I said." He managed to calm me down and then Friedrich said that he wanted to continue to work with me. So I said, "OK I will go back, but for Mozart's sake, not for yours."

I do think that this blowup knocked the blinders off his eyes. He was so busy criticizing me and making snide remarks about me being a former Juilliard student that he had been unable to see my development and the progress that I had made during the rehearsal period. After I confronted him he actually looked at me and saw my work—and the fruit of our work together. I had actually been trying to do what he asked of me. José and I made a very good couple and I was energetic, believable, and had a good sense of timing. After the final dress rehearsal he called me over and said, "Thank you. I saw my Susanna tonight, you are the Susanna of my dreams, this production is being carried on your shoulders." That was an exaggeration with such a cast, but I was happy that he finally had acknowledged my work.

At the opening night party, Fischer-Dieskau whispered into my ear, "I do not believe that you have never sung the role before." I took this as a compliment—after all, he was a family friend and had known my husband, Martin, since he was a little boy. He even had a son about the same age also named Martin.

I was completely unknown and had a big success in Berlin. "Who is Barbara Hendricks?" was the title of an article by a political journalist who had come to one of our performances, which was also attended by several top German politicians. He had brought an applause meter to measure the applause when the politicians entered the hall but to his surprise it was I who received the most applause that evening.

Barenboim had decided to use the original Mozart manuscript and in the trio of the second act the Countess and I sang the original lines, contrary to the common tradition. I can imagine that in some production somewhere in the past the Countess had been unable to sing the high Cs so some of the lines were given to Susanna. When Daniel Barenboim spoke to me about this original trio I found it quite logical that the Countess should sing the higher line at that moment in the opera because she had every right to be a bit hysterical—she had hidden an amorous and sexually awakened young man in her closet because her husband arrived earlier than expected from a hunting trip.

"Barbara Hendricks is obviously starting to have vocal problems because she did not sing the high C in the second act trio" was a review that I received because of the change in the trio. He did not know what was in the score, and rather than question why that musical choice had been made he used his ignorance as an excuse to give me a negative review. This was another sign to me that reviews did not deserve to have any place in my life.

I was in Berlin for rehearsals of a reprisal of *Figaro* when Friedrich called me around noon and asked me to step into a production of his *Figaro* in Hamburg. Their Susanna had suddenly fallen ill. I made my debut in Hamburg without any rehearsal. I arrived at 5:00 for a performance that began at 7:00. I just had enough time to do a fitting for the costume. I did not care if the costume fit but it was imperative that the shoes should fit since I would be on my feet nearly four hours. Friedrich had told me that it was the same production as in Berlin, and it was, except that the set was a complete mirror image. This meant that all of the furniture and the doors were on the opposite side of the room.

The Countess, Gundula Janowitz, had always sung the traditional version of the act 2 trio, without the high C. I had learned both versions so I asked to have a score hidden behind a folding screen that was on stage so that I could look at the score when I was not singing to check which line I should sing next and then stick my head out to sing it. It must have seemed to be a strange bit of staging. The performance was a success because everyone was so focused and wanted to help me get through it. However I am sure that a second performance, where everyone would have settled back into their routines, would have been artistically horrible.

I sang many performances of Susanna in the production in Berlin. When I visited Berlin for the twentieth anniversary of the fall of the Berlin Wall in 2009 I saw a brochure from the Deutsche Oper and this production is still in the repertoire.

Bernard Lefort, for whom I had auditioned in New York, engaged me to sing my French opera debut as Susanna in the summer of 1978, in the Aix-en-Provence production of *Le nozze di Figaro* with my other favorite Figaro, Samuel Ramey. The cast was, like me, young and mostly unknown. Ann Murray sang Cherubino and Valerie Masterson sang the Countess, the conductor was Neville Marriner, and the director was Jorge Lavelli. The atmosphere was much more relaxed and fun than the production in Berlin, and I had nearly twenty performances under my belt when I arrived in Aix. I could start to refine and fine-tune my Susanna. The performance was televised live on French television and my career really took off in France after that.

Susanna is such a full character, and I continued to fine-tune my interpretations of her in productions on three continents. During this time my two children, Sebastian and Jennie, were born—in 1981 and 1984 respectively—and they accompanied me and my Susanna on tour in Japan and at the Metropolitan Opera.

After having recorded it with José, with Sir Neville Marriner conducting, I felt very well prepared for my opera debut in the role at La Scala. I had already sung many recitals there but in 1987 I would sing not only a recital, but also a concert in the Duomo of Milano of Beethoven's Missa Solemnis with Carlo Maria Giulini conducting, as well as my debut as Susanna in the Giorgio Strehler production conducted by Riccardo Muti.

I arrived in Milano in May; the flowers had started to bloom in my garden back in Montreux. Riccardo Muti had a reputation for being very difficult so just before my first meeting with him I thought about my children at home and the flowers in my garden. I had already had a few experiences with some "difficult" conductors and directors and I thought, It is so beautiful at home and the train ride from Milano to Montreux is a bit more than three hours, so if he becomes unbearable I'll just return home and spend the month with Sebastian and Jennie going on picnics in the mountains and enjoying the beauty of the wildflowers.

The day of the first rehearsal we all gathered in a room with a long table and a piano at one end. Sam Ramey and Ann Murray from my cast in Aix-en-Provence had already sung with Maestro Muti on many occasions. Ann seemed to be very nervous and anxious before he arrived and I thought, Oh no, if she is frightened already he must be a real ogre. I started to visualize myself on the swing in my garden overlooking the most spectacular view of Lac Leman.

The entire cast had understudies—mine was an Italian soprano who came made up and dressed as if she was about to go on stage any minute for a performance. Ann's understudy for Cherubino was the Swedish mezzo Anne Sofie von Otter.

Maestro Muti entered the rehearsal room and took his place in front of the music stand at the end of the long table near the piano. I had placed myself at the other end of the table, the furthest point away from him. He looked around the room and greeted everyone then looked directly at me and made a sign with his finger that indicated that I should come and sit next to him. I looked around and said, "You mean me?" and he said, "Yes, you." So I had to move to the seat nearest him.

My opening recitative begins with my line to Figaro, "Cosa stai misurando, caro il mio Figaretto?" We rehearsed this phrase and the rest of the short recitative with Figaro for at least thirty minutes. It seemed like hours and of course everyone in the cast and their understudies seemed to be holding their breath and watching me, especially my Italian understudy who obviously assumed that being Italian gave her some advantage over me. I found it absurd to be afraid of an opera conductor: was he going to hit me or harm my children? If he did not like my work maybe he would never work with me again. So what? But that was not the case. Maestro Muti was very demanding about the Italian language that he seemed truly to love. He was not personal in his criticism; he only corrected my Italian declamation. As the rehearsal progressed my own ego seemed to leave the room and I began to concentrate only on Susanna, not on myself or even on him, and certainly not on my understudy. I was not always in agreement with him but I was willing to try in earnest whatever he asked me to do. I had already performed Susanna so many times that I had lost count and now I was working on the role as if for the first time. It was a luxury and a gift to be able to start anew with a role that I had considered mine and to see it with fresh eyes. During the month of rehearsals with Muti I was able to go deeper into the character than I had done before. I did less and Susanna did more and Susanna became herself. The famous Giorgio Strehler production had been first produced in 1980 with the great Mirella Freni as Susanna. Strehler however did not come to our rehearsals. One of his assistants excellently directed them. When we gathered for the curtain calls I met our director for the first time. The baritone who was singing the Count asked me during the curtain calls, "Who is that white-haired guy?" I answered,

"Giorgio Strehler, our director." This is a very peculiar habit in the opera world. Opera productions can run for many years but the director leaves a production after its premiere and sometimes never revisits it. It then passes into the hands of someone who may not even have been present during the original rehearsals and has no relationship to the original director. In our case, at least the assistant director had worked closely with Strehler.

During the rehearsal period we received visits from the representative of the *loggionisti*, passionate opera aficionados who stand in the upper reaches of the theater, the cheapest tickets in the house, and do not hesitate to boisterously let their judgments be known to all. They have also been called the *claque*.

I had heard about the *claque* as a part of opera folklore but thought that it was a relic of the distant past. When I sang Nannetta in *Falstaff* with Giulini in Florence, Sir Thomas Allen, who sang Ford, came to my dressing room and said, "You may receive a visit from someone from the *claque*. They expect to receive money so that they should shout 'bravo' or at least not boo when we take our curtain calls." He added, "I refuse to pay, how about you?" I said, "Of course I will refuse." When a very shady looking person came around, Thomas came to my door and this person passed by without asking me for anything. There was never a problem.

This time I was not so naïve so I decided to speak to the other singers about it as soon as I saw the visitor going from one dressing room to another. It was not so easy. Most said, "Oh, I already gave something last time, and it isn't so much. It's like inviting them for a beer." I said, "I want to decide to whom I offer a beer." The representative came around a few times but only asked for autographed photos for the *loggionisti*. I signed the photos and gave them to him. Then I completely forgot about him. On opening night when it was time for Cherubino to go out for her curtain call, I remembered, Oh . . . the *loggionisti*, what if they boo? OK, I thought, it will certainly be unpleasant but I am well, all the members of my family are well, and I know that I have given one hundred percent of myself in this production both musically and dramatically. Cherubino came back and when the Countess went out I took a deep breath and waited; when she came back I strode out in front of the curtains to tumultuous applause. There were no boos. I do not know how I would have handled them, but I was very clear about the priorities in my life. I had accepted early on in my career that applause and glory is like a mist that you cannot grab or hold on to.

As the entire cast gathered for the last curtain calls I said to Muti, "I am going to miss the rehearsals very much," and he said, "I will too." What I learned working with Muti on the recitatives in *Figaro* I immediately applied to the recitatives in my beloved Mozart concert arias. I began to relish long recitatives as much if not more than the arias themselves: they became really dramatic monologues.

In that first rehearsal he had informed me, "I do not follow singers." I did not say anything. Many years later when he invited me to the Philadelphia Orchestra to sing Berlioz's *Les nuits d'été* in Philadelphia and Carnegie Hall we spoke about this first performance and he said, "I have a good friend who has been going to La Scala for more than fifty years, since he was a child, and he told me that Susanna's 'Deh, vieni, non tardar' with you was one of the most magical moments that he had ever experienced." I reminded Muti of his statement about not following singers and I said, "I know that you were not following me nor was I following you, as I tended to sing this with my eyes closed, but I do believe that we were both following Mozart."

The following year I came back to La Scala to sing a Schumann recital and I met the *loggionisti* again. I was surprised to see them there because I thought that they only came to the operas. But after my recital they were waiting for me at the stage door with a gift, a framed official La Scala poster, to which they had attached two commedia del arte masks; when I turned it over there were the signatures of all of the *loggionisti* on the back side.

The Giants of the Orchestra 7

A liberal is a man or a woman or a child who looks forward to a better day, a more tranquil night, and a bright, infinite future.

—Leonard Bernstein

Music can name the unnameable and communicate the unknowable.

—Leonard Bernstein

I have been fortunate to have collaborated with most of the greatest conductors of my time. In addition to those already mentioned are Rafael Kubelik, Kurt Sanderling, Kurt Masur, Zubin Mehta, Seiji Ozawa, James Levine, Jorma Panula, Herbert Blomstedt, Erich Leinsdorf, Yuri Temerkanov, Paavo Berglund, Michael Tilson Thomas, Bernard Haitink, and Wolfgang Sawallisch. But the three who had the most influence on my artistic and personal development were Leonard Bernstein, Carlo Maria Giulini, and Herbert von Karajan.

Observing conductors in rehearsals with their orchestras and soloists has been a privilege. I came to the conclusion that it takes at least thirty years for a talented and bright young musician to develop into a great conductor, for even the most exceptionally gifted musician must acquire an in-depth knowledge of the vast orchestral and opera repertoire, accumulate the experience of rehearsals and performances, and gain a degree of the humanity necessary to earn the place on the podium as *Maestro*. I believe that if one wants to achieve the maximum result in even the smallest task one must adhere to a natural, almost organic, time frame necessary for performing that task. This makes all the difference between the real and the faked. The real thing gradually comes to possess a kind of patina like an antique piece of furniture or the floor of an old house; it manifests not only the time that has passed but also the human activities that occurred during that time. It is like the difference between cooking food instantly in a microwave or over a slow fire for hours. The finished dish may look the same, but the taste reveals the truth. In our stressful society it can be difficult to resist the temptation to go faster and to accept expedient substitutes for true quality. But to become a true artist you must give the necessary time to each piece of music to allow it to reveal itself. I needed to devote at least the first twenty years of my career to learning and expanding my repertoire. Only afterward did I begin to feel that I was slowly progressing from being an artist-in-the-making to being an artist-at-work. I had to make a conscious decision to control the tempo of my career in balance with the other aspects of my life in order to give myself the time to develop not only as an artist but also as a human being.

———

Herbert von Karajan was touring in America in 1974 with the Berlin Philharmonic and CAMI took the opportunity to organize a cattle call audition at the Town Hall on Forty-Third Street.

At least thirty of the very best young singers in New York City, most from the CAMI roster but some from other artists' agencies, were called that day to audition. Backstage at Town Hall the excitement was unusual. I knew that Karajan was a famous European conductor but I had no idea that he held such an important position in the international world of classical music. Since we were so numerous we were told that he would only have the time to hear one aria. I had only brought with me my standard audition, Mozart's "Vorrei spiegarvi, oh Dio!" and not my other competition-winning aria, Charpentier's "Depuis le jour" from

Louise. My agent Michael was in the hall sitting next to Karajan. When I finished the Mozart, Karajan said, "Mr. Ries tells me that you sing Micaëla, from *Carmen.* Do you have the aria with you? Can you sing it for me now?" The role was listed in my repertoire as a probable role but I had never sung it and did not even know her aria. Since I had been more interested in learning recital repertoire in school I had only learned a few opera arias for competitions and auditions.

"I do not have the music with me but I could ask if anyone backstage has a score with them," I replied. He agreed and asked me to come back after a few minutes. I went backstage and said, "If any one of you have the score of *Carmen* or the Micaëla aria do not say so or I will kill you." I was pleading more than threatening. I had just a few minutes to decide what to do. After the audition I was going to a rehearsal for a recital and luckily had the music with me so I decided to sing a French song, "Oh! quand je dors" by Franz Liszt. I said to my pianist, "When I announce what I will sing you must start to play immediately and not allow anyone time to object." So I returned to the stage and said, "Maestro, no one has a score of *Carmen* here and I live too far away to go and get my score so I would like to sing a very beautiful French song by Franz Liszt and I am sure that you will like it." At that moment my pianist stared to play and I sang. It was clear that Karajan had never heard the song before. At the end of the audition he asked to hear three of us again on his way back to Berlin.

Maria Ewing, Carol Neblett, and I met Herbert von Karajan this time at the Juilliard School concert hall. He had asked me to prepare the soprano part in the Brahms Requiem and he sat at the piano to accompany me. The Japanese conductor Seiji Ozawa sat next to him and turned pages. After the audition he asked me to come to Berlin during the Christmas holiday time to work with him.

My sister Ruthie had moved to Frankfurt and was working for the US military as a psychologist. So I spent Christmas with her and her family and then went on to Berlin to meet Karajan. But when I arrived in Berlin and called the number that I had been given, I was told he had taken ill and no one knew when he would be available to see me. I did not have the means to wait longer than planned because my ticket could not be changed so I went back to Frankfurt and took my flight back to New York.

I never heard anything from him, and I told my agents when I came back to New York City why the meeting did not take place. I forgot all about it until one day in 1978. As I was leaving the CAMI building I ran into agent Sam Niefeld, who said, "Hello, we were just talking about you with Herbert von Karajan. He is back in New York and he was wondering what had happened to the little girl who sang Liszt for him." I said, "Here I am." I told Martin that Karajan was interested in me and he contacted him.

Karajan engaged me immediately for my first recording with EMI, "La voce del cielo" in Verdi's opera *Don Carlo* with the Berlin Philharmonic. The cast included José Carreras as Don Carlo and Mirella Freni as Elisabeth de Valois. I had exactly two pages to sing and I felt that the size of the role was perfect for me for a first recording in such an illustrious production. I did not long to be singing a bigger role: I just wanted to sing my two pages of this very beautiful music on the same level as the rest of the cast, the conductor, and the orchestra. We were recording in the Philharmonie that had been built for the Berlin Philharmonic according to Karajan's strict demands.

Karajan was known for being a singer's conductor because he had a unique way of supporting the voice on a cushion of orchestral sound; this allowed singers room for freedom and flexibility in their phrasing. I was not placed on the stage of the Philharmonie next to the violins but above the orchestra in one of the balconies to the right of the conductor. The distance from the stage and that balcony seemed enormous. At first I followed his beat exactly but I was always ahead of the orchestra and soon realized that the orchestra played a bit after his beat. The fraction of a second difference was actually helpful to prepare the entrance of a phrase. I had one long phrase that I wanted to sing in one breath and I was worried that I would not have the time that I needed to prepare it. Because I was stressed I did not take the time to take a good breath and he heard my difficulty. He said, "Take all the time you need, I will wait for you." I took a comfortable, unrushed breath, and when I listened to the playback afterward I could hardly hear that I had breathed at all. Jennie Tourel had often said, "The taking in of the breath is an integral part of the expression," and Karajan had substantiated this.

That day was the beginning of a very strong musical relationship. He offered me, a budding artist, a psychological support that was as reassuring as his musical support, a cushion of orchestral sound that enabled me to glide effortlessly from phrase to phrase. After the recording, he asked me to come with him on tour in Japan the following November to sing the soprano solo in six performances of Beethoven's Ninth Symphony with the Berlin Philharmonic. When I received my contract and the necessary papers from the orchestra to apply for the visa I was in Chicago with the Chicago Symphony, singing Debussy's *La damoiselle élue* with Gennady Rozhdestvensky conducting. I had to get my visa there because I was to go directly to Japan. I went to the Japanese consulate in the morning before my rehearsal, wearing jeans and sporting my big afro hairdo. I was summarily refused. The consul refused to leave his office or even examine my papers. The man at the counter said that I could not be a professional singer—and even if I was, I certainly did not know Herbert von Karajan. I arrived at Orchestra Hall for my rehearsal in tears. I had only a few days to get the visa or I could not go to Japan. I told this to Solti's secretary, who was horrified at my treatment, and she said, "I will take care of this. We have just returned from a tour in Japan and I know them very well at the consulate—we had to get visas for the staff and the orchestra." After the rehearsal she came to me and said that I should return to the consulate after lunch. I did so, was politely ushered into the office of a very embarrassed consul, and was given my visa right away. He tried to mumble something about my papers not being clear but I knew and he knew that it was the color of my skin that had stopped him from even reading the contract from the Berlin Philharmonic.

When Martin and I arrived in at the Okura Hotel in Tokyo, Maestro von Karajan greeted us very warmly. The next day we had a piano rehearsal for the fourth movement with all of the soloists in Karajan's hotel suite. The following morning orchestra and dress rehearsals took place in Fumon-kan Hall in Tokyo, a great Buddhist Hall that was being used for the first time for a concert because, so I was told, the head Buddhist was a great admirer of Maestro von Karajan. It was very impressive, with about five thousand seats. I had never sung in such a large hall before. I assumed that we would rehearse only the fourth movement with the soloists, the choir, and the orchestra, but he began the symphony from the beginning and he rehearsed the orchestra as if they were playing the piece for the first time. I could hardly believe that I was sitting there listening to him rehearse in such minute detail; I felt a mixture of joy and gratitude to see his approach to a score that he had performed and recorded with this very orchestra many, many times. He seemed to be forcing the orchestra to see the symphony with fresh eyes and to hear it with fresh ears, even though they already had an intimate knowledge of the score. When the quartet started to sing in the fourth movement he said to the orchestra, "If you cannot hear her,"—pointing to me—"you are playing too loud." When I sang he would point to me as if to indicate that my line was the most important at that moment. This attention embarrassed me but it was clear that it was not about me personally. He wanted to hear the phrase that I sang because it was important for Beethoven's sake, not mine. He was like a sculptor who realized the image indicated in the score and gave it three-dimensional form; the musicians were partly his clay. Yet I did not feel that I had to be passive material in his hands. He was sculpting while also reacting to our input as if in an improvisation. Not only did he accept my input but also he encouraged me. Don't misunderstand me—he had very precise ideas about what he wanted—but if my input was serious and made sense to him, he could be open and flexible too. He is often referred to as a musical dictator, and he may have been with others who found it normal that musical process meant accepting a dictator's rule. This was not the case with me.

He often conducted with his eyes closed but sometimes he would open them and look in my direction. I do not know what he had imagined or expected to hear, but his expression made me feel as if I were singing just for him, and in that moment, it was the most beautiful sound that he had ever heard. I knew that this was not true because he had worked with some of the most beautiful voices and accomplished sopranos of his time—Leontyne Price, Gundula Janowitz, and Mirella Freni, just to name a few. But those moments that we shared were very empowering and humbling at the same time.

After the tour in Japan he invited me to perform Mozart's C Minor Mass with the Berlin Philharmonic Orchestra in Berlin, and we recorded it directly afterward. I edited my own part since Karajan did not want to have a producer. There was only a sound technician present, and Karajan himself decided which takes he wanted for the orchestra. So I asked for the tapes of all of my work, indicated the takes that I wanted for the record, and he accepted my choices. I do not know who decided for the others.

———

"The Lord works in mysterious ways" was one of my mother's favorite sayings. I was so happy when I learned that I was pregnant that I told everyone I knew about it. I had been engaged by Bernard Lefort, who had just become the director of the Paris Opera, to make my Paris debut as Zerlina in a new production of Mozart's *Don Giovanni*. I was scheduled to give birth at the time of the opening. I had met Gerard Mortier, one of Lefort's assistants in the corridors of the opera while attending a performance there, and he asked me if the rumor was true—that I was pregnant and would be giving birth about the time of the *Don Giovanni* production. I said yes, but I would wait until the fourth month to cancel my contract. Nevertheless he immediately engaged another singer to take my place. I had a miscarriage after the second month, so when Martin called to say that I was no longer pregnant Mortier informed him that he had replaced me with another singer. At that moment Opera et Concert, the agency for whom Martin worked, was in conflict with the Paris Opera about a German baritone who had canceled his contract. I assumed that I was maybe paying the price for being the wife of his agent. I accepted that. Since I benefited from my husband's friends, I also had to deal with his enemies and adversaries. It could have been that Mortier simply did not want me and wanted someone else; his reasons really did not matter to me. Martin proposed that we oppose them and insist that I sing. I was quite devastated that I had lost my baby and I thought that it was better to let it go and to ask for something else later. Some days later Maestro von Karajan called.

After the performance in Japan, Martin had sent him a radio recording of a concert that I had sung in Germany at the Schwetzingen Festival, a program mostly of Mozart arias but also an aria from Puccini's *La rondine*. He called Martin and said, "After listening to the Puccini aria I became aware of a quality in her singing that I had not heard before, an expressive quality that would make her an ideal Liu." He asked if I was free in May and would like to record Liu in *Turandot* in Vienna with the Vienna Philharmonic. I was free because the recording was to take place exactly at the same time as the *Don Giovanni* production.

Karajan had chosen a first-class cast of singers: Katia Ricciarelli as Turandot, Placido Domingo as Calaf, and Ruggero Raimondi as Timur. The choice of Katia had been controversial as the role was usually sung by steely voiced Wagnerian sopranos like Birgit Nilsson. But I understood what he wanted from Katia. He was looking for a voice that could express the vulnerability of the spoiled and cruel child princess. Seeking revenge for her ancestor, the Princess Lou Ling who had been brutally murdered by an invading prince, she feared love and vowed never to be possessed by any man unless he could answer her three enigmas. The aria "In questa reggio" certainly demands a lot of sound but the rest of the role, in order to be credible, demands a softer, more intimate sound that Katia could do perfectly. However, when she arrived for the recording her voice was not at all in its usual good shape. Karajan, who had taken a risk to cast her in the role, was quick to show his displeasure and was neither kind nor supportive. Katia and I had only one recording session together. The cast was placed behind him on the floor of the parquet of the Musikverein and whenever I sang he turned around and smiled. But when Katia sang he just looked at the orchestra. This must have been horrible for her: after all he had chosen her for the role, not the inverse. I was in heaven working with him on the beautiful role of Liu, but his treatment of Katia made me very uncomfortable. She knew that she was not singing well so she also felt some responsibility.

After recording my third act aria I said to Karajan that we would have to do it again and he asked why and I said because we were not together in the final measures. When we listened to it he agreed but everyone around us was so shocked that I would dare say that to him. I had spoken with a colleague, Edith Mathis, during a recording of a Haydn Opera about my upcoming recording with Karajan and she advised me, "If you want to repeat something, drop your pencil or make a noise because he will not do it just because you are not happy."

During lunch that day with Domingo and Ruggero a representative from Deutsche Grammophon said, "You have a lot of nerve to ask the maestro to repeat something that he seemed pleased with." I said to him, "I know you are not going to write on the record jacket that 'she sang this better under the shower this morning but we did not dare ask the maestro do another take,' so this is my only way to make sure that we record the best that I can do." They all laughed. Besides, Karajan did not seem to be at all upset with me. I always spoke to him in a simple and natural way and he seemed to appreciate that I gave my honest opinions about my work. This was in sharp contrast to the sycophants around him and maybe he respected the fact that I did not fear him.

When I came back to Paris we went to see *Don Giovanni*. The production was awful! The most memorable moment came when the droppings of the live horse made what I considered to be a poignant critique of the whole production. What a blessing to get thrown out of it!

Before arriving in Vienna for the recording I learned that I was pregnant again and I was doubly happy because of my earlier miscarriage. I did not tell anyone, even Karajan, until I had passed the fourth month. Many times in my life unjust and unpleasant events have morphed into positive and revealing experiences. Little Sebastian was on the way, my relationship with Karajan had deepened, and the direction of my repertoire had veered for good away from the *Fach* of soubrette roles such as Zerlina and Despina toward Puccini, Verdi, Massenet, and Bizet, just as Jennie Tourel had predicted.

On his next tour to America, Karajan was asked in an interview for *Newsweek* magazine about the young talents with whom he worked, and he spoke about me, saying that I had a talent and quality that reminded him of Maria Callas. He did not elaborate and I was the first, but not the only person, to be surprised. Of course, Maria Callas and I have completely different instruments—in vocal color, repertoire, and temperament. But I remembered what he had said to me when he engaged me for the role of Liu, that he heard an ability and range of expressiveness that was very rare in my voice type. He said to me, "Never abandon the Mozart and Strauss repertoire—your voice is perfectly suited for this—but you must develop the Puccini roles and you will become a true lyric soprano with a slim but penetrating sound." When I was offered the role of Marzelline in Beethoven's *Fidelio* at the Salzburg Festival, Karajan said to Martin, "Nein, Sie ist kein kleines Deutsches Mädel" (She is not a little German maiden).

Karajan and I did not have a relationship outside of the concert hall. I went only once to his home outside Vienna; it was for a rehearsal just before the recording of *Turandot*. I sang through the role and he did not have very much to say. I think that he wanted to make sure that he had made the right choice. I did not seek a social connection with him and I avoided his fawning and parasitic entourage like the plague. Maybe I did not want to know if the man was as great as the musician.

In 1974, after my second audition of the Brahms Requiem, Ronald Wilford invited me to Karajan's concert in Carnegie Hall of Brahms's second and fourth symphonies. I sat for the first time in a box as a guest of the maestro. I could hardly grasp the richness of the sound that filled the hall that night. I left several feet above the ground, my head full of the colors and dynamics that he had brought out in the music. After the concert I passed by to see some friends and I could not contain my enthusiasm. One of them confronted me. "How can you listen to music conducted by a Nazi?" I did not know that he had been a Nazi so I had no argument and I did not want my friend to destroy my euphoria. I had to deal with this information about him and weigh it with the music that I had just heard. I replied, "I don't know what responsibilities he had during the war. Or what crimes he may be guilty of. Do you know for sure what he did? I can only tell you that the performance I heard tonight was full of light—not darkness. I can only speak for myself tonight. And I know I would always fight for your human rights and to protect your right to exist if you were being threatened because you are Jewish and I hope you would do the same for me if my life was threatened by racists."

It was true that Karajan had joined the Nazi party in 1933, at the age of twenty-five, when he was appointed to a post in Ulm, Germany. In 1942 he married Anna Maria Sauest, née Güter-mann, whose grandfather was Jewish. His membership in the party might have been a protection for her. Just before the end of the war Hitler indicated that he wanted to eliminate everyone who had a single drop of Jewish blood. Fearing for her life, Kara-jan and Anna Maria fled Germany to Italy with the help of the Italian conductor Victor de Sabata. It seemed that he was not a man of deep political convictions but of enormous personal ambi-tion. I would have preferred that he had left Germany in 1935 like Toscanini or had confronted fascism in Italy like Giulini, but life is not like an American movie.

In 1974 all I knew about him was that he had been a very strong supporter of Leontyne Price when she began her career as she pushed past the doors that Paul Robeson and Marian Ander-son had hammered on so hard.

After working with him it was impossible for me to judge whether his early ambition was purely to obtain personal power or if it was a tool to enable him to best serve the music, which he did like no other person I had met since Jennie Tourel.

I wondered how Miss Tourel would have reacted to him, hav-ing escaped from Nazi terror. She had sung Baba the Turk in the 1951 world premiere of Stravinsky's *The Rakes's Progress* with Elisabeth Schwarzkopf, whom the *New York Times* had called "the Nazi diva," singing the role of Anne Truelove. I met Schwarzkopf after a master class in France. When I told her that my teacher had been Jennie Tourel, she said, "A great singer but she was awful to me."

Would Jennie Tourel have approved of the place that Karajan had filled in my musical life? I do not know, but I think she would have approved of the lessons that I learned from working with him. She would certainly have recognized the same dedication and musicality that was the driving force of her life.

I had not yet found a voice teacher to replace Miss Tourel and I could have been tempted to seek in Karajan a teacher or guru, but working with him spurred me instead to want to be even more artistically independent and responsible. He encouraged my development and my trust in my own ability to match his rigor as a musical partner in the search for the truest sound, color, and dynamics indicated by the composer in the score. I still had no idea what I was capable of, where my limits were, and what heights I could scale. I went trustingly along with him on these musical journeys and achieved more than I knew I could. I always tried to give the best of myself no matter with whom I sang, but I seemed to have more to give with him. I wanted to maintain that effortless effort, not only when I sang with him and a great orchestra, which was easy. I began to gain the confidence that I could make the same demands on myself, maintain the highest level of music making and achieve the best results whenever and with whomever I sang. For the first time I felt that I had moved to another level in the continuation of the work that I had started with Miss Tourel. I would let my own voice and sensibilities dictate the direction I would take.

When I arrived in New York I was twenty and was searching for the meaning of my life in music and I became interested in the teachings of Zen Buddhism. I learned that there comes a moment when the student must become her own master. After the birth of Sebastian I stopped searching outside of myself for that someone who would fill the gap left by Miss Tourel. I had a clearer picture of the goal and I was ready and willing to go alone if necessary.

As soon as they leave their studies, solo instrumentalists and conductors are expected to take full responsibility for preparing a score before they arrive at the rehearsals for a concert. An instrumentalist certainly speaks with the conductor before a rehearsal but never expects the conductor to coach him through a concerto or how to play every phrase. Singers are often treated like babies. They are spoon-fed interpretations by conductors and pianists until they retire, and most expect and accept this. They begin to go to coaches when they are students and continue as professionals, often passing through an additional rehearsal pianist and finally the conductor before going into a rehearsal with the orchestra for a concert or an opera.

Working with Karajan I acquired the self-confidence to take the musical responsibility for my part in a score like any other professional musician.

I never became part of the inner circle of musicians and singers who always worked with Karajan. Neither was I with the agents with whom he worked (he himself was with Ronald Wilford at CAMI and most of the singers who worked with him were with the Glotz agency in Paris), nor was I an exclusive artist with his record company, Deutsche Grammophon. However he spoke regularly to Martin and sometimes engaged some of Martin's other artists. Even though I was an outsider I continued to work with him on a regular basis.

I sang the role of Die erste Blumenmädchen (First Flower Girl) in Wagner's *Parsifal* for the Easter Festival that was recorded live. The other five Flower Girls were all excellent singers. But during the rehearsals he embarrassed me by showing a little favoritism toward me. He obviously liked the timbre of my voice and he made it very clear that he wanted the others voices to match mine like the violins in an orchestra vibrate with and follow the lead of the concertmaster.

He put me on a pedestal so high that it made it very difficult for him to accept even the slightest weakness in my performance. He staged and conducted *Parsifal* himself and had decided that he wanted the Blumenmädchen to sing from the orchestra pit underneath the stage, and to have dancers on stage. This was fine with us because it meant that we did not to have to put on costumes or makeup. We sat in a restaurant eating dinner while the opera was finishing. I would like to have worked with him on a role that demanded some character development because I was very curious to know if he worked on that or if he only approached directing from the score and his musical point of view. It is understandable that he wanted to direct as well as conduct. How painful it must be for one who has such insight and reverence for the score to have to work with a director who is unable and/or unwilling to interpret the musical aspect of the opera. The influence of opera directors was becoming more important than conductors as the great generation of conductors was dying away. This was not in my opinion an advance for opera. I believe great opera must be both great music and great theater.

In the spring of 1983 Karajan invited me to record the Brahms Requiem again in Vienna with the Philharmonic; José Van Dam, my first Figaro from Berlin, would be singing the baritone part. Karajan's health had gradually deteriorated. He was in pain and suffering most of the time. The atmosphere was not as easy as previous performances and recordings. But the recording went well and he seemed pleased. He asked me to consider singing Donna Elvira in *Don Giovanni* with him and I answered immediately that I thought not, because even though I was sure that I could sing the part, especially with him conducting, I believed that it demanded a noble stature and a certain maturity that I could not yet command. Elvira is very often staged as a stereotypical hysterical woman but for me she is the only major character in *Don Giovanni* who acts out of love, and she must not be ridiculous. He also asked me to look at Verdi's Requiem and to please him I decided to give it serious thought. I bought the score when I came back to Paris. When I had sung through the part at the piano I called him and said, "Maestro, I do not think that this is for me at this time." He asked:

"Are you afraid you will not be heard over the orchestra in the ensembles?"

"No," I said, "not with you conducting. Basically the dynamics of the soprano part are mostly piano and pianissimo and I know you will make sure the orchestra adheres to Verdi's score. But I do feel that the color of the vocal sound that Verdi wants in the recitative of the 'Libera me' is something that I cannot yet deliver."

"Think about it. I am on my way to Boston for a very serious operation that I hope can help me because I have unbearable pain in my back. I will wait for your answer when I return."

I was afraid that he might not survive the operation, and I decided that if he did then I would accept his request. I did not get to make this mistake because a few days later Karajan called Martin and said that while listening to the Brahms recording with the producer Michel Glotz, he heard that I was an eighth of a tone low on one note and maybe I was beginning to have a bit of a vocal problem. After his enthusiasm about new projects I could not understand where this new reluctant attitude was coming from. I called Michel and during the conversation I realized that there was something else going on. I could not know what intrigues were around Karajan at his weakest moment. Maybe someone in his entourage wanted to separate us. Or maybe I was indeed on the verge of having a vocal problem that he had heard—but if so, "one eighth of a tone too low"? I knew that he worked often with singers who had serious vocal flaws and to whom he remained loyal. I was quite confused but I knew that he was seriously ill and in constant pain so I looked for the problem in myself.

I had felt slightly uncomfortable during that Brahms recording because I had been having a problem with my shoulder for about six months. I slowly lost the ability to raise my arm above my shoulder and I wondered if that could account for the sense of tightness and loss of muscular freedom in my vocal production. One of the trademarks of my singing is that it always sounds and looks easy and free of tension. But even though the slightest movement in my shoulder was painful I did not hear a difference in the sound of my voice. I did not know where this problem had come from—maybe lifting and holding Sebastian since his birth in 1981. When the problem with my shoulder occurred I had been a little afraid to do something about it. But if Karajan was able to hear some problem in my singing then I had to fix it before it became worse. I became afraid that this might be the beginning of something serious. I canceled a few concerts to take the time to see a doctor. When I sat down in his office he said to me, "Oh, the last time I saw you was during the dress rehearsal of *Romeo et Juliette* at the Paris Opera. I remember that just before you started to sing the second aria, 'Amour, ranime mon courage,' you had a bad fall. I was so impressed that you stood up immediately and started to sing as if nothing happened in such a natural way that I wondered if that might have been a part of the staging." Eureka, I thought, this was the cause of my problem, this was why I have had such pain. The stagehands had waxed the stage floor, my costume was a long chiffon gown, and when I stepped on it I skated across the stage. I obviously had tried to break my fall with my right hand. All of my attention had gone into getting up and starting my aria, so I had completely forgotten that this had happened. Somehow when I had learned the reason for my problems the tightness on that side of my neck began to relax.

I was diagnosed with a frozen shoulder and had daily physical therapy sessions. I wanted to be in my best shape for my next encounter with Karajan in Salzburg during the festival for the two performances with José of the Brahms Requiem. We were also to perform and record the Beethoven Ninth Symphony in September in Berlin and he wanted to make sure that I could still sing the high B natural with the same ease as I had in Tokyo. He was calling all the time and really making a big deal about it so I went to meet him in Saint-Tropez in June and sang through both solos. This went well, but when we came to Salzburg I felt as if he was looking at me through a microscope—everything I did and every note that I sang was being scrutinized. I felt no joy at all. I sang two good concerts and even received the praise of Elisabeth Schwarzkopf, who was in the audience. I was also pregnant at the time but I did not know it and had a miscarriage in September.

We went to Sweden from Salzburg as we always did for our summer vacation and Karajan called Martin again and this time said that my B flat was slightly off during the second concert in Salzburg. I decided that this was enough. So I wrote him a letter to cancel the Beethoven in Berlin. I do not have a copy of the letter but it went something like this:

Dear Maestro,

During the years that I have had the great privilege to work with you I have been able to arrive at the highest level of musical collaboration and partnership, something rarely obtained in one's life. You have inspired me to grow and to surpass myself. In Salzburg I made an unforgivable error; I was more concentrated on you and what you might be thinking when I sang than I was on the demands of Brahms. I will not and you should not ever accept anything less than what we have been able to obtain together and so it is with great regret and sorrow that I cancel my participation in the performance and recording of the Beethoven Ninth Symphony with you and the Berlin Philharmonic next month.

So our story ended as it had begun, with the Brahms Requiem and the Beethoven Ninth. What a journey this had been, a beautiful musical love story that I could not bear to let turn into an ugly marriage.

Karajan had come into my life at the end of his best years and I was able to really witness and absorb the fruits of his musical maturity. He had passed on to me what he had to offer and the time had come for me to move on. I will never know what exactly happened, and it is unimportant. Within the group of sycophants that were slinking around him I only saw people trying to prepare a place for themselves after his death. I must give thanks to whomever or whatever pushed us apart. Our collaboration had been a great blessing, and I mourned the end of this relationship. But I again felt that I was advancing further on my own path. It was indeed the right time to turn the corner, and I was saved from making a decision that I would have regretted. I am so lucky that I did not agree to sing the Verdi Requiem with him at that time, not because I would have damaged my voice, but because I would have accepted singing something against my better judgment. My own self-esteem and credibility would have suffered.

I saw him briefly in Salzburg in 1985 when my daughter Jennie was nine months old. I had come to work on *Le nozze di Figaro* with Jeffrey Tate in preparation for my recording with Sir Neville Marriner later in the year. Martin asked for a meeting with him and convinced me to go along. I was not sure that I wanted to meet him again. However, he was very kind, asked how I was, and seemed genuinely happy to meet my two children, though he seemed a little embarrassed and uncomfortable.

The last time that we met was on the Concorde to New York some years later. I always preferred to sit in the second part of the Concorde. There seemed to be some kind of stupid prestige about being seated in the front, and Air France usually gave me a seat on the coveted first row in the first section next to some French minister or some obnoxious businessman who wanted to show how important he was. So I always asked to sit in the back section where I might be able to have two seats to myself. I went to my seat as usual without looking around to see who was on the plane. About twenty minutes after takeoff a large one-armed man came to me and said, "Mrs. Hendricks, I saw you pass by. I am the personal doctor of Maestro von Karajan and I have heard you so many times with him and I was wondering if you would like to change seats and sit next to him. We are seated just two rows ahead of you." I replied, "No, thank you, I don't want to bother him." He insisted, "Oh, I am sure that he would love to spend some time with you." So I said, "Fine, lunch is about to be served, so I will come as soon as the lunch service is finished." After eating, I went, not without a bit of trepidation, to exchange seats with the good doctor. Karajan greeted me warmly. I could see how weak he was and it made me sad to see him so diminished. He asked if I was going to sing in America and I said, "No, unfortunately I am going to the funeral of my nephew who died in a military plane crash over Canada on his way back from a peace-keeping mission in Egypt." "I am so sorry to hear that," he said and I asked the same question: "And you, Maestro, are you going for a concert?" "No," he answered, "I am on my way back to Boston for more surgery. This has been hell for me and I am still in so much pain." I showed him pictures of Sebastian and Jennie that I carried around with me and he spoke to me with pride about his daughters, Arabel and Isabel. I saw that he was tired so I said, "I will let you rest now," and went back to exchange my seat with the doctor. As we were leaving the plane I moved along in the aisle and said goodbye. We wished each other the best and at the moment when I was just past his row the movement toward the exit stopped for a few minutes so I could see him out of the corner of my right eye as he struggled to get his coat on, refusing help from his one-armed doctor. I wondered if I should offer my help but I looked straight ahead because I felt that he did not want me to see him so helpless. The scene was tragic and almost comical at the same time. He was trying to put on his coat and his one-armed doctor was also trying in vain to assist. When the line moved I moved with it out of the plane. The tears welled up in my eyes. I knew that I would never see him again and I was so grateful to have been able to say goodbye and in some way to say thank you.

I wanted to keep as my lasting image of him his eyes closed, completely transported and in total service to the music. I left the plane and never looked back.

———————

Carlo Maria Giulini was the natural successor to the great Italian conductors Arturo Toscanini and Victor de Sabata. Because his career was interrupted by the war he was already in his mid-thirties when Toscanini first heard him conduct in 1950. The two men became close fiends until Toscanini's death in 1957. De Sabata brought Giulini to La Scala where he became music director and conducted some of Maria Callas's early triumphs. He became known for his perfectionism. He refused to perform a work in public unless he had spent enough time preparing it so that it had become a part of his being. In the opera house he demanded to be given adequate time for rehearsals with the orchestra and the cast. He was constantly at odds with theater directors who wanted to take shortcuts and make compromises and who allowed star singers to be absent from rehearsals because they were jetting around, squeezing in performances elsewhere. Some singers only showed up for the dress rehearsal and sang their standard performance with little or no regard for the score or the audience. He never conducted Puccini or Strauss but seemed to have Mozart and Verdi in his blood. After a dispute about Mozart's *Don Giovanni* in 1967 he announced that he had decided to never perform in an opera house again since it was impossible for him to do proper work there. He recorded a few operas for Deutsche Grammophon and kept his word until Ernest Fleishmann, the manager of the Los Angeles Philharmonic, persuaded him to perform Verdi's *Falstaff* in 1982, staged by Ronald Eyre. Giulini was then music director in Los Angeles and knew that Fleishmann would give him the conditions for rehearsals that he wanted. I was thrilled when Fleishmann asked me to sing Nanetta in the coproduction of Verdi's masterpiece with the Los Angeles Philharmonic, Covent Garden, and the Teatro Comunale in Florence. A recording was also planned with Deutsche Grammophon.

Maestro Giulini's reputation as a conductor and musician was well known. He not only shared Verdi's mother tongue but was also the greatest living master of Verdi's musical language. I was aware of the importance of being a part of his return to the opera but I did not know how much his attitude and mine about music and opera would coincide. We shared the same belief about the necessity to be totally faithful to the score and our demands for proper rehearsal time. Nor could I have guessed that I too would come to the same conclusion as he had done and start to refuse opera productions that did not offer me serious rehearsal time with all the members of the cast present from the beginning of the rehearsal period until the end. I understood that his decision not to perform opera in staged performances must have been very painful to him when I too felt compelled to make a similar decision. It was my love for opera that forced me to greatly limit my work in the opera house and to concentrate more on my orchestral and chamber music repertoire. I could not bear to cheat on that love with inadequate rehearsals and the usual opera traditions that were substitutes for the real work. When opera is done well it can be the maximum art form. I do not know how Giulini dealt with the loss of his beloved opera repertoire and the fact that he would never again satisfy his desire to conduct Verdi's *Otello*. I felt the loss of the great masterpieces and the roles that I would not be able to incarnate in staged performances but I knew that it would be a greater loss for me to compromise my own standards.

Sebastian was born December 6, 1981, and I had already canceled all of my concerts in the first months of 1982, except for a recital at La Scala. I was still breast-feeding and I had Sebastian with me backstage because I had to feed him just before the beginning of the concert. I was paid in cash before the performance and just as Sebastian was falling asleep I placed the money underneath his mattress, locked the door to my dressing room, and went out on stage. Sebastian was still asleep at the intermission when Martin went backstage to check on him, and he awoke right after the last encore. The intendante, Cesare Mazzonis, was waiting backstage during the encore and watched very bemusedly when I went directly from the stage to feed Sebastian. The concert had gone well but I felt some fatigue during the last songs of the concert.

At that time I still did not know if I would be able to perform in the historical production with Guilini or in the *Romeo et Juliette*, my delayed debut at the Paris Opera later in June. Even though I was tired after the recital, my voice had come back almost better than before. It lacked some strength at the very top but every day I was improving. The role of Nanetta did not demand a big sound and the very top notes were always sung in pianissimo so I hoped to have the strength and breath control to sing those long lines by the time we came to the performances.

Since I had planned to breast-feed Sebastian for at least six months I needed to bring his babysitter with us to Los Angeles. We had engaged the adopted daughter of a Swedish-French couple, Marianne and Jean-Paul Latouche, who were very close friends of ours. She had just finished her studies in puericulture, the care of babies. Siantak Latouche, originally from the Gilbert Islands, was a French citizen. I was totally unprepared for the difficulties at the American embassy when I went to apply for her visa to accompany us to L.A. I was shocked to see that she had to fill out her "complexion" on the application and ever more shocked when the consul with whom I had been given an appointment turned out to be a black woman. She insisted that she could not accept Siantak since she had not been working for me for at least a year. I said, "This is impossible because my son is only four months old now." She wanted to make sure that she did not intend to stay in the United States. After promising to come by her office upon my return to Paris with Siantak to show that we had indeed returned together, Siantak finally received her visa. But it came too late to use the ticket that I had bought for her to travel with us to and from L.A., so Sebastian and I left without her and she followed a week later.

Vocally I still had not arrived at my maximum capacity but I had nearly two months of rehearsals before the opening performance to get back in shape. I decided that if after the first rehearsal with the orchestra I still felt unsure, then I would consider pulling out so that another singer could be found for the role.

The other members of the cast were European and mostly Italian—Renato Bruson, my first Rigoletto when I sang my first Gilda at the Choregies d'Orange in 1980, sang Falstaff; Katia

Ricciarelli, from the *Turandot* recording with Karajan, sang Mrs. Ford; Leo Nucci, with whom I would sing *Rigoletto* at the Vienna State Opera, sang Ford; and Lucia Valentini-Terrani, with whom I later sang in Mahler's Second Symphony with Claudio Abbado and the London Symphony Orchestra, was Mrs. Quickly.

We all lived in the same apartment complex in downtown Los Angeles. Sebastian, Siantak, and I settled in. It was in no way luxurious, but this was Southern California so there was a big swimming pool for everyone. Sebastian and Siantak spent much time at the pool while I was in rehearsal.

Verdi's *Falstaff* is based on Shakespeare's *Merry Wives of Windsor* and scenes from *Henry IV*. The opera has many difficult vocal ensembles that are woven together like fine lace and demand in-depth musical and staging rehearsals. Giulini had engaged a famous choir director, Roberto Benaglio from La Scala, to be in charge of the musical rehearsals. This white-haired elderly gentleman was obsessed with rehearsing the complicated and intricate fugue that ends the opera until it reached perfection. Whenever he would meet more than three of us together in the hallways of the apartment complex he would pull us into his apartment that had been equipped with an upright piano for a "fugue rehearsal." Once I received a call in my apartment to come immediately to his apartment for one of his impromptu rehearsals. I said that I was not free to come at that moment but he refused to listen to me and insisted. I arrived a few minutes later with Sebastian and proceeded discreetly to continue to feed him. He turned red with obvious embarrassment and said, "Signora, I can see that you are indeed busy so you may be excused from this rehearsal."

For Giulini and his wife, Marcella, their family was their highest priority. He had even refused long engagements far away from home when his sons were growing up.

One day at the end of the scheduled staging rehearsal Benaglio came in just as we were preparing to leave and said that since everyone was still in the rehearsal room we should all assemble around the piano so that we could rehearse the fugue. I had managed to fit the needs of Sebastian very well into our scheduled rehearsal periods. I had rented a car so I could drive back to the apartment for lunch and also be back in time to give him food in the late afternoon after his nap. I knew that it was soon time for Sebastian to eat again and I was also feeling quite tight in my breasts as the milk had filled them according to my son's hardy appetite. I said, "I am not so sure that I can stay but I can call to the apartment and ask how things are there." I called and Sebastian had not yet awakened from his afternoon nap. So I returned and said, "I can stay maybe another fifteen minutes but then I really must go." We rehearsed the fugue a few times and then I ran to my car to drive back to my apartment. The next day as I left the parking lot and started to cross the street toward the rehearsal room I saw Maestro Giulini approaching me in the same intersection. He was tall and slim and his noble bearing would have made him stand out anywhere in the world, but in downtown Los Angeles he seemed to glide along the street with an otherworldly timelessness and authority. He was in appearance and demeanor the personification of the Italian *Signore*. He was, as usual, meticulously well dressed in a three-piece suit and his ubiquitous wide-brimmed black hat and scarf. Always the gentleman, he lifted his hat as he passed me and said, "Buon giorno, Signora." I answered, "Buon giorno, Maestro." He then stopped and with great sincerity, apologized profusely for the impromptu rehearsal of the fugue the day before and said, "You know, signora, il bambino always comes first." He lifted his hat again, smiled, and continued on his way.

The cast was a jovial crowd and we had many evening meals together, barbecuing outside near the pool with Sebastian, who was at that age a natural swimmer, as the star of the party. I had not seen Katia since the recording of *Turandot* with Karajan in Vienna the year before and I was hoping that she would not hold it against me that he had displayed obvious favoritism toward me during the recording. She never mentioned anything about it and we became good friends rather than rivals.

When I took my place for the first time in the rehearsal room with the orchestra I was a little nervous because I had set this as the deadline for myself. I had no way of knowing if I was going to be able to get through the performances five months after Sebastian's birth while still breast-feeding. When I finished my aria with a long diminishing pianissimo, I saw the look of satisfaction on the face of Giulini and I felt great letting my voice soar over the orchestra. I knew that I would not have to cancel.

Working with Richard Eyre on the character of Nanetta was also a source of joy. I probably could have gotten away with just playing a generic young ingénue and singing well; maybe all would have been satisfied. But that would certainly have bored me after a while and it would have felt like cheating. I wanted to give a fuller portrayal of Nanetta.

I need to allow the character of a role or even a song to evolve constantly and to be in motion, ever so slightly moving toward a complete realization of the composer's intent. I concentrated on her relationships with her mother, her father, and her beloved, Fenton.

In order to present a full-blooded character I take note of what she does and says, paying particular attention to how she speaks musically, that is to say, the evolving character of the musical line. The score gives me dots to connect into lines and gradually these lines start to take on a three-dimensional shape and the character becomes a flesh-and-blood person with a past, present, and future, desires to fulfill and obstacles to overcome.

During the rehearsal period Giulini was under the strain of dealing with the recent stroke of his beloved wife, Marcella, whom he had met as a young musician in Rome. Giulini had been an officer in the Italian Army during the war but became a pacifist and anti-fascist. He deserted and there were posters all over Rome with his picture and instructions that if seen he should be shot on the spot. While in hiding Marcella smuggled scores to him so that he could continue studying. She became his business manager and closest confidante. The stroke left her partially paralyzed, and shortly after the *Falstaff* production they moved back to Italy. I met her a few times and in spite of her illness she was always very enthusiastic about the music; it seemed to help her cope. She had always taken care of everything for him and I was often worried that he did not take such good care of himself, sometimes forgetting to eat or only eating just to stay alive.

The premiere went well and then I packed up Sebastian and Siantak and moved back to Paris. I had one month to prepare for my postponed debut at L'Opera de Paris as Juliette in Gounod's *Romeo et Juliette*. Things turned out for the better for me: Juliette was an ideal role for my debut and since Mortier was a little flustered during the negotiations with Martin he mistakenly quoted a fee that was double what I had been offered for Zerlina!

We then moved to London for the performances of *Falstaff* at Covent Garden. In London the cast lived in different apartments throughout the city. The fact that we had lived almost communally added to the strong sense of ensemble that is a given in the theater but rarely encountered in the opera world. This was absolutely necessary for the great ensemble opera *Falstaff*. During the nearly eight months—two months of rehearsals in Los Angeles, several weeks of rehearsals and performances at Covent Garden in London and at Teatro Comunale in Florence later in the year— I was able to work closely with Maestro Giulini and his beloved Verdi and we developed a mutually enriching relationship.

After *Falstaff*, Giulini invited me regularly to sing with him in orchestral concerts all over Europe of mostly sacred music: Bach passions and masses such as the B Minor Mass, Fauré's Requiem and Beethoven's Missa Solemnis. We performed with the La Scala orchestra in the Duomo in Milano, and Marcella was able to attend. During these concerts I saw even more of the monk in him. He did not turn his conducting into an outward spectacle. Since he was so tall, he did not need to jump up to tower over the orchestra. He used minimum movements, with his graceful hands indicating what he wanted, even just a glance. He, like Karajan, often closed his eyes when conducting.

I had a different kind of contact with him than I had had with Karajan. He always asked about my family and told me how Marcella was doing. I sent him some recordings of mine at Christmas time and he called me at home to tell me how much my record of Negro spirituals had meant to his wife. He was extremely kind and caring to everyone. On one occasion, we were rehearsing the B Minor Mass at the Teatro Comunale in Florence and the mezzo-soprano was having very severe vocal problems. I had known her since we were students in New York and she spoke to me about it. She had had a horrifying experience with another conductor in Philadelphia. He had humiliated her in front of the orchestra, other soloists, and the choir. She left the stage in tears and was fired on the spot. Afterward she went to see her doctor and found out that a medicine she had been taking for a thyroid problem was the wrong dosage and had been causing her problems; but she was only slowly coming back. Maestro Giulini spoke to me about her and asked if I knew what her problem was because she had always been a most reliable singer. I told him her story and he asked me, "So what can I do for her?" I said, "Since the problem with her medicine has been corrected, most likely a big part of the problem now is the psychological trauma of not being able to know if her voice would work when she tried to sing, but also the fear of repeating the horrific experience in America. If she feels you are on her side and encouraging, that may go a long way." He worked with her in a very gentle and caring way and she regained a lot of her confidence, sang quite well for the concert, and fully recovered afterward.

Maestro Giulini spent a great deal of time studying his scores and simply thinking about the music. I sang Gilda in a production of *Rigoletto* at the Monte Carlo Opera in January 1983, shortly after the *Falstaff* with Giulini, with a completely unknown young Korean conductor, Myung Whun Chung, who had been an assistant to Giulini in Los Angeles. We spent a lot of time over many meals speaking about the great man and he told me a wonderful story. He had asked the maestro about the beginning of a Schumann symphony that he found difficult. He said, "Maestro, I do not know how to conduct this entrance, what do you suggest?" He did not hear anything from Giulini for several months and he assumed that Giulini had forgotten about it. But one day the maestro called him over after a rehearsal and said in a quiet and measured voice, "Mr. Chung, I have been thinking very much about that entrance of the orchestra in the first movement of that Schumann symphony and you are right, it is very difficult." This answer came from a Zen master. He was the most spiritual artist that I had ever encountered. He was completely at the service of his art and led all of us—the choir, the orchestra, the soloist, and the audience—into a prayer-like communion with the music as a collective experience. He was the consummate artist, the most loyal of friends and colleagues, and just a great human being. After his very humane treatment of my colleague in Florence, I said to him, "Maestro, to make music with you is always the greatest pleasure and honor, but knowing that such a being as you can exist in my profession is an even greater gift to me. Thank you for being who you are."

———————

Leonard Bernstein was my direct connection to Jennie Tourel, his muse and close friend. They met at the Tanglewood Festival in Massachusetts where he was asked to accompany her and they immediately became friends. In August 1943, Jennie Tourel sang the world premiere of his song cycle "I Hate Music" during the festival. She later sang his songs in her Town Hall recital debut on November 13, 1943, thus helping him to be recognized as a composer. The recital was an enormous success. Virgil Thomson, the composer and critic, wrote that it was "the best recital debut since Kirsten Flagstad in 1934." After the recital they were up until the early hours of the morning celebrating. After only a few hours sleep Bernstein called, waking her. She was the first person to know that he had just received a call from the New York Philharmonic telling him that he would have to fill in that evening for Bruno Walter, who had suddenly fallen ill. The concert was broadcast nationally on the radio and America was introduced to its first soon-to-be internationally acclaimed conductor. Overnight, at age twenty-five, he became known worldwide. He and Jennie Tourel had just experienced very successful back-to-back debuts, and this reinforced the bond between them. Jennie Tourel sang the world premiere of his first symphony, *Jeremiah*, and his third symphony, *Kaddish*, which he composed for her in memory of JFK. She sang with him in many of his legendary performances of Mahler songs and symphonies with the New York Philharmonic Orchestra and in Israel. His mother was also named Jennie.

Leonard Bernstein wanted everyone to call him Lenny. He was known for his passion for learning and his desire to share his knowledge with others, especially young people. He was a natural born teacher. He came from a line of rabbis and often quoted Jewish stories, both secular and religious, to illustrate a point. His legendary series of Young People's Concerts that played in prime time on CBS from 1958 until 1972 was seen on television screens all over the country. I had seen some of the programs myself so I knew who he was before meeting him. Miss Tourel always spoke of him with great admiration and love in her voice. She had a picture of the two of them on her piano. I now have that picture signed by Lenny for me in my office.

The first time that I sang for Leonard Bernstein, I did not leave a very good impression. One day out of the blue, during my second year at Juilliard, Miss Tourel called me and announced, "This afternoon I am going over to see Lenny and I want you to come and sing for him." I said, "But Miss Tourel, you know I am just getting over a bad cold and I am not at all in the best shape to sing for such a musician." She said, "Never mind, he will still be able to hear that you have a great talent and what you will be able to do." It was not a request but a gentle order. "Be at my apartment at four o'clock and we can go over there together; I have two other students coming, too." I reluctantly pulled myself together and met them at her apartment on West Fifty-Eighth Street and proceeded to Lenny's office nearby. I was also worried that he might have remembered me from the episode when I tried to slip in to hear the *Fidelio* performance, but thankfully he did not seem to recognize me at all. I sang as best I could and he was very complimentary to us and to her. I left, thinking to myself, I can forget about singing with him anytime soon; that was nowhere near what I am able to do. Since Miss Tourel must have been bragging about us, I felt that I had not lived up to the expectation she had prepared.

The first time that Bernstein invited me to sing with him was in Mahler's Second Symphony, the *Resurrection* Symphony, in January 1984 with the New York Philharmonic Orchestra. This was the same symphony that I had sung as a member of the chorus in Aspen in 1969 with Jennie Tourel as mezzo-soprano soloist. He had started with great passion the Gustav Mahler renaissance and he was single-handedly responsible for placing the works of this Jewish composer into the standard orchestra repertoire on a par with Mozart, Beethoven, and Brahms.

Before arriving in New York City I received a request from Bernstein to come first to Washington, DC, to sing the same symphony with an ad-hoc group assembled from the National

Symphony and the Baltimore Symphony at the Washington Cathedral in a concert sponsored by Musicians Against Nuclear Arms. I agreed to come. I did not have much time to spend with Bernstein and to speak with him after the rehearsals during this first engagement because I had come with my son, Sebastian, who had just turned two and was quite a handful. He sat in the back of the hall for the rehearsals but when he came up at the end of the rehearsal and started to wave his arms in imitation of a conductor he made quite a hit with Lenny.

In 1951 Leonard Bernstein had married Felicia Montealegre, a Chilean actress with whom he had three children. After the illegal overthrow of the democratically elected government of Salvador Allende and his assassination on September 11, 1973, there was a reign of terror throughout the land. The military government's rule was marked by the most horrendous human rights abuses. Thousands were tortured, executed, or "disappeared" during the first years after the coup. Lenny and Felicia were very concerned about the plight of their family members and friends, some of whom were victims of the regime. Anyone who was suspected of being a political activist was targeted. The Bernsteins' concerns about human rights abuses led them to begin a long and supportive relationship with Amnesty International. After the death of Felicia from cancer in 1978 Leonard Bernstein established the Felicia Montealegre Bernstein Fund of Amnesty International USA in order to continue their struggle for human rights. This fund helped human rights activists around the world. Lenny felt that we could come closer to living in peace if all of us who want it work for it. That first musical collaboration with him would also bring together our shared connection to the work of Amnesty International and our dedication to the promotion of human rights.

After those concerts he invited me to go with him and the European Youth Orchestra on a Journey for Peace tour that began in Athens and went to Hiroshima, Budapest, and Vienna in August 1985 in commemoration of the fortieth anniversary of the bombing of Hiroshima. He had chosen to perform his third symphony, *Kaddish*. Although Jennie Tourel had been a mezzo-soprano, the score suited me perfectly. The other soloist on the tour was a very young Japanese violinist, Midori, who played a Mozart concerto in the first half of the program. I had been on vacation with my family and I was not looking forward to leaving Sebastian and Jennie, who was just nine months old. It would be the first time that I would be away from her for more than a week. I left them with Martin and his parents. Martin joined me after the first week and the kids were to be with their grandparents and the Swedish au pair, Amelie, in Sweden until we arrived from Vienna after the last concert on the tour. I arrived in Athens together with a good family friend from Paris, Ragnar Grippe, a Swedish composer. It was 40 degrees Celsius in the shade and I had just checked in and was on my way to my room when I ran into Harry Kraut, Lenny's business manager. He welcomed me to Greece and said, "It's great that you have arrived. Lenny is here, so why don't you come over and say hello?" I waited for my bags to arrive and went immediately to Lenny's suite.

A handsome young man opened the door and on the couch in the middle of the room sat Lenny in red bikini underwear sipping a drink, very comfortable and totally at ease. There were a few other young men in the room who were fully dressed. Lenny greeted me warmly and naturally as if we were sitting at the swimming pool. I said, "It's so hot here, the air conditioning is obviously not sufficient. I need to take a shower after my long trip so maybe I will see you later." I then slipped out and went back to my room where I unpacked my bag, wondering what was in store for me.

When I returned some time later with Ragnar, Lenny was fully dressed and we proceeded to go over the score of his *Kaddish*. I told him that I was honored to work with him again but especially to sing with him a piece that he had composed for Jennie Tourel. He said that my pronunciation of the Hebrew text was good and he was very impressed that I had memorized the score.

Lenny was never considered to be a singer's conductor like Karajan and Giulini and I do not think that he really understood the voice so well. I do not exactly know why he chose me for this concert, for my vocal qualities or because I was interested in human rights. Maybe it was both. I was certainly interested in singing a piece that had been written for Jennie Tourel. He was thrilled that it suited me so well. He spoke with great admiration about his "dear Jennie, a great friend and a great artist."

Lenny really seemed to just love people, women and men; he was a true social being and needed to have people around him because he had so much to share and to teach. I was not interested in his private life and did not even want to know the details, but I was fascinated that he was so accessible. After a rehearsal or concert his door was always open to the young musicians who wanted to talk with him about politics or life in general. He spoke several languages and was well versed in history, philosophy, and even science. He was a true renaissance man. He was a pianist, a conductor, and a composer, all on the highest level that one could achieve. But it was his energy and curiosity that interested me the most. His energy knew no boundaries and was matched by his unlimited desire to continue to learn until the end. He was open to whatever life presented to him.

The performance in Athens was in a big arena by the sea. We had several days to rehearse with the European Youth Orchestra and a local Greek chorus. There had been a recent terrorist attack on a TWA plane some weeks before and the Greek government wanted to assure Lenny that he would have first rate security, so a warship was docked off the coast near the arena. We were given police escorts to and from the hotel and the venue. One night after the dress rehearsal Lenny decided not to get into his car with us because he wanted to ride on the back of one of the police motorcycles. No one dared say no to him, so that is how he rode back to the hotel. So much for security, but he had fun. During the rehearsals and performances the orchestra was under his spell. He was known for his exuberance but there was so much more to what he did. He knew how to get exactly what he wanted from us and we gave an electrifying performance. He could stay up until five in the morning and be completely ready to go for a 10 AM rehearsal. Of course I could not keep up with him, but I would have loved to take part in the late night philosophical or political discussions with him. We gave a press conference in Athens about the tour and the need for peace in the world. The Greek minister of culture, Melina Mercouri, was present and Lenny did not see anything wrong with disagreeing with her about Socrates and Aristotle live on Greek television.

I left one day earlier than Lenny and the orchestra to fly to Hiroshima because I needed more time to adjust to the time zone change; I met Martin in Frankfurt so that we could fly to Japan together. The day before the concert there was a ceremony for the victims of the bombing. I did not go because no non-Japanese were honored on the monument. I felt that given the horror of the event, discrimination against some of the victims was an insult to all of them. Lenny did not seem to mind my protest but he did not speak to me about it. During the dress rehearsal in Hiroshima that was being filmed for television the sprinkler system started in the hall and the cameras had to leave. Once the problem was solved we resumed the rehearsal and Lenny was in a bad mood. I missed an entrance during the rehearsal and he gave me a nasty look. I leaned over to him and said, "Lenny, that is what rehearsals are for, to highlight the weak spots so that I will not have this problem in the concert." He looked at me and smiled.

We flew from Hiroshima to Budapest. This was my first time in the city. Hans Landesmann, the manager for the orchestra, had stayed in hiding with his family in the city during the war. He gave Martin, Ragnar, and me a tour of the city through his eyes. I was very curious to know if he had met Raoul Wallenberg, the courageous Swedish diplomat who had managed to save so many Jews in Budapest from the Nazis and who had disappeared in Soviet custody after the war. "We had little knowledge about anything happening outside of this place," he told me.

The last stop on the tour was not far away, down the Danube in Vienna. Lenny was very much loved and appreciated there. Our concert was in the Vienna State Opera and we had to adjust to a stage that was smaller than the previous ones. I was placed in the middle of the orchestra instead of in the front, near the first violins. During the rehearsal I could not hear the first violins and I had always listened to them for one entrance during my solo. I thought that it might be better to get a cue from Lenny and since he had not given me a cue during the previous concerts I wanted to ask him to do so. I knew that once he arrived at the theater there would be scores of people around him so I decided to go to him before he left the hotel.

I went to his room and knocked on the door. I told the young man who opened the door that I needed to speak to Lenny before the concert. He said that Lenny was in the bath, and I said, "I will come back in a few minutes." "No, no," he said, "Lenny likes to receive in the bath." "Well, I do not like to be received in the bath, so I will see Lenny in the theater. Please tell him that I must speak to him before going on stage." I found Lenny pacing around backstage before the beginning of the concert with a lit cigarette hanging from his mouth and one of the firemen of the Vienna State Opera following him with a bucket of water underneath his cigarette to catch the ashes. It was *strictly forbidden* to smoke in the Staatsoper! But Lenny was so beloved that the rules were bent for him.

I was very honored to be invited to participate in his seventieth birthday celebration in Tanglewood a few years later. It was a weekend extravaganza, a four-day love fest organized by the festival that he loved and that loved him. The program was to cover the full range of Lenny's career, both his conducting and his classical and popular compositions. I was on stage with some of the artists who had played an important part in his life. The Boston Symphony, the Boston Pops, and the Tanglewood Festival Chorus were conducted by Seiji Ozawa, Michael Tilson Thomas, John Williams and John Mauceri. The solo artists included Lauren Bacall, Yo-Yo Ma, Christa Ludwig, Midori, Betty Comden and Adolph Green (with whom he had done *On the Town* in 1944), Kitty Carlisle, Gwenyth Jones, Frederica von Stade, Van Cliburn, Phyllis Newman, and Mstislav Rostropovich.

I sang a movement from *Kaddish*, with Ozawa conducting, and "I Feel Pretty" from *West Side Story* with the Tanglewood Chorus and Michael Tilson Thomas conducting. It was a crazy four days and Lenny was happy and effusive; he hugged and kissed everyone.

We were all waiting to go out for the finale with Lauren Bacall, who had the last performance. I was standing next to her and noticed that she was petrified with stage fright. I found myself holding the hand of this legend, trying to calm her down before her entrance. "How do you do it?" she asked. "I don't know, I have never had stage fright." I got her to take a few long easy breaths until it was time for her entrance and she was great.

Lenny had decided to record all of the works of Gustav Mahler again and he wanted me to sing the soprano solo in the Second Symphony with Christa Ludwig, the solo in the Fourth Symphony, and the second soprano part, the most beautiful part, in the Eighth Symphony. I had already sung both of the other soprano parts in the Eighth Symphony—the Mater Gloriosa with Sir Georg Solti and the Chicago Symphony and the first soprano part in Paris with Seiji Ozawa conducting. We recorded the Second Symphony with the New York Philharmonic in 1987. He decided to record the Fourth Symphony with a boy soprano. I did not agree with his musical decision because I believe that Mahler wanted an adult's view of heaven from a child's perspective, an adult who had experienced life's difficulties, sorrows, and disappointments. I was looking forward to recording the Eighth Symphony with him.

In 1989 Lenny invited me to Poland to participate in a commemoration concert for the fiftieth anniversary of the beginning of World War II as well as the forty-seventh anniversary of the Warsaw Ghetto Uprising, the largest single demonstration of resistance and revolt by Jews against their deportation from Warsaw to internment camps. I had followed with great interest the rise of the Solidarity movement in Poland begun by the nongovernmental trade union led by Lech Walesa since its beginning in 1980 in Gdansk. I supported their efforts and feared for them during the repression of the subsequent martial law. I still have my Solidarinosc pin given to me by a Polish journalist who interviewed me in Paris for a Polish newspaper. The regime tried to destroy the movement but by 1989 it had been forced to negotiate with the union and elections were held; just one month before I arrived in Warsaw with Lenny a new government led by Solidarity was formed. However, Jaruzelski, who had presided over the years of repression, was still president. The big change would occur a year later in December 1990 when Lech Walesa was elected.

Lenny and Harry Kraut were taking a private plane from London and Martin and I met them there to continue to Warsaw.

I was very happily surprised to see that we would be the only four on the plane since Lenny usually had so many people around him.

He was a chain smoker and announced that he would make an effort for me on the plane because he knew that cigarette smoke was dangerous for my voice, especially since I am allergic to smoke and pollution. He really made an effort. But it was equivalent to counting to one hundred between cigarettes instead of lighting a new cigarette directly from the previous one, which was his habit. He and I had never had so much time before to speak in depth about Jennie Tourel. Since it was rare to find Lenny alone I had to accept that the price I would have to pay for these exclusive, precious moments with him was putting up with his uncontrollable need to smoke. I took the opportunity to finally thank him for the beautiful and true eulogy that he had given at her funeral in 1973. I told him how much she had meant to me and that he had captured perfectly the woman that I had grown to know and love. I said, "In the nearly twenty years that have passed since that day I have strived every day to live up to the legacy she passed on to me, entrusting me to continue by adding my own personal commitment and contribution." He spoke about her recital debut and how much she had meant to him as a close friend and muse for some of his best compositions. I reminded him that he had saved me from being thrown out of the Avery Fisher Hall for his performance of *Fidelio* when I was a student, and that I had never told Miss Tourel about it because I was too embarrassed.

I had just started to work for the United Nations High Commissioner for Refugees as a goodwill ambassador and I wanted to organize a big classical concert for the organization's fortieth anniversary in order to help bring awareness to the organization and its important agenda. I spoke to him about my ideas on human rights and refugees and he asked me to write him a letter about what I wanted him to do. He and Sir Georg Solti were the only conductors who answered me right away about conducting a concert for the UN—even though they declined my offer, they did at least answer me and swiftly. The others, all among the most well-known conductors of the day and with whom I had performed numerous times, did not even bother to answer.

In Warsaw I sang the "Lacrimosa" from Penderecki's *Polish Requiem* conducted by the composer himself. I had previously sung his *Dies Irae* in Los Angeles so I was not unfamiliar with his works. After the concert a group of us met in a small dressing room and were in the midst of a little informal reception when in walked President Jaruzelski to congratulate us. We were stunned to see him just like that, because he was the face of the communist oppression and the villain in the struggle with Solidarity. But Lenny was not fazed for long and he quickly launched into a very fiery discussion with him, with the help of an interpreter, about the merits of freedom and democracy. Jaruzelski seemed genuinely interested to hear what Lenny had to say. In November, a few months later, we would all marvel at an event that we thought that we would never see, the fall of the Berlin Wall. When I hugged Lenny and said goodbye at the end of our trip back to London, I could not have imagined that this would be the last time that we would see each other. Lenny died in October 1990 before finishing his recording of all the Mahler symphonies. The performance and recording of Mahler's Second Symphony, the *Resurrection* Symphony, with Christa Ludwig and the New York Philharmonic in 1987 was my last performance with him.

I returned to Poland to sing my debut recital in the opera house after Lech Walesa had become president in 1990 and I received two large bouquets of flowers in my dressing room, one from President Walesa and the other from ex-president Jaruzelski, both of whom were in the hall.

Lenny was one of the greatest all-around musicians of our time. He was the rare bird who could be both a great classical musician and a true political activist despite the very negative picture of him that Tom Wolfe painted of him in his "Radical Chic." Lenny was a successful political actor because he was constantly reaching out to others through his lectures and concerts; he performed in Germany after the war when others were still boycotting the country, and even though he was troubled that he loved the work of an anti-Semite, he continued to conduct Richard Wagner's works. He believed that music is a force for good. And those of us who were privileged to experience his passion and love are all the better for it.

My Family 8

My earliest memories are of belonging to an important unit—my family—where I had my own place and in which I gradually became an active participant. People and ordinary objects around me seemed gigantic and strange but I felt secure because I was nourished in my family's warm bosom. The majority of our celebrations—our large family gatherings in Stephens, Arkansas—were connected to the big family holidays like Christmas, Thanksgiving, and Easter, and to other church activities. In those years I was completely unaware of the difficulties that my parents had to confront just to provide us with shelter and food in a climate of inequality and segregation. They always emphasized to us the importance of getting a good education because we would have to carve out a place for ourselves in our society. They did not take the time to celebrate birthdays or even their own wedding anniversary. I tried to establish some of our own family traditions and enjoyed organizing surprise parties with my sister and brothers for our parents' birthdays and anniversaries. They appreciated my efforts but considered them unnecessary. Neither my parents nor my sister and brothers cared about pursuing these traditions further, so after going away to university I gradually gave up trying.

When I lived in New York I established a family of friends with whom I celebrated most of the big holidays. We gathered for Halloween or Valentine's Day and shared the tasks of preparing traditional meals at Thanksgiving and Easter, but most of us still went home for Christmas. I realized that family could indeed extend past bloodlines because it was most important for me to spend quality time with those who, like me, were seeking true meaning in their lives and who enjoyed sharing ideas over a good home-cooked meal. Maybe I was trying to recreate the ambience of my earliest family gatherings at my maternal grandparents' farm. In any case I invested much time and care in the preparation of the culinary specialties that I offered on those occasions. Expectations were always high when I showed up with my basket of homemade delights.

I had not enjoyed cooking meals at home when I was a teenager because we could only afford the cheapest goods and my father, who decided everything, had very conservative taste. He did not want anything new so I had to learn to be creative. Once I came home from shopping with carrots and he said, "Why have you bought carrots? You know that I do not like carrots."

"Yes, I know," I replied, "but there are four persons here who like carrots and I can make extra potatoes for you."

To prepare a meal for my family and friends is an act of love whether it is the simplest daily meal or a dinner with guests. I enjoyed being alone in my kitchen in Clarens, cooking and listening to the radio—French and Swiss channels, as well as NPR and the BBC on shortwave before the Internet made streaming possible. I have never had a television in my kitchen.

Dinnertime with the family should be festive. Our kitchen has always been a gathering place and the most used room in the house. Ever since my children were able to speak, the dinner table has been the scene of the most animated, interesting discussions.

When I was a young woman at Nebraska Wesleyan University, getting a husband was furthest down on my list of immediate goals. I watched many girls in their junior year start to panic because they were not engaged and had no immediate prospects. There seemed to be an unwritten scenario for girls on campus: in the second year you were "going steady" with a boyfriend, in the third year you would be "pinned," which meant that your steady boyfriend had given you his fraternity pin to wear, and finally in the fourth year, you got engaged to be married soon after graduation. At first, I thought that it was just the age difference between me and my older classmates that accounted for my total disinterest in the dating game; but I realized that I did not want to participate in it because it was so incredibly artificial. I have always had close male friends and the masquerade that I saw the girls in my dormitory go through as they prepared to go on a date seemed absurd to me. They and the boys that they were dating seemed to be playing a role. I sang at many of my friends' weddings and although most of those relationships ended in divorce there are one or two that are still going strong. I saw myself as a new liberated woman whose personal and professional life would not be defined by whether I did or did not have a husband. However, I had always had a strong desire to have children. That I would someday become someone's mother was a natural and self-evident idea, even for the feminist that I was. Children possess an insight, a strength and energy that I love to be around, and they speak directly to the child in me. That little barefoot girl in rural Arkansas who enjoyed building a doll's house and furniture with the red clay in her backyard recognizes and relates to other children on their level.

When I met Martin I moved to Paris against the wishes of my agent at CAMI because I wanted to follow my heart. I thought about the stark loneliness that I had sensed in Maria Callas and even Jennie Tourel, who had married at least twice but was alone in her later years. For several decades she had held court at her apartment on Fifty-Eighth Street in New York City for all of the major artists and intellectuals of the 1950s and '60s because she was an impeccable hostess. Invitations to her Russian dinners that she sometimes prepared herself were the most coveted in town among the artistic community. At the end of her life she did have her students, but she lived alone in her apartment with two small dogs for company. I could not be sure that I would not have the same destiny but if so it would not be because I had refused to listen to my inner voice. I moved to Paris and took full responsibility for my choice. I said to Ronald, "I know that you think that it is a bad idea to move away from New York City at this time but I must do what is right for my life. My career will just have to follow." In 1977 my career was already quite well established in the United States. I had already sung with all of the major orchestras and had a full calendar with recitals and concerts. All I needed was to be near an international airport.

We lived on the rue Richelieu in a small studio facing Molière's statue. The kitchen and refrigerator were so small that I had to shop almost daily at the market before I could prepare our evening's dinner. I enjoyed our simple Parisian life. Until I could speak French I found the Parisians to be "rude, crude and barbaric," but I did not feel that they were racist because they treated one another in the same way. We went to Stockholm during the summer and for Christmas to spend time with Martin's family, who welcomed me with open arms. Since Torolf and Inge were both interested in and very knowledgeable about classical music they understood what I was doing and were very supportive. And I bonded immediately with Martin's sister, Marion.

Martin wanted to have children soon after we married, but I assured him that he should benefit from the time that the two of us had together. Afterward, I would be completely devoted to our children.

In 1981, after a miscarriage, I was pregnant with Sebastian Amadeus. During my pregnancy I often wondered what I would do if I did not like the person that had chosen me for his mother. Do you automatically love a child just because you give birth to him? As much as I adored children I did not like all children. Some I found unbearable and even evil. This was fortunately not the case with either of my children. If it is indeed the child who chooses its parents then I felt blessed that they had made a good match. They have taught me as much or more about life as I have been able to teach them.

Sebastian Amadeus was born in Paris on December 6, 1981, a few minutes before midnight. He was due on the seventh, and has always been punctual.

We had moved from Martin's studio apartment to a small two-bedroom apartment on the rue Hérold near La Place des Victoires. It was not the chic *quartier* that it has become today. The apartment was near Les Halles and I continued to go to the nearby markets to find inspiration for my dinner menu. At that time fruits and vegetables were only available when they were in season and my greengrocer would give me suggestions like "the first fresh peas came in today." I knew that the season would not last long and so fresh peas were on the menu that evening. She told me about some local food traditions, such as making a wish when I ate the first cherries of the season.

Jennie Victoria was born in 1984, named after Jennie Tourel, and Victoria because I thought I might lose her. I was diagnosed with toxoplasmosis in my fourth month. My doctor, Pierre Simon, called me in London to say that Martin was on his way with an antibiotic that I should take right away, and that I should come directly to his office upon my return to Paris. When I walked into his office he said, "What shall we do about this pregnancy?" I was horrified! I did not know exactly what he meant. When he saw my reaction he said, "We can perform a relatively new test that is called amniocentesis; we will take blood from the baby in the uterus and test it. But this can be done only after the fifth month. You must wait one month for the results and we can also follow the baby's progress with ultrasound to see if it is in any way deformed. If you have been contaminated by the virus during the first two months your baby might be born blind or stillborn, but if it was later there might be nothing at all out of order." I decided to wait and take the test. I had frequent ultrasound tests and things seemed to be in order, and I agreed to let them tell me the baby's sex. I was happy that it was a girl because I had the ideal girl's name ready. We went to Sweden for the summer and expected to receive the results from the laboratory in the middle of August, but of course at that moment all of France was on vacation and the lab was closed. Finally in September when I was in the seventh month we received the good news that our little girl was victoriously healthy. Jennie Victoria was born November 2, a Scorpio like her mother.

Just before her arrival and after a very disheartening search we moved into a duplex apartment in a building just across the street from La Banque Nationale on the Avenue Colonel Driant, still in the first arrondissement. We were the only tenants who lived there—the rest of the building was offices and after 5:00 PM we were alone. Whenever I watched the frequent patrol of the police on the roof of the bank I falsely assumed that we were also protected. However our apartment was robbed twice within a three-month period.

Since I believe that life gives us signs, I thought that two robberies in such a short time meant that it might be time to move on. As much as we both loved Paris, it was not a easy city for small children. I was running all the time: to rehearsals, to and from the kindergarten, taking care of the needs of Sebastian and Jennie. It was even difficult to find a bit of greenery on which it was not forbidden for them to run around. So we usually went for long walks with them in the Bois de Boulogne on Sundays. I was always learning new pieces for my concerts, recitals, and opera roles; it seemed that whenever I went on stage I was singing something for the first time. It took me many years to build a large repertoire. I worked with a wonderful pianist, Irène Aïtoff, who lived in the seventeenth arrondissement, and on the days when I went to her the entire day was gone.

After the second burglary, although little was stolen, we decided to leave the city. We wanted to live in the country, but we did not want to leave France. We had recently bought a ruin without electricity or municipal water near Les Baux-de-Provence and seriously considered moving there. I wanted my children to have a bilingual education since they had already inherited two languages. Martin spoke to them only in Swedish, and I began speaking English to them but changed to French after Jennie started school. Close friends of ours who lived in that area sent their children to Paris to school. Sending my children away to school was not an option for me. I did not want to be in a big city, but I needed to be near an airport. And I needed to have access to an infrastructure that would not complicate my travels to and from home.

I had always had a soft spot in my heart for Tuscany since my first travels to Italy as a student, but living in the middle of the country there would have presented a logistical nightmare for my travels.

Martin spoke by chance to a colleague who lived in Montreux about our situation and he suggested that we come to Switzerland. I had sung there many times and loved the area around

Montreux-Vevey, but I thought of it as a lovely place to go to retire. We made what I thought was just an enquiry about residence in Switzerland and then the entire affair seemed to take on a life of its own. The commune of Montreux sent an immediate response that they had accepted our "request" and shortly afterward we received the same response from the Canton de Vaud. I did not have time to decide if this move was really what we wanted to do and I did not know how or if I should try to stop the momentum. The second robbery of our apartment had taken place at the end of August while we were in Sweden on vacation and we moved into our house on the Avenue Chantemerle in Territet above Montreux on the 19th of December 1985.

For the five years that we lived on a high ridge overlooking Lac Léman the view never ceased to take my breath away. We could see France from our windows and I was happy to continue to speak the French language and live in a French culture. When I lived in Chattanooga I discovered the beauty and majesty of the Smoky Mountains of Tennessee and later relished my two summers in Aspen in the Rocky Mountains of Colorado. I could hardly believe that I was going to live and raise my children surrounded by the grand Alps. The juxtaposition of the mountains and the beauty and calm of the lake was a source of peace and serenity for me. I accepted the pull of destiny toward a greener and calmer life for the entire family. Jennie and Sebastian would know that milk was not made in cardboard cartons but actually came from cows that they could see everyday and that fish were not originally rectangular shaped. The rent was cheaper than our apartment in Paris. I especially appreciated the punctual trains that I took to and from the Geneva airport. And living in the very center of Europe meant that I was no more than two or three hours from all of the major European cities.

My children have given me a chance to learn some new lessons of life and to review others that I had not really learned well. They have been mirrors of my actions and motives and have forced me to face myself on a daily basis.

I did not accept the idea that motherhood must be synony-mous with sacrifice and abnegation and some idealistic uncondi-tional love. I worked for a relationship with Sebastian and Jennie that would be based on truth, trust, and mutual respect fostered by constant and open communication and active participation. I had few rules but those were based on values that were non-negotiable. In other matters I was willing to be convinced to change my mind on the merits of their arguments, and they were quite good at defending their points of view.

I did not repeat like a parrot the same rules that my parents had used with me. They depended more on strictness and pun-ishment to make us bend to their will than on any real authority that they possessed. They were products of their time and of our mutual history of the cruel and brutal system of slavery that broke up families, separating children from their parents at birth to be sold as farm animals or a bale of cotton, resulting in the disen-franchisement of the family unit.

I made a conscious choice to build a reciprocal relationship with Sebastian and Jennie in which they would enjoy the affection and intimacy that I had missed and longed for as a child. And the voice of my inner child, little Barbara Ann, was my guide.

Whenever my mother called me, "Barbaraann, come here," saying both names together as if they were one word, I knew that I was in hot water. I could never completely separate myself from my own upbringing or the presence of my parents' voices, but Barbaraann's voice was by far clearer and stronger.

Parenting is so exciting because each child presents a unique challenge. I was curious to get to know the person waiting to be revealed in their small, delicate bodies. Sebastian and Jennie are very different personalities and I could not allow myself to go on automatic pilot. I had felt that I was "child number two" for my parents, somehow a generic child that should have to abide by exactly the same rules as child one, three, and four, regardless of the circumstances. I resented that they could not see "me." I could not understand when my father asked me, "Did you do this?" and I had given my answer, "No, sir, I didn't," that he could return with the same question again—"Barbara Ann, did you break this lamp?" My reply was, "Is this the same lamp that you asked about five minutes ago? Well, my answer is the same as five minutes ago." I did not use the word *lie*—it was too strong coming from a child's mouth addressing an adult. But by the end of this exchange, I could not hide my exasperation with him; he should have known me better than anyone, but he treated me as if I were a stranger. I was usually punished for my insolence. They seemed to have forgotten the broken lamp. It was more important to keep me in my place than to get to the truth about it.

It seemed that centuries separated the time of my childhood and that of my own children. I believe that relationships that are based on control of the strong over the weak are unhealthy and unproductive regardless of whether they are within families or in society or between citizens and their governments. I chose a more homeopathic approach to parenting. I did not use the strongest medicine and did not expect immediate results. I wanted to help them to fulfill their own destinies as well as to lay the ground for a long-lasting and meaningful relationship between us. I also believe that life in the family unit is the most important preparation for them to be able to survive and prosper in a larger community. Therefore my greatest responsibility to them was to prepare them to leave me. I held them for myself for only nine months but from the day they were born I had to start to enable them to become independent and productive members of society.

From the time that we could converse together I wanted them to understand that love, respect, and trust go hand in hand. I said to them, "There is nothing, no matter how horrible, that you will do in life, that will be worse than the lie that you tell me; we can find solutions together to whatever problems that may arise but if I cannot trust your word we cannot have a true relationship. I too will abide by this same rule." The trust that we build over time in a relationship allows us to be who we truly are. Of course they have not told me everything that they have done, which is normal—we all need our own private gardens.

The questions that they posed to me about problems at school or with their friends forced me to re-examine some of my own beliefs. I had to be an active guide sometimes and other times step back and just be a benevolent observer. I tried to give them the maximum freedom to search for their solutions and to reach their own conclusions as they navigated away from me. I did not treat them as if they were my property or the embodiment of the fulfillment of my wishes and my "cherished outcomes."

When Sebastian was about ten he came to me with a dilemma. He had promised to sleep over during the weekend with one of his best friends from school but then had received an invitation from another boy whom he had hoped would become a friend. He wanted to cancel his night with his old friend. We had an in-depth discussion and he came to the conclusion that this would not be the correct thing to do. I explained to him how important it is that others trust you when you give your word and that friendship is something truly valuable and deserves to be treated as such.

When he started to be interested in girls I used the opportunity to talk to him about respecting a woman's rights within a relationship. In my twenties I had defended a woman's right to choose how she wanted to live and to be treated as an equal in every part of society—at home, at work, and on the streets. Being an emancipated woman did not at all mean being like a man and behaving as men do. I learned after some experimenting that the freedom and respect I sought had to begin within myself and be manifested in any relationship that I would have with the man in my life. I talked to both Jennie and Sebastian but felt a particular responsibility to make my beliefs clear to my son by relating some of my own painful experiences and broken hearts. After he had broken off with his first girlfriend he refused to speak to her. She called at home and I answered the phone but he refused to take her call. I went up to his room and explained how much my experience of being dropped without explanation by a boyfriend had not only hurt me but had also made me lose a lot of time trying to understand what had happened and of course assuming that the breakup was due to my shortcomings. I said to Sebastian, "Of course you mustn't stay in a relationship with someone if you do not want to, but even when we must make choices that do not please another person, we can always remain true to ourselves if we treat others with a respect and kindness that leaves them with their dignity intact." Today the ex-girlfriend is still one of his closest friends and Laetitia, his wife, jokes, "All of Sebastian's ex-girlfriends are still his friends." I believe that addressing the small episodes in our daily lives was better than giving a lecture at the dinner table about human rights. For me the desire to promote and defend human rights must begin at home with those we love and for whom we should not be afraid. I have admired some "human rights activists" before meeting them, but after seeing their behavior toward their wives, children, and staff I lost all respect for them because they were imposters, human rights activists in name only.

While I was pregnant with Sebastian I sang Pamina in Mozart's *Die Zauberflöte* at Les Chorégies d'Orange and in 1984 when I was pregnant with Jennie it was Micaëla in Bizet's *Carmen* that I sang at the same festival. I have always wondered if the music of Mozart and Bizet somehow affected their personalities. In any case it seems to me that the music of *The Magic Flute* corresponds to Sebastian's reflective outlook and the passionate music of *Carmen* could be Jennie's theme song.

Before they began primary school they both traveled extensively with me. Because we wanted them to speak Swedish as well as French and English we had many Swedish au pair girls during their early years who lived with us in Paris and Montreux and accompanied us when I was on tour. Most of them—Maja, Ylva, Ylva's sister Amelie, and Brigitta—became like close family members and we still have contact with them. I packed the folding baby beds, food warmers, diapers, toys, favorite blankets, and teddy bears in with my concert dress, makeup, scores, and a miniature keyboard. My children have been with me on tour throughout Europe, Asia, North and South America. They have sat through my rehearsals in opera houses all over the world. When they were two and five they sat quietly through the entire performance of *Der Rosenkavalier* at the Metropolitan Opera.

After one of those performances I was walking back to the apartment that I had rented a few blocks from the Met and ran into a member of the staff who looked after artists who were not from New York, helping with finding apartments, etc. She was used to seeing opera divas arriving and leaving in oversized limousines and she asked me, "Are you walking home alone after the performance? Where is your entourage?"

I said, "I love walking these few blocks after the performance. And as far as my entourage is concerned, they are supposed to be asleep at this hour. Besides I have just bought this ice cream bar and I have no intention of sharing it with anyone." She left laughing but she should not have been surprised. When she had asked me if I wanted to rent a limousine to arrive for my debut on opening night, I said, "First of all, I live only a five-minute walk from the theater and I always arrive more than two hours before the performance. Who would be there to see me arrive in a ridiculous limousine at five o'clock in the afternoon?"

Once Sebastian started school I decided that it was best to leave both of them home during the school year. I did not want to disturb their education. Even though he had always traveled with me at her age I knew that Sebastian would not understand why I would take Jennie and leave him alone with his father and the au pair. I never counted the times that I was away from home on tour because I wanted to concentrate on the quality not the quantity of the time that I spent with my family.

I enjoyed having them on tour and European airports were all much smaller then. The connection times were longer and most airports were for taking off and landing airplanes, not the huge shopping malls that they have become today. Recently I arrived at the Munich airport on a flight from Budapest that was twenty minutes late and had to run as fast as I could in order to make my connecting flight. I arrived quite out of breath only to be greeted by an impatient lady at the check-in scolding me about being late as if I had been personally responsible for the late arrival of my plane or as if I had been shopping instead of trying to break an Olympic record. When I sat down in my seat I tried to imagine how it would have been that day if Sebastian and Jennie had been with me; getting all of our coats on, looking for toys that had fallen under the seat, waiting for the stroller, and then running with Sebastian while pushing Jennie's carriage past all of the shops to get to the gate. Of course we would have missed the flight.

Going away to work and then feeling guilty about it is a useless and self-indulgent emotion that I tried to fight off. I certainly missed them when I was away but it was also a positive feeling to long to be with them again. Maintaining a healthy balance by accepting the positive and negative sides of things is a great challenge. I told them that singing is a vital part of my identity, and that being their mother was another vital part. I did not try to justify my absences by saying, "Mommy must go out to work so that she can buy you the new bicycle that you want." I explained that I did not go out to work only to provide us with material things—a house to live in, food, clothing, and toys—but because singing is what I have to do. "I love you and want to be with you all the time but if I were to be home all the time and all the energy that I put into my work were to be focused solely on you, you would both end up in psychoanalysis."

I toured extensively in Europe and one of the major advantages of living in Switzerland is its central location. I usually took the last flight that was possible from home and the very first flight back home the morning after a concert. When they were in primary school I tried to arrive before they came home for lunch at noon. This meant taking flights as early as six the morning after a performance. I never came home bearing gifts because I did not want them to think that I needed to buy their acceptance of my absence. If I had bought gifts for them when I traveled I hid them away until a birthday or Christmas.

As soon as I sat on the train that took me directly to the airport, I began an inner transition, changing from mother to the performer on the way out and the reverse transition from the stage to the kitchen on the train ride home. I never had anyone helping us on weekends because I wanted to protect as much as I could the quality of true family time. This was my choice and I assumed it—going to do the shopping for the food, looking at schoolwork, preparing dinner, cleaning the house and doing laundry. I remember many times, arriving home on a Friday afternoon from the United States or Asia, tired from a long trip, how hard it was to make that transition during that hour on the train from the Geneva airport. I made it even more difficult for myself because I wanted to take over everything as soon as I came home. I did homework with them even on tour. When Jennie was having a hard time with her mathematics course she would send me her homework to my hotel by fax and I would correct it, send it back before going to the theater, and call her to explain to her what she had not understood before going on stage. I was never quite able to get either of them to see the beauty of mathematics as I had, but having a mother who had studied math did come in handy.

I knew when every vaccination was due, when it was time for an appointment with the pediatrician or the dentist. I jealously guarded this domain for myself. I didn't even ask Martin if he minded, and this was perhaps to the detriment of his role, partly because I had to organize my own schedule and fitting a dental appointment into it was an easy thing to do and partly because I needed to be present and to participate in all of those little moments.

In spite of my desire to be involved in every aspect of their lives I had to be careful to leave them enough room to develop on their own.

One morning when Jennie was in second grade I noticed that she was reluctant to go to school. I was perplexed because she usually liked to be there and had many good friends among her classmates. She finally told me that the teacher had not been nice to her. I called the teacher and made an appointment to see her. I said, "I have not come here to tell you how to teach your class or how to discipline my daughter who often needs it. However Jennie loves to come to school and to learn so whatever you are doing in your class that makes her not want to come anymore is an indication that your methods are not working. I will not accept it if you destroy her enthusiasm for learning because it will require an enormous effort to restore it. So please find a way to get what you want in your class without killing her positive attitude toward learning." She listened attentively and I do not know or care how she managed it, but the smile came back to Jennie's face when I helped her get ready to go to the school the next day. She has never lost her curiosity and love of learning.

My friends back in Paris could not believe that I was not missing the big city and often asked me how I could stand to live in a small town where there was nothing happening. Besides the peace and quiet and the trains that run on time, if something breaks down in my home on a Sunday morning, a plumber or electrician shows up fifteen minutes after my call, fixes what is broken, and leaves with a smile saying, "Au revoir et à votre service, Madame." Our lives slowed down to another pace and the small town kindness and politeness was a welcome change from the big city life and noise. When we lived in Paris I had no interest in taking part in Parisian social life and I turned down so many invitations that gradually they stopped coming. I preferred to invite our close friends home for dinner or to meet them in a neighborhood bistro.

My life in Switzerland was completely oriented around my family. My friends tended to be mostly the parents of my children's friends. We bought our new home in Clarens a little above Montreux, nearer Vevey, in 1990 and bought a golden retriever that we named Figaro. I enjoyed being at home more than going out and the house was always filled with Jennie's and Sebastian's friends. I never gave formal dinner parties, and was seldom invited to them, because in my professional life I had my share of receptions and official dinners. But if friends dropped by on their way down from the mountains at dinner time I was always happy to stretch what I had planned for dinner and to set more plates at the table. At Christmas time I spent days on end in the kitchen preparing our two Christmas dinners. First was the Swedish one on the twenty-fourth, with the traditional Swedish Christmas smörgåsbord: Christmas ham, herring, marinated salmon, meatballs, etc. Then the American Christmas on the twenty-fifth: turkey with cornbread stuffing, made with my own homemade sausage, sweet potato gratin, homemade cranberry relish, etc. I started to organize for this in October. I ordered the fresh cranberries from a shop in Paris and there was a butcher in Lausanne that prepared the ham the Swedish way, since there is a large Swedish community in the Canton de Vaud.

I performed often in my neighborhood so my neighbors were able to hear me at the Festival of Classical Music Montreux-Vevey as well as at the Montreux Jazz Festival or at Vevey's Chamber Music series, which had brought me to Switzerland for the first time. I campaigned passionately with other musicians who lived in the region, like Michel Dalberto and Nikita Magaloff, for the new Stravinsky Concert Hall in Montreux. The region of Montreux-Vevey had always attracted many great musicians—Richard Strauss and Igor Stravinsky had both lived in Clarens, and my neighbor across the street was the widow of the great conductor Wilhelm Furtwangler. Charlie Chaplin and writers Graham

Greene, Ernest Hemingway, Dostoyevsky, and Victor Hugo had also lived in my neighborhood. For many years I organized a Christmas concert in the small, local hospital in Montreux for the patients and doctors, a tradition that they continue to this day. I, like other parents, had rushed with my children after—thankfully—minor accidents to this small hospital for care and comfort. When I proposed to do these concerts my conditions were that there was to be no press prior to the concert and that no outsiders would be allowed to come into the hospital for it.

When Jennie and Sebastian were five and eight they were nearly hysterical in anticipation of the Christmas presents they might receive. They were echoing the prevailing commercial message of unlimited consumerism that was in complete contrast with my beliefs. I realized that we should focus more on what for me was the universal meaning of Christmas: peace, solidarity, and brotherhood. My Christmas concerts have as their theme: Let there be peace on Earth, and let it begin with me. Thus from then on our holiday season always began in the local Montreux hospital.

The only social event that I organized at home was an annual Swedish glögg party during the holiday season for my neighbors, friends, and colleagues from the UNHCR. I invested a lot of time preparing meals for my family. Sebastian and Jennie loved my homemade pizza so I had to get up at six in the morning in order to prepare the pizza dough just as they liked it—it had to rise twice before cooking it for our Saturday lunch. I cooked varied dishes and tried to make vegetables attractive and tasty. This resulted in them being very open about trying new food, especially vegetables. One Saturday I had a lot of work to do and I was in town shopping so I suggested to them that I pick up something for lunch for them at the new McDonald's in Vevey. They replied, "Oh, Mom, couldn't you cook something at home?" I could not refuse.

Sebastian asked me one day if he could change schools. When I asked him why, he told me "The head of the school and most of the teachers are all hypocrites." Sebastian was always interested in the world around him and when we would watch the evening news together he commented on the hypocrisy of most of the politicians that we saw. "I am not sure that that is true, but if indeed it is then your school is a wonderful learning experience and will prepare you well for the life that will confront you later. The world is full of hypocrites and cowards and you will need to know how to deal with them." He stayed in that school.

When we bought our home in Clarens we had to sell the ruin in Provence at a big loss in order to collect enough money for the down payment. I wanted my children to have a place where they could have the memories of family life firmly anchored in the walls of one home. I had spent my childhood traveling around from place to place following my father's appointments to various churches and I thought that the stability of one place, one anchor, would be an added element of serenity and security in their lives.

My memories of my childhood are much harder to piece together because we moved so often. I had to learn early on to let go of places and eventually to let go of the people in those places. In Clarens we lived practically in the countryside. The landscape of the Alps and the lake offered us immediate contact with nature every day of the year. I feel like I gained an extra ten years to my life by leaving the hustle and bustle of the city. During the week Sebastian and Jennie were very busy with school, homework, and after-school sports—horseback riding and dance for Jennie and tennis and football for Sebastian. They were not allowed to watch television during the week unless they were home sick from school. This was the cause for many disputes, but recently Sebastian said to me, "Mom, you remember how I fought about not being able to watch TV during the week? Well now I thank you because I was forced to use my own imagination and that certainly helped me to develop my own creative instincts." I was pleasantly surprised to hear this. On the weekends when I was home we went to the mountains for skiing in the winter and long promenades during the other seasons.

Our home was an open house to friends—full of children and Figaro running in and out. It was filled with music, disputes, and lively dinner conversations. When I was away on tour I longed to be home sitting around the dinner table with my family. I made a point of cooking a special meal on Sundays, and I cherished our animated conversations, which were always punctuated with laughter. We spoke openly about what was happening at school and with their friends. Sebastian and Jennie both have a distinct sense of humor that disarmed me whenever I was annoyed with them—we would eventually all dissolve in giggles.

When Jennie was nine she was confronted with a difficult choice between her enthusiasm for horses and her love of ballet: if she wanted to continue to study the latter she had to begin to work *en point*. She explained, "Ballet demands me to be turned out at the hips and to accentuate that daily, but when I go to ride I have to counter that turnout in order to control the horse. What should I do?" I had spoken to my friend John Neumeier, the director of the ballet school at the Hamburg Ballet, who had choreographed the moving ballet to Mozart's Requiem that I sang in Salzburg. He had advised me that she should not wait longer than about age ten before starting to work *en point*.

Discussions that began at the dinner table often reached their denouement at night with me sitting on the side of their beds before putting out the lights. That night I sat on Jennie's bed and asked her, "How much do you love to dance? I have many close friends from my Juilliard days who are dancers and I know from them what a hard yet enriching life it is. But you cannot expect it to bring you fame and fortune. I can assure you that you will be in constant pain somewhere. You can never take a vacation from dancing or the pain is even more acute when you start again. But if your first thought when you awake in the morning is, I want to dance, I must dance, I want it to be my life and the pain and all the rest does not matter, then you must chose ballet over being an equestrian and dedicate your life to it."

She did not say anything for several days about our conversation and I had nearly forgotten about it when she came to me said, "You know, Mom, I have thought about it and I really do love to dance. But the truth is I do not love it enough to devote my life to it."

She eventually stopped her ballet class and spent more time riding and even wanted to buy her own horse; but as the demands of her schoolwork grew she eventually had to give that up too. She consoled herself with some modern dance classes.

From the time Sebastian was about twelve I made many visits to his school to talk with his teachers about some trouble that he was causing in class. In one of those meetings the head teacher said that Sebastian was leading the other students to disrupt the class. When I asked him about this, Sebastian's defense was, "I am only stating the truth to the teacher and haven't you always taught me to say the truth?"

"Yes, of course," I answered, "you must tell the truth but not always at the moment that you think it—don't forget about timing and purpose. Is it right to tell the truth in order to just cause someone pain? Life is so much more complicated than telling someone that they have on an ugly jacket just because that is what you think. You are going to have to develop and use your ability to think and reason in order to go deeper into the questions that you have." I also told the teacher that even though I agreed that Sebastian needed to be more self-disciplined, I did not want them to completely destroy the very qualities that made him a headache in class because they would help him to become a critical thinker and hopefully a productive member of society. His teacher agreed with me.

If he did not like a teacher he would say, "I do not want to do the work for her," and I would say to him, "You are not doing the work for her, she already has passed her Maturité Fédérale, Sebastian." ("La Maturité Fédérale" is a series of written and oral federal exams that are taken during the last two years of high school on two different occasions and in two different locations within the Federation, neither in the students' own school nor administered by their teachers.) One day when he was sixteen he announced to me, out of the blue, "Mom, I have decided that I am in school to work for myself and not for the teachers." "Eureka," I said, "and not a moment too soon."

I found it particularly interesting to listen to Sebastian and four of his classmates who were at home for dinner and were talking about their preparations to take the very difficult exams. One mentioned a student who was known, since he was in primary school, for cheating in class. One asked, "I wonder how he will make it because it is impossible to cheat on the final exams." This led to a discussion about cheating, not only on exams but about cheating in life in general. I said that cheating is a plague on our society, corporations large and small do it, politicians do it, sportsmen and sportswomen do it, endangering their health and sometimes paying with their lives, and of course professional criminals do it.

I posed the question, "When you cheat, whom do you cheat?" The discussion was very animated. Everyone had an opinion, but by the time we started to eat dessert we all agreed that the cheater cheats himself most of all.

"If you cheat on these exams and you succeed to get accepted to Harvard, Oxford, or La Sorbonne, even if from that moment on you work honestly, you will always doubt that you deserve the success that comes because you know that you cheated to get where you are. It is the same principle in life as for the runner who wins the Olympic gold medal and knows that he or she has cheated by doping. Can he truly enjoy the fruits of his dishonesty?"

Dealing with Sebastian's growing pains at home and at school were complicated by his struggles to deal with a kidney disease that was diagnosed just before his twelfth birthday. I had assumed from the time of the diagnosis that if he would ever eventually need a transplant, I would be the donor. When he became an adult the relationship between his doctors and me changed. I was informed about his condition but the decisions were his to make. He had been admirably taking responsibility for taking his medicine and following his doctors' orders. When he was nineteen he was told that he would eventually have to go into dialysis, but I held out hope that his kidneys would miraculously be cured. At age twenty-two his kidneys were failing and there was no other choice. He chose a method of dialysis that he could do himself at home. I accepted then that he indeed would have to have a transplant and I prepared myself to be the donor. But when I learned that our blood types were different I was forced to accept an unusual role in my son's life of being a supportive spectator but not the fixer. Eventually the acceptance of this role had an unexpected calming effect on me. The distance from which I was forced to view the problem also helped me to allow Sebastian to cope as an adult with his own destiny. I have never discussed his illness to the press, firstly because I am a very private person and I do not believe that my children have any duty to be in the public eye unless they choose to be, and secondly, I never wanted there to be the slightest suspicion that I would use his illness or any other aspect of my private life as a part of my own public relations. At first he did not want the emotional complications of a living donor. After three years of dialysis he finally received a transplant from his father at age twenty-six. He continues to manage his illness and its complications with great courage and a certain rage that keeps his nemesis, his mortality, at bay. He is a constant subject of my admiration. He plans to write his own story about his illness, but as soon as he recovered from his operation he began to work on his first short film. It was accepted at the Cannes Festival in the Short Film Corner in 2012. He entered under his family name, Engström, and was selected without anyone knowing that he was my son. He and Laetitia have a baby boy, Marlon, born in 2012, and he will start in the masters of fine arts program in the Cinematic Arts Film and Television Production program at USC in the summer of 2013.

Since she was fifteen Jennie has worked during the summers at the Verbier Festival, and she became Martin's assistant. She finished her studies in Lausanne, went to university in London, and then worked two years in New York City at PBS in the music documentary division. She is back in Switzerland and works in Geneva with a mentor program for artists.

A woman is free when she can organize her life with or without an outside career or job just as men do with or without children. This is what I was fighting for as a student feminist. I did not want to wear a uniform or fit into a mold that had been determined or dictated by someone else, whether it be my parents, society, or my own government. But women are often asked to pay a higher price for the choices that they make.

On more occasions than I can count I was asked during a reception or a dinner after a concert: "You are so often on tour; do you ever see your children?" What could I answer? "No, in fact I only had them because it looks good on my CV," or "No, I do not care to see them at all. They just serve as good tax deductions." However, I just answered, politely, "Yes, I see them more than you might imagine." Of course I never heard any of my male colleagues being asked such questions, and some of them had left a trail of offspring all over the world. At a fund-raising dinner for the Verbier Festival I was asked by the director of a very big Swiss bank, "Don't your children miss you terribly when you are out on tour?" I answered, "Probably not more than yours miss you when you are away on business trips." He retorted, "But I have a wife at home." I looked in the direction of his wife as I answered, "And I also have a husband at home." She could not resist chuckling quietly and that ended that line of questioning.

I know that most professional women who try to juggle a career with the responsibility of motherhood are also confronted with this double standard, especially women in the public arena. The fantasy about the glamour of public figures incites all kinds of ridiculous remarks. I have met so many mothers all over the world, from refugee women to heads of state, and these working mothers are confronted with some of the same problems as they attend to their responsibility to raise their children and they share similar hopes and fears concerning their children's well-being. All mothers are working all the time either at their workplace or in the home and most are doing both.

When we moved from Paris, Martin and I had decided that he would continue to work at Opera et Concert for me and only four other artists. He was to commute to Paris with the new TGV train, stay three days, and work from home the rest of the week. He had developed into one of the most successful agents in the classical music world in the ten years he had been working in Paris.

However after a year in Montreux and without discussing it with me, he decided to abandon that idea, saying that he wanted to stay at home full-time with the children. Being an at-home father was certainly a plus for him and the children, but it did eventually contribute to the breakup of our marriage some years later. I still do not know what happened exactly to force him to give up the other artists for whom he worked because he liked them as friends and appreciated them as artists.

I met Martin in 1974 and began my relationship with him in 1977. As a young feminist I was fighting for women's equality in society and in the workplace, but most importantly equality in our personal relationships at home. I was hoping to meet a man who shared those same values. Martin and I did not speak so much about what we wanted from a relationship because we felt that we already had so much in common and our mutual passion for music was an enormous bond. But I did say to him that it was important for him to know about the necessary values that I had for my life, not so that he would adopt them for himself, but so that we could be a support for one another in times of need. I said to him, "I am a pretty strong person and I know the road on which I must travel, but there will certainly be a few occasions, in moments of doubts and weakness, when I might be tempted to go another way and then I will need you to remind me about who I am and what my purpose is. I will need you to ask me the question, 'Are you being true to your purpose?'"

I had not agreed with his decision to leave the office and to only work for me from home. I thought that this was a waste of his talent and abilities—he was the director the Paris office of Opera et Concert at the age of thirty.

On the one hand it lightened a little bit the responsibility that I felt as a parent. But on the other hand, I felt it was not good for him. In retrospect I do believe that during this period, which lasted nearly ten years, he might have been in a bit of a depression that I was not able to see.

The more I expanded my activities in the outside world, the more he turned inward toward me, the children, and our home. I started to work for the United Nations High Commissioner for Refugees (UNHCR) in 1987 and continued to search for new horizons in my work and repertoire. After some time we grew apart and it was clear that we were traveling slowly, albeit without apparent strife or conflicts, in different directions.

When we lived in Paris he had spoken to me about his dream to run a festival together with an academy of music, and somehow when he realized that our relationship was in trouble he began to work to make that dream come true. This effort forced him out of the place he had been hiding in for ten years and he embarked on the adventure that would become the Verbier Music Festival and Academy.

Gradually I felt that the relationship had run its course. As hard as I tried I could not see a future for us together. I knew that I could never leave him if he was not standing firmly on his own feet, so I did everything that I could to help him make the festival a success: the countless dinners with potential sponsors, lending my name to the project in order to open the necessary doors, and of course singing many concerts each year during the festivals. During those first years my concerts were the only ones with full houses and they earned the only profit for the festival. In 1996 we divorced amicably and for at least two more years Martin continued to live at my home whenever I was away on tour. We also celebrated two Christmases together with his mother after the divorce. The festival has prospered and evolved and I occasionally still perform there. The festival was Martin's idea and the success is his. I was only an enabler.

He had worked hard with me to help me build my career and build a family. We worked well together: he openly offered his opinions, which were often good, but he never tried to impose his ideas on my artistic decisions. He kept a keen eye out for opportunities for me and took care of the logistics of my career. As my agent, particularly at the beginning of my career, he often made the first contact with promoters and conductors, but of course I had to ensure by the quality of my work that I would be invited back after the first concert. I never had to ask about the fee; my first questions were always, "What is the repertoire, with whom, how much rehearsal?" I did not have a strategy to advance my career—I was mostly interested in working with artists from whom I could learn and advance in my artistic development. I accepted with a Zen mind that I benefited from Martin's friends and sometimes suffered at the hands of his enemies. In any case, all of the strategic planning for a career is useless. I believe that the only strategy that counts is to be prepared, open, and ready to seize the opportunities that present themselves.

Our marriage of twenty years ended with the rise of his festival. We shared a love and passion for one another, music, and nature and a very strong sense of family with two beautiful little angels that came to our lives. I considered our marriage up until that point to have been a success. But we had grown apart and were beginning to pull in opposite directions. I felt strongly that to continue together while traveling on separate inner paths would be a certain recipe for the destruction of all that we had built together.

I had to learn to deal with separations while I was growing up, going from one town or one state to another following my father and his work. I learned to adapt quite well to leaving good friends behind. My divorce was the most difficult and painful separation that I have ever endured. I had to assume my responsibility for the divorce to Sebastian and Jennie and worried that they might not understand why I made the choice that I did. I hoped that they would see that sometimes in order to remain true to yourself you must make a decision that will certainly cause disappointment and pain to others, but if you do so respectfully you will not infringe upon their dignity. I had an obligation to follow my path but also an obligation to Martin, Sebastian, and Jennie not to allow the process to become ugly and destructive.

Martin and I had the same lawyer and he drove me to the courthouse in Vevey. Not only was this civilized but it was much cheaper than most divorces. It took less than fifteen minutes to be finalized and Martin drove me afterward to the train station so that I could fly to Stockholm. I was about to begin a tour with a Christmas program that I had previously performed in 1994 in Stockholm at the Globe with Eric Ericson and his choir.

I went to Stockholm for rehearsals with the choir and the orchestra before proceeding to Copenhagen, Paris, Cologne, Vienna, and Turku in Finland. Johan Englund, who had produced the previous concert, had asked his cousin Ulf Englund, who had been the light designer in 1994, to be released from his work at Dramaten (The Royal Dramatic Theater in Stockholm) in order to go on this tour. Christian Hagegård, the son of the baritone Håkan, was working on the tour and had asked Ulf back in October about the tour but had never confirmed it with him. When Christian called Ulf on Wednesday to say, "We are leaving tomorrow for the tour with Barbara Hendricks," Ulf replied,

"I can't go anywhere tomorrow. I have not heard a word from you since October and at this late date I will never get a release from Dramaten." Ulf had designed the lights for the production of Bertolt Brecht's *Puntila* directed by Thorsten Flinck and he was running the lights himself for the performances. Ulf asked all of the colleagues and friends that he knew to go in his place but could not find anyone on such short notice to leave for a ten-day tour. Knowing that his assistant could run the two remaining shows of the run but expecting a negative answer he reluctantly asked the head of the lighting department if he could get away for the period. To his surprise the answer was yes.

At the beginning of the tour I was feeling sad and kept mostly to myself when we were not in rehearsal or performance. Johan was the only person who was aware of my private situation, and he was watching out for me so that I would not get down or depressed.

I do not remember it but I obviously had said hello to Ulf at our first production meeting in 1994. I did not see him again until we arrived in Paris at the Palais des Congrès for the rehearsals. I was walking backstage and saw that he was focusing some blue spotlights on the front of the stage. I asked the stage manager, "Can I speak with the lighting designer?" When he came down, I said, "Are you planning to focus blue lights on my face? Because if you do it will turn my skin green and I will look like Kermit the Frog." He laughed and assured me that I would not look like Kermit the Frog. I spoke briefly to him at the reception after the concert and he assured me that I had not been at all green. On the plane Ulf usually sat with Christian and Johan so whenever I went to speak to Johan I also greeted him. After the other concerts I saw him briefly at the receptions but I usually went directly back to my room and ordered room service if I was hungry.

When we arrived at the Konserthaus in Vienna their technical crew informed Ulf that they had planned for their usual lights for a concert, so he did not have anything to do. I saw a few projectors that were not in use and asked him if he could do something with them. This was the longest conversation that we had ever had.

From Vienna to Helsinki the orchestra had been booked on one SAS flight that went through Stockholm. Eric, the choir, and I were booked on another SAS flight that went through

Copenhagen. When we arrived at the airport in Vienna, Johan suddenly became aware of a big problem: the plane to Stockholm was a Fokker and could not take all of the orchestras' instruments in its baggage compartment. Johan had to negotiate with SAS to take some of the instruments on our plane. He had very little time because our plane was leaving first. He gave my carry-on bag that he was carrying to Ulf and said, "You must take care of Barbara until we get to Turku. I have to settle this and take the later flight with the orchestra." So there we stood and I said, "OK, see you in Turku. Good luck with the instruments."

I sat next to Eric Ericson on the flight and we talked a bit and I slept. Ulf was sitting with the choir. When we arrived in Copenhagen he came to my seat and took my bag from the overhead compartment. We had a few hours to kill before taking our connecting flight to Helsinki. It was just before Christmas—I had already bought some herring for our smörgåsbord in the airport shop on my way to Paris and had left it in the SAS lounge where they kept it in the refrigerator for me. I went to pick up my package and helped Ulf buy a Christmas present for Ninni, from whom he had recently separated and with whom he had a six-year-old son, Malkolm. (He later changed the spelling to Malcolm.) He wanted to buy a face cream but I convinced him to also buy the tonic and a cleanser.

When we arrived in Helsinki the airport was covered in snow. The ride to Turku took more time than usual because it was snowing the whole time. Eric was seated in the front of the minivan and Ulf and I sat in the back and talked all the way to Turku, about everything and nothing in particular. Upon arrival he went straight to the venue and worked late into the night. Some hours later Johan, the orchestra, and the instruments arrived safely. I ate dinner and went to sleep. I saw Ulf the next morning at breakfast and then had my usual uneventful concert day: a little walk, lunch, a nap, the sound check, and the concert. Turku was the last concert of the tour and Ulf said to me much later, "I watched your oversized image projected on the video screen in the large hall and I realized that I might never see you again and I was sad because I felt that we had connected with one another during our day together."

After the performance we had a farewell dinner with Eric, the orchestra, the choir, and the technical staff. Ulf and I were up talking until the wee hours of the morning while I packed my bags. I had to leave at 5:00 AM to get my flight from Copenhagen back to Geneva to prepare for Christmas with my family: Martin, Sebastian, Jennie, and Martin's mother, Inge. Johan had planned to accompany me to the Helsinki airport because he also needed to organize the return flights to Stockholm later in the day for everyone else. Ulf decided to come along in the car and I fell asleep with my head on his shoulder. Because of the snow that had fallen during the night we arrived later than planned; Johan had to deal with the later departures right away and sent Ulf to the gate to see me off to Copenhagen. We wished one another a Merry Christmas at the gate and had a long hug before I went reluctantly on the plane to take my seat.

When the plane started its ascent I started to cry for the first time since I had left Switzerland and I could not stop my tears. I assumed that I was tired after so little sleep and a very intense tour, but I later realized that I had also been very touched by Ulf and that I was already missing him. The last thing I was looking for or expected at this very sad moment in my life was that I had just met my soul mate.

We both returned to our respective homes and ex-partners to spend the Christmas holidays. We called each other often just to talk and he was the first person that I called on the twenty-third of December to tell about the brutal murder of Sophie, the wife of one of my closest friends, Daniel Toscan du Plantier. We spoke daily during the holiday period and decided to start to meet one another whenever we could. I assumed, of course, that the first relationship that one has after a breakup or divorce can never be the true, lasting one but I had felt a real connection to him. How wrong I was and how blessed I have been to not have felt the need to control anything but to just go with the flow. The beginning was logistically difficult. I lived in Switzerland with two children and he lived in Stockholm and alternated custody of his son on an every-other-week basis. We took one step at a time and everything just fell into place. Even Sebastian, Jennie, and Malcolm related well from the beginning, whether they were all together or just two at a time.

We started a conversation in 1996 in the Vienna airport, talking about unimportant things that one speaks about to a stranger, but that conversation has never ended. It is ongoing all the time, every day and all day. It is about life: our children, how we confront obstacles, how we love, politics, and art. We start up again every morning from the night before, in the sauna and of course through all our mealtimes.

Everyone in the family treasures and looks forward to mealtimes together: long breakfasts outside in the garden during the summer, dinners at home or in the boathouse, picnics on the boat or grilling on an open fire on a small island in the archipelago, or seated all around hot fondue after a day of skiing. Around our table we love to include members of our extended family and friends including Martin and Ninni, who are welcome for informal gatherings as well as for the traditional meals at Christmas, Midsummer, etc. But it is that one-on-one dynamic that we have grown to nurture and cherish that makes our relationship so rich and engaging.

I have never known anyone with as much integrity as Ulf has, and this asset I cherish the most. But his sense of humor comes in a close second and is a perfect balance to his rigor. He helps me to search even deeper for my own truth and to stay faithful to it. He is the first person with whom I want to share the news of the world or an interesting encounter, a joke or just a simple silly story.

When I divorced I did not think that I would ever marry again because being married had never been my goal, but when Ulf went down on one knee on Fjällgatan overlooking Stockholm after buying me an ice cream cone and asked me to marry him, I answered without hesitation, "Yes." He had not planned to ask me and his question came out as spontaneously as did my answer. Our wedding brought together friends and family for a journey on a steamboat through the islands of the Stockholm archipelago. We wanted to show them its beauty; after nearly four hours we arrived at the two-hundred-year-old church where we exchanged our wedding vows. I had invited Inge, Martin's mother, with whom I kept in contact, Ninni, her husband Jean-Louis, Martin, and his wife Blythe. It was an unforgettable and joyous day and after the first dance, to Aretha Franklin singing "You Make Me Feel Like a Natural Woman," we danced into the wee hours of the morning. After the last guest had left for Stockholm we boarded our small boat with Sebastian, Jennie, Malcolm, and their friends from Switzerland and Stockholm, and sailed back to our summer cottage under the bright morning sun.

We have come together with our own baggage and vulnerabilities. We help each other to be open and receptive as artists because we protect one another. I have often wanted to protect myself from the difficulties of life, but I knew that if I did that too much I might sacrifice the fragility that enables me to be a vessel of the raw and purest emotion on stage. The contrast between the peak emotional experience that one shares with the audience during a concert and the sudden emotional plunge into the abyss of everyday life the next day can be a schizophrenic experience. Whenever I have arrived with my Swedish jazz quartet at the passport control at an airport in Germany only *my* Swedish passport was thoroughly examined. Once I looked the agent directly in the eyes and said in German, with a smile, "I know that I do not look like a Swede, but I am." He looked at me almost embarrassed that I had guessed exactly what he was thinking. It is always so surprising that people think that I do not notice their racial profiling. I once thought that I should travel with a secretary who could answer stupid questions and be a buffer for me, but then I thought about frightened and poor refugee women who in the same situation have to accept far more humiliating treatment and are powerless to defend themselves. So in order not to lose contact with reality I continue to travel on my own. Being in a relationship that is so supportive enables me to expose myself to humiliation and know that I will be able to rise above it. When Ulf looks at me I feel his gaze deep in my soul where I find strength.

Ulf is a self-taught and true artist. He can do every kind of work involved with the lights and sets. He started at the bottom and evolved slowly from apprentice to master. Before he started to do lighting he toured extensively with rock tours such as Rock-Tåget as a part of the crew. Once he started to dedicate his attention to light design it was a great advantage for him that he had the opportunity to work with and to watch the work of great artists such as Ingmar Bergman and the Canadian director Robert Lepage with whom he has done several productions at Dramaten, including Strindberg's *Dreamplay*. The first production that I could watch him work on was Tom Waits's *Black Rider*, directed by Rickard Günther. I had never been so aware of the lights in opera productions because since I was in the light I could never judge if they were good or not. I could only comment on whether the lights bothered me, not if they complemented my acting. Most concert halls consider any discussion about lights just a nuisance. We were told in one hall, "We have two light cues, on and off." Sometimes it is better to choose "off" and stay with the work lights, because "on" is usually worse. In addition to his work at Dramaten Ulf collaborated with some of the great talents of his generation at various free theater groups such as Galeasen Plaza and Theater Tribunalen. I take every opportunity to sit in on his rehearsals when I can. Ulf gives me a copy of the scenario to read so that I can follow the dialogue and this has helped me improve my Swedish.

He decided to leave the staff at Dramaten and completely freelance, which made it possible for him to work with Efva Lilja's dance company, Circus Cirkör, and in all of the major theaters in Sweden. He also has time to work more with me. We met through our work together and it is only natural that we continue to work with great joy on recitals, jazz, choral, and orchestra concerts in Asia, South and North America, Africa, and extensively in Europe. He designed the lights and décor based on the lights for a concert of opera arias and duets with the French baritone Ludovic Tézier on the vast Roman stage at Chorégies d'Orange conducted by Michel Plasson. I decided to risk putting the orchestra in the pit where they are for the operas. When I was alone singing the Countess's aria from Mozart's *Figaro* I felt his artistic support in the lights that bathed the stage in a painting made up of colors and varied shades of light and shadows. It was the first time that the famous wall had been lit in that way for a concert. Raymond Duffault, the director of the Avignon Opera and the Orange Festival, was so impressed with his work that he invited him to come the following season for a concert without me of Carl Orff's *Carmina Burana*, also conducted by Michel Plasson.

We most recently toured with a staged production of Schubert's *Winterreise* with texts that I wrote in French based on Müller's poems that I recited in between some of the songs. We wanted to make it easier for the French-speaking audience to assimilate Schubert's music and Müller's poetry during the intense seventy-five-minute duet between the voice and the piano. Ulf designed the set using the lights and a backdrop on which he projected subtle images of photos that he had taken of Swedish winter landscapes. I cannot see myself in his lights so I must have complete confidence in Ulf's artistic choices.

What a treat for me to have an artistic partner who shares my ideals about the meaningfulness and necessity of art in our lives as well as the dedication to authenticity in whatever we do. There is never any element of competition between us. We are both in our right place when we work together. He prefers to work in the shadows. He focuses light on others and he is satisfied painting his images on the stage and the actors and does not need to share the limelight.

He has so many interests. He rebuilds vintage cars and motor-bikes from parts that are dispersed throughout the garage and races his 1972 Triumph motorbike that he built from parts when-ever he has the time. He plays the guitar and sings; he has a group with whom he performs a few concerts. We have actually sung together for fun at family gatherings and our local Christmas con-cert on the island in Sweden. In 2012 he joined me on stage in Paris at Unesco's International Jazz Day.

Although I had been coming to Sweden since 1974 I did not know Stockholm's archipelago at all. Ulf introduced me to the places he had spent the summer with his family since his birth. I felt immediately at home in the serenity of the landscape. The naked rocks surrounded by the sea create a great sense of calm in me. From the time that Ulf could row a boat he and his friends explored the waterways of the thousands of islands. We continue this tradition on our modest family boat with our children and friends every summer. I particularly enjoy late summer excur-sions with just the two of us when the tourists and summer guests have gone home.

When we renovated our summer home in Sweden he stud-ied and read all he could about old wooden Swedish houses and became quite an expert. He spent much time getting the right details in his search for authenticity in a windowpane or a floorboard. We share the same taste and our home reflects our desire to live in an environment that is in harmony with us and with the surrounding nature in a truly organic way.

I inherited a wonderful family with Ulf: his son Malcolm, who gave me my last chance to learn Swedish and who fit together with Sebastian and Jennie from their first meeting without the slightest problem; his paternal grandmother, Hild, who died at the age of ninety-four in 1999; his parents, Margareta, a librarian, and Björn, a physicist, who treat me like a daughter and are genuinely happy to have two more grandchildren in Sebastian and Jennie; a lovely younger sister, Eva; aunts, uncles, many cousins, and two nephews. His cousin Annika lives in the Canton de Vaud in Switzerland with her husband and their lovely daughters, and we have formed a Swiss branch of the family that are very close. After Sebastian's transplant in November 2008 they joined us in Montreux to celebrate Christmas with Martin, his second wife Blythe, and their daughter Rania.

With our three children Ulf and I have formed a family together like I wanted to have since I was a little girl. It was quite natural that he and Jennie, who have the same blood group as Sebastian, were the first to offer to donate him a kidney when he needed his transplant. Martin, Jennie, and Ulf were the only family members whose kidneys were compatible with Sebastian.

Ulf is truly a man of light. He has shone light on me on stage in our mutual search to serve art and in our private life in our mutual search to live truthfully. Thus he illuminates my soul daily.

———

From the time I lived in New York, close friends have also been cherished members of my family. Whenever I am asked what my most positive trait is, I proudly say, "I am a very good and loyal friend." My friends know that I will always be there for them. I longed to have an older brother when I was growing up, and I have had close male friends since I was in high school—friends like Chuck Cahn in New York, Daniel Toscan du Plantier in Paris, Sergio Vieira de Mello at the UNHCR, and Pasqual Maragall, ex-mayor of Barcelona and president of Catalonia, have been "brothers" to me. But I have always highly treasured my relationships with my girlfriends. Feminine solidarity has been a source of strength and support for me. My grandmother Tumaie, my grandfather's second wife Miss Ethel, my mother Della, my sister Ruthie, Jennie Tourel, my daughter Jennie, and my mother-in-law Margareta: strong and nurturing women have accompanied me with love from the cradle through childhood to being the free woman that I am today. They were an example for me and enabled me to find my own voice and to dare to make it heard. Because of them I see that the positive side of being female far outweighs any minor negative side.

Genuine sisterhood has been important to me since I was in first grade and found my first best friend. Listening and sharing my innermost thoughts, fears, and hopes with my sisters has helped me through the most difficult moments in my life and it is with them that I have shared my greatest sorrows and joys.

I have always found it a silly notion to be in competition with another woman for the affection of a man or even for a role in an opera. If a man wants to be with another woman and not with me then it is a waste of my time to want to be with him. If I am not chosen to sing a role or a concert that I have wanted to do I accept that it was not meant for me. When I was fifteen years old, I had just moved from Memphis to Little Rock and was also very unhappy that my parents refused to allow me to be a part of the social life of the other students in my class. The parents of one of my close friends were more urbane and more open than my parents. She was pretty and always wore beautiful clothing although she was not at all a very good student. One afternoon, after spending some time at her place, I returned home, prepared dinner, and then got into an argument with my parents about going to see a film the following weekend. I went to my room and cried and thought, I would give anything to be her, to have her parents, to live in a beautiful home and to wear beautiful clothing. But what do I have to give? I do not own anything, I have never inherited anything, even the clothing on my back does not belong to me. I thought for a while, I have my intelligence and I have my talent and I would never give up either for anything in the world. This is the last time that I have ever been jealous of anyone or their possessions.

When I started my career I was sad to find that some of my older colleagues felt threatened by a newcomer. I want all of my colleagues to be as good as they could be because they inspire me to perform better. The opera world is full of petty rivalries that are just a waste of time. I have never considered another singer to be my rival because I am the only person who stands in my shoes at a given time and I cannot and have no desire to stand in someone else's place.

When we worked on *Falstaff* together in Los Angeles, Katia Ricciarelli and I became good friends. I had been concerned that Katia, whom I had not seen since the recording of *Turandot* with Karajan in Vienna the year before, might hold against me the obvious favoritism that he had displayed toward me during the recording. In Los Angeles we spent a lot of time after the rehearsals talking about relationships and affairs of the heart. At the beginning of the rehearsals with the orchestra she had a problem hearing her starting pitch for a phrase that she had to sing. Since I was standing on the stage directly over the instrument that played the note I hummed it to her. She was surprised that I would help her and that sealed our friendship. It was not planned that I should sing in the production in Florence since I was not free for the first performance. Giulini cast a young Italian soprano who was so openly in competition with Katia that the atmosphere became counterproductive. Giulini called me and asked me if I was free to do the rest of the performances. When I answered that I was, he asked the young singer to leave the production after the opening. I arrived in the middle of the opening night performance and as I was crossing the stage during the intermission, Katia saw me and came running and hugged me as if I was her long lost sister. "I am so happy to see you and to have you back in the cast," she said.

In another production of *Falstaff* at the Paris Opera directed by George Wilson and conducted by Seiji Ozawa, I felt that I had to stand up for my colleague Sylvia Sass, with whom I had sung in a concert version of *Turandot* in London. She came into the cast at the last minute to replace an ailing Christiane Eda-Pierre in the role of Alice Ford. Sylvia was learning the role as we went along. She was an excellent musician and learned very quickly. We spoke a little bit during the rehearsals and I learned that she was going through a difficult time in her life. She had defected from Hungary and missed her family and her country terribly. We were two different casts and the organization of the rehearsals was a complete mess. One day I arrived to rehearse with the Alice of the second cast and I complained. I was tired of changing casts with every rehearsal. The assistant, Charles Fabius, called me over to confide that Sylvia was being sent away from the production because Ozawa thought that she was not suited to the role. I couldn't believe what he said. I thought that Sylvia was doing a great job and I knew that this was the last thing that she needed. I decided to speak to Ozawa. "Maestro," I said, "I do not dare question your artistic decisions but I want to give you some information that you certainly do not have. I have gotten to know Sylvia a little during the rehearsal period and she is going through a very difficult time in her personal life and being sent away from this production will be a cruel blow to her. Of course you must do what you believe is right for the production but I ask you to consider the human element in your decision." He listened to me and thanked me. The next day Sylvia received a phone call from a secretary who informed her that she was fired. The replacement was an American soprano from the CAMI roster who was so unbelievably inadequate that she was finally relegated to the second cast. I sang with the Swedish soprano Helena Döse.

My relationships with my "sisters," women who search for a meaning in their lives and with whom I have met and traveled on a common path, have always been a priority in my life. Lorraine Nubar, Jennie Tourel's assistant, has been a constant friend since my first summer in Aspen in 1968. She knows my voice better than anyone and is the only singing teacher that I have ever recommended to anyone. Lorraine has been always available whenever I have questions about vocal production or repertoire. At the beginning of my career I often sang for her when I was in New York and she would give me her valuable opinions. Sometimes we do not speak to each other for an entire year and then our next conversation continues as if we had spoken just the night before.

When I was a student at Juilliard I wanted to study the Alexander Technique with Judith Leibowitz in the drama department, but she had no time in her school schedule for me and I was unable to afford to take private lessons with her. She sent me to one of her students, Rachel Zahn, an excellent Alexander teacher and a Gestalt therapist. She eventually moved to Paris and is one of my closest friends.

Soon after Sebastian's birth the Korean violinist Young Uck Kim came to Paris and introduced me to Sheila Brennan, an American osteopath living there and in Santa Barbara. She worked with me during my pregnancy with Jennie and is her godmother.

Marianne Scheja, the ex-wife of my piano player Staffan Scheja, and I met in Gotland during the festival and I call her my Swedish sister. She is a playwright, an actress, and a TV director, as well as a certified therapist. She works with autistic adolescents and young adults on theater projects, writing and performing. Her two children with Staffan are my goddaughter Rebecca and Leonard. They, Sebastian, and Jennie are as close as cousins. Even after her divorce we continued to meet for holidays and important events such as birthdays and school graduations. Marianne has now recomposed her family together with her soulmate Lars and his two children, Sara and Joseph, and together with Ulf and Malcolm, our extended family has grown. If anything ever happened to me I know that Sebastian, Jennie, and Malcolm would be able to count on Marianne to be there for them, as I will always be for her children.

My sisters and I have spent countless hours discussing everything under the sun through tears and laughter. We have been present for one another in the toughest and happiest hours of our lives. I sang a spiritual, "Glory, Glory, Hallelujah," in Arlington National Cemetery when I said goodbye to my dear sister Ruthie who was buried near her son Billy (William Hansen Jr.) in 2009.

Most of my agents are women and are supportive of my artistic development but have have also become my friends: Diane du Saillant in France, Almudena Garcia-Ortega in Spain, Aino Turtianen in Finland, Marianne Maurer in Switzerland, and Ulla Sändö in Denmark (who has just retired). All of them have been with me during the good and the bad times. We have talked about our marriages, our divorces, our pregnancies, our children, breast cancer, burying our parents, the kilos gained and the kilos lost, and the value of music in our lives.

From the time I was a twenty-year-old woman I thought that the struggle for equality between the sexes had to begin in the primary relationships based on mutual respect between men and women. The fight was not just going to be won in the boardroom. A man who treats his wife and daughters with respect at home will do the same with his female colleagues at work. Previous generations' struggle for gender equality have won many judicial and social victories, but I am disheartened to see that Jennie and her friends are faced with a very different situation and one that is maybe more exasperating than what we faced in 1968. They are confronted nonstop with ubiquitous degrading and superficial images of women and girls dictated by the mass media. Women and girls are the victims of more violence in and outside of the home than ever before. When I speak to Jennie and her friends I am hopeful that they will meet these challenges head-on, having learned from our mistakes while enjoying some of our gains.

I was also influenced by the multitude of courageous women that have come before me like black congresswomen Shirley Chisholm and Barbara Jordan but even the anarchist Emma Goldman, whose strong sense of justice led her to make some radical decisions that she later renounced.

I have been able to have a successful career on my own terms and to have a family life with children and two successful marriages. I consider my marriage with Martin a success until our journey together ended. I believe that I have the right to make choices for my own life and the duty to seek to manifest the expression of my inner being. I have been able to maintain a balance between the different aspects of my life: as a woman in my relationships with my partners, as a mother with my children, as an artist, and as citizen of the world, all under the watchful eye of the little Barbara Ann from rural Arkansas.

My Repertoire and My Musical Families 9

True genius without heart is a thing of naught—for not great understanding alone, not imagination alone, nor both together, make genius—Love! Love! Love! that is the soul of genius.

—Nikolaus von Jacquin to Wolfgang Amadeus Mozart

My repertoire has grown from the few songs that I learned for my first recital in Lincoln, Nebraska, to a vast and varied collection of opera roles and vocal music dating from the eleventh century up until the present including orchestral, choral, recital, chamber music, and jazz. Never content with what I have already learned, I continue to be hungry for new repertoire to perform for my audiences all over the world. Lately I have become accustomed to juggling different styles of music within a short period of time. Once within a two-week period I sang Strauss's *Vier letzte Lieder* with orchestra, a jazz concert, opera arias of Handel and Purcell with the Drottningholms Barockensemble, as well as Schubert's lieder cycle, *Winterreise*, with piano. Singing recitals had accustomed me to minor stylistic and linguistic changes within a program, but this schedule was mentally exhausting. Even though the task had been excellent mental gymnastics I decided to avoid such planning. I also want to enjoy each concert and give myself more time to change stylistic gears. Each composer has his distinct musical language. I strive to sing it with all of its nuances as I do when speaking actual languages—Italian and German or the ones that we alternate constantly at home, English, French, and Swedish. Thus I adapt to the demands of each composer's style while maintaining the integrity of my own vocal personality.

———

In 1968 I discovered chamber music at the Aspen Music Festival with the Juilliard Quartet. I listen to different styles of music at home but when I want to recharge my spiritual batteries I listen to chamber music. A simple Schubert trio has the power to directly nourish my soul. I began my relationship with chamber music as an avid listener but from the first time that I performed it with others I found my musical home in the inspirational process of sharing ideas, listening, and reacting to one another during the rehearsals and performances.

I participated in my first chamber music series at the Festival dei Due Mondi in 1975. Charles Wadsworth was in charge of chamber music at both festivals in Spoleto and Charleston, South Carolina, and was also the founder of the Chamber Music Society at Lincoln Center. He invited me to the festivals in Charleston and Spoleto and subsequently to perform with the Chamber Music Society in New York over the years. That first summer in Charleston I also discovered key lime pie—and performed with and listened to some great young musicians, including the adolescent Yo-Yo Ma, Richard Stoltzman, Peter Serkin, and Richard Goode.

Making music with others in this way became a model for all of my work and in every style of my repertoire, including opera. I try to work together with all musicians like I do with my partners in chamber music.

During my student years at Juilliard I had fantastic opportunities to hear most of the greatest artists of that time performing chamber music and recitals in the concert halls of New York City. I went to hear Dietrich Fischer-Dieskau, Elisabeth Schwarzkopf, Adele Addison, Victoria de los Angeles, Gundula Janowitz, Christa Ludwig, Elly Ameling, Hermann Prey, Peter Schreier, Régine Crespin, and Dame Janet Baker among others.

I never missed a concert of the violinist Nathan Milstein or pianists Alicia De Larrocha and Radu Lupu—nor my favorite quartet, the Guarneri Quartet. One Friday evening in 1972 I was just about to leave school for the day when I met my friend Staffan in the cafeteria. He told me that the line was already forming outside the Metropolitan Opera for the limited number of tickets to Vladimir Horowitz's comeback concert—they were to go on sale the next morning. So around 5:00 PM we decided to go there too and took turns standing in the line during the night. I left just before midnight to get some sleep. When I returned in the early morning to relieve Staffan with some sandwiches and coffee, he told me, "You won't believe this but right after you left, Horowitz himself came by with cookies and coffee for us. He had seen us on the television news and was touched that we were willing to stand in line overnight to buy tickets, just like for a rock concert." We were able to buy two tickets and to hear this legendary artist in an unforgettable performance. He, along with Jennie Tourel and the artists of that generation, were like beams of light showing me the way toward my goal. I was not interested in becoming a carbon copy of any of these masters, not even my dear Miss Tourel, although it might have seemed at the time the easiest route. Not only did she discourage this but I longed to find my own voice. Maybe with much hard work and dedication I would be able to pass on to others the great tradition that I had received from them.

My opera repertoire can be put into four basic categories: Mozart and Strauss, Italian, French, and a miscellaneous group: Stravinsky, Tchaikovsky, and contemporary opera.

I have already spoken about Mozart's Susanna, my most important debut role. I identified easily with this young woman who knew exactly what she wanted: to have the right to marry Figaro, the man she loved. Yet she was very aware of the obstacles in her way in the person of her employer, the Count, and the system of aristocratic privilege that he incarnated. Her resistance to that unjust system foreshadowed the French Revolution. It is one of the longest roles in the repertoire and the hundreds of performances that I sang in Europe, America, and Japan gave me a solid foundation for all the roles that I performed afterward, especially the Mozart roles.

I had prepared the role of Pamina from Mozart's *Die Zauber-flöte* in the 1973 production at Juilliard but I didn't sing the role then. When I was engaged to sing it in 1981 at the Chorégies d'Orange I felt ready even though I was five months pregnant with Sebastian. During both of my pregnancies I listened carefully to my body and continued to sing as long as I felt well. I even felt as if the additional bulk provided more support to my diaphragm. I recorded Pamina with Sir Charles Mackerras conducting.

When I was in Glyndebourne singing in Cavalli's *La Calisto* I had a lot of free time between my performances to attend rehearsals of Mozart's *Idomeneo* and I loved it immediately: I did not miss a single one. I was so interested to observe the work of George Shirley, the first black tenor to sing leading roles at the Metropolitan Opera. I was mesmerized by the intensity of his performance. He incorporated the text and music so organically. His interpretation of *Idomeneo* was on a par with the best Shakespearian actors. The wonderful choral music in this opera awoke a nostalgia for my early choral singing. I later performed Ilia with conductor Sir Colin Davis in Munich, followed by a recording for Philips with the Bayerischer Rundfunk Orchestra.

I was never even asked to sing Mozart's soubrette roles Zerlina and Despina, except for the horrible production of *Don Giovanni* in Paris, where I was thankfully dismissed. Although I never sang the entire role in a staged performance I am closely associated with the Countess from *Figaro* because I have sung her arias in concert for more than twenty years. The arias of Fiordiligi, Donna Anna, and Donna Elvira also make up a big part of my active concert repertoire and I recorded them in the early 1990s for EMI.

Sophie in Strauss's *Der Rosenkavalier* was my debut role at the Metropolitan Opera and the Vienna State Opera. Sophie has the most exquisite music to sing but I wanted to do more than just sing well. I wanted to get outside of the box of the standard ingénue and to reveal her fighting spirit: she refuses an arranged marriage and insists on marrying Octavian whom she loves. I recorded the role in Dresden with Kiri Te Kanawa and Anne Sofie von Otter, with Bernard Haitink conducting.

At my Metropolitan Opera debut in 1988 I was surrounded by a fantastic cast: Brigitte Fassbaender was stunning, the most credible Octavian that I have ever seen, and the renowned Swedish soprano, Elisabeth Söderström, was making her opera farewell as the Marschallin.

I had met Elisabeth when I sang my European debut in Glyndebourne in 1974. She became a wonderful example for me and a faithful supporter and friend. She was a very beloved artist at Glyndebourne and was singing the countess in Richard Strauss's *Capriccio.* I was curious and enjoyed watching the rehearsals of the other productions that were in preparation, but after seeing Elisabeth in one rehearsal I attended all of her rehearsals and all of her performances that I could. I was so impressed—her acting was so natural. She was not just an opera singer; she also spoke many languages and was a consummate recitalist. Elisabeth was generous and had a great sense of humor: we laughed a lot together. I once sang a New Year's concert with the Stockholm Philharmonic in Stockholm's Konserthus and Elisabeth was the master of ceremony. She told a story to the audience that I had never heard. "I was in France singing at the Opera de Paris and took a taxi from the opera back to my apartment. The taxi driver asked me if I was an opera singer, I said, 'Yes I am.' Then he asked, 'Do you know Barbara Hendricks?' And I said, 'Yes, very well.' When we arrived at my destination I wanted to pay the fare but the driver refused. 'No, no Madame, you know Barbara Hendricks so this ride is on me.'" I made my debut at the same time as Elisabeth was singing her farewell opera performance. It was like a blessing from her; as if she were passing a flame of an important tradition of singing Richard Strauss's music to me. Elisabeth nominated me to be a member of the Swedish Academy of Music and beamed like a proud mother during the induction ceremony.

Although I never sang any other Strauss opera roles his music occupies a central place in my repertoire. His songs make up a big part of my lieder repertoire. For nearly thirty years the *Vier letzte*

Lieder and the "Schluss-Szene" from *Capriccio* have formed the basis of my solo repertoire with orchestra. This Mozart–Richard Strauss axis was the one that great sopranos at the Vienna State Opera, such as Sena Jurinac, Imgard Seefried, Lisa Della Casa, and Elisabeth Schwarzkopf, pursued. At the beginning of my career I thought that I should follow the example of these singers. They evolved slowly and sang opera, lieder, and even operetta, but stayed within this axis. But after Gilda in Orange and Liu with Karajan I also turned toward the Italian operas of Puccini and Verdi.

Mimì in Puccini's *La bohème* stole my heart in 1974 in Aspen, Colorado, and I performed the role while at Juilliard and the Met Studio. But I did not return to Mimì until I filmed the role in 1986. I had decided to wait until my voice had matured more throughout my range so that I could do justice to the role. There will be more about Mimì later.

In 1980 Jacques Bourgeois, the director of the Chorégies d'Orange, invited me to sing Gilda in Verdi's *Rigoletto,* which was based on Victor Hugo's *Le roi s'amuse.* At first I thought that the role was not for me because I had always associated Gilda with light coloraturas who I had often heard sing the aria "Caro Nome" in competition and auditions. But when I studied the score I realized that they had in effect deformed the true meaning of the aria into a showoff piece of technical fireworks. I wanted to stress Gilda's desperate desire to know her true identity, to have a name. During the aria she repeats the name of her beloved, Gualtier Maldé, over and over as if to make it her own. On closer examination of the rest of the score it was clear to me that Gilda makes an enormous transformation, and this is evident in Verdi's handling of her vocal line. Gone are the staccato notes, the breathlessness, and the questioning of the first act. At the end of the opera she sacrifices her own life to save her father from murdering the duke (Gualtier Maldé) who has betrayed her. The demands of the last two acts were proof that the role is definitely for a lyric soprano. Verdi does a similar vocal transformation with Violetta in *La Traviata.* My cast in Orange was Renato Bruson as Rigoletto and the grand Spanish tenor Alfredo Kraus as the Duke. I had made my Carnegie Hall debut in Donizetti's *La favorita* conducted by Eve Queler, with Alfredo and the great mezzo-soprano Shirley Verrett. When Alfredo learned that I was singing the role for the first time he was so thoughtful and helpful. During the dress rehearsal we had to fight against a terribly cold mistral, the wind that passes through the Rhone Valley in the south of France. In the photos of that rehearsal one can see that I am wearing long underwear underneath my costume. Fortunately, the opening night was completely calm. I will never forget the feeling of suspension that I felt during my death scene as I looked up into the stars before singing my last notes that the famous wall of the Chorégies carried up to the last row. Jacques told me over dinner afterward that it was good that I had been unaware of the gossip back in Paris that I, a Mozart singer, was going to be a terrible flop as Gilda. After the success of that magic night the noisemakers would just have to get used to me not living up to their expectations. I sang Gilda many times after Orange: in Monte Carlo with a young Myung Whun Chung conducting, on tour in Japan with the Hamburg Opera with Kazushi Ono conducting, and in Vienna. I went back to Berlin to sing in two different productions, both with my favorite Rigoletto, Ingvar Wixell, the most beautifully and movingly sung Rigoletto that I have ever heard. Hans Neuenfels directed the latter production.

Alfredo Kraus had been very gracious and helpful during my first production of Verdi's *Rigoletto*. He was known for his elegant French roles. I will never forget our work together in Offenbach's *Les Contes d'Hoffmann* and a duet from Gounod's *Romeo et Juliette* for the inauguration of the Bastille Opera in Paris in 1989 during the celebration of the French bicentennial of the storming of the Bastille.

I thought a lot about Alfredo when I was rehearsing that latter production of *Rigoletto* in Berlin because unlike many singers, and especially tenors, he never marked—that is to say, to sing less or even whisper the part—in rehearsals but always sang out and played fully. During the six weeks of rehearsals in Berlin, I never heard the voice of the young tenor who played the Duke until the dress rehearsal, where he was magnificent. However, at the premiere he cracked every high note and canceled the rest of his performances. It is very unsettling not to know what to expect from a colleague during the entire rehearsal period. I have always found that whenever I mark I have a tendency to diminish the intensity in the acting as well.

The recording of Liu in Puccini's *Turandot* with Karajan in 1981 consolidated my turn toward this repertoire. After that I performed the role often: twice at the Chorégies d'Orange, in concert in London with Silvia Sass and Franco Bonisolli, and fourteen performances in Bonn, Germany. The latest production was in 1999, with Zubin Mehta conducting the Teatro Comunale di Firenze orchestra and chorus, was directed by the Chinese film director Zhang Yimou. It took place in Beijing, in the real décor of the Forbidden City. Karajan had tried hard to organize a production of *Turandot* in the Forbidden City and had even been in contact with the Chinese authorities on many occasions, but he was never able to realize his dream. The many performances were divided amongst three different, rotating casts. The first cast sang the opening night, and a recording and film was made with the second one. I was very happy to be in the opening night cast as I had already recorded the role with Karajan and felt that I was fulfilling a little of his dream by bringing his Liu to Beijing. The first day of the staging rehearsals I was taken to a movement coach who was working with the three sopranos singing Turandot on the physical attributes, such as typical hand movements of a Chinese princess of that period. I asked why I should learn the same movements because Liu is a slave and probably not even Chinese. I met Zhang Yimou a short time afterward and so I asked him, "Where does Liu come from?" He answered, "From stage right." I said, "I am not talking about her first entrance, I mean from which country does she come? Persia or some other Asian land?" He had not considered the question, so I said, "It is only important for me to choose something concrete for my work as an actress, not necessarily something factual for the audience to know." With three different casts and a thousand extras he had his hands full. I was asked about this production in an interview afterward and I said, "Well, it was more Cecil B. DeMille than Ingmar Bergman."

One of my most successful competition and audition arias was Charpentier's "Depuis le jour" from *Louise*, and I knew that my love for the French song repertoire would eventually lead me toward French opera just as Miss Tourel had predicted. In 1982 I sang Juliette in Gounod's *Roméo et Juliette*, another role often sung by a light voice because of the first act aria, "Je veux vivre"; but there is a second aria, "Amour, ranime mon courage," that had usually been cut because it is definitely not for a light soprano. I insisted on adding it to our production because it is needed to fill out the character of Juliette.

Micaëla in Bizet's *Carmen* is thought of as a one-dimensional, uninteresting character. It was important for me to indicate her evolution from the young obedient girl of the first-act duet with Don José to the determined young woman who sings the aria of the third act. By then she no longer loves José, or at least has given up on marriage with him, but she shows enormous courage and a sense of duty when she goes to search for him in the bandits' den. I sang this role in Orange in 1984 when I was pregnant with Jennie and in the 1992 production Sebastian and Jennie sang in the children's choir. Sebastian took his role very seriously, guiding me to the bandits' den before my third-act aria. The only Bizet role that I have sung and recorded was Leila in *Les pêcheurs de perles* at the Nice Opera, but I have been singing Carmen's arias in concert and might consider doing the role in an interesting production.

Cinq poèmes de Baudelaire introduced me to Claude Debussy's music in 1969 and led me to sing his mélodies on an album with Michel Béroff. I also recorded *La damoiselle élue* with Daniel Barenboim and L'Orchestre de Paris. I sang his masterpiece *Pelléas et Mélisande* at the Paris Opera. I have always wanted to sing this score because of the perfect marriage of Debussy's music with the magnificent texts of Maeterlinck. However that production left a lot to be desired. It was a reprisal of an old production directed by Gian Carlo Menotti, and his vision of the opera was more suited to Puccini than Debussy. But most of the problems came from the orchestra pit. One evening as I lay on the stage waiting for the curtain to rise I thought that something horrible had happened there. I did not recognize the music at all. Later during the intermission I asked the conductor what had happened and he said, "There are twelve persons sitting in the pit that I have never seen before in my life. Some orchestra members have sent their own replacements without informing me, and some are their students!" The result was catastrophic for us and above all for Debussy.

During the intermission of one of the performances I had a very unexpected visitor. I had just sat down at my dressing table to prepare for act 2 and there was a timid knock on my dressing room door. I opened the door and there stood Serge Gainsbourg. I greeted him and invited him in. He was very shy and did not really seem to know what to say. After a short silence, he showed me the cigarette that he had in his hand and said, "I suppose that I can't smoke in here." I said, "Yes, you are right." He mumbled something about my performance and I said, "I must prepare for the next act; maybe we can talk after the show." He mumbled something again and then left. He did not come back afterward.

When I was a student at Juilliard I discovered Massenet's *Manon*. I listened often to the recording with Victoria de los Angeles and Jussi Björling, one of my favorite tenors. I liked Manon's music but it was difficult for me to sympathize with her. I found her frivolous and egocentric. I thought that it would be impossible to play a character without having some sympathy for her. One day I was watching Jennie play with a bracelet of mine and I saw the child, Manon, in her gestures and in her fascination with things that glittered. I decided to look deeper into Manon's character and realized that she is a victim of all of the men in her life: her father, who sent her away to a convent; Des Grieux, who professed his love for her but who wanted her as an object of his fantasies; and Lescaut, her unscrupulous cousin who used her to advance his own ambitions. I began to understand her better and to have a real affection for her. I spent wonderful hours with this character in the production at the Parma Opera in Italy. Parma is known for its opera house and everyone in town seemed to have an opinion about the opera and opera singers. You could ask any taxi driver about what was being performed at the opera and not only could he tell you what was playing but also who was singing and then give an in-depth critique of the performance. There was a rumor that an underground tunnel had been built to skirt away unlucky tenors who had missed a high note during a performance. This is probably not true but adds to the opera folklore of Parma. Parma is also known for delicious food. I can still taste the wonderful ravioli with pumpkin and the Parma ham. I exercised every morning just so that I could enjoy the delights of the local cuisine.

I loved every note of Antonia's music in Offenbach's *Les Contes d'Hoffmann* from the first time that I opened the score. She is still one of my favorite roles and I returned to Parma to sing it with Alfredo Kraus.

The last new role of the traditional repertoire that I learned was Tatiana in Tchaikovsky's *Eugene Onegin* in 2000 at the Nice Opera. I felt as if every single role that I had performed up until then was in preparation for this one. Tatiana touched me immediately and it was a great challenge to reveal the very subtle evolution of her character. She is a very young country girl who reveals her love for the worldly Onegin in the passionate and famous "Letter" aria. He rejects her and after a duel where he kills his best friend he is forced to go away. Tatiana grows up and eventually marries a nobleman. After a long absence Onegin returns to Moscow and, seeing Tatiana, declares his undying love for her. Out of duty to her husband and her place in society she rejects Onegin even though she still loves him.

I was completely taken with her and was impatient to sing her story. Since working on Rachmaninoff songs with Miss Tourel I have been singing Russian songs in my recitals and never had problems memorizing them. But it took a much longer time than I expected to memorize the long scenes of the opera. I had to memorize the words and the translation at the same time. I had parallel tasks going on in my brain: the words and their meaning, the music, the vocal demands, and the staging. I received a lot of support from the Croatian conductor Ivo Lipanovic and from my Onegin, Vladimir Chernov. Vladimir was surprised that I put so much time into getting the Russian pronunciation just right. I loved the Pushkin work and felt truly frustrated not to be able to read and understand this masterpiece in the original language. The long scene that includes the "Letter" aria is more than twenty minutes and it was very hard for me to keep the intensity and concentration at a maximum. Finally, in the first dress rehearsal, it all came together as if by magic, and Tatiana was present and strong. I never want to leave Tatiana, so I often sing the letter scene and the final duet with baritone in concert with orchestra.

When Jean-Pierre Brossman became the director of the Theatre du Châtelet in Paris he changed the complexion of Parisian musical life and everyone sat up to take notice. Every year he invited me to present a different aspect of my repertoire: chamber music with Shostakovich's *Blok Songs* for piano trio, a program of opera arias with the Croatian Radio Orchestra conducted by Ivo, two recitals with Love Derwinger: Spanish songs and Schubert's *Die schöne Müllerin*, and a jazz concert with the Magnus Lindgren Quartet, all lit by Ulf. In 2004, his last season before retiring, he offered me a crown jewel, the role of the Angel in Tony Kushner's *Angels in America*. I have sung contemporary music since I was a student and I was honored to work with the Hungarian composer, Peter Eötvös. He composed his opera to a libretto written by his wife Mari Mezei that reduced the six-hour play to three hours. I never expected to be included in the composition process but I met with Peter many times while he was composing my part. He listened to me speaking my part, and as soon as he had composed a portion of it he would send it to me so that I could try it out. He composed the most beautiful music for the angel and for me. I had seen the play in a television production with Meryl Streep and Al Pacino and was looking forward to performing it. I was most curious about how I would fly in and out for my scenes. When the director, Philippe Calvario, showed me what he had in mind I was petrified. I told him that I would try it but that he would have to accept a no if I could not do it without passing out. We went five stories above the stage and they fitted me into a harness; on a musical cue I had to jump into the void and start to sing as I descended to the stage. The first time that I tried it I could not stop trembling from fright for at least an hour afterward. But I gradually mastered my fear. Having to sing at the same time made it much easier for me. Sebastian, Jennie, and Ulf could not believe it when they saw me on opening night flying around as if it were something I did everyday. When I met Tony Kushner after the last performance he said, "I want to have you in every production of my play." I understood that he was not just speaking about my performance but felt as I did that the music that Peter had composed was proof that a singing angel was what Tony had intended all along. Working with Peter while he was composing and rehearsing with him was an invaluable farewell gift from Jean-Pierre that I will always cherish. I know that he is enjoying a well-deserved retirement and I am so grateful for the friendship and work that we have done together.

I love to perform opera. And it is because I love it so much that I, like Maestro Giulini, decided to give up most staged productions. I get no enjoyment out of rehearsals that are just a kind of *mise en place*, no more than traffic directions so the singers do not bump into each other. When I was twenty and full of the impressions from Stanislavski's books *My Life in Art* and *An Actor Prepares*, I thought that my generation would make the same revolution in opera that Stanislavski had done in the theater some one hundred years before. It did not happen. There have been some magnificent productions during the last forty years and I have been in a few of them, but in general the great evenings of opera as true theater have been the exception and not the rule. Not much has changed since Giulini decided to stop with staged performance. After the birth of my children my priorities shifted. When I have had the choice between singing in an "instant" opera production or a concert that I could assure would be well rehearsed, whether with orchestra, chamber music, or a recital, I chose to accept the latter. Or I simply chose to be at home with my family. So as not to abandon the wonderful opera roles that I love to sing I sing them in concert and I know that I can be true to the music and the libretto.

The piano is the instrument most intimately associated with a singer's work. When I began to study music at Juilliard I had to learn to play it well enough to learn my musical scores. I choose to sing all of my recitals and most of my orchestra repertoire from memory. After having learned the score I like to work with a pianist. I don't want to be distracted by my efforts to sing and play the piano part. The pianists with whom I've worked have been my most important partners on stage in recitals and chamber music but were also necessary partners during rehearsals prior to a concert, where the real work takes place, a process I jealously covet.

Many of the piano students and some of the conducting students who attended Jennie Tourel's repertoire classes offered to play for her students, but she was very demanding and chose her pianists very carefully. I remember her stopping a pianist at the end of the introduction to a song, just as I was about to start to sing. She said, "Stop! It is impossible for her to sing even the first note of this song if you play those first measures like that. The song begins before you play the first note, not when she starts to sing. Now do it again and think about your role in the song." Most of the pianists were aspiring soloists. They were not planning to become professional accompanists for singers, but they and the conducting students who attended her class wanted to benefit from what "the musician's musician" had to say not only to the singer but also to the pianist about the interpretation of a score. She was able to coax her student and the pianist into breathing life into the score together because Jennie Tourel was more than just a singer with a beautiful voice—she was a complete musician and linguist whose instruments were her voice and her intelligence.

When I began to give recitals at Juilliard I sought out pianists who were as curious as those students who came to our repertoire classes every Tuesday afternoon, who were seeking to learn how to become a true chamber musician. But I found that the usual relationship between the pianist and the singer was more like that of a singer and her coach.

If a singer does not read music his coach will have to teach him the music from start to finish and then correct musical and diction faults as well as give advice about phrasing and the overall interpretation of the song. This is most common in the opera house, where singers are coached in every nuance, first by the rehearsal pianist and then by the conductor. Most singers begin their careers much later than instrumentalists and like me have had no formal musical training of any kind before beginning to study singing. I had so much catching up to do compared to my friends who were instrumentalists, so I worked extra hard to learn to read music and to play the piano. Today many singers have a good musical education or come to singing after having studied one or more instruments, but some pianists and conductors still act as if they should indicate every single phrase to them. This never happens with instrumental soloists. How often have I have heard in a rehearsal situation a stage manager addressing the group as "singers and musicians." I have always found this distinction to be a bit condescending because I consider myself a musician whose instrument is the voice. I hope this patronizing attitude toward singers will gradually change.

When I started, I followed the same trend, coaching with excellent pianists for operas and recitals, but I gradually began to seek out pianists who were interested in making music with me rather than teaching me how to read the score, since I was more than capable of doing that on my own.

Tommy Thompson was also Staffan's agent at CAMI and he arranged a few of our first recitals together, but since Staffan was busy trying to get his own solo career off the ground he did not have the time to play all of my recitals. I met an excellent young pianist, Lawrence Skrobacs, with whom I began to work almost exclusively. Larry understood and appreciated how I wanted to work on a score. We worked together on opera and concert repertoire and he played recitals with me all over the United States, in the CAMI Community Concerts Artists series as well as my Town Hall debut in 1976. We became very good friends and he was one of the members of my New York City "family."

When I moved to Paris I had to begin my career in Europe from scratch and there were no Community Concerts associations. I was not yet being engaged for big tours and often the promoters could not pay for Larry's air travel to and from New York for just one concert. I had to find a Europe-based pianist.

Martin suggested that I work with one of the leading singers' accompanists of the time who lived in Europe and who could easily come to Paris for rehearsals with me. I should have known from the very first meeting that it was not going to work for me. It was not a rehearsal. It was a coaching session where he sought to find something to criticize or correct. He often wasted time trying to teach me something that I already knew. He once spent ten minutes telling me that the "Herz" is pronounced like Hertz in "Hertz-Rent-A-Car." I knew how to pronounce the word but when I sang it it was not as clear as when I spoke it. He was basically treating me like a stupid child. These were not real rehearsals between two musicians, since he was concentrating only on me and not on his own playing. He prepared the piano part alone and I only heard his musical intentions during the concert! I was no Liza Doolittle in need of a Pygmalion but he wanted to play that role. The recitals that we performed together went well but I did not enjoy them and actually came to dread the "rehearsals" with him. Rehearsals in preparation for a concert with Larry and Staffan had been precious and joyful moments and were almost more important than the performances. During those working rehearsals I had the freedom to explore the score together with my partner, stretching the limits and discovering the many possibilities that the score reveals. But with him I was unhappy and did not feel like I was advancing artistically.

I once asked him to play his part from memory in the rehearsals as I was doing so as to force him to concentrate on his participation and less on me. But he refused; he did not want me to listen to him work, and he had never played anything from memory. He had certainly played a song like Schubert's "Gretchen am Spinnrade" a thousand times in his twenty-year career and surely should have been able to play it without looking at the score. He was not interested in a partnership but in having an empty vessel that he could fill with his ideas, taking credit for the result. He had another annoying habit that made me very uncomfortable as well. He loved to gossip about other singers with whom he worked. He seemed to think that everyone was as envious of others as he was and that by telling me negative stories about my colleagues I would somehow feel better and bigger.

Once after a rehearsal with a well-known French singer he arrived in my apartment in Paris and immediately began to tell me about what bad vocal shape she was in and how badly she had sung. I stopped him in mid-sentence and said, "You know, she is a very great artist for whom I have an enormous respect and admiration. I have no interest in hearing about your work with her, so keep it to yourself and let's get on with this rehearsal." I continued to work with him for a few seasons, trying hard to make it work, until January 1982.

Georg Hörtnagel, the German agent and concert promoter, engaged me to sing my first "Liederabend" in Germany in his concert series at the Herkules Saal in Munich. Martin and I were on vacation in Schloss Elmau in Bavaria, a place where Martin's family had been going for three generations. Georg heard me practicing Berlioz's *Les nuits d'été* as he was walking by the house of the hotel's pianist, who had allowed me to rehearse at his home. He did not know me and asked around and found out that I was married to Martin, whom he knew well. He engaged me directly for a recital in Munich in January 1982.

When I learned that I was pregnant with Sebastian I waited until I was past the fourth month before calling to tell him that the baby was due around December 7, 1981. Neither my doctor or any of my colleagues could give me advice about how soon I would be able to sing again after giving birth, but one and a half months seemed to me to be a bit optimistic. Georg did not want to cancel and suggested that I should wait and see. A little bit more than a month after Sebastian's birth the accompanist came to me for a rehearsal. After trying for thirty minutes it was clear that I would not be able to do the concert in two weeks. I wanted to tell this directly to Georg so I told the accompanist that I would call him myself. Georg was away in Poland and it was impossible to reach him there. This was during the Cold War and it was difficult to call from the West to countries that were behind the Iron Curtain. His secretary asked me to wait a few days for him to return to Germany. But before I was able to reach him the accompanist had already spoken to the agency and offered another singer to take my place. I called him and told him exactly what I thought of him. I have never seen or spoken to him since.

I had to find a new pianist for my recital debut at La Scala Milano six weeks later.

Of course there have always been and still are many pianists who have dedicated their work to the singer's repertoire and are great musicians whose concerts I have immensely enjoyed—Gerald Moore and Geoffrey Parsons are two—but this very negative experience forced me to find another way.

I was still missing Miss Tourel very much and I had accepted that teacher-student relationship with the "accompanist" in order to fill that gap. This experience coincided with the birth of my first child and forced me to accept what a famous Zen Buddhist master says to his student: "It is time to become your own master and to teach yourself." I had to move on to another level and to take the responsibility for my instrument and for my artistic footprint. I did not want to make that journey alone but together with like-minded musicians: conductors, instrumentalists, and singers. I began to find my musical family in my musical home: chamber music.

I had heard the Finnish pianist, conductor, and composer Ralf Gothoni play Schubert's *Winterreise* in Paris with the great Finnish bass, Martti Tavela, and not only was it a fantastic concert but the relationship between the two seemed to be mature and was very inspiring. I immediately told Martin that I would like to work with Gothoni. We went backstage afterward to greet them both. Martin worked for Martti, whom I had met often at the Deutsche Oper in Berlin, where he was a member of the company. I spoke to Ralf and asked shyly if he might be interested in working together some day; he answered yes.

So Martin contacted Ralf and he was free and happy to play for my recital debut at La Scala, only six weeks away. After ten minutes of our first rehearsal together I knew that the relationship that I had longed for since working with Larry was possible. What a difference in style and intellect! Ralf has perfect pitch and speaks German fluently, and he did correct faults that he heard—in order to enhance the music, not his ego. I also felt free to share my thoughts about the interpretation of the music. Our collaboration continued for many years until he decided to devote himself full time to composing and conducting.

A very important encounter for me was with the great Rumanian pianist Radu Lupu, whom I met in Tel Aviv in 1979. We were both guest artists with the Israel Philharmonic, conducted by Zubin Mehta. Radu played a Beethoven piano concerto in the first half of the program and I sang Mahler's Fourth Symphony in the second half. After performing several concerts we recorded these pieces with the orchestra for Decca. After the last concert Radu asked, "Do you sing Schubert lieder?" I answered, "Yes, of course." Then he asked, "Would you like to sing some concerts of Schubert songs with me?" I could not believe my ears and I called Martin immediately to tell him. He asked Radu if he was indeed serious about this request and when Radu confirmed that he was, Martin began to organize a tour for us. Radu was not free before 1981. When I became pregnant with Sebastian we had to cancel the tour. We postponed the first project to a period three years later when Radu would be free. But I was again pregnant, this time with Jennie, and we had to postpone it again. Finally in 1986, more than seven years after his request, we began our rehearsals of the Schubert songs. Getting us together for this project was more difficult than giving birth.

I had heard Radu play several times when I lived in New York City and was already a fervent admirer when we met in 1979. I had always found his playing moving and was taken by his unique presence and conviction at the piano. But it was during our rehearsals at my home in Clarens, with him seated at my piano, that I was able to truly appreciate the actual breadth and depth of his mastery of his instrument and his reading of the score. To hear up close the audible difference between a *ppp* (pianississimo) and *pp* (pianissimo) and to hear his phrasing develop with each playing of a song was light-years away from being told, "Just say 'Herz' like in Hertz Rent-a Car" and the other silly remarks I had been hearing.

The work with Radu propelled me into the depths of my task and I enjoyed it immensely. He was a great inspiration to me. Instead of playing power games, he was actually shy and a little tortured. Our relationship was one of give and take as we searched together to get closer to Schubert's intentions.

We toured the recital in Europe and eventually recorded my first album of Schubert lieder. We met again in 1993 and repeated the same process; rehearsing, touring, and recording a second album of Schubert lieder.

My work with Ralf and Radu gave me the courage to seek out other great artists with whom I could collaborate. I have since, except on one occasion, worked with pianists who were soloists and who performed chamber music on a regular basis. Whenever I heard artists whose playing touched me I wanted to share a music-making experience with them.

When I lived in Paris, the French pianist Michel Béroff and I met through our mutual friends Marielle and Katia Labèque, duo pianists with whom I had performed and recorded Gershwin songs for Philips. I had heard Michel in concert and especially appreciated his interpretations of the French repertoire. When I asked him if he would be interested in working on Debussy songs with me, he accepted right away. After a tour of several concerts we recorded my first recital LP for EMI in 1985. Michel and I became friends. He is one of Sebastian's godfathers and we have continued to work together on and off since then. He had a long period when he had problems with his right hand so we were not able to work together although he continued to play piano repertoire for left hand only. When he started to play again with both hands the first concerts that he played were on a small tour with me. Another French pianist with whom I had the pleasure to work was Michel Dalberto. Michel had won the Clara Haskil competition in Vevey, Switzerland, and lived there for a while, not far from us, and that made rehearsals very easy to plan. I performed many concerts with him and recorded a recital of Gabriel Fauré songs, a bestseller in my catalogue, and a collection of French songs by various composers, *Mélodies Françaises*. Michel's touch was perfect for this repertoire, especially for the simple yet difficult songs of Gabriel Fauré, whom I consider the French equivalent of Franz Schubert.

André Böröcz, our friend from the Menton Festival, organized every year classical musical cruises on the "Mermoz" and he often invited me to participate. During one of the cruises I heard the Portuguese pianist Maria João Pires for the first time. I was so moved by her seemingly effortless playing that I went up to her immediately after the concert and asked her if she would like to work with me. This resulted in a European tour and a subsequent recording of Mozart lieder.

There was a wonderful piano series at the Théâtre des Champs-Élysées where I heard the best piano talents of our time. I was always on the lookout for someone with whom I might enjoy working. Richard Goode is a pianist whom I admired and with whom I had briefly worked at the Chamber Music Society in New York, but we were never able to plan a recital tour together in Europe. I tried hard to plan concerts with one of my favorite pianists from my student days, Alicia de Larrocha. We met and spoke about repertoire at her home in Coppet, Switzerland, not far from Geneva. We read through a few Robert Schumann songs but we could never get our schedules to coincide and unfortunately the tour never materialized.

I have sung many times with Daniel Barenboim; he conducted the Orchestre de Paris with me, we performed *Le nozze di Figaro* in Berlin, and I appeared with him leading the Israel Philharmonic. Only on one occasion did I have the pleasure to work with him as a pianist—when he invited me to sing a chamber music concert with him in Paris, an early piece by Olivier Messiaen, who was in the audience.

The only European concert that Larry Skrobacs and I performed together was in Dresden, Germany, in 1976 and it was the only time that I had sung behind the Iron Curtain before coming to the Soviet Union/Russia, the birthplace of Jennie Tourel, in August 1978. Martin asked me if I wanted to do a chamber music tour with the great Soviet violinist Liana Isakadze and pianist Alexander Slobodyanik, with whom he had become friends when he was working for Lodding in Stockholm. Liana had organized the tour with the official Soviet artists' agency, but the month of August was a little off-season. In my American passport it stated that American citizens should contact the embassy when visiting certain countries such as the Soviet Union. So I did, but the cultural attaché was away for summer vacation and no one at the embassy seemed to care. Liana had asked Alexander's wife, Natasha, to play the cello but due to additional concerts in the United States he had not returned and Dmitri Alexeev was the last-minute replacement. He was the son of American Jews who had immigrated from New York to the Soviet Union in the 1930s, seduced by the idealist goals of communism. I wondered if they had known Emma Goldman, anarchist and feminist of Russian origin, who was expelled from the United States at about the same time. I had read about the American emigrants in her autobiography, *Living My Life*.

The initial plans were for us to rehearse in Moscow a few days and then go to Riga, Latvia, and Vilnius, Lithuania, before going to Pitsunda in Georgia, Liana's home, and then to Sotchi on the Black Sea. Upon arrival our "guide" (KGB agent) Larissa handed us train tickets and announced that we were to go directly with the night train to Riga and would rehearse there. I was not at all pleased because I wanted to visit Moscow and was starting to make a big fuss when I read the look on Liana's face: it meant, "Don't say anything more or I am in trouble." I accepted the change and kept my thoughts to myself during the next two weeks. Due to the sudden change in plans no one had thought to get a train ticket for Dmitri. When we boarded the train we did not even know if he had been able to get a ticket. About an hour after departure he showed up in our compartment in time to share the delicious Georgian picnic that Liana had prepared for us.

Upon arrival in Riga we went to the hotel and then directly to rehearse. During one of our breaks we had to wait in another rehearsal room while the harpsichord was being tuned. Dmitri sat down at the piano and began to play some jazz. I couldn't believe what I heard because he was really good. We improvised a few spirituals together and decided to add them to the program. The concerts went well and we even had some time off to go to the beach in Sotchi. It was a very strange setup with Larissa, the musicians, and us. Soviet citizens were not allowed to live in the same hotels as foreigners without special permission. Since we were on tour together there was no problem for the musicians, but if other Russians—friends of Liana or Dmitri—tried to come into the hotel restaurant with us after the concerts they were denied entrance. Somehow, after a little while, they always managed to get in and Larissa appeared to look the other way.

Liana invited us to her home in Pitsunda for a sumptuous Georgian meal accompanied by delicious local wine. I remember an incident in the car with one of her cousins, a well-known pianist. I said something to Martin in English and Liana kicked my foot. Later when I asked her why, she said that she had not quite understood exactly what I had said, but just to be sure it was better that I kept my thoughts to myself around others. I said, "But it was only you, Martin and your cousin in the car. Can't you trust him?" She said, "He is like a brother to me, he has been in our home since he was a baby, but I do not know if I can trust him." A cold shiver ran down my spine.

The tour was the beginning of a long collaboration and friendship between Dmitri and me. Whenever I was invited back to the Soviet Union for recitals in Moscow and Leningrad it was he who sat at the piano. Together we recorded *Negro Spirituals*, my first solo album for EMI.

Youri Egorov was on his way to having a great career when he was struck down at age thirty-three with AIDS. We had just started to work together and had done one tour with Schumann songs. This was the first time that I had done a program devoted mostly to Schumann. I struggled with Schumann because I expected his songs to be as accessible as Schubert's, but it took me many years to feel as at home in his universe. Youri and I performed our last concert together at the Fondation Gianadda in Martigny, Switzerland. I remember that after the concert I was not so happy with the Schumann songs but he was very encouraging. "It was not a bad concert at all; you felt some discomfort, but don't worry, it will come." He was a very sensitive human being and a great pianist and was often compared to the great Dinu Lipatti, who also died aged thirty-three. AIDS took Youri, Larry Skrobacs, and too many others away from us too soon. I would have liked for him to hear me now because with time and patience Schumann and I came to a rewarding and mutual understanding of one another. Fortunately Youri lived in the Netherlands and was able to plan his own dignified death.

When I arrived in Europe song recitals were composed mainly of German lieder and French mélodies, and these still occupied a big place in the classical music universe. I had the benefit of hearing so many singers performing the repertoire as they passed on the tradition and the passion for the genre. The decline has been rapid and unforeseen. Most of the singers, in particular female singers of my generation, with the exception of Dame Felicity Lott, have completely abandoned the recital. They preferred opera and large "events," concerts in large stadiums that instead of promoting classical music to the masses have rather contributed to its marginalization. My recitals still sell out concert halls all over the world and I have been able to impose programs composed of lesser-known or completely unknown songs. Without knowing the specifics my audience knows what to expect from me and is confident that I will always present an interesting program with an integrity that reflects my own personal commitment. It makes me sad that my younger colleagues seem to not even be aware of this rich cultural heritage. When they do leave the opera house to sing a recital it is a mixture of popular songs and opera arias.

I invite my audience to go on an emotional journey with me during a recital and so I ask them to not applaud after each song but to respect the integrity of the group of songs as I have organized them. I want to help them come into their own concentration, not to think or to analyze, but to allow the music to work its own magic. Sometimes the promoter is embarrassed to make an announcement and adds, "Barbara Hendricks asks you . . ." I think that the audience wants to know the protocol for the evening and it works. The silence between songs is a vital part of the journey that I want all to experience and is as important as the notes.

My programs are a result of my own desires to sing a certain cycle or to put certain songs together to form a group. Most likely a great deal of the program will be new to the audience but from my experience from my first Community Concerts in the United States to my yearly recitals in Paris, Munich, New York, or London I have been able to gently impose the programs that I love on my audience. One recital that I sang at the Théâtre des Champs-Élysées sold out so quickly that it had to be doubled and the program included Alban Berg and Schönberg songs.

When I sang my first Schubert songs more than forty years ago I had no idea how rich two minutes of music could be. I just knew that I loved to sing the songs. The more I worked I realized that my task was not just to sing the music with good diction but,

In 1999 I met in secret with Aung San Suu Kyi, who was under house arrest. She asked me if the people of Burma could use the example of the American civil rights movement led by Martin Luther King Jr. to get their rights. We were happy to meet on her first trip outside Burma in Bern, Switzerland.

Kofi and Nane Annan have been close friends with Ulf and me for many years.

Bishop Desmond Tutu, Nobel Peace Prize laureate, and I met at the inauguration of Nelson Mandela. He has been the moral conscience of many generations. He says, "My humanity is bound up in yours for we can only be human together."

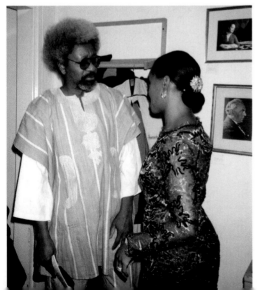

Wole Soyinka, the first African to receive the Nobel Prize in literature, and I became friends at the 1993 Nobel ceremony.

Prague, 1994, in the office
of ex-dissident President
Vaclav Havel.

Danielle Mitterrand was
very interested to learn
about my life growing up
under Jim Crow in the
South and during the civil
rights movement. She often
invited me to participate in
events organized by her
foundation, France Libertés.

Audrey Hepburn, goodwill
ambassador for UNICEF
who also lived in the Canton
de Vaud. We were very
supportive to one another in
our respective work.

On tour in South Africa with Mama Africa, Miriam Makeba, in 2004. We had hoped to do a European tour together, but she passed away in 2008.

I was the soloist for the Nobel concert, ceremony, and gala dinner in 1993 when Toni Morrison received the Nobel Prize in literature.

Lauren Bacall, Hedy Lamarr, and I at the Moulin Rouge at the hundred-year gala, organized as a benefit concert for Danielle Mitterrand's foundation, France Libertés.

Quincy Jones and I at the Montreux Jazz Festival. Quincy was very
supportive when I began to include jazz and blues in my repertoire.

Dee Bridgewater and I in1993 at Chateau Versailles
for a benefit concert for needy children.

The great drummer Ed Thigpen and I on tour in France. Ed was a great support to me during my first years singing jazz.

In concert in Stockholm with Swedish jazz musician and composer Magnus Lindgren and with bassist Ira Coleman.

In Venice with Daniel Toscan du Plantier on our way to meet Luigi Comencini.

The jury for the Cannes Festival 1999, presided by David Cronenberg, with Jeff Goldblum, Dominque Blanc, Holly Hunter, and Yasmine Reza.

Filming of Puccini's *La bohème* in 1986, directed by Luigi Comencini.

I filmed Stravinsky's *The Rake's Progress* in 1995 for SVT (Swedish Public Television) with Greg Fedderly and Håkan Hagegård, directed by Inger Åby, and conducted by Esa Pekka Salonen.

With Martin, my first husband, holding Jennie; I am holding Sebastian.

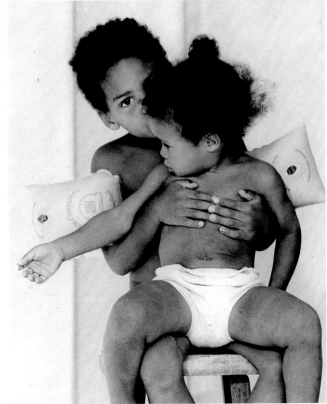

To be a mother has been one of my great privileges and the source of my greatest joy. Here: Sebastian holding Jennie

With Ulf, the light in my life, on his vintage motorcycle on vacation in Gotland.

Malcolm, Sebastian and his wife, Laetitia, and Jennie preparing dinner in our garden in the Swedish archipelago.

The family, including Ulf, his parents, and I, went to see Jennie receive her degree from Richmond University in London. Here: Jennie, me, Malcolm, and Sebastian.

My life has as its leitmotif the struggle against the sham glitter that eclipses the inner light, the complexities that kill simplicity, and the vulgar externals that diminishes true grandeur.

in the words of Dietrich Fischer-Dieskau, I was actually striving to "speak the music and sing the poetry." My choice of songs for a recital are as often based on a poet that I want to explore as on the music of a particular composer. Eager to learn as much as I could I kept adding more songs to my repertoire every season. Schubert alone composed more than six hundred songs and I have to accept that when I retire I will not have had the time to learn and sing many of them, not to mention songs of other composers. I did not, however, want to finish my voyage with Schubert without traveling with him through his two great masterpieces written to poems by Wilhelm Müller, *Die Schöne Müllerin* and *Winterreise*, written for tenor but most often sung by baritones. I think that for a true lieder singer *Die Schöne Müllerin* is the equivalent of *Hamlet* for a Shakespearean actor. Thus *Winterreise* becomes the equivalent of *King Lear*. Very few women singers have included these two cycles in their song repertoire, but I did not let this stop me from delving into these magnificent dramatic monologues.

The overwhelming majority of lieder texts are taken from poems written by male poets, but for me their poetry is universal and transcends gender. I try to relate the human emotions that are depicted in the poetry.

I began first with *Die Schöne Müllerin* and I toured it for several years all over Europe before recording it. I have just finished a tour in Sweden, Spain, Belgium, and France with *Winterreise*, which Schubert wrote at the very end of his young life.

I do not believe that the audience needs to speak the language of the song that I sing in order to feel a connection to it, but for cycles like these it can be an added advantage. I will never forget the long silence at the end of a performance in the Herkules Saal in Munich that suspended the work in space and into an immeasurable time frame. This was so much stronger a response from the audience than the applause that broke that silence.

When I added *Winterreise* to my repertoire I had a long tour planned in France, Switzerland, and Belgium. I was aware that fewer and fewer audiences knew this repertoire well. Ulf and I devised *Winterreise* as a theatrical piece with the backdrop of a light design and projections conceived by his subtle hand. In between some of the songs I recited short poems that I had written myself in French based on Wilhelm Müller's German text in order to help the French-speaking audiences come into the atmosphere of the piece from the first song.

Winterreise is about seventy-two minutes long and I could feel that the audience was a little unsettled during the first twenty minutes; I could see one woman playing with her hair, another changing her position from side to side. But after a while it seemed that they came closer to me and into the world of Schubert and Müller. The attention was palpable and they were completely with us on Schubert's winter voyage until the last note. This is quite an achievement in this zapping society in which we live.

For more than forty years I have defended with all of my being the art of the recital, and I will continue to carry that torch until I sing my last note. In spite of the lack of interest today I believe that, like baroque music, the classical song recital will too make a comeback when we realize that our souls have been running on empty for far too long.

The great solo pianists with whom I worked had very heavy schedules and many demands on their time so I was very happy when they found time to rehearse and tour a recital program with me. In the 1980s and '90s I was performing as many as forty to fifty recitals a year in addition to my orchestra concerts and opera performances. Staffan Scheja was willing to give me the time in his schedule to perform the majority of my recitals with me. Our musical partnership began in 1974 and lasted more than twenty years.

Staffan is an excellent pianist who enjoys playing chamber music. He went through a very difficult time in his life in the beginning of the 1980s, a rather self-destructive period, and I was starting to wonder if his playing might be affected. But then he met and fell in love with a beautiful and positive young woman, Marianne, who was working in Visby on the island of Gotland in Sweden. While visiting her he came up with the idea to do a chamber music festival there during the summer. This was the birth of the Gotland Chamber Music Festival in Visby in 1985. At the beginning it took place in various small venues in the city—a cinema, the Roxy, and a school—before it found its home in the Saint Nicolai ruin in the medieval Hansa city. Staffan and Marianne did everything: booking artists, flights, and hotels; printing up posters; going around town putting them up; and moving around chairs and music stands on the stage during the concerts. I was so happy to see this metamorphosis that in my opinion literally saved Staffan's life. It was a very special arrangement: all musicians agreed to play without pay but were invited to come with their families for a week together on this beautiful island. It was a joyful atmosphere with lots of children. We were making music, discovering new repertoire, and, unlike in our touring life, had the luxury of enough time to listen to many wonderful concerts and to interact with other good musicians who also gradually became good friends. All of us participate because we love chamber music and know how necessary it is to ensure that it continue to exist. The festival expanded to include some other towns on the island and this gave us an opportunity to discover the rest of Gotland. I have performed in the festival nearly every two years since then and it was there that I met so many wonderfully talented and dedicated Nordic musicians. Many of them have formed my Swedish musical family.

Staffan's piano teacher at the Stockholm Conservatory (Musikhögskolan in Stockholm), Gunnar Hallhagen, seems to have been for several generations of Swedish pianists the kind of inspiration and example that Jennie Tourel had been for me. Although I never had the privilege to meet him he is very important to me as the father to three generations of Swedish pianists who have formed an integral part of my Swedish musical family.

One of them is Roland Pöntinen. He has played an incomparable role in the success of the Gotland Festival since its beginnings. He is a curious, open-minded, and enthusiastic musician and is happiest when he is playing music. Shortly after hearing him for the first time at the festival I asked him to play some concerts with me. Staffan had often spoken to me about Hallhagen, but when I started to sing concerts with Roland, who was in the next generation of his students, I began to understand the determining impact that he had on his pupils. Staffan and I recorded

Hommage à Jennie Tourel for EMI, which could also have been a tribute to Gunnar Hallhagen.

Roland and I recorded two CDs together for EMI, one of lieder of Hugo Wolf and the other Nordic songs, including some by Grieg, Sibelius, Rangström, and Nielsen. But Roland became a father and was getting busier every year with his career. I needed to find someone for a concert in Norway with the Vertavo Quartet that neither Staffan nor Roland were free to play. Roland suggested his younger colleague and best friend, Love Derwinger, who had also been a student of Hallhagen. After working with him I was convinced that there really was a "Hallhagen effect and philosophy." It is no coincidence that they make music on the same high level as any of the more internationally known pianists with whom I have worked. I continue to work with Roland when he has time and we have recorded three additional CDs—Brahms lieder, Schumann lieder, and Schubert's *Die Schöne Müllerin*—all on my own label, Arte Verum. But Love has now become the pianist that I work with most and is an ideal partner. We have been touring together all over the world since 2000 and have already recorded for Arte Verum recitals of *Canciones Españolas,* Poulenc, Beethoven lieder and Volkslieder, and Schubert's *Winterreise;* we have three more recordings—Shostakovich's *Blok Songs,* chamber music of Ravel and Fauré, and Mahler lieder—waiting to be released.

But there is one more! Love was not free for a recital in Montreal, nor was Roland, and Love suggested a friend and fellow Hallhagen student, Anders Kilström, and it happened again. Ulf was in the audience and he came backstage and said that the concert was "pure magic." Thank you, Gunnar!

The Gotland festival also introduced me to other instrumentalists with whom I would perform and tour all over the world. The great trumpet player Håkan Hardenberger and I toured extensively in Germany and recorded Bach's Cantata no. 51 for my Bach recording in East Berlin with Peter Schreier conducting. After one concert in a small town the only place open where we could get something to eat was a funky local hamburger joint. When we saw how it looked from the outside, Håkan said, "I'll go in and buy something to take away but you stay in the taxi and protect my trumpets."

Sweden's greatest classical guitarist, Göran Söllscher performed and recorded Mozart with me. Another regular during the early years was the trombonist, composer, and lately conductor Christian Lindberg. I have been a soloist with him as he conducted Last Night of the Proms at Konserthus with his brass ensemble, and we toured together with the Swedish chamber orchestra, Musica Vitae, in Sweden, Cyprus, and Greece. I also sang with his Arctic Philharmonic Orchestra in Norway, but sadly our tour in Japan was canceled due to the Fukushima nuclear disaster in 2011.

After some years I had quickly exhausted the repertoire of chamber music for voice and instruments. The Gotland festival commissioned the Swedish composer Sven-David Sandström to compose the Mölna Elegy for soprano and piano trio that we premiered in 2000 in Visby. The French composer Bruno Mantovani composed *Das erschafft der Dichter nicht* for me and six instruments; I premiered it with the Ensemble Intercontemporain at La Cité de la Musique in Paris in 2002. Arvo Pärt composed *L'abbé Agathon*, a simple and moving piece for eight cellos and soprano, which I premiered at Rencontres d'Ensemble de Violoncelles in Beauvais, France in 2004. The chamber orchestra in Jonköpings Sinfonietta commissioned *Fyra Kärlekssånger* using poems of Niklas Rådström for me in 2006. I began my career singing contemporary music so it feels good to support composers of my time.

I have also organized mini chamber music festivals with other friends such as the Emerson Quartet and the Orpheus Chamber Orchestra in Sweden, Switzerland, and Belgium.

Esbjörn Svensson, jazz pianist and founder of the jazz trio EST, was a great artist who died much too young in a tragic diving accident. I heard him for the first time in Gotland and it seemed that the music he played flowed directly from somewhere deep within himself out from his fingertips on to the piano keys. One of the great advantages of a festival like Gotland is that we all feel free to suggest repertoire to one another for the concerts at breakfast. "I brought a score that we could do together. Would you like to perform this with me?" When Esbjörn and his trio came back to Gotland we improvised an unforgettable "My Funny Valentine" together. We met afterward at his home to talk about doing a project together and we both thought that we should try to first work just as a duo. His career took off and every time we would run into each other, usually at the airport, we both said, "We have to get together and think about our project." We both thought that there would be much time ahead of us. Sadly Sweden and indeed the world have lost one of the most interesting, innovative musicians to come along in a long time.

I became a jazz fan in the living room of Arthur Porter in Little Rock, Arkansas, as I indulged myself in his vast collection of jazz albums. I dabbled in jazz for fun and to earn a little extra cash while studying at university, where I sang the standards with a jazz trio. I later bought some LPs and would daydream as I looked at the album covers of artists who had recorded live at famous jazz festivals such as Newport or Montreux. I can still see in my mind an Ella Fitzgerald cover, *Live in Montreux*, and thinking, Oh, what a treat it would be to go to hear a concert at the Montreux Jazz Festival one day. When I moved to Montreux one of my first thoughts was, Now I will go to the all of the festival concerts every year. Already that first year in Montreux I was there. I eventually met the founder and director of the festival, Claude Nobs. He lived up above us in the mountains and we often passed by his exceptional home on our Sunday promenades. Sebastian and Jennie absolutely hated to go on promenades but they loved to stop by Claude's. He was always the first person in Switzerland to have the very latest in sound and video equipment, like the first Walkman, as well as other gadgets such as old jukeboxes, and the children found it amusing, a fun museum. I enjoyed watching concerts in his video archives and discovering some of the legendary performances of musicians such as Oscar Peterson, Miles Davis, B. B. King, Ella Fitzgerald, Stan Getz, Stéphane Grappelli, and Nina Simone. We often spoke over a meal of his delicious pumpkin soup, good wine, and Swiss cheese about the rich history of jazz and of the festival. One of those conversations led us to speak about the great Duke Ellington. I said, "I love the music of Duke Ellington and I admire him not only for

his musical genius but also as the great human being that he was."
Claude then said, "Why don't you come to the festival and do a
tribute to him?" And I agreed. Claude spoke to Quincy Jones,
who had been coproducing some previous festivals; he thought
that it was a great idea and I was on my way. My dream had been
to hear a concert in Montreux, not to sing there myself, but I
thought that it could be fun just this one time.

I took two years to make the project happen. I wanted first to
make up a program. Claude had lent me several large cardboard
boxes full of vinyl recordings of Duke Ellington. I listened to
hours of Ellington conducting only his instrumental arrangements
spanning a period of four decades, although none with singers. I
wanted to absorb myself in his musical universe without any vocal
influences. I did not want to even unconsciously copy anyone. I
wanted the inspiration to come directly from Ellington himself.

Claude and I were hoping that I could do the concert with
Oscar Peterson, but he was very ill at the time. Claude suggested
a trio with Monty Alexander on piano, Ira Coleman on bass, and
Ed Thigpen on the drums. Monty lived in Orlando, Florida, and
at Easter time 1994 I was to perform some concerts of American music by Aaron Copland and Samuel Barber with Michael
Tilson-Thomas in Miami (we later recorded them in London).
Before going, Monty and I worked several days together and the
rehearsals went well. I continued to work for the next three months
on my own. We met again to rehearse for a few days in Montreux
before meeting Ira and Ed, who arrived some days before the festival began.

I was a bit nervous for this first encounter with them. Ira was
an in-demand rising star and I knew that Ed had had an illustrious career, playing in the Oscar Peterson Trio for many years and
touring extensively and recording with Ella Fitzgerald. I remember this rehearsal as if it were yesterday. I started the first song,
"Duke's Place," and they were just listening, but by the time I was
finishing the third song I turned toward Ed and saw a big warm
smile on his face—he was enjoying it. I glanced over to Ira and
he too was smiling. I breathed a sigh of relief and continued the
rehearsal feeling that I was on the right track because of the enormous support and encouragement that they gave me.

Next I had to face the Montreux jazz audience. I had been so involved with Duke Ellington and his music that I had not thought at all about the response I might get. I had previously sung "Summertime" from Gershwin's *Porgy and Bess* with orchestra at the festival in a guest appearance for a gala concert some years before. But now I would be stepping into unknown territory as a jazz singer with a new and different audience who had their own specific demands.

I said to myself, "What are you doing? You are not going to be facing your usual affectionate audience, who might indulge your whim to sing jazz. This is an audience who has paid for and expects a jazz performance." Then I thought, "Never mind, this is just a one-off and if they don't like me they can certainly appreciate the wonderful music and the playing of the trio." I have never wasted any time listening to the "noise" in the business so I had no idea nor did I care about what was being said about the fact that I was doing a jazz concert at the festival. But the audience was another matter.

Quincy Jones came to listen to our sound check and when I heard his enthusiastic introduction just before my entrance I felt that he was not just introducing me to the audience but also welcoming me into the jazz family, albeit as a beginner. I was honored to stand on the stage and be a part of such an illustrious tradition even though I never expected to repeat the experience. The concert was a success: the audience seemed to love the show. I had a lot of fun and by the end of the concert I realized that I had felt quite at home with the music and in the context of the jazz festival. Everything about the process from beginning to end had been enjoyable and an enriching learning experience. I wanted to continue to sing jazz regularly for jazz audiences. I knew that I would need the demands of a discerning audience to help me grow and develop into a true jazz artist.

I met the pianist Geoff Keezer in Japan just before a tour that had been organized by my Japanese agent, Mr. Kambara. Kambara told me that when he was a young man he had started his career because of Duke Ellington, who had allowed him to organize his tours in Japan. He wanted to close the circle by organizing a tour of my "Tribute to Duke Ellington" there and it was one of the last tours that he arranged for me before retiring. Some weeks before leaving for Japan Monty called and unexpectedly canceled his appearance on the tour. My agent in Europe suggested the young pianist Geoff Keezer, who was living at the time in Yokohama. I found myself on the way to Japan with Ira and Ed but without knowing anything about our pianist. We arrived in Tokyo a few days early for rehearsals. Monty's cancellation proved to be a wonderful blessing for me. Not only did the tour go well but Geoff and I also started a collaboration that led to nearly forty concerts together and a recording of Gershwin songs that Geoff arranged for orchestra and jazz trio.

Rehearsing and performing jazz became just an extension to the chamber music branch on the tree of my varied repertoire and it was helping me stretch my own musical possibilities. I wanted to sing jazz and with no intention of becoming a "crossover" artist: no jazzy version of Schubert's "Ave Maria." I use my instrument as it is without distorting it while bending it and adjusting it to the stylistic demands of jazz. But that is exactly what I have been doing for years, adapting to the many different styles of classical music that I performed.

Each composer or style has a distinct language. Schubert and Schumann are close but different; the same goes for Debussy and Fauré, or Puccini and Verdi. Each jazz composer also had a language that I wanted to learn and to master.

Ira lived in New York and was just starting a family, Geoff lived in San Francisco, and Ed in Copenhagen. So if I was to continue seriously with jazz I knew that I needed to have more rehearsal time with my musicians than we were physically able to do.

In order for the travel costs from the United States to be covered our agent could only accept tours of three or more concerts in Europe with the trio. During our tour with the Gershwin concert during the summer of 2000 I needed a saxophonist for the concert in Stockholm for the *Porgy and Bess* duets. The producer suggested an up-and-coming young artist named Magnus Lindgren, about whom I had just read an article in a Swedish magazine. During the first rehearsal I was blown away by his sound and his natural dexterity. He was brilliant at the concert and I was thrilled to work with him. Some months later in 2001 I was offered a concert in Holland and the American musicians were not free to come a week earlier to rehearse some new songs for the program beforehand. The promoter could not pay the travel costs for the musicians for just one concert. I called Magnus and asked him if he and his quartet (with Mathias Algotsson on piano, Fredrik Jonsson on bass, and Jonas Holgersson on drums), would like to do it. He answered me immediately, "Yes, sure." Shortly afterward we met and rehearsed and that was the beginning of a new important partnership. We performed close to one hundred concerts together in Canada, Europe, Asia, and North Africa. Over the years I have met and worked with many Swedish artists but the last place I expected to find my jazz and blues musicians was in the north. I was totally unaware of the strong jazz traditions and great musicians who exist there. I knew that France had welcomed jazz and its greats with open arms but the discovery of the Nordic jazz tradition was a welcome surprise that would enlarge my Swedish musical family even more.

I have always had a close relationship to the composers whose music I sing. When I started to enlarge my jazz repertoire I looked into the different composers of the great American songbook, the jazz standards that comprise the major part of a jazz musician's repertoire. Each of them also had a language I wanted to master. The songs were mainly composed for the Broadway musical theater and Hollywood musicals. I had begun with an entire program dedicated to the songs of Duke Ellington, and my next stop was George Gershwin. I had recorded "Summertime" in 1975 and felt that I was not going so far away from familiar repertoire as I set out on this new musical adventure. I continued with songs of Cole Porter and Richard Rodgers, songs that I had heard as I was growing up or had sung in the school choir and with my little jazz trio in Lincoln, Nebraska.

My latest venture has been to go further back to the roots of jazz in order to connect to its deepest traditions. This search led me to the blues. Without realizing it I had already been nurtured on the roots of the blues and jazz as a child in my father's church with the songs of the slaves, my beloved Negro spirituals. These songs are the true roots of this American music that we call jazz. For the first time after nearly ten years of singing jazz I listened again to recordings of jazz singers, searching for songs for the blues project. I felt that I had developed my own way of singing jazz and that there was little chance that I would try to copy or imitate someone else.

The Magnus Lindgren Quartet and I recorded *Barbara Sings the Blues*, my search for the roots of jazz. It is a luxury to have the quartet so close, to be able to rehearse whenever we feel the need, as we continue to evolve together from concert to concert in the perfect chamber music tradition. The blues project took many years to develop in performance as I gradually found my own way into the music. I continue to evolve this project and I have formed a new band, Barbara's Blues Band, with the wonderful and versatile pianist Mathias Algotsson, guitarist Max Shultz or Staffan Astner, bassist Kristian Lind, and drummer Jonas Holgersson. Sometimes when Jonas is not free, drummers Morgan Höglund or Calle Rasmussen have joined us. I heard Staffan play with a good friend, the great American blues and folk singer and guitarist Eric Bibb, in Stockholm and immediately asked him to join us too.

Sometimes I perform my latest program *Blues Everywhere I Go* with only Mathias and Max because this works very well in smaller, more intimate spaces. The entire band plays when we go into large outdoor venues such as the Cognac Blues Festival or in concert halls like the legendary Olympia in Paris. In March 2011, *Blues Everywhere I Go* was the fourth program I performed at the Olympia after Ellington, Gershwin, and *Barbara Sings the Blues* with Magnus Lindgren.

Magnus and I continue to work together and he has revealed to me another aspect of his vast talent. During the recording sessions for the *Barbara Sings the Blues* album I asked him, "Have you ever performed classical music?" He hadn't. "I am the artist in residence this year up in Piteå," I told him, "and one of the concerts that I am doing is an all-Schubert program. The clarinetist that was supposed to perform with me has just canceled on very short notice; would you be interested in performing Schubert's *Der Hirt auf dem Felsen*? Here is the score."

He looked at it during one of the breaks and said, "I would love to try it." He performed the piece as if he had been playing it for years. I was so impressed with his curiosity and ability to step outside of his safe box of being only a jazz musician.

Improvisation is an important part of jazz performance and integrating it into my own performance style has pushed me further, but not only in the jazz repertoire. Whenever I returned to my classical repertoire right after singing a few jazz concerts I felt a new freedom. I saw my recital repertoire and my orchestra repertoire of Berlioz, Strauss, and Mozart concert and opera arias, particularly those with long recitatives such as the long opening recitative of Mozart's *Idomeneo*, in an entirely different light. The dimension of time suddenly became more fluid. I seemed to have more time to pronounce and color the words. This is in part the reward for the time that I have spent with the score during preparation and performance; but spontaneously embellishing during jazz improvisation also opened up an unexplored space from which the interpretation could organically evolve.

Every concert is a unique experience not only for the audience but also for the artist. The performance can never be repeated exactly even though the score is set. But in jazz and baroque improvisation I never sing exactly the same thing. I listened to several different recordings of Ella Fitzgerald singing the same song on different occasions and the improvisations were absolutely identical. It was remarkable and I don't know how she did that, because the only way that I can improvise is to allow the music to come out freely, and I am surprised myself where it leads me.

The flexibility and freedom in the performance of baroque music is quite similar to jazz improvisation. I made my American and European opera debuts singing in baroque operas: Cavalli, Monteverdi, and Gluck; and among my first recordings were Handel's *Serse* and Vivaldi arias with La Grande Écurie et la Chambre du Roy conducted by Jean-Claude Malgoire for Sony.

During my studies at the Juilliard School I met and worked with Albert Fuller, the harpsichord professor and a major force in the baroque music revival at the very beginning of the international movement, to bring back this rich and neglected repertoire into the mainstream of classical music. In 1972 he invited me to sing with him the first Aston Magna Festival that still takes place in Great Barrington, Massachusetts, an idyllic setting in the Berkshires. The local residents were apprehensive when they heard about this new festival. No one knew what "baroque" meant and if they had looked the word up in the Merriam-Webster dictionary they would have found "characterized by grotesqueness, extravagance, complexity or flamboyance," or in the American Heritage dictionary, "extravagant or bizarre," and better yet the 1913 version of Webster's, "in bad taste, grotesque, odd." Maybe they expected long-haired hippies playing some kind of "ba-rock" music. However, the quality of the concerts of the festival obviously overcame these initial prejudices since Aston Magna is now the oldest annual summer festival in the United States dedicated to the performance of classical and baroque music performed on period instruments. I went back often after that opening season to sing the works of Purcell, Handel, and Rameau.

I am very grateful for the scholarship of the baroque specialists who followed Albert Fuller but I had little use for their sectarian activism because each camp claimed to know the whole truth about performance practices. For me making music is about communication and openness. I found little pleasure in working with conductors who considered that all music composed after Mozart and before Schönberg was vulgarity personified and that other specialists were to be dismissed as dilettantes. I slowly gave up the baroque repertoire, the songs and arias I had performed in Great Barrington. I made one exception: Bach. I cannot live without singing Bach and I continued to do so, although with modern instruments, recording with Håkan Hardenberger for EMI in East Germany. The dust has now settled in the baroque world and some of these same sectarian musicians are now conducting repertoire that they used to consider to be vulgar, such as Verdi's Requiem and the *Symphonie Fantastique* by Berlioz.

The Drottningholms Barockensemble has become the latest addition to my Swedish musical family. It is a small orchestra consisting of about twenty musicians led by their first violinist, Nils-Erik Sparf. The orchestra's knowledgeable harpsichordist Björn Gäfvert has been a great help to me with the specific performance practice of baroque music. The orchestra plays without a conductor and our performances together are pure chamber music with the first violin or I taking the lead when necessary.

We recorded two CDs for my label Arte Verum, one dedicated to Purcell and Handel and the other of Pergolesi's *Stabat Mater,* which had brought me to Paris in 1976. Every year we perform many concerts in Europe together and since 2010 have produced a Christmas concert, "Let There Be Peace on Earth." The concert is sent live to cinemas in the Nordic countries and features guest artists such as the Swedish actors Michael Nyqvist and Anita Wall, or the American Eric Bibb. Since 2012 the concert has taken place in Stockholm's Stadshuset the weekend following the Nobel ceremonies.

It was probably a good thing that I had been singing jazz for more than ten years when I came back to the baroque repertoire having acquired a natural freedom to improvise. I had always composed my own cadenzas for Mozart arias and now I really had fun to see how the improvisation developed with every performance.

Singing in the choir has been one of my greatest joys since I was ten years old. My repertoire is full of great choral masses, requiems, and passions and I still enjoy singing with choirs as much as when I was a child.

The first time that I worked with Eric Ericson was in the late 1980s when he invited me to sing a concert in Falun, Sweden, with the Swedish male a cappella choir Orphei Dränger (OD). At that time Eric was their principal conductor. The choir invited me back to Sweden to perform with them in one of their annual Caprice Concerts at the university in Uppsala. In 1993 Toni Morrison received the Nobel Prize in literature and I was the guest artist for the traditional Nobel concert the evening before and during the Nobel ceremony together with the Stockholm Philharmonic. I topped off the Nobel festivities with OD, who asked me to sing some Swedish folksongs with them during the banquet.

Eric Ericson was a giant in the choral music world; most other choral conductors considered him the unsurpassed master, known as an innovator of choral singing and repertoire. I am only one of a multitude of musicians whose lives he touched and to whom he was an inspiration. I remember that Riccardo Muti told me that he did not want anyone other than Eric to be in charge of the choir whenever he performed or recorded a choral work. I was very fortunate to work with Eric on two recordings: *Sacred Music* and my first Christmas album.

Eric lived right across the street from Martin's parents. I had just to walk a few steps to meet him whenever we were preparing for a recording or a concert tour. We were very happy with the Christmas recording and decided to do a concert of the program. He conducted the first of two sold-out Christmas concerts at Stockholm's Globe Arena in 1994. We toured that Christmas concert with orchestra, his choir, and a children's choir in 1996 to Denmark, France, Germany, Austria, and Finland, where I met my husband Ulf.

I was very happy with the concerts and recording of Negro spirituals that I had done with Dmitri Alexeev. But I longed to get back to the a cappella tradition that I had learned in my father's church and in my junior and high school choirs. Since so many people, especially in Europe, confuse Negro spirituals with gospel singing I also wanted to make the distinction. The former sprung up out of the souls of the American slaves, sung in harmony, a cappella, and was transmitted orally from generation to generation. The latter has its roots in the spirituals but began later in the 1920s as an expression of life in the Jim Crow South. I was in Atlanta, Georgia, to sing Strauss's *Vier letzte Lieder* with the Atlanta Symphony and the radio in my hotel room was as usual tuned to National Public Radio. A concert of Negro spirituals was already underway when I put the radio on. Although I did not hear who the performers were, I did hear the choral sound that I had been longing for. After some research I found out that it was the Moses Hogan Singers from New Orleans. I contacted Moses and asked if he and the choir would be interested in performing and recording with me. We recorded the album *Give Me Jesus* in New York City and did two European tours together. I was really happy to be back in the bosom of the songs of my youth and the roots of my people. Moses had devoted his life to keeping the Negro spiritual alive and he managed this with simple yet effective arrangements. Sadly, Moses died suddenly from a brain tumor at the age of forty-five and his choir ceased to exist. I did not want to give up singing this repertoire with choir so I have been performing it with a Swedish choir. I had performed a few spirituals with OD on the *Sacred Music* album with Eric Ericson; Gustaf Sjökvist, the music director at Storkyrkan in Stockholm, agreed to teach his choir the songs and this led to many concerts together. My latest expansion of this repertoire has been with Eric Bibb.

Destiny had led me to Sweden where I have found love and family but it has also given me a wonderful big musical family of great inspiring artists. I have always only wanted to work with musicians whom I appreciated not only as musicians but also as human beings, without endless and ego-boosting musicological discussions. We are able to develop a kind of musical telepathy that allows true moments of grace to occur.

Behind the Scenes 10

When I sing, I don't want them to see that my face is black. I don't want them to see that my face is white. I want them to see my soul. And that is colorless.

—Marian Anderson

My entire being is my instrument, not just the area around my vocal chords. I have always sought a holistic approach to my vocal health by trying to maintain an equilibrium between the mental, physical, emotional, and spiritual aspects of my being. I try to lead a healthy life by being physically active, eating healthy foods, and being in positive company. I choose to spend time with, work with, and eat meals with people that I love and admire. Flying, changing one's environment often, air conditioning, and, of course, air pollution can cause problems for a singer. I have some simple allergies that I would not even notice if I had another profession. However, I am immediately aware of the big blob of mucus forming near my windpipe just waiting to fall onto my vocal chords during a concert or recording. I have tried different solutions such as giving up dairy products and cheese some days before a concert. This is a real sacrifice for me because I love cheese. But I have come to accept that phlegm is an occupational hazard and I have become very adept at navigating around it.

I listen to my body and really try to respect what I hear. When it is time to stop and rest I must do so, but this has not always been easy for me. I tried to fit the image that my generation of feminists imposed on itself—of the superwoman who is also a perfect wife, mother, and professional. I also had to overcome the strict Protestant upbringing and work ethic that made me feel guilty about taking time off for myself. With the encouragement of my husband Ulf, I am learning to slow down and to simply enjoy gazing into the sunset. I give one hundred percent of myself to everything that I do at home, on stage, and as a citizen of the world, but in order to be able to give to others I must not neglect to give to myself the opportunity to replenish my core being. I have been practicing yoga on and off since I was a student and have recently taken it up again and practice almost daily. Just being in nature and soaking in its splendor has also been an important healing meditation for me. My instrument is a gift that came with a responsibility to serve it. I have treated it like precious capital, have nurtured it and allowed it to grow. It has given me dividends that can be measured neither in success nor celebrity. For more than a half a century it has allowed me to be in communion with that which is divine in our human existence through unique peak experiences. Having this talent means that I have been chosen to serve a most noble cause: art. And I have strived in all that I do to earn the right to be worthy to serve.

I began my career singing with major orchestras in major cities and at the same time with Community Concerts in some of the smallest towns in the country. I have kept this balance between big cities and small towns throughout my career. I could not live only on a diet of the major capitals of the world. I need to go to the people with my music.

I am often asked, "Why have you chosen to come to sing for us in such a small town?" The answer is simple. I tell them, "First, because you have invited me to come, and second, because I need to come to you in order to share the music that I sing with as many people as I can." I have experienced some of the most unforgettable concerts in the most unexpected places. I sang my first recital in the Eastern Bloc in 1977 in Dresden, East Germany. The hall was packed, but it could not have been because of me: I was completely unknown. It had to be because there was a real collective need to experience the music as food for the soul. It made life there a little more bearable. I asked to return every year to give concerts behind the Iron Curtain because I in turn needed to have contact with an audience for whom music was a necessity. These visits were difficult and paid very little but I gained so much and could see that I was fulfilling a higher purpose rather than my own aggrandizement.

Singers seem to be at the mercy of their health. A drafty room or a sneeze on an airplane can jeopardize an entire production. I have been blessed with a very solid constitution. I think of myself like an athlete and try to take care of my health holistically, for both my body and soul comprise my instrument. I have rarely had to cancel performances, and only on one occasion have I announced to the audience that I was ill, although this is a common practice in the opera world ("Mme X is indisposed tonight but will sing anyway"). If I am too sick to sing then I cancel because I don't want to make the audience nervous for me and often they cannot even hear that I am not well. I sang with a soprano in Berlin who had a habit of announcing that she was indisposed, especially when the press was in the audience. I never took her seriously because I never detected that she had even the slightest cold.

I sang the small role of Amore in Gluck's *Orfeo ed Euridice* in Amsterdam at the Holland Festival in 1974. Although Amore has only one aria to sing, the stage director, Rhoda Levine, had staged me in every scene from the beginning to the end. I fell ill after the opening performance and was really unable to sing, but I felt that I could not cancel because the performance would have to be canceled. There was no understudy and a replacement would have not been able to learn all of the intricate staging in time. An announcement was made and I walked through my part and the orchestra skipped over my aria.

Speaking of Amsterdam and being sick, I was to make my recital debut there in the 1980s accompanied by András Schiff. I remembered the story that Miss Tourel had told me about her recital debut there, where there was hardly any audience. The reviews the next day were so fantastic that the promoter asked her to stay to do the recital again the following weekend, and of course it was to a full house. I arrived two days before the recital and fell ill on the evening of my arrival with a high fever and a very sore throat. I did not know what to do. The concert was to be broadcast live on the radio. I went to see a throat doctor who said that if I stayed very quiet that I might be able to sing the following day. The next day I went to rehearse on stage in the Concertgebouw. Martin and Daniel Toscan du Plantier were with me and each said after listening to the rehearsal that they could hardly hear that I was sick. I decided to sing the concert.

Just as I was waiting to go on stage I heard an announcement. András Schiff was not playing on a Bösendorfer but a Steinway. (He had a contract with Bösendorfer but was unhappy with the piano that was delivered to the hall.) I thought to myself, I hardly have one working vocal chord and he has to announce this about his piano? At least he has a piano. Near the end of the concert I started to cough uncontrollably and when I tried to speak to the audience to say that I needed to go out to get some water they heard that I could barely speak. In fact, I said to them, "This is probably the first time that the singer coughs more and louder than the audience." I returned to the stage and finished the concert and was even able to sing one encore to a standing ovation, but Amsterdam audiences are known to be generous with standing ovations.

I have never canceled an engagement to take on something that might have been better or more prestigious. Riccardo Muti once called me to do four performances and a DVD of *Le Nozze di Figaro* at La Scala. I was free for all the performances except the first; I had a recital in Zug, Switzerland. I asked to change the date but it was not possible. I called Riccardo and said, "I am so sorry not to be able to sing *Figaro* with you again but I hope you understand that I cannot cancel in this small town, even to sing with you at La Scala." As it turned out, the orchestra went on strike and the first three performances were canceled.

When I leave my hotel room on my way to a performance, I am focused and not at all accessible to anyone who is not directly involved in the work that I am on my way to do. I do not want to make small talk in the hotel lobby nor sign autographs outside the stage door. I do not want anyone to see me in my costume or concert dress before going on stage. These hours before the performance belong to me and although I can joke around with the musicians I am rather closed to others.

The last thing I want on the way to the concert is to be tortured by the horrible pandemic of noise impersonating as music that plagues us everywhere we go. I ask taxi drivers to please turn off the radio when I am on my way to a concert. We are innundated nearly everywhere with a horrendous noise pollution that is undemocratic and frustrating—even on the beach, on the ski slopes, and places where we should be enjoying the beauty of nature. I sang a very complicated program in Torino once, and after an intense dress rehearsal with the orchestra I left with my mind filled with diverse arias in several styles and languages. I went back to my hotel to eat lunch but already in the lobby I felt aggressed by the loud music that managed to beat the simplest tune from my head. I went to the restaurant, and it was even worse. I had to go to my room and order room service in order to not go mad. How and why has this happened? When many different persons, each with his or her own musical taste, are gathered in a public space, who gets to decide that each person must listen to the same music. Who is this cruel dictator? I have refused to eat dinner after a concert in a restaurant that plays music and I have walked out of shops that play music without buying anything. I cannot take it anymore. Is there some conspiracy to make it impossible for people to speak to one another, for one to think or just let one's mind wander? I can imagine that poor composers must find their creativity shut off when they go out in public. This constant aural pollution is almost like torture, and the only way to fight back seems to be to stay at home and hope and pray that the cruel dictator will soon decide that silence is a necessity. Then we can fill our brains with whatever noise we choose. I hope this will happen sooner rather than later. I feel that people are losing their capacity to listen during a concert because they hear too much constant noise. Silence may be one of our last luxuries.

In Carcassonne, France, in 1982, five minutes before the beginning of the concert, I was already standing backstage with the pianist, Michel Béroff to prepare for our entrance when a man approached me and asked if he could take my photo for the local newspaper. I said, ""Here and now? I am going on stage soon." He insisted, so I said, "OK, take it quickly please." He then said, "No, no I want a photo of you standing in front of the piano." I said, "The audience is already in the hall and that is impossible. If you must have that exact photo I can do it at the end of the concert." He looked at me as if I was an idiot and said, "Madame, I have no intentions to stay for the concert." So I said, "In that case take your photo now or leave without it."

This episode should have prepared me for what was to come; some photographers who come to take photos at a concert are insensitive to the audience, to me, and above all to the music.

During one concert in Spain, the photographer walked all over the hall during the first three songs of Strauss's *Vier letzte Lieder.* I turned from side to side in order to avoid seeing him. I finally had to close my eyes in order to concentrate. I opened them during the last of the four songs, "Im Abendrot," the most delicate and moving of the four. I could not believe what I saw; he had placed himself in the middle of the center aisle and just one minute before the end he noisily packed up his equipment and left the hall.

After that experience it became clear to me that I had to control photographers during my concerts. At the Verbier Festival I was very strict with a very insensitive photographer who was always disturbing the artists backstage and during their rehearsals. One evening his wife met me backstage just before my concert and said, "I hope that you will let my husband do his work tonight." I answered, "If your husband does not get in the way of me doing my work tonight then he is more than welcome to do his."

I try to be accommodating and give them permission to take photos during a limited amount of time during my concerts, but they must respect my instructions and are forewarned that if they do not I will stop singing and order them to leave the hall because I can't let them destroy the entire concert for everyone. I find it hard to believe that someone who does not have any respect for me or any interest whatsoever in what I do would even want to take my picture.

At an outdoor concert in the south of France all of the photographers left after the first aria, except one woman who noisily continued to take photos during the entire first half of the concert. At the intermission I told the promoter to ask her to leave. She was still there when I came back but did not have her camera out. As soon as I opened my mouth to sing, however, she started again. I tapped the conductor on his shoulder and stopped the concert. "Madame, you have disturbed me and the audience around you throughout the entire first half of the concert. Now I want you to leave the venue." She packed her camera and sat down where she was on the steps. I said, "I did not ask you to pack away your equipment but to leave the venue now or I will not sing another note." She reluctantly left, accompanied by the tumultuous applause of the audience.

I was the guest editor for a local newspaper in France and had a great time working all day with their photographer. He was covering the festival where I had several concerts and he said, "I know that you do not allow photographers in your concerts. You are very hard on us poor photographers; but you needn't worry, I will take a photo where you look good." I explained to him, "This has nothing to do with my vanity, this is about my work. I strive to be as professional as you and to give my best every time that I am on stage. Unfortunately, too many of your colleagues are insensitive, disrespectful, and/or deaf, so I cannot take a chance any longer. My principal goal is to sing a good concert for my audience. The audience and I need to be able to concentrate on the music without distraction. Your goals and mine do not coincide, they collide. So the best thing for me is to say no to all: the good, the bad and the ugly."

Maybe it is my strict Protestant upbringing, but I am not taken in by flattery. I tend to run as far as I can from those who attempt it. However, genuine comments that come from the heart touch me deeply and encourage me to continue. After a concert in Carnegie Hall, a young African American man in his thirties approached me timidly and said, "Your voice brought me back to life." I looked at him astonished and speechless. He continued, "I was lying in the hospital in a coma for many months. My friends brought me some of your recordings and played them nonstop. When I awoke after some weeks it was your voice, your instantly recognizable voice, that was the first thing that I heard. I wanted to share this with you." When he finished I had tears in my eyes. I hugged him and thanked him for the gift that he had given to me.

I receive so many wonderful and thoughtful remarks from members of the audience who have been moved by the concert and have felt a strong connection to something powerful yet intangible in the music. I am genuinely touched by sincere expressions of affection that have nothing to do with "stargazing" and blind admiration.

I can compliment myself when I have learned something difficult or have finally achieved something that I had been working toward for a long time—and then I feel joy.

After a concert in Los Angeles a friend of mine who had come backstage remarked, "You have already changed back to your clothes. I work a lot with musicians and I have never seen someone change as quickly as you do. Why do you do that?" I had never given it any thought before she mentioned it. I imagine that I need to get back as quickly as possible from the world of the stage, to leave behind the ephemeral trappings such as applause, so as not to confuse the performer with the person in the dressing room. Backstage I become Barbara, a real person, not a role. As closed as I can be before a performance, I am just as open afterward to meet and speak to audience members who ask me to sign autographs or records. When I sign I try to take the time to look at the person before writing his or her name. I do not have fanatical groupies following me but I do have many loyal fans who have been coming to my concerts for more than thirty years. I am always happy to see them after a concert and we greet one another as old friends, but they have always respected my privacy.

After meeting the audience I always look forward to a meal: a natural ending to my evening with good food, good wine, and good friends.

Before coming to New York I thought that an artist's relation to reviews was similar to what I had seen in films about performers waiting in a restaurant until the wee hours of the morning for the verdict of the critics that would spell success or immediate failure.

But the reality is entirely different. Critics' reviews can have an effect on the career of an artist, especially when she is unknown, but should never, ever affect her artistic evolution. CAMI always wanted quotes from reviews on the artist brochures, but I said, "If you take the good ones seriously then you must take all of the bad ones seriously as well and I am not interested in quoting any of them."

A review of my performance is totally useless in teaching me about myself. Reviews reveal so much more about the reviewer than they do about the artists. Until her death Miss Tourel was my most demanding critic, and since then I have had to assume that task myself. I learned during my first year as a professional singer that a review was not the right criteria to determine how well I had done my work, whether I had done what I had set out to do. I know my repertoire and I know when I have done my best work.

There are many stories about critics who have reviewed an artist who had canceled and not the one who performed. I remember a scandal in Switzerland. The reviewer from a Geneva newspaper wrote a scathing review about a pianist: "Mr. X played Beethoven as if it were salon music." The pianist in question had not played Beethoven, he had played Chopin, and an announcement was made at the beginning of the concert. Either the reviewer was not present at the concert or he could not hear the difference between Beethoven and Chopin!

Early Sunday morning December 22, 1988, the ringing of the phone awakened me. It was my friend Lorraine Nubar. "Have you seen today's *New York Times*?" she asked me.

"No, I haven't, why?"

She said, "I am sorry to call so early but I wanted to talk to before you saw the unusually nasty and untrue review of your performance of Susanna at the Met. I am absolutely furious because it is completely false. You would think that he was paid to do such a review. In any case I wanted to let you know before you read it alone in your apartment."

"Thanks, Lorraine, I'll get the paper and call you back."

I got out of bed and went to the front door and took up the paper. My performance had been at the beginning of the week and I had not even thought about a coming review.

I fetched the paper and went straight to the culture section and read the review. Lorraine was right. It was cruel and unjust. I felt as if I had received a heavy blow in my stomach. But when I turned to the first section of the paper to read the news I immediately called Lorraine back.

"Hi, I just read it and you are right, it is pretty awful. But have you seen the front page of the paper?"

Pan Am flight 103 was totally destroyed by a bomb over Lockerbie, Scotland, killing all 243 passengers and 16 crew on the plane and 11 persons on the ground.

"You know Lorraine, I am probably going to feel a little bad about the gratuitous meanness of the review until around lunchtime but those who are at JFK airport this morning waiting to greet loved ones coming home for Christmas will never recover from their loss. Let's meet for lunch and put this review, like all reviews, in the perspective that they deserve in our lives."

On Monday night she and I went to a concert at Alice Tully Hall. As we were leaving she whispered to me, "Barbara, that's him, that's him."

"That's who?" I said.

"The *New York Times* reviewer."

He was slight, had thinning hair, wore very thick glasses, and did not look like a happy person. I started to laugh and said, "You see, Lorraine, his review is as insignificant as his appearance. I almost feel sorry for him. I will go on to do my best in my next performance, just as I did in my last one."

I do need to hear an honest evaluation of my work from those persons who follow my progress, but not from someone who hears me during one concert from time to time or maybe even only once in my career and who is looking for something to criticize. It is essential to hear the opinion of someone who understands my goals and values and has true knowledge of the music that I sing. I receive these true evaluations from other musicians with whom I work and especially from those who have followed my career over many years. Miss Tourel told me, "Always keep your blinders on; don't listen to those who are incapable of teaching you something."

I imagine that critics serve some purpose and I do not want to do away with them. But I only wish that they would see that they have the possibility to inspire interest in live concerts and not just to find something wrong with the performer. Negative and mean reviews discourage readers and can kill their desire to go hear concerts.

After an Alice Tully Hall recital in New York, Ralf Gothoni and I went on to London to Wigmore Hall. The program was Schubert, Strauss, Debussy, and Poulenc. It was one of those rare concerts where from the first note to the last we felt completely in the zone. We did everything that we had wanted to do and the audience was with us from beginning to end. We both felt as if we had really established a strong bond between the audience and the music. They gave us a rousing ovation at the end of the concert and we performed at least seven encores. Martin was not in London for the concert; we were to meet at the Amsterdam airport the next morning to go to Moscow for a recital there with Dmitri Alexeev on my way to Japan for a recital tour. I wanted to share with Martin what I had felt about the concert the night before but I could not just say, "I was great," because so much more had taken place. While I was waiting for him in the airport I stupidly decided to buy an English paper. The review was bad. I thought to myself, That's OK, I will get another one. I bought two more papers and it was farcical because one was worse than the other and they contradicted each other. One said that I did not know anything about Schubert but Debussy was fine, the other said that my French was not at all idiomatic but my German was good. I sat with these papers in front of me and began to laugh out loud. They were absurd. But then I read from the one that disliked me the most: "It seemed that I was among the few persons in the hall that was not under the spell of Miss Hendricks and Mr. Gothoni last night but I suppose it was her pleasing appearance." Something extraordinary had happened during the concert and he, the expert, had obviously felt completely left out; he could hardly contain his frustration. I understood that he and the audience did not have the same purpose for being at the concert and that he had not been able to tell the audience beforehand what they should think. We artists do not need the critics in order to exist—but they do need us.

The audience never sees many of the people who are active behind the scenes in a musician's life. Before arriving on the stage to perform a concert we have to go through teachers, agents and managers, as well as theater, opera, and orchestra directors. Fortunately for me many directors of orchestras and opera houses with whom I have worked think for themselves and do not need to read a review to know if an artist has performed well or not. They are the ones who care about nurturing young artists, not using them up and squeezing them dry before throwing them away. I worked often with Raymond Duffault, director of the Avignon Opera and the Chorégies d'Orange, where I regularly sang operas, concerts, and recitals. I developed an artistic relationship not only with Raymond and the public of Orange but also with the people of Provence. In 1995 the Conseil Général de Vaucluse informed me that after an election of the students, the new college (junior high school) was to be called Le Collège Barbara Hendricks if I accepted. I was very touched that the students, ages twelve to fourteen, had chosen my name among the other candidates who were dead French white males. In the spring of 1995 the adults of Orange chose their mayor from the far right xenophobic party Le Front National. There was much discussion about whether I would accept, but I could not let the students down. I have kept in close contact with the school and visit it regularly.

Jean-Pierre Brossman became one of my most active supporters. There was a kind of anti-star attitude in some opera houses in France but Jean-Pierre was interested in having artists and had nothing against one who also had become a star. The collaboration with him and the Opéra de Lyon was the most valuable to my evolution in my operatic career. He was a director whose healthy philosophy about developing young talents was coupled with a knowledge and love of music and musicians that was rare and overrode the "talk and gossip" that came from Paris.

I started in Lyon with Donizetti's Norina in *Don Pasquale* in 1990 in a coproduction with the Aix-en-Provence Festival and La Fenice in Venice, with Gino Quilico and Luca Canonici from the *La bohème* film cast and the incomparable Gabriel Bacquier in the title role.

When we were making plans about the next production in Lyon of Donizetti's *L'elisir d'amore* Martin said to me, "Maybe you should do *La bohéme* instead." Alain Lanceron, the head of EMI France, echoed this sentiment. I assumed that Jean-Pierre had changed his mind and I called him to ask what was going on. He said that Martin and Alain were worried because I had received bad reviews for the performance in Aix from some of the Parisian press. They did not want me to take a chance with another Donizetti role. I thought to myself, How bad can the reviews be? I knew that I had sung well and that the audience had liked our performances. It had been many years since I had bought music magazines or read reviews of my performances, so I asked Alain to send me copies of the reviews in question. One said that I was an ideal Mozart singer but that I lacked the legato for the bel canto repertoire. This didn't even make sense—how could Martin and Alain take this seriously? Another said, "Singing Norina is the biggest faux pas of her career." You would have thought that I had sung Wagner's Isolde. I asked Alain, "What do *you* think? You tried to get the recording away from Erato after hearing the performance in Lyon!" He could not answer me. However, he had planted the seeds of doubt in my mind. I called Gino at home in Canada—he had sung Malatesta in Lyon and in Aix—and Lorraine, because she had heard the performance in Aix. I knew that I could always count on them to tell me the complete truth. Both assured me that I could be proud of my performance. Finally I asked Jean-Pierre, "What is your opinion?" He said, "I loved your portrayal of Norina. I listen to the recording for my own pleasure and you can sing whatever you want, Adina or Mimì or both." I sang Adina and had great fun with Gino and Gabriel.

Singing Norina and Adina enabled me to grow as a singer and actress. I will never leave it up to critics to determine how I should evolve. I was so grateful to have the invaluable support from Jean-Pierre at a time when I was feeling down and most alone. I began to think that I was traveling on a different path from Alain professionally and from Martin spiritually.

Jean-Pierre asked me to sing Antonia from *Les Contes d'Hoffmann* for the reopening of the opera house in Lyon in 1993 after its renovation. The cast included a young debutante, Natalie Dessay, and José van Dam, who like me was a kind of honorary member of the ensemble at the Lyon Opera. In 1997 I sang *La bohème* with his young ensemble. I had always refused to be a permanent member of an opera house but I was proud to be a part of an opera house that had an intelligent and artistic policy that coincided with my beliefs about opera, music, and art.

Just a few years ago, my mother-in-law, Margareta, asked me worriedly after a recital with Roland Pöntinen at Konserthus in Stockholm, "Barbara, was your recital amplified?"

"No, of course not, why?"

"Well, I did not want to say anything to you but I read a rather unkind review in *Svenska Dagbladet* yesterday that said that the only reason that one could hear you in your diminishing vocal condition was because you were using a mike."

"Critics, Margareta, you should never waste time reading them! Although he should hear the difference between an amplified sound and a real sound, he actually gave me the biggest compliment. This article is more about his preconceived ideas and shows his musical snobbery and ignorance."

Neither the existence nor the nonexistence of critics should concern the artist. The media obviously believe that they serve some purpose but teaching an artist about whom she is or should be is not it.

In 2000, when the Juilliard School gave me an honorary doctorate degree, I was chosen to give the commencement speech to the graduating class; I spoke about critics:

Classical art, whether it be literature, music, dance, theater, or the plastic arts, is being forced into a "culture ghetto" where it is less accessible and diminished in its impact on the lives of the majority of the members of the community. Art should not only be used as a showcase for tourists but is the heart and soul of the community and should participate in the enrichment of the lives of all. It is becoming more difficult every day to fight against the tendency to concede to the prevalent theory that art should be managed like a commodity that fluctuates on the stock market, dictated by a demand that has been influenced and manipulated by media pressure and hype. What shall you do with the legacy that you have been given in today's world? How will you continue to reach out while maintaining your artistic integrity?

You have your task before you and I challenge you to take risks and to dare:

Dare to know yourself and to be true to who you are.

Dare to live, to experience life fully, to love, to feel.

Dare to stay curious about every aspect of life and art, not only your own discipline.

Dare to give up the cherished outcome of becoming the next Heifetz, Nurejev, Toscanini, or Callas.

Dare to become yourself, the one and only you, wherever your path may lead.

Dare to refuse to take shortcuts and the easy way even when the pressure from agents, record companies, and the like seem too strong to resist. We have yet to invent a substitute for time.

Dare to challenge the false premise that life and art are competitive sports. We are only in competition with the best of ourselves.

Dare to put yourself in constant question.

Dare to be vulnerable, it will keep you receptive.

Dare to be an informed, participating citizen, respecting the rights of all with whom you come in contact.

Freedom is not given but earned by constant vigilance.

Above all, seek the truth and speak it from your hearts, have faith and never lose sight of the power of love.

Cinema 11

There is no end, there is no beginning. There is only the infinite passion for life.

—Federico Fellini

My love affair with the cinema dates back to Chattanooga, Tennessee, when as an adolescent I went up to the balcony reserved for "Colored Only" for the first time with my friends, a bag of popcorn, and a soft drink. We waited in the darkened theater with great anticipation for the magic to begin. The seventh art took us on many journeys far away from Chattanooga and made us believe that countless possibilities were waiting for us, yet to be discovered. I continued to find great films from all over the world at U of N, in New York, and of course in Paris.

In 1980 the director Jean-Jacques Beineix sent me the script of his first feature film, *Diva*, and asked me to play the role of Cynthia Hawkins, an American opera singer who had always refused to record her repertoire. One of her most enthusiastic fans was young Jules, who not only had made a clandestine recording of the diva during one of her performances but also had stolen an evening gown from her dressing room. The story becomes more complicated for Jules when a prostitute places a tape of her recorded testimony against a corrupt police chief in the bag of his scooter just before being murdered. I read the script and liked it but I did not think that it was a good idea for me to play the role of an opera diva in a film before I had established my own professional identity as a singer, so I reluctantly refused. When the film was released I saw it and loved it; it looked like it had been so much fun to do. The film was not an immediate success in France: it was dismissed by the critics and only played in one cinema in Paris. But news of the film spread by word of mouth; it soon became a cult film, eventually receiving four Césars (the French Oscars); and it went on to have a big success in the United States. I met Jean-Jacques at the Cannes Festival some years later and I told him, "I enjoyed the film very much and am truly flattered that you wrote the screenplay with me in mind. I hope that you understand my reasons for refusing it at that time. However, now that my own audience knows who I am I know that I could act the role of a singer without the audience confusing that character with me. If you ever think about doing a sequel or the *Daughter of Diva* I would be delighted to do it."

My decision to not accept the role was based purely on not wanting to have to fight for the rest of my career against the image of the opera singer depicted in the film and to be known as "the girl who played in *Diva*." As it turned out, so many people think that it was I who performed in the film that I have given up saying, "No, it wasn't me," to people who say, "Oh, you were in *Diva*. I loved the film." I just say, "Thank you very much."

I was in Milano for a recital at La Scala when I discovered in the cultural pages of *Le Figaro* an article entitled, " 'My Next Opera Film Will Be Puccini's *La bohème* with Barbara Hendricks as Mimì and Placido Domingo as Rodolfo,' Says Daniel Toscan du Plantier"; the article was accompanied by a photo of me and Placido Domingo. This was news to me. I had seen Toscan du Plantier on the television and had found him arrogant and full of himself. I later met him briefly at a reception after a concert of the Brahms Requiem, conducted by James Conlon at the Basilique St Denis just outside Paris. He had asked me what my next opera projects were and I answered that I had plans to sing Mimì in Avignon the following year. I was shocked to see this interview with him. How dare he announce this without first asking me if I wanted to sing the role or if I wanted to work with him? I asked for a meeting with him upon my return to Paris. He received me in his office in Paris and I let him do all the talking—from what I had seen of him on the television he liked the sound of his own voice. He began to explain to me very seriously why he wanted me to play Mimì. He described to me the qualities that he had seen and heard in my performance of the aria in the Brahms Requiem. He spoke about the character of Mimì, describing her to me and then describing me to me! He spoke about me and my vocal sound almost as if he were speaking to a third person, saying, "Of course you can sing the role well but you have so much more to offer than just a beautiful voice. You have a singular voice that is immediately recognizable after you have sung only two notes—and a strong stage presence. You have the capacity and intelligence to incarnate the emotional and inner life of Mimì perfectly. The expression that you have comes from within and this is ideal for the camera. These are the reasons why you are my only choice to play and sing the role of Mimì in my film of *La bohème*." He was not talking about typecasting—I did not resemble Mimì physically—but he thought that I could act the role. I did not say much because I was very moved, not for the compliments that I had received but because he saw me as an artist—or at least he saw the seed of the kind of artist into which I was striving to grow. I thanked him and left his office quietly. No stage director had ever spoken to me in those terms and only Karajan had ever inferred my interpretive qualities when speaking about me. I was speechless and I knew that I absolutely wanted to work with him.

Daniel had not yet chosen the director so he sent me to New York to meet Woody Allen, with whom he had discussed the project. I spent an afternoon talking to him about *La bohème* and Mimì. He was very interested and I believe that he was tempted to take on the project, but he finally turned down the offer.

Daniel then decided that it was maybe better to have a director who spoke Italian and asked the great Italian filmmaker Luigi Comencini; the latter liked the idea and agreed to meet with us. I went to Venice with Daniel to meet Comencini for the first time. Although we spoke very little about the opera and the role of

Mimì it was clear at the end of that dinner that Comencini would be our director.

When it was announced that Comencini had cast a black soprano as Mimì for the film it created a bit of an uproar in Italy. Daniel told me laughingly that Franco Zeffirelli had actually said that the only reason that Daniel wanted a black Mimì was to help sell the opera film in African cinemas (indeed, given the abundance of cinemas in Africa)! Comencini diffused all the criticism when he responded in an interview during a press conference in Rome, "Oh, is she black? I never noticed that she was black! She is my Mimì and the color of her skin has no bearing on her work or her capacity to portray her character."

Daniel and Comencini chose the youthful José Carreras to play Rodolfo. Although I have always preferred baritones to tenors, José's singing has moved me since the first time I heard him, when he sang a wonderful Nemorino from Donizetti's *L'elisir d'amore* at the Met (I was at Juilliard then; I had later sung Micaëla to his Don José in Bizet's *Carmen* in the summer of 1984 at the Chorégies d'Orange). Gino Quilico, the most beautiful baritone voice of his generation and a great natural actor, was to sing Marcello. He had sung Mercutio with me in *Roméo et Juliette* at the Paris Opera in 1982. By some unbelievable coincidence James Conlon, who had conducted my performance at Juilliard and the Brahms Requiem that Daniel had heard, was chosen to conduct. The first step was to record the soundtrack over which we would act.

Even though I had often sung Mimì before, it had been at least twelve years since the last time. I approached the score as if I were seeing it for the first time. I looked very closely at Mimì's words and at Puccini's setting of her music. She is an independent and strong woman who loves life. She is not the pitiful, weak victim she is often portrayed as. She is active and decisive: she arrives in the first act, leaves in the third, and returns in the fourth all at her own will. Mimì is never sentimental nor self-indulgent about her fate; she accepts it and tries to make the best of it. She is the only one of the "bohemians" that has steady work and her lines are even more poetic than those of her young beloved Rodolfo, a struggling poet. I spent six months getting to know her better—her language and her way of expressing herself. Some singers and conductors do Puccini a great disservice by not respecting his exact indications, especially the *a tempo* after the *ritardando*; this makes the music sentimental and diminishes its true emotions. I was studying some Schumann lieder at the same time and I noticed that Puccini is far more exact in his notation than Schumann. I wanted to anticipate on the recording the emotions that I would later have to act before the camera, thus creating as many different layers of expression as possible.

I gathered the whole family and we moved to a hotel outside Paris for the month of July 1986. We began the filming with the third act in Paris in an outdoor location that had been prepared with artificial snow. We had to have giant fans to cool us off so that we would not perspire in our heavy winter clothing. It was clear that Comencini was not in the best health and we wondered if he would be able to finish the film (he lived until 2007). But the bad news came where we least expected it. On Friday, at the end of our fifth day of filming, we had just arrived at the point when Mimì sings "Addio" (Goodbye) before her third-act aria when we stopped for the day. We were to resume on Monday. During the weekend Daniel called me to give me the disturbing news that José would have to leave the film because of a very serious illness that had just been diagnosed. We did not receive more details than that. Daniel and Comencini had to decide whether to stop the filming, postpone the project, or try to continue. They received a message from José giving them permission to find someone to act over his recorded voice. A desperate search was started for a young tenor who knew the role and was available to fill in immediately. We had mixed feelings about continuing without knowing José's fate. Luca Canonici was chosen to play the part. We had to refilm the third act from the beginning again with Luca. He was fun, easy to work with, and fit well into the cast. It was very strange to hear José's voice and to have to react to another person's face and body, but we adapted gradually.

We filmed acts 1 and 4 in a studio near Paris, and by the time we arrived at Cinecittà in Rome the situation did not seem strange at all. Rome was calm in the languid August heat, devoid of most of the Romans, who were away on vacation, and it was a pleasure to walk the streets in the evening after the filming.

Gino had lived in Italy as a child and knew Rome inside and out. My most vivid memories of Rome were from 1978, when I sang a concert with the Santa Cecilia orchestra around the time that the body of Aldo Moro, the Italian prime minister who had been kidnapped and murdered by the Red Brigades, was discovered in the trunk of a car. Since then I had never felt comfortable in Rome and did not know the city at all. Gino rented a motorcycle and every day after the filming he showed me a different aspect of the city; I fell in love with it.

Daniel arrived at the end of that first week and was livid that I had been riding on the back of a motorcycle in Rome. Before the filming began we had signed an agreement with the insurance company not to participate in the most unlikely activities: hunting of ferocious animals, jumping from an airplane, etc. But there was absolutely nothing about riding a motorcycle. Gino gave his motorcycle back and I was confined to my chauffeured car to go to and from Cinecittà. When we had some time off I wandered into some of the other studios and was thrilled to stand in the very same one where Fellini had made films such as *La Dolce Vita*. Each day we filmed at most five minutes of the opera, spending eight hours working just on that scene over and over, searching in every take to get deeper into the work. This demanded an incredible concentration and mental energy and I loved every minute of the work. Learning to do the playback, lip-syncing to the prerecorded soundtrack, demanded a lot of time. We had a coach who worked with us every day because it was a very exact science to get a perfect match with the music and this very difficult technical task had to be mastered before the camera began to roll. Every evening I worked on the playback for the following day's filming. I arrived very early the next morning and listened to the soundtrack on a small tape recorder during my makeup session. It seemed to me that my personal acting technique was well suited for the camera; the origin of even the smallest physical movement that showed in my face and body came from within. This is probably why some opera stage directors like Cacoyannis and Götz Friedrich had only been able to see and appreciate my work when I came close to the dress rehearsals because I never imposed gestures or facial expressions on a character in early rehearsals. I let them develop slowly and organically, allowing the necessary time to find the true expression. The film was finished at the end of August. I had spent a year in the presence of my beloved Mimì and *La bohème*, and I was grateful for the rare luxury of spending such a long time to go to the depths of a character.

Daniel was very possessive about his artists and the women in his life; he was also used to having intimate relationships with some of his leading ladies. However, he and I only developed a very close friendship and he became a wonderful brother to me. During the filming of *La bohème* and the promotional tour in France for the release of the film I came to know, appreciate, respect, and love him. During an intense period of filming one has the impression that everyone is your closest friend. But soon afterward everyone goes on to the next project and we find ourselves surprised that we cannot remember the name of someone we saw every day and in whom we may have confided our innermost secrets. It was only after the release of the film that Daniel and I became really close friends. At first Daniel was surprised that I would call him just to hear how he was doing and not ask him for anything. We met regularly whenever I was in Paris, and he never missed my performances. We spoke about our private lives and our work. He shared with me his passion for the films that he had produced and the artists with whom he had worked—Ingmar Bergman, Roberto Rossellini, Federico Fellini, Maurice Pialat, and Luigi Comencini. He loved them for their art and talent, and was totally devoted to them throughout the filming process. He was distraught when things did not go well and went to all lengths to satisfy their artistic needs. When Pialat's *Van Gogh* had gone way over budget, he sold artworks from his personal collection to finance the film, at a time when he and Maurice were not even on speaking terms. Daniel trusted his artists completely and the film was the most important thing. I loved him for his unselfish love of art. There are impostors who appear to be something but are completely fake, and those who are genuine, authentic, and true. In a world of impostors Daniel was the genuine article.

He was a man on a mission to put opera on film. He knew that opera had started as a "popular" entertainment before becoming enclosed in the museums reserved for the elite. He believed that opera could again appeal to a much wider audience if the camera was allowed to show the inner emotions at play. He was passionate about filming opera, and to his credit he has done more for the genre of filmed opera than anyone else: Joseph Losey's *Don Giovanni* (1979), staged in and around Venice; *La bohème* (1988) by Luigi Comencini; *Boris Godunov* (1989) by Andrej Zulawski; and, later, *Madame Butterfly* (1995), directed by Mitterrand's nephew Frédéric, and *Tosca*, directed by Benoît Jacquot (2001).

After the success of *La bohème* Daniel received a request from a producer at PBS in New York for me to make a television film about the life of Marian Anderson based on her autobiography *My Lord, What a Morning.* We were in contact with the producers in New York City and I reread her book and was looking forward to filming her story, but after several months the PBS project was abandoned due to lack of funds. By this time Daniel and I had become so attached to the idea of making a film about this great lady that we decided to continue with the project.

Marian Anderson was one of my "Negro heroines" that I learned about in school. When I came to New York City in 1969 one of the first things that I wanted to do was meet her. I was fortunate to be at a concert in Carnegie Hall that she attended and the black mezzo-soprano Betty Allen, with whom I worked on *Four Saints in Three Acts,* introduced me to her. She had retired from the stage in 1965 and was genuinely interested in young singers, especially young black singers. She was very gracious to me so I kept in contact with her about how I was progressing at Juilliard. I sent her an invitation to my debut recital at Town Hall in 1976 and the telegram that she sent to me wishing me good luck is one of my most cherished possessions.

Daniel thought that we should abandon the idea of doing a biographical film about her entire life and instead just concentrate on the events around the concert at the Lincoln Memorial in 1939. By then Marian Anderson was at the height of her career—she had conquered Europe on her first tour in 1930 with the beauty and warmth of her voice and had toured extensively, singing recitals and concerts with the major European orchestras and conductors. Arturo Toscanini said to her after a recital in Salzburg, "Yours is a voice one hears once in a hundred years."

In the small towns and villages of Scandinavia she had thousands of fans whose enthusiasm for her was called "Marian fever." Her Finnish pianist Kosti Verhanen introduced her to the Finnish composer Jean Sibelius in 1933, who was so moved by her singing that he dedicated the song "Solitude" to her. She received invitations from many European opera houses but refused because she felt that she did not have sufficient acting experience. In America she was one of the top-selling concert artists on the roster of the renowned impresario Sol Hurok, but her successes in America did not exempt her from the same discrimination that other Negro artists had to endure. She was often refused accommodations in hotels, restaurants, and even concert halls. Sol Hurok wanted to book her for a concert in Constitution Hall in Washington, DC, a segregated city at that time. Negroes who attended events there had to sit at the back of the hall. Constitution Hall was owned by the Daughters of the American Revolution, who refused to rent the hall for a Negro artist. Because of this decision many members of the DAR, including Eleanor Roosevelt, the wife of the president of the United States, resigned from the organization. Mrs. Roosevelt was so incensed that she persuaded Harold Ickes, the secretary of the interior, to arrange an outdoor concert for Marian Anderson on the steps of the Lincoln Memorial, where Martin Luther King would give his "I Have a Dream" speech twenty-four years later. Anderson began her concert with "My Country, 'Tis of Thee," also known as "America," accompanied by Kosti Verhanen, on Easter Sunday, April 9, to seventy-five thousand people of all races while millions listened on the radio.

In the research that I did in preparation for the film I realized that Marian Anderson and I had so many things in common, including our connection to Scandinavia and the fact that we both sang Schubert's "Ave Maria" as an encore at the end of our recitals. (I had always avoided singing what I considered to be "obvious repertoire," but when I sang Schubert's "Ellens Gesang," I–III, of which "Ave Maria" is the third, it became my standard encore.)

Daniel contacted many writers in search of someone who could write a scenario that would do justice to Marian Anderson's story. I went to Danbury, Connecticut, to visit her at Marianna Farms, where she had lived since the 1940s. She was planning to move to Portland, Oregon, to live with her nephew, conductor James De Priest, with whom I had sung when he was the music director of the Monte Carlo Orchestra. She was a beautiful ninety-five-year-old, very lucid, and was as regal and noble as she had appeared in her photos at the Lincoln Memorial. I waited for her in her living room and she arrived elegantly dressed, beautifully made up, and manicured. I proceeded to explain our project to do a film about her and the Lincoln Memorial concert and humbly asked her permission to play her in the film. She told me, "I have been following your career since your Town Hall debut and you have become a truly great musician. I am very proud and there is no one else in the world that I would rather have play me in a film. I am honored." I was very moved by her words. I spoke with James DePriest after her move to Portland because I hoped to visit her again, but she had a stroke in March 1993 and died a month later. Daniel tried in vain to get this project going and had not given up on it when he died.

Swedish Television, SVT, was one of the last European Public Service television channels to continue to produce high-level drama, culture, and music programs, including Ingmar Bergman's *Scenes from a Marriage* in 1973 and his interpretation of Mozart's *Die Zauberflöte* filmed in the Drottningholm Theater with Håkan Hagegård as Papageno. I sat through this film absolutely fascinated in a Los Angeles movie house during the summer of 1975. Now that the media in Europe has been opened up to private competition to give us more choice, the arts, when they exist at all on television, have been relegated to time slots late at night suitable only for insomniacs. *Public service* has become just *public*, without the *service*.

SVT invited me to come to Stockholm to film Anne Truelove in Stravinsky's *The Rake's Progress* with Håkan Hagegård, Greg Fedderly, and Eric Saedén in 1995. I was happy to be in front of the camera again. The opera is no longer considered difficult; it is still modern yet accessible. The film was directed by Inger Åby and was conducted by Esa Pekka Salonen.

Because of my experience filming *La bohème* over a prerecorded soundtrack, the work was easier for me this time around.
Inger insisted that we have several weeks staging rehearsals before
recording the soundtrack, and this was an excellent idea. When I
was standing still in front of the microphone I could relate inwardly
to some movement that I had done on the set. I knew that there
were certainly going to be many changes when she started to film,
but these rehearsals intensified the underlying dramatic intent of
the music. I was able to refine my work with the character before
recording a single note. Stravinsky's music invites me to dance
and to improvise movements that correspond to Anne's emotional
life. We filmed in the SVT studios in Stockholm and on location
in the old town and around the city. We had the great fortune to
have one of the world's best cameramen, Gunnar Källström. He
and Inger fostered a true atmosphere of innovation and openness
that allowed me to lift out the inner life of my character, and at the
necessary moment Gunnar's expert eye captured it on film. *The
Rake's Progress* received the Prix Italia in 1996.

My voice preceded me to the Cannes Film Festival in the film
Don't Kill God, directed by Jacqueline Manzano in 1984. Ennio
Morricone, the Italian composer, had been commissioned to
compose music for the film. He contacted me and asked me to
record one song for the soundtrack. I had actually forgotten about
this first appearance at the Palais des Festivals until very recently
when I was asked by the organizers of the Swedish Polar Music
Prize in Stockholm to sing a musical tribute to Ennio Morricone.
He and the Icelandic artist, Björk, were the two recipients of the
2010 prize.

When Gilles Jacob invited me to be a member of the Cannes
Festival jury in 1999 I had already gone up the red carpet on several previous occasions, albeit as an outsider in the film industry.

Jack Lang, the French minister of culture, had invited me to the
festival for the first time in 1988 some months after the release of
La bohème for an evening dedicated to opera films. When I arrived
at the bottom of the red carpet, the announcer said, "Barbara

Hendricks, the star of Comencini's *La bohème*," and I started up the stairs; the applause of the crowd increased when I arrived at the top. My escort up the red carpet was baritone Ruggero Raimondi, who had sung in the *Turandot* recording with me and who been in several of Daniel's opera films. I was taken aback by the unexpected fervor of the crowd waiting behind the barriers as they screamed my name and applauded when I turned to face them. I thought to myself, "They must think I'm someone else." Jack Lang asked me to sing two songs in a gala the following evening, and I sang Gershwin's "Summertime." When I finished I said to the audience, "I would also like to sing a song in French but I am not so sure of all of the words and I know that there is someone here tonight who could be my prompter if he will come to the stage and sing along with me. Yves Montand, would you be so kind to come and help me out?" He was gracious and charming and came onto the stage. We sang a duet of "Les feuilles mortes." It was an unforgettable moment that was the equivalent to me of dancing a pas de deux with Fred Astaire. I had spoken to Daniel in the afternoon during my rehearsal about asking Montand to sing with me and he said, "If you ask him he will certainly refuse. He is a lot like you and insists on having a proper rehearsal no matter where he performs. But maybe if you use all of your charm and ask him nicely to join you on stage he just might do it." After the dinner I went over to Simone Signoret and Yves Montand's table and said, "You have fulfilled one of my dreams tonight and I hope that you are not angry with me for putting you on the spot." "Au contraire," he said, " I was delighted to sing with you but relieved that you had chosen my key instead of the higher key that you probably sing."

After that I always gave him a call to say hello whenever I passed through Saint Paul de Vence, where he lived. Since then "Les feuilles mortes" is one of my standard encores of my jazz concerts. The last time that I saw him perform was on the stage of L'Olympia in Paris. I always think of him, the artist and activist, whenever I sing that song. And when I stand on the stage of the L'Olympia I feel his presence with me.

When Daniel called me to say that Gilles Jacob, the artistic director of the Cannes Film Festival, wanted to invite me to be a member of the jury in 1999, I looked at my schedule and immediately agreed. David Cronenburg, the Canadian director, was to be president of the jury. I arrived in Cannes with Ulf, Jennie, and Sebastian (Malcolm, Ulf's son, was in school and could not attend). We had two adjoining rooms at the Carlton Hotel that were just down the hall from Daniel's room. I was given strict instructions by Gilles not to reveal anything concerning the jury's discussions to anyone, especially to Daniel. The other members of the jury were André Téchiné, Jeff Goldblum, Dominique Blanc, Yasmina Reza, Holly Hunter, Doris Dörrie, George Miller, and Maurizio Nichetti. Sebastian and Jennie had been looking forward to going up the red carpet and to be in the middle of the adoring crowd as they had seen many times on the TV. They were so excited when we left the hotel to go to the opening ceremony. But once we were in the car inching our way toward the Palais, the roar of the crowd actually frightened them. I had done this many times but they did not know what to make of people following the car, looking into the window, and screaming, "Barbara, Barbara." When the members of the jury advanced at a snail's pace up the red carpet they had to walk behind us while the photographers shouted hysterically from all sides for us to turn in their direction. I turned to one side, then to another. Finally we arrived at the top where Gilles greeted each member of the jury and we smiled for a group photo and escaped inside. Ulf had not been enthusiastic about the idea of going up the red carpet from the beginning and once we arrived inside he, Jennie, and Sebastian vowed never to do it again. After the opening ceremony we always entered the hall from backstage and avoided the activity out front.

Once the formalities of the opening ceremony were over the jury settled in and began the serious business of watching the films that had been selected. The Cannes Festival exists on several levels—the red carpet, the business stands, and the late-night parties—but the most important event is the screening of the films in competition. As a member of the jury I had little time or energy for much else other than eating, sleeping, and watching the films. Every day we had one screening in the morning, one in the afternoon, and, for a few films that had not been scheduled during the day, there was an evening screening as well. I was happy to discover the wide variety of films from every corner of the world, so many films that I would never have known existed if I had not seen them in Cannes. There are many passionate filmmakers in the most remote places in the world who are striving to produce meaningful films on a shoestring budget.

I had been afraid that I would not be able to take in the more than twenty-five films during the eleven days of the festival, but it was easier than I thought. Only those films or performances that moved me or resonated within me lingered. Being a morning person I was much more attentive to the films that I saw in the morning than the ones that I saw after lunch, but since many of my other fellow jury members were tired from their evening social life they were the opposite, so I assumed that this evened out the chances for all. I saw many well-made films but few continued to live on afterward and leave a trace behind. Some I had already forgotten before leaving the hall. One of the films that I still think about is *Kadosh*, a very moving love story directed by Amos Gitai, with whom I worked later, in 2008, on his film *Disengagement* with Juliette Binoche and Jeanne Moreau (I sang "Abschied" from Mahler's *Das Lied von der Erde* in an arrangement by Simon Stockhausen, the son of the German composer Karlheinz Stockhausen).

The film that received the Palme d'Or that year was *Rosetta* by Jean-Pierre and Luc Dardennes. When the lights came on after the screening we knew that we had just seen our Palme d'Or and it received unanimous approval. It was more difficult to arrive at a consensus for some of the other prizes and I was happy that Pedro Almodóvar received the best director award. Since I am not allowed to discuss the details of our deliberations I will only say that in both the international and French press the articles that I saw about our decisions were completely off. One said that all was decided beforehand and another that the French members of the jury insisted on a French-language winner. These conjectures could not be further from the truth.

Being a member of the Cannes Festival jury was an unforgettable and unique experience. After the announcement of the prizes I was finally able to speak openly to Daniel about my thoughts about the 1999 selection of films.

Daniel was the head of Unifrance and his commitment to his mission to support and promote French cinema was unwavering. During our many conversations he spoke to me with affection about the different women who had been a part of his life. He loved women, appreciated their strengths, and was fascinated by their complexity. After his divorce from Francesca Comencini and a few relationships that did not work out, Daniel met Sophie Bouniol, whom he married in 1991. They lived together with her son, Pierre-Louis, and his son with Francesca, Carlo. His relationship with Sophie was never dull; she was always a bit of a mystery to him and kept him guessing. I think that because of that he was totally fascinated and devoted to her. I also confided in him when Martin and I decided to divorce. Sebastian, Jennie, and I spent that summer vacation with him, Sophie, and the boys at his home near Toulouse. He was an enormous support to me during that time.

My divorce was finalized in December 1996 and Daniel and I had planned to go to Senegal with our families to celebrate the New Year. On December 23, shortly before midnight, the phone rang and woke me. It was Daniel. "I do not want you to hear this on the news tomorrow morning or read it in the paper. Sophie was murdered tonight in Ireland!" I was in shock. A few minutes later, I rang him back. "Daniel, I think that I have had the strangest dream that you called me to say that Sophie has been murdered; please tell me that this was a bad dream." I had just met Ulf but I wanted to speak to him; I called him to relate the horrible tragic story. Instead of packing to go to Africa, Sebastian, Jennie, and I left Switzerland where we had celebrated Christmas together with Martin and his mother and flew to Toulouse. Daniel's closest friends rallied around him to give him support; his first wife, Marie Christine, their two children, David and Ariane, his second wife, Francesca, and their son, Carlo, Isabelle Huppert, and Maurice Pialat, who had a home nearby (Sophie had been very instrumental in bringing the two friends and collaborators back together after the filming of *Van Gogh*). For her funeral Daniel asked me to sing "Pie Jesu" from Gabriel Fauré's Requiem, the same that I had sung at Notre Dame for Mitterrand's funeral in January 1996. This was a great contrast—an intimate funeral in the small church at the foot of the hill down from the house that he had bought for himself and Sophie.

After the funeral Sebastian, Jennie, and I went with Daniel and a few friends to Nimes to the home of Nicolas and Marie Seydoux for our New Year's celebration. It was a sad New Year's Eve, but Daniel told funny stories about Sophie and their life together, many of which I had heard during our many lunches together in Paris.

He was devastated by her loss, and became obsessed with the idea that now that I was divorced, we should marry. I said, "Daniel, why would we want to destroy a perfectly good friendship with marriage? You know that we lead such different lives. I am a morning person, love the mountains, and you are an evening person and you hate the mountains. Besides, I hate to go to dinners and receptions and that is a necessary part of your life; after two weeks you would start to hate my neat little organized way of life. We have the best possible relationship in the world—let's cherish that." It was difficult to see him so vulnerable and injured and to realize that he could not bear to be alone.

Sometimes I had stayed with Daniel and Sophie in their house on the Cité Malesherbes in Paris. The last time that I saw Sophie alive, I had been visiting my agent, Diane, who lives in the same street, and met Sophie outside their house. She pulled me into a magnificent house next door to theirs and said, "This is so beautiful and it is for sale—you must buy it." I said, "Sophie, I am not interested in owning another house. And if I were I could not afford this one. I sing classical music, not pop music." She laughed and said, "Yes, I know that it is too expensive, but it would be great to have you and the kids next door to us."

In May 1997 I went to the Cannes Festival to be with Daniel for a few days. He was singing the same song about us, but by the end of the festival he had met a young girl, Melita. When we met in August at Nicolas Seydoux's home near Nimes he was with Melita, who was pregnant, and had thankfully forgotten all about his idea of marrying me. I was relieved that I did not have to reject him in his most weakened and vulnerable state because he was beginning to convince himself that this was a good idea. I was one of the few of his starring actresses who had not yet had an affair with him, and maybe he thought that there was still time. His meeting with Melita saved our friendship. This was just as well because I had met Ulf the previous December and had invited him to come to hear my last performance of Liu in Puccini's *Turandot* at the Orange Festival. Knowing how jealous Daniel could be I was very concerned that he would make life miserable for Ulf when he arrived in Nimes. Ulf was not only to meet Daniel for the first time but also Sebastian and Jennie. The meetings went very smoothly but Daniel surprised me because he was unusually gracious to Ulf. Maybe he saw what a special person Ulf is and sensed even before I did that he was going to become someone very important in my life.

After Daniel's marriage to Melita in 1998 we had no more family gatherings with all of our children but I could always count on him to be present whenever I sang in Paris, and we cherished our lunches together, where the subject of Sophie always came up. To this day her murder has not been solved and Daniel needed to be able to speak openly about it to me. Even though he thought he knew who was guilty of the crime, Daniel could not have any closure. In January 2003, at the Berlin Film Festival, his sixty-one-year-old broken heart stopped beating, much too soon for all of us who loved him and for the kind of European cinema that he defended almost single-handedly.

I stayed in the back of L'eglise à la Place de Madeleine because I knew that I would not be able to control myself if I had to sit through the beginning of the mass and listen to all of the tributes to him. As soon as Isabelle Huppert had finished speaking I walked up and sang "Pie Jesu" from Gabriel Fauré's Requiem, as I had done for Sophie. Afterward I went to my place next to Jennie and Sebastian. I could no longer control my tears; they both held me as if I was a baby. It was the first time that they had ever seen me in such sorrow. Ulf was in rehearsal at Dramaten in Stockholm and could not be with us. Although he had only known Daniel for five years he felt a strong connection to him and, like all of us, felt that Daniel had left us too soon. I miss him terribly. He touched so many of us so deeply. It was Daniel's destiny and it was his time to go—and maybe even his desire.

In addition to my own personal experiences with the "seventh art" I believe that the cinema has not only a cultural role but also an important social role to play in our society. In 2002 Sergio Vieira de Mello and I became the patrons of the first Festival du Film et Forum International sur les Droits Humains in Geneva (the FIFDH).

Sergio had just been appointed commissioner of the UN Human Rights Council and brought in the council as a partner to the festival with the aim of providing a forum for filmmakers, human rights activists, and the general public to express and share their ideas in an open forum. The festival fearlessly denounces human rights abuses wherever and by whomever they are committed. There is now a network of human rights film festivals in association with Human Rights Watch and Amnesty International around the world, with several in Europe, in North and South America, Africa, Asia, Australia, and New Zealand.

After Sergio's death in 2003 a prize was given in his name by the city of Geneva, but after a disagreement with his widow over the festival's right to invite the participants of their choice without interference and outside pressure, the prize was withdrawn. This festival meant so much to Sergio and I know that he would not only defend the festival's independence but would want to be present in some way. Since 2008 the Barbara Hendricks Foundation for Peace and Reconciliation gives the Sergio Vieira de Mello prize every year in Sergio's honor at the festival in Geneva and since 2009 in the festival Ciné Droit Libre in Ouagadougou, Burkina Faso, that is now called the Gilda Vieira de Mello Prize in honor of her son Sergio."

Juliette Binoche and the Mauritanian filmmaker Abderrahmane Sissako have formed an association, Des cinemas pour l'Afrique, and have started a vast campaign, Un fauteuil pour l'Afrique, to save the cinemas in Africa that are rapidly disappearing. Juliette wrote me a letter about their association and asked me for my support of their efforts. We met at the 2010 FIFDH festival when they presented their project. I have, as a private citizen, bought one of the first *fauteuils* in Bamako, Mali, that will make it possible for them to build a polyvalent cinema there. I am sure that Daniel looks down and smiles and thinks that maybe they will finally be able to see me in *La bohème* like Zeffirelli insinuated.

Arte Verum 12

When a truth is not given complete freedom, freedom is not complete.

—Vaclav Havel

When I began my recording career in the 1970s it seemed to me an unwritten rule in classical music that only those artists who had achieved sufficient knowledge and mastery of a score were considered ready to leave behind their vision of that score for future generations by setting it in vinyl as a record of that moment in their artistic evolution. This was contrary to the tradition in pop music where an artist prepares a recording, sometimes for many years, and then tours the repertoire afterward in order to sell the record.

I have always felt that I had to earn the privilege to go into the recording studio to record my repertoire. This meant that spending the necessary time working on a score and then performing it many times before a live audience was essential to allow the music to evolve naturally into a mature interpretation. Every performance of a score is unique and as different from those that have preceded it as it is from those that will succeed it on its continual movement toward an unobtainable perfection. Only when I feel that my interpretation of a piece has reached a certain maturity do I decide to record it. Even so the recording is also just one unique performance that is the sum of the multitude of unique performances that have gone before it.

After having recorded a piece I always feel that subsequent performances of it are even better than the recording, and that is how it should be: a live concert should always be superior to a record. I know that I have not exhausted all of the possibilities within the score, but the recording process can be like a fertilizer enhancing a continual evolution.

I began to record early in my career, but slowly and in very small roles. The first was Clara in *Porgy and Bess* with Lorin Maazel and the Cleveland Orchestra. Clara's role consists of the famous "Summertime," sung twice, and a few small lines. The next role I recorded was "La voce del cielo" in Verdi's *Don Carlo,* conducted by Herbert von Karajan. This role consists of two pages of music. Both of these roles were well within my abilities, and I did not in any way covet the bigger soprano roles in these operas. I felt that I was completely in the right place at that time in my career.

Too many talented young musicians today are eaten up by their record companies, chewed up and spit out before they have had the time to establish their true artistic identities. I have seen so many careers begin with a lot of fanfare and disappear after only a few years. I read an interview with one such singer who wanted to record her entire repertoire while her voice was young and fresh. She recorded everything that she could but since she had not performed nor experienced the repertoire, she produced lovely sounds with no personal imprint. After a short time her career ended and the recordings are now forgotten. The record company exploited her talent and then abandoned her.

We all have to deal with our own impatience. When I made my New York City recital debut in 1976 a week before my twenty-eighth birthday, I had already been touring for two years in the Community Concert series with the repertoire and I felt that I was very well prepared. Yet when I was on the stage of Town Hall where Jennie Tourel, Lotte Lehmann, and Marian Anderson had stood I was almost painfully aware of what a rank beginner I was. This was a source of much frustration because I wanted to fast-forward to the time when I would be a "master singer." I longed for the foreign languages in which I sang to be already second nature to me. I did not want to think about exaggerating the muscles in my mouth as I formed foreign consonants and vowels. I wanted to be a long-distance runner before mastering the smaller distances. I wanted to be where I am today. I had to accept that I was still in the starting blocks, but it took a long time for me to tame my impatience and to enjoy the present moments of each unique performance. Gradually I was able to enjoy even the tiniest steps on the voyage toward my goal as I improved with each rehearsal and with each performance. This evolution was what I wanted to represent when setting down one unique moment in vinyl.

When I look back it is so clear how important and essential each step along the way has been, how far I have come, and how necessary it was to advance slowly. I remember distinctly a recital in New York's Alice Tully Hall in the early 1980s with the pianist Ralf Gothoni. I sang a mixed German and French program: Schubert, Wolf, Debussy, and Poulenc. The German diction was no longer a physical and mental effort for me and even the French diction that has always been easier seemed more fluid. The interpretation was like a train in motion, the notes propelled by the energy of the rhythm as they glided along on the rails of the language and diction. When I walked off the stage at the end of the concert I felt different and realized that I had arrived at another level in my work. I felt that I was ready to start to record some of my French and German recital repertoire. In 1986 I recorded my first German lieder album, *Schubert Lieder*, with Radu Lupu.

Many singers record themselves during rehearsals and performances and listen afterward in order to evaluate their work. I have also recorded myself but somehow conveniently forgot to listen because something in me did not want to. I preferred to sense my instrument from within. However, during the recording process having to listen to myself has proven an excellent teaching and learning experience that has made me more demanding about my vocal production when I returned to the concert hall. I have profited from my time in the recording studio and actually learned more about my natural singing technique. I always listen to the first takes of each song to verify if the tapes are registering my intentions. Sometimes the pianist and I are greatly surprised to hear what the tape plays back to us. A "take" that we felt was great sounded like an exercise in self-indulgence in the playback. The tempos were too slow or too fast or it was downright sentimental and we heard this immediately.

During the first recording session with my producer, Nicolas Batholomée, I let him know that he could be very demanding with me. I do not want him to accept sloppy or scooping entrances, and of course no bad intonation. I give him permission to be most severe without being counterproductive. After the first take I usually tell him what I want to hear from myself in subsequent takes and then I have to trust him completely until the end of the recording session. He knows when he could ask for one more take of a difficult passage or if we should leave it and pass on to something else, returning to it at a later time. It is essential to have an independent listener like Nicolas whom I can trust. Besides having an excellent ear he also has very good taste.

During the recording process we are constantly stopping and listening and making corrections, unlike a live performance. Therefore one of the most difficult tasks in recording is to *give* a live performance. We prefer to use long complete takes with minor corrections so as to avoid a clinical and cold, albeit more correct, version of the piece.

If I look back at the nearly forty years of my recording career I must admit that I have been very privileged. To this day I have recorded more than one hundred albums of the greatest music with the greatest artists of my time and have sold more than fourteen million records. At the beginning of my career Martin stressed not only the importance of striving to be a successful concert and opera artist but also of being a recognized recording artist. He said to me, "Whenever the record companies plan to record your opera or concert repertoire, you should be on their short list for the role."

I began recording with many different companies. After *Porgy and Bess* I recorded Mahler's *Fourth Symphony* with Zubin Mehta and *Final Alice* with Sir Georg Solti and the Chicago Symphony for Decca, as well as Debussy's *La damoiselle élue* with Daniel Barenboim and the Orchestre de Paris for Deutsche Grammophon. My first solo album of French opera arias with Jeffrey Tate conducting and Gershwin songs with Katia and Marielle Labèque were for Philips. For Sony I recorded Handel's opera *Xerxes*, Vivaldi Cantatas with Jean-Claude Malgoire, and Mahler's Fourth Symphony with Esa Pekka Salonen; with Karajan I recorded *Don Carlo* for EMI.

In 1980 Alain Lanceron, the director of EMI France, offered me my first exclusive contract for solo recordings. *Negro Spirituals* with Dmitri Alexeev was released in 1983 and *Debussy Songs* with Michel Béroff was released in 1985, a recording that stayed in the catalogue and continued to sell for nearly twenty-five years. I was, however, free to accept offers for recordings with other companies for large orchestral or opera productions if EMI could not offer me the same project. I recorded twenty-one opera roles but only four for EMI. I recorded Bizet's *Les Pêcheurs de Perles* (Michel Plasson), Gluck's *Orfeo* (John Eliot Gardiner), and Enesco's *Oedipe* (Lawrence Foster) for EMI France. Peter Alward, the artistic director for EMI London, was not at all interested in me as an opera singer though and Strauss's *Der Rosenkavalier* conducted by Bernard Haitink was the only opera that I recorded for EMI Classics.

Alain gave me complete control over the artistic production of my solo recordings: the repertoire, my partners, and eventually the technical and production staff with whom I wanted to work. I was able to record as I chose and when I felt ready to record. Every year I was performing at least two completely new recital programs and when it was time to plan a new album I could choose the repertoire that I felt was most ready. The majority of the repertoire was recital and chamber music, but I also recorded opera and operetta arias, sacred music, Christmas music, spirituals, and an album of Disney songs for children. I chose the programs for these albums with the same rigor and curiosity as I did my recital programs. When I started recording LPs on vinyl the duration of an album was about forty-five minutes but the CDs could contain more than sixty minutes of music. Because some music magazines considered it to be an added value for the money Alain insisted on a program of at least sixty minutes.

One of my first gold records for EMI was *Sacred Music* (Ave Maria) with Eric Ericson conducting. I researched a long time for the songs for this recording. I added Schubert's "Ave Maria" to my repertoire for the first time. Although I had chosen to learn songs that I had heard in class at Juilliard or in concerts I tended to stay away from the most popular songs. I made up for this belated start with "Ave Maria" when it became a signature piece for me just like it had been for Marian Anderson.

I worked very well with Alain and especially with Aude de Jamblinne, the press attaché who is still a very close friend. I was very happy with my collaboration with EMI France and we made many excellent recordings. When the classical section of EMI France was phased out it was decided that I should go to EMI Classics in London and my contract was transferred to them. It is a bit difficult to explain how the company worked. EMI was a decentralized company and each country had its own company, producing its own recordings with its own local artists. This was sometimes counterproductive since each local company was in competition with all of the others within the same parent company. I was considered a "French" artist. The other companies, such as Angel in the United States and EMI London, could choose whether or not to take and promote the CD of an artist from another subsidiary of EMI. This seemed to me to be a great weakness in the company because the other major companies—Deutsche Grammophon, Sony, and Decca—worked as one company and their artists received simultaneous worldwide distribution and support.

While I still worked with the French office concerning the repertoire and the preparation of the recording, the follow up outside France was to be done from London. I do not know why, but this never really worked well for me and I never became a true EMI Classics artist. I was, however, still quite happy as long as I was able to continue to record "my" repertoire. I was singing concerts and opera all over the world and had very good contact with most of the EMI representatives in the countries where I usually sang. The recording industry in general and the classical companies in particular benefited greatly from the arrival of the CD. It was a shot of steroids to them. Classical record companies like EMI had an enormous back catalogue that they transferred to CD with little or no cost. As soon as this cow had been milked dry we began to hear about a crisis in the record industry and the result was cutbacks in everything. The local EMI companies were no longer able to produce records and the classical division was often reduced to one person who had to take care of everything. Eventually many of the offices were closed. The companies had become accustomed to their steroid diet and had forgotten what the essential industry was before the CD.

After World War II and up until the mid-1980s, when a star artist such as Herbert von Karajan sold ten thousand copies it was considered a "gold record." After 1990 the major companies began to look only to the bottom line, and their appetites had become insatiable. This forced them to scrape the bottom of the barrel to look for gimmicks that would produce big sales in the short term. Gone were the criteria for recording that had existed when I began to record. "Ask not what an artist is ready to record, ask only what can we persuade her to record that will give us immediate sales." The success of the "Three Tenors" (Pavorotti, Carreras, and Domingo), who together represented nearly a hundred years of career and thousands of performances, prompted many in classical music to try big "rock and roll events" and the abomination called the "crossover" was born. Recording based on faith in the artist and in the classical repertoire went the way of the steam engine, consigned to the past. The record companies lost their way.

I have always been able to strike a balance between the repertoire that appeals to a smaller "specialist" audience and that which appeals to a wider audience because I have such a varied and wide ranging repertoire, but I have based my solo recording repertoire solely on my actual performance repertoire.

When EMI Classics asked me to record a CD of Disney songs, the only solo recording request that I received from that office, I refused because there was no opportunity to have a concert with the songs and I was not at all interested in the repertoire. Martin thought that it was a good idea and while discussing it at the dinner table both Sebastian and Jennie said, "Mom, you should record the Disney songs for us; you have never done a recording just for us." This was an argument that I could not refuse so I went to work to put together the best program that I could. I decided to record the songs that I had heard and knew by heart from my own childhood, and the songs that had come from the films that I had watched with Sebastian and Jennie. This is the only recording that I have done singing to a prerecorded orchestra track, because EMI Classics told me that this would be the easiest way to proceed. I insisted, however, to be present at the rehearsals and recording of the soundtrack, and to sing with the orchestra before they recorded. My children loved the record and I still receive messages from parents from all over the world who tell me, "My children fall asleep listening to you and adore this record."

The Disney record was exactly what EMI Classics said it wanted but they proved to be grossly incapable of promoting the record properly. They had expected the CD to sell itself. Just four months before the release, two of the promotion representatives from London came to Paris to speak to the director of Disneyland Paris, Philippe Bourguignon. They made what they assumed was an offer that he could not refuse and obviously expected him to fall on his knees in gratitude for offering him the possibility to sell the CD at Disneyland. But he did refuse and they did not seem to have had any other plan, so nothing more was done. Philippe called me afterward to explain that due to exclusivity rights at Disney he could not sell my CDs. But had he been able to, he would not have wanted to because of their unprofessional and arrogant attitude.

Richard Lyttelton came to Montreux to negotiate my last contract with EMI Classics. During the meeting we talked about how to deal with the difficulties that the recording industry was starting to face and what each of us could do to help solve those problems.

I questioned him about EMI's marketing strategy—or lack of a strategy, as I saw it. In my opinion this should be discussed at the same time that the recording is decided upon. I also wanted to know why a lieder recording that I had just released had not been marketed at all. I was told, "Since we knew that the record would not receive a good review in *Gramophone* magazine we decided not to invest in it at all." I was shocked. How did he know that before the record was released—and did they actually wait until then to begin to think about a marketing strategy? I had always wondered about the nebulous relationship between the record companies and the magazines that review their records while at the same time depending heavily on advertising from the record companies

to exist. Lyttleton's remarks did not in any way assuage my sus-
picions and should have been a wake up call for me about EMI's
insidious intentions and lack of vision.

We agreed that I would continue to record my repertoire as
I liked and I promised to keep a balance in the repertoire that I
offered. He assured me that my recordings would not be taken
from the catalogue.

When EMI celebrated its one-hundred-year anniversary in
2002, I said to Lyttleton, "I am extremely proud to be included
in the first hundred years of EMI and honored to be in the company of some of the greatest classical music artists of all times.
But I fear that the next hundred years will not be nearly so glorious." He dismissed my remarks as pessimistic. I came to London
to meet EMI Classics' artistic director Peter Alward and we too
spoke at length about the difficulties facing the industry; he found
nothing wrong with the approach that they had to the music nor
to the artists but longed for a new technical revolution like the
CD, some new technical steroid that would artificially dope the
industry again. I felt that the solution lay with the artists and our
great classical repertoire. "I sing every week to sold out halls in
front of enthusiastic audiences. I know that they are interested to
hear the repertoire that they have discovered during my concerts
and would be willing to purchase my CDs of the same repertoire." He did not think that my relationship with my audience
was enough to translate into the record sales that they wanted. In
disbelief, I said, "Which clientele are you trying to attract? From
where should they come? If you do not even bother to inform the
concert audience of the existence of a new record, can we be surprised that a record does not sell?"

My arguments did not convince him and it became clear to me
that the artistic decisions were being molded by the marketing or
rather the non-marketing staff, who could have just as well have
been working for IBM as for EMI. I have always joked that maybe
EMI Classics was a front for something else since they seemed to
be so uncreative and unsuccessful at selling their records.

A short time after signing my new contract I was in Copenhagen to sing Berlioz's Les nuits d'été and received a phone call
from the EMI press representative in Denmark, with whom I had

worked very well over the years. "I am so exasperated I can't get a single CD of Berlioz for the concert tomorrow. I have tried everything—I even called the office in Paris—but there was nothing that they could do. There is nothing available and it seems that it has been erased from the catalogue. I cannot even order copies to be produced."

I could not believe what I heard, so I called London and spoke to Lyttleton, who first of all denied that he had ever said that nothing would be taken from my catalogue and then insulted me. "How many orders have you received for your new release?" I answered, "I don't know and the release was just a week ago." "Well," he said, "we have another soprano who has received orders for sixty thousand records." I was shocked that he would speak to me about another artist but even more shocked when I found out that the "soprano" that he was talking about was a twelve-year-old crossover singer.

I then looked at the EMI Classics website to see which of my records remained and when I saw how they had gutted my basic repertoire from the catalogue I was shocked and hurt. I felt as if someone had taken a portrait of me and begun to erase small parts, leaving a bit of nose here and a bit of an ear there. This was a mutilation of my artistic portrait that represented twenty-five years of work. I had planned each recording with care and thought, but it was worth nothing to them. At one point only five of my recordings, the bestsellers and some compilations, remained, out of about fifty. This was very painful.

Even the new releases underwent the knife of commercial expediency. The last CD that I recorded for EMI was *Nordic Songs* with Roland Pöntinen, but it faded away as quickly as it had appeared. I had been singing in the Nordic countries since 1974 and I wanted to dedicate an entire CD to the music of my first audiences in their own languages. I had also become a Swedish citizen and this was an added incentive to make the record. I had been singing songs of Edvard Grieg and Jean Sibelius for many years and I added Türe Rangström and Carl Nielsen songs to a recital program that I toured a long time before going into the studio. I knew this was the very kind of repertoire the London office had no intention of supporting, but on the other hand I knew that I could count on the enthusiasm of the local EMI offices in the Nordic countries. The CD was to be released in October. I was in Stockholm for a concert in May and was surprised that Inger Forsblom from the Stockholm office, with whom I had always worked very closely, did not come to my concert. I knew that her mother had been ill so I called her. She informed me that she had been fired along with other colleagues within EMI, the office in Stockholm was closed, and that her colleague in Denmark would be responsible for Sweden. I will not bother to go into the details. Needless to say, to this day very few persons in the Nordic countries have ever heard of the CD and it was taken from the catalogue just some months after its unnoticed release. This was the last straw. I had had enough. Even though I was still under an exclusive contract I decided that I was not going to ever record another CD for EMI— or any other major recording company for that matter.

In hindsight I think that I should have never signed a new contract with them, but I have a very strong sense of loyalty. EMI was my family, my label, and I believe that in a relationship one must take the good with the bad and I wanted to be a part of the solution. However I had to accept that I was not a priority for EMI Classics and I painfully realized that it was futile to remain.

A finished recording represents many years of research, work, and touring and is a part of me, and I do not want to give it away to people who are neither interested in my repertoire nor capable of appreciating my work. It felt like giving birth to a child and then abandoning her in the wilderness. I suppose that EMI kept me on so that I might do another bestseller. As a matter of fact during those last years they were asking me to make another *Sacred Music* recording. I refused. "When I made my recording of sacred music it was because I wanted to sing that music and since then everyone has released a CD of sacred music. I do not need to copy those who have copied me—no thank you."

But when I had suggested to EMI Classics that I was ready to record Schubert's *Schöne Müllerin*, I was told, "Schubert does not sell anymore." In a sense they were saying that they no longer believed in an important part of our common cultural heritage. I did not agree with them and I still had quite a lot of my repertoire that I wanted to record. I decided to record that repertoire for my own archives. Whenever I felt that I was ready with a group of songs I recorded them, even though I had no idea what I would later do with the tapes.

I had worked with Nicolas Bartholomée for the first time when I recorded *Hommage à Jennie Tourel* with Staffan Scheja. The CD introduced us to the new digital sound. I have always been frustrated with digital recording technique because it changes the sound to fit within a technical parameter that is far from the truer sound of the analogue recording that I still remember from my first recordings. Nicolas and I have had many lengthy discussions about how to obtain as much of the analogue sound as possible even though we had no choice but to work within the framework of the digital system. He has constantly been trying to get closer to the "true" sound. When I decided to record my archives I called on him. I had discovered a wonderful hall in Stockholm, the hall of the Royal Swedish Academy, known as Nybrokajen. The acoustic is just perfect for recording chamber music and we wanted to make recordings where the listener would feel as if she is sitting in the middle of the hall. It had been some time since I had decided to have the piano lid open to its fullest for my recitals, contrary to the tradition with the lid on the lowest position. I want to hear the full sonority of the instrument since I sing with excellent pianists who could and wanted to play the dynamics indicated in the score. For recitals with piano we use the same microphone for both piano and voice. The balance between them that the listener hears on the CD is exactly the same balance that we perform—it is not manipulated in the control room.

I used my own resources to finance all the recordings; I did not even have the means to edit the tapes. The most important thing for me was that my work exist. During a three-year period I recorded Schubert, Brahms, and Schumann lieder with Roland Pöntinen. I recorded Spanish songs (*Canciones Españolas*), Shostakovich's *Blok Songs*, and Beethoven *Lieder and Volkslieder* with Love Derwinger. It was the equivalent of six CDs of music. Nicolas then asked me what I had planned to do with all of the work that we had done. I answered, "I don't know, maybe leave it to my children and they can decide. But under no circumstances will I give my work to one of the major record companies."

He suggested starting my own label. I looked at my contract with EMI and realized that I had one year left so we began to make plans. Nicolas introduced me to Olivier Vannieu, his cousin, who had already worked on a similar project with Jordi Savall.

On March 15, 2005, the last day that EMI could have renewed my contract, I called Olivier and Nicholas and said, with obvious glee in my voice, "I am free, let's go!"

Olivier had suggested that I come up with a name for the label that began with the letter A. "It is easier to find," he said. I was sitting in a car and passed a sign for a concert of Mozart's Ave Verum Corpus and I thought that Ave Verum would be a great name; but on second thought it seemed a bit pretentious. However, it would not go away, and one day I said to myself, "Not Ave Verum, it must be Arte Verum." *Arte Verum*: art and truth—authentic sound and balance.

My label is about the search for truth in my art and my life. Starting my own label was much more of a financial risk than just recording my archives but I knew that it would have to be a long-term investment. Recording my archives gave me the greatest satisfaction because I was preserving the repertoire that I love. But I cannot explain what a strong sense of freedom I felt when the first CD was released. I have always been a free spirit and have chosen the paths that I felt I had to take without self-consciousness. I act according to my convictions and following them is a liberating act. With the launch of Arte Verum I felt and could say to myself, You are truly free, free of the artificial demands and machinations of the "business" of artistic endeavor.

In January 2006 Olivier and I introduced the newborn label to the recording industry at Midem in Cannes with the release of *Canciones Españolas: Canciones Amatorias* and *Tonadillas* by Enrique Granados and *Cinco Canciones Negras* by Montsalvatge. I sang from the score that Montsalvatge signed for me after a performance of the work in the Palau de la Musica in Barcelona a few years before his death.

This first release was dedicated to the great Victoria de los Angeles. I was about to go on the stage for the last of three concerts with the Barcelona Symphony on January 15, 2005, when I was informed that she had died that afternoon. When I was a student at Juilliard I listened to recordings of great singers and she was by far my favorite soprano. I spent hours listening to her records because her singing touched me deeply, her voice was immediately recognizable, and I loved her natural, unaffected style. I only heard her perform live twice, in recital at the Théâtre Athénée in Paris in the 1970s and some years later at the Nice Opera at the very end of her career. I met her after the Paris recital and I tried to persuade her to teach me or coach me but she said that she was not teaching. It was from listening to her Spanish songs that I came to love the Spanish repertoire that she championed in her recitals. The evening of her death I dedicated my performance of Mahler's *Rückert Lieder* to her. The next day I had planned to meet my close friend, Pasqual Maragall, the president of Catalonia and the previous mayor of Barcelona, for lunch on my way to the airport. He called me and asked me if I could come earlier so that we could go to pay our respects to Victoria where her body was lying in state. I expected to arrive at one of the churches in Barcelona but Pasqual's car pulled up to the seat of the Catalonian government; I could not even see the end of the line of the people who had also come to pay their respects to her. She was so loved by people from all over the world. I was honored to be there at that time to be able to say thank you and farewell to a great inspiration.

Olivier and I had hoped to buy my catalogue from EMI but were categorically refused. Alain Lanceron, who had replaced Peter Alward at EMI Classics, also blocked the transaction for us to get the rights to license and to release my recordings on Arte Verum, even though EMI would have earned royalties.

Arte Verum's second release was *Schumann Lieder* with Roland Pöntinen. The third release was *Endless Pleasure*: George Frideric Handel and Henry Purcell arias with the Drottningholms

Barockensemble. Olivier had the idea to follow the example of the British pop group Radiohead, who had made one of their albums, *In Rainbows*, available for free download from the Internet. I thought that it was a great idea and we decided to allow each person the discretion to pay whatever they could or wanted to pay for the music, thus setting his or her own price or not paying anything at all.

This was the first time that this had been done by a classical music artist. I agreed to try this experiment but I wanted to make it very clear to those who downloaded the music that I believe that the mp3 players can never do justice to the sound that we have researched and strived to acquire in our recordings. I hoped to inspire the young listeners who downloaded the music to want to listen to the actual CD or better yet to have the optimal experience of hearing a live classical concert—not even necessarily one of mine.

The overwhelming majority of music users of the Internet are young people who may have never heard a concert of classical music, either in the concert hall or on television. I wanted to give them a chance to have access to the music composed by two great geniuses, Handel and Purcell, but I also wanted make it clear to my young listeners that only the artist has the rights to her own work. I can decide to offer my work with the conditions that I have chosen myself but I would not look kindly on someone stealing my work or the work of others—besides it is unjust, immoral, and I hope illegal. The campaign was a success: more than five thousand Internet users downloaded the CD and 60 percent paid a price that was more than we had expected.

Too often I hear young people say, "I don't like classical music," when they have never had an opportunity to hear a live concert. This is a sign of the cultural poverty of our society today, where ignorance tends to breed a kind of comfort. I do not think that everyone will like or feel a connection to the music that I like, but it seems so sad that our children are completely unaware of the existence of so much that is the cultural heritage of all humanity. I have been so disappointed to hear politicians say, "The classical arts—music, dance, opera, and theater and even literature—should have to compete on an equal footing with popular art forms and if it cannot support itself then it should become extinct like the dinosaurs." If a parent were to present a child a choice at the dinner table between ice cream or cake and spinach or broccoli, she would be considered irresponsible. A society has a responsibility for the cultural nutrition of its citizens, and especially its children.

When I started my career in Europe, each country in Western Europe had at most three television channels. Classical music and the other fine arts had a place in the audiovisual landscape. But shortly after the opening up of the media in Europe, the European cultural scene was abandoned to include only pop culture and sport in the mass media.

In most European countries cultural programming disappeared from the mainstream channels or was relegated to the wee hours of the morning. This means that children who should be in bed before midnight can grow into adulthood without ever having had any exposure not only to classical music, but also to dance and theater, unless their parents have taken them to performances or if they have had exposure to cultural activities in school. The transmission of many of my performances of operas and concerts live on European public service television and radio during prime-time contributed greatly to the unique prominence and celebrity that I have among all classes of Europe's citizens. It is impossible for my younger colleagues to get that exposure today.

The record industry is still struggling. In 2012 Universal bought EMI and the classical catalog was sold to Warner Music. The label EMI Classics ceased to exist. In the last ten years I have recorded fifteen CDs. Arte Verum has released eleven of them since 2006, and I continue to record at least two new CDs a year. I feel as if I have been resurrected from the EMI burial ground where my work had been consigned by some marketing guru. When EMI was in its death throes, due to the positive attention that Arte Verum has garnered they rereleased most of my recordings, albeit in very cheap versions, with poorly photocopied photos and no booklet. At least they exist. My artistic portrait is filling out again with my repertoire and on my terms. My recording career is in the best health ever—vocally, mentally, and musically. I plan to keep Arte Verum moving ahead at full speed as long as I am able to perform well. I am enjoying every minute of the ride.

Encounters 13

Only the individual can think, and thereby create new values for society—nay, even set up new moral standards to which the life of the community conforms. Without creative, independently thinking and judging personalities the upward development of society is as unthinkable as the development of the individual personality without the nourishing soil of the community.

— Einstein

I have no special talent. I am only passionately curious.

—Einstein

Kofi Annan

Today, in Afghanistan, a girl will be born. Her mother will hold her and feed her, comfort her, and care for her—just as any mother would anywhere in the world. In these most basic acts of human nature, humanity knows no divisions. But to be born a girl in today's Afghanistan is to begin life centuries away from the prosperity that one small part of humanity has achieved. It is to live under conditions that many of us in this hall would consider inhuman.

I speak of a girl in Afghanistan, but I might equally well have mentioned a baby boy or girl in Sierra Leone. No one today is unaware of this divide between the world's rich and poor. No one today can claim ignorance of the cost that this divide imposes on the poor and dispossessed who are no less deserving of human dignity, fundamental freedoms, security, food, and education than any of us. The cost, however, is not borne by them alone. Ultimately, it is borne by all of us—north and south, rich and poor, men and women of all races and religions.

With these words Kofi Annan began his Nobel Prize acceptance speech on December 10, 2001. Some minutes earlier, and without having had the time to confer with him, I had walked to the stage with the help of crutches and sang, "Sometimes I Feel Like a Motherless Child." It was a magical coincidence.

Kofi and I had met on a few occasions in Geneva and in some international forums in Europe before he became secretary general, but we had never sat down together for an in-depth conversation until I met him at UN headquarters in New York in the spring of 1998 with a message from Aung San Suu Kyi, who brought us together for our first policy meeting.

During Kofi's tenure at the UN, Ulf and I became close friends with him and his Swedish wife, Nane Lagergren, a jurist, a painter, and the niece of Raoul Wallenberg.

Whenever Ulf and I were on our way in or out of New York, Kofi managed to squeeze in a brief meeting with us and we quickly covered the issues of the day. Sometimes he could only manage a quick early breakfast at their home on Sutton Place in New York. We sometimes were able to meet when he came to Geneva to meet with UN agencies there. I often wanted to get his feedback about events happening in the world and in turn to give him encouragement. Whenever I called he always called back as soon as he had the time. In addition to talking about the challenges that the UN and the UNHCR faced daily, we also spoke about our families.

Kofi and I have both have Swedish spouses, but we also have other Swedish connections in common that extended beyond our affairs of the heart.

Before I ever met Nane, Raoul Wallenberg had been an inspiration to me. I was moved by his courage and determination to save Hungarian Jews from the Holocaust, and by the mystery surrounding his disappearance after he was arrested by the Soviet army in 1945. When I was president of La Fondation pour l'Action Humanitaire in Paris, I tried to get permission from his family to name a think tank on human rights defenders after him. We did not receive the permission—at the time, I did not know Nane or her mother, Nina Lagergren, Raoul Wallenberg's sister.

I almost did not make it to Oslo. I had fallen on the stairs at home ten days before and had to cancel a concert with Yuri Bashmet in Moscow because I had sprained my right ankle and had pulled a muscle in my right thigh. I was to sing two Christmas concerts at Carnegie Hall in New York entitled "Let There Be Peace on Earth" in honor of the victims and heroes of the September 11 tragedy.

Kofi and Nane had been planning to attend the Christmas concert for a long time, but when I called to congratulate him and the UN on being the recipient of the 2001 Nobel Peace Prize he said, "Unfortunately this means that we will not be able to come to your concert at Carnegie Hall on December 4 because we must already be in Oslo at that time. Maybe you can come to Oslo." Shortly afterward I received the invitation to sing for the Peace Prize ceremony and the gala concert.

I travelled on the Concorde from Paris and back for the last time. I had done this trip before with crutches and a leg brace, but I did not expect to catch a terrible cold on the flight over. I had two days to try to recover before the first rehearsal, but I had with me my usual potions, mostly homeopathic, that have always worked for me, so I was sure that I would be able to sing. Though it is uncomfortable, I am used to singing with a common cold and have sung well in spite of it. Having a cold had hardly ever caused me to cancel a concert. I went to the orchestra rehearsal with the New York Pops Orchestra conducted by Skitch Henderson and was certain that after warming up a bit I would manage. To my stupefaction I could not even sing a single complete phrase of "Silent Night"—some notes came out and others did not sound at all. After trying and hoping during the first part of the rehearsal I asked the orchestra director to call a throat doctor at the break, and we left to see him immediately. The doctor only confirmed what I had feared during the rehearsal: I had more than a cold. I had laryngitis and would neither be able to sing the first concert the following day nor, most likely, the second one. He gave me a shopping bag full of medicines, charged me nearly one thousand dollars, asked for an autograph, and wished me well. I looked into the shopping bag, took out the medicines, and, after very carefully reading the labels, decided to discard them. I have never taken such strong medicine. I knew that the medicines he had given me were not going to produce a miracle and might even cause me some damage. I have always pushed myself to my limits but have maintained great respect for my body and accepted its verdict when it refuses to go further. The orchestra manager said that he hoped that I would be able to sing the second concert, but by the end of the afternoon he had already replaced me and rehearsed with a new singer.

I immediately tried to get a flight back to Europe because I had to rest and get well for the Nobel ceremony and gala concert. It was Christmastime and there was not a single seat available on any Air France flight in any class back to Paris. I had bought my ticket with my Air France frequent flyer miles and could not change airlines. So there I was, stuck in my hotel, and the trip was becoming expensive. On the day of the second concert, the sun was shining, and I hobbled across the street to a French bistro where I often ate when I was in town; they greeted me warmly and gave me some sympathy. When I returned to my room it was being cleaned so I went back down and tried to take a little walk across the street just to kill some time. On previous trips I had enjoyed looking in the window of an antique jewelry shop, and I lingered in front of the window for a while before venturing inside. I began trying on bracelets just for fun, but I kept looking longingly at one really beautiful bracelet. The owner noticed this and asked me if I would like to try it. I said, "Yes, but it is too expensive for me." He said, "Business is so bad since September 11 because the tourists have not come back to the city. If you really want this bracelet I am willing to sell it to you for only a little more than I paid for it." He called his assistant who brought a book with his purchases and he showed me what he had paid—a great deal less than his asking price. We made a deal and I bought it. He saw that I was a little hesitant and he said, "Take it now and think about it. Come back tomorrow if you change your mind. I will take it back." I left with the bracelet and called one of my best friends, Sheila, in Paris and told her the story. I said, "You know I am not earning a single penny here and running up a very nice hotel and room service bill as well." She said, "Keep the bracelet, you deserve it." When I called Ulf later in the day he said, "I agree with Sheila."

So I stepped up to the podium in the Oslo city hall with my new bracelet hidden under the sleeve of my dress. I walked with crutches up to the podium and had enough time to get into position and discard my crutches while the camera was on the person who was introducing me. I had worn my navy blue hiking boots because they were the only shoes in which I could manage to walk a few steps without the crutches since they held my ankle firmly in place. When I settled into position I looked down and saw my boots peeking out from under my long concert dress, so I gingerly lifted the front of the dress and placed it over the tip of the boots. I noticed that the Norwegian princess, who was seated on the front row, giggled when she saw my shoes. I stood there full of pride for all of my friends, my colleagues, the refugees, and all who have supported UN ideals since 1945. It was a great honor for me as a member of the UN family to lift my voice in song for the United Nations organization.

Dag Hammarskjöld, the second secretary general of the UN, was possibly assassinated on his way to negotiate a ceasefire in the escalating civil war in the newly independent Belgian Congo in 1961, and received the Nobel Prize posthumously that year. JFK called him "the greatest statesman of the century." He has certainly been a light to many of us who try to put one step in front of the other on the road to making the world a better place. Hammerskjöld once remarked, "The pursuit of peace and progress cannot end in a few years in either victory or defeat. The pursuit of peace and progress, with its trials and its errors, its successes and its setbacks, can never be relaxed and never abandoned." He later said, "Everything will be all right—you know when? When people, just people, stop thinking of the United Nations as a weird Picasso abstraction and see it as a drawing they made themselves." Now, forty years after Hammarskjöld's death, Kofi Annan, the seventh secretary general, was receiving the Nobel Prize for the

UN, and he still had to deal with internal strife in the ex-Belgian Congo, where instability and violence continue today.

The Nobel Peace Prize was for all of the dedicated people working in the field who are responsible for the success stories that never get covered by the media. They were finally receiving just a few minutes of gratitude and appreciation in the international limelight. Little did we know that the consequences of September 11 would result in the Iraq War and that the lead-up to that war would itself be almost the undoing of the organization.

Aung San Suu Kyi

In 2007 I wrote an article titled "From Little Rock to Rangoon" that was printed in several European newspapers. This is an excerpt:

> I have been following with great emotion the celebration of the fiftieth anniversary of the desegregation of Central High School in Little Rock Arkansas. I found myself reliving this frightening and revelatory event at the same time that courageous monks and ordinary Burmese people were marching for freedom and pleading for our support. I waited for a reaction from the International Community and since the UN General Assembly was taking place in New York City, I thought that the timing was perfect for a serious response. Once more, the Security Council showed its ineffectuality. A scream of indignation stuck in my throat every time I heard yet another head of state or foreign minister say the right words of support without showing the necessary will to act on them. And as they were talking the Military Junta in Burma started to crack down on the demonstrators with its usual tactics.
>
> The American and European neoconservatives did not hesitate to support sending troops to Iraq to fight an illegal war in the name of democracy and freedom but are content with mere declarations of support for the suffering people of Burma. Maybe we should drop our hypocrisy and just say, "We do not want to jeopardize our oil and commercial

interests." President Eisenhower was not prointegration but he made a courageous decision that changed the course of American history and the bell tolling for justice can be heard from Little Rock to Rangoon. Here in the European Union, where is our courage, and how are we living our conviction to defend human rights?

How many times can we stand by and do nothing like we did in Budapest in '56, Prague in '68, Soweto in '76, and Tiananmen Square in '89? What exactly—other than offering statements of disapproval or moral outrage—are the Security Council and the European Union proposing to do in response to the repression and massacre of innocent people? Where is the Security Council? Where is Europe?

> Barbara Hendricks, Musician
> President, Barbara Hendricks Foundation for Peace and
> Reconciliation

Aung San Suu Kyi is the only daughter of Aung San, who is considered the father of Burma. She is the leader of the National League for Democracy party and in the 1990 general election her party won 59 percent of the vote and 81 percent of the seats in the parliament. But the governing junta refused to respect the election results. She was under house arrest from 1989 until 2010. She received the Nobel Peace Prize in 1991. I have followed her since that election because her conviction and courage deeply moved me. Her plight and the total inability of the international community to help her and her people were so hard for me to passively accept. In 1998 I was on tour in Asia and had several days free between a concert in Singapore and one in Hong Kong. I had spoken with the Swedish Foreign Ministry to help me contact her in Burma, but there were no Nordic embassies there—the nearest was in Thailand. I arrived in Bangkok with a few hours to wait for my connecting flight to Singapore and decided to take a chance and call my friend Hubert Védrine, the best foreign minister that France has had in our time. I was lucky because not only was he in his office, he was also free to take my call. I told him what I wanted to do. He said that he would do whatever he could and assured me that I would have a message waiting for me when I arrived at my hotel in Singapore. And indeed upon arrival I was handed a message from the French ambassador in Rangoon. I called him back and he assured me that he could help me. I had gotten a tourist visa with no problem before leaving Geneva and had booked a round trip flight to Rangoon from Singapore. The French ambassador met me at the airport and was able to facilitate my entry into the country. I expected him to take me to a hotel but he insisted that I stay at the embassy with him and his wife. At that time, in spite of the fact that Aung San Suu Kyi was under house arrest, she was allowed to go to a few embassies from time to time, and as chance would have it she had been studying French with the ambassador's wife. She usually came on Fridays. When the ambassador heard that I wanted to meet her he very cleverly got a message to her that it was imperative that she be there for her lesson. We sat waiting for her, not knowing if she had received the message or if she was going to come.

When I heard the car pull up outside the embassy, my heart raced. After a few minutes Aung San Suu Kyi walked through the door, beautiful and serene. We spent several hours together talking about her struggle and her sacrifices. We both have two children, although hers are a bit older than mine, and as I listened to her and absorbed her aura of calm, I could not imagine sacrificing the opportunity to watch my children growing up. Her conviction was so solid, so true, and so Zen. The way she fought for her beliefs and even embraced her singular and difficult destiny was a great inspiration to me. She asked me if I thought that she and her people could use the example of Martin Luther King and the civil rights movement to fight for justice in Burma. I told her how the civil rights movement had taken form in the churches of the south where blacks were free to attend even when their right to assemble elsewhere was denied. "Buddhists do not assemble on a regular basis and without the possibility to have contact with the people and to get your message to them, I think that organizing the masses in the same way would be extremely difficult," I said. However, in 2007, when the Buddhist monks took an important lead in the rebellion against the junta, I thought to myself that maybe she was right after all.

She asked me to take back a message, rather a plea for help for her people. She wanted sanctions against the government and travel restrictions for the members of the junta and their families.

After my concert in Hong Kong I went to New York to record the *Give Me Jesus* album with the Moses Hogan Singers. As soon as I left Rangoon I contacted Kofi's office to ask for a meeting with him because I had a message for him directly from Aung San Suu Kyi.

He received me in-between meetings with the weapons inspectors Richard Butler, chairman of the UN Special Commission for Weapons Inspections in Iraq, and Scott Ritter. Both of them would later oppose the invasion of Iraq in 2003. I did not have very much time so I went directly to the point.

I not only related her message to Kofi but also personally to Manuel Marin, the European Commissioner, whose portfolio of External Affairs included Burma, and to Mary Robinson in Geneva, who was the head of the UN Human Rights Commission. Everyone who listened to me agreed to do what they could but were helpless because within the international community, and in particular the Asian countries, the will was totally lacking to deal seriously with the Burmese dictatorship and their hold on the Burmese people. I cannot say it enough: without the full support of the Security Council, nothing ever gets done in the political arena at the UN. During this time under Kofi's leadership the UN worked hard to establish a dialog between Aung San Suu Kyi and the military junta and worked tirelessly for her release, which finally came in November 2010.

When I returned home from New York I sent her messages and some of my Mozart recordings by diplomatic courier. I called her husband Michael Aris in England, who had just been diagnosed with cancer, but he was more concerned about her. "How did she look, is she well?" he asked me. "Having never met her before I cannot really say, but I found her to be fine, strong, and beautiful." He seemed relieved but did not ask more questions. When it was known that his cancer was terminal he asked the

Burmese to give him a visa to visit her. Instead they offered her the possibility to leave Burma to visit him but she refused, knowing that they would never let her come home again. She felt that she had to be with her people and that she would be more effective continuing her struggle from within the country than from exile in London. In spite of pleas from Kofi, Pope John Paul, and others, Aris was not allowed to enter Burma to see his wife before his death in 1999. I wrote a letter to her when I heard about her husband's passing but do not know if she ever received it.

In 2002 Aung San Suu Kyi was temporarily released and I was thrilled. Since 1998 I had always hoped to go back to see her again but it was very difficult. I had never made public my secret visit at the French embassy but I felt that it was so important not to let the opportunity of her release slip by. I wrote an editorial in *Le Monde* begging the world not to let their guard down, not to assume that the fight was over and that she had won because she had been released. A year later she and her convoy were attacked and many of her supporters were massacred. She escaped unharmed but was arrested and spent three months in prison before being returned to house arrest for the next seven years. During this time the UN worked tirelessly for her release, which finally came in November 2010. I watched the news on the Internet and when she walked out of the house to greet her supporters I could not see any signs that time and isolation had put a single line in her brow. The political situation changed rapidly after her release and she had a chance to run for office. In April 2012 she was elected to the lower house of Parliament. I hope that she will use her voice to speak up against the injustice, violence, and oppression suffered by minorities in Burma.

Aung San Suu Kyi's first trip to Europe after her release from house arrest was to Switzerland. On June 14, 2012, the president of Switzerland, Eveline Widmer-Schlumpf, invited me to a reception where Aung San Suu Kyi and I had a brief reunion.

The struggle for democracy is not over and we do not know how important a role she will be allowed to play in the future of her country, but we must stay vigilant because she will never give up and we should not either.

Vaclav Havel

In 1992, during George H. W. Bush's presidency, I was invited to sing at the White House after the state dinner given in honor of the newly elected president of Czechoslovakia, Vaclav Havel. This was his first state visit to the US capital. Havel had been a great inspiration to me for many years and I jumped at the chance to honor him, his vision, and his courage. He was a man of the theater and a dissident who chose not to go into exile but to stay and fight for his beliefs from within the country. He was a passionate believer of nonviolent resistance and his motto was "Truth and love must prevail over lies and hate." I had been asked to perform previously for state dinners but my schedule had not permitted it. I was not at all free for this concert but I twisted myself into a pretzel and shifted my schedule around in order to be in Washington that day. I had a rehearsal the following day in London with Sir Colin Davis and the London Symphony Orchestra. I explained the situation to Sir Colin and he accepted that I would arrive a little late. The concert in Washington would not finish in time for me to catch the regular flight from Washington to London, but luckily I was able to hitch a ride on a private plane.

At the black-tie state dinner I was seated opposite Havel but it was a little difficult for me to speak to him directly because Barbara Bush and another person were seated between us. On my name card, "entertainment!" was written. I wondered if someone expected me to jump out of a cake. Mrs. Bush was presiding at our table and President Havel was seated on her right. Her staff had obviously informed her that I had made a special effort to perform at the state dinner. She said to him, indicating me, "Mr. President, Mrs. Barbara Hendricks, who is our entertainment for this evening, is a great fan of yours. She has flown in from Europe just for this occasion and will be leaving immediately after her concert to go to London for a rehearsal there tomorrow. She is probably the only person at this table who has read some of your plays and books." He looked at me with wide eyes and acknowledged me with a smile and a nod. And I thought to myself, "Not only at this table but also in this room." Neither any great American playwrights nor any writers had been invited to the dinner.

As far as I could tell the only other artist in the room was the actor Leslie Nielsen, who had starred in the *Naked Gun* films. I managed to say to Havel that I had read everything of his that had been translated into French and English and that one of my favorites was his "Letters to Olga" (written during his longest stay in prison, from 1979 to 1984). After the dinner I performed a short recital of American songs and a song cycle by the Czech composer Antonin Dvořák, *Gypsy Songs*, that I usually sang in German. But that night I sang the most well known song of the group, "Songs My Mother Taught Me," in Czech for him. I had studied the Czech pronunciation with Olga Pavlovska, the widow of the painter Oskar Kokoschka, who had fled the Nazis during World War II and settled in Montreux.

After the concert, I changed quickly and we rushed to our car to go to the airport but I nearly missed my plane; just as we were driving out of the White House grounds we were stopped by White House security because Mrs. Bush was walking her dogs, and no one could be on the grounds at the same time. So we had to sit in the car thirty minutes before leaving for the airport, and we barely made it in time for take-off.

After that first brief meeting I met President Havel again in Prague in his "White House." In 1994 I was invited to sing a benefit concert for the Olga Havel Foundation in the beautiful Spanish Hall of the palace that also houses the president's office. I was thrilled to finally meet the famous Olga, to whom the "Letters to Olga" had been written. She turned out to be even more impressive in person than the woman I imagined from the letters. I felt as if I already knew this truly extraordinary woman. I sang Mozart arias from *Le nozze di Figaro*, *Cosi fan tutti*, and *Don Giovanni* in the first half of the program. During the intermission President Havel went back to his office to wait for an important call that continued through the beginning of the second half of the concert. I was then waiting in my dressing room when his secretary came in and said that President Havel wanted to invite me to visit him in his office.

His presidency was still young, but in 1991 he had already ended the Warsaw Pact, the mutual defense treaty between the Soviet Union and eight Eastern European countries. This achievement meant a great deal to him; he was quite proud the Soviet counterweight to NATO no longer existed. It seemed as if he could still hardly believe that everything was real and not just a dream that he was having in his prison cell. He showed me around his office and we spent an unforgettable hour speaking about the politics of the past and his vision for the future of his county. I politely drank the very strong sparkling Czech wine that he offered me as he smoked nonstop. When Martin and Olga joined us for the reception after the concert, I could feel a little buzz in my head from the wine, and I asked myself if I, too, were in a dream.

Olga's death two years later was a terrible shock to me and a great loss to her husband as well as the many whose lives she had influenced. He too had serious health problems and after Olga's death he finally stopped smoking. After he left the presidency he wrote more plays, supported a dissident theater group from Belarus, and worked for human rights and tolerance in Europe. He and his second wife Dagmar came to my concerts whenever I was in Prague.

I was in my kitchen making preparations for Christmas when I heard of his death on December 18, 2012. I was very affected by the loss of one of my great inspirations and I know that the world is a better place because he walked among us for seventy-five years.

Maya Angelou

Sometimes it takes only one meeting with a person for her to mark you for a lifetime.

The wonderful renaissance woman Maya Angelou was born April 4, 1928. You cannot classify her in one category because she has done so many different and varied things. She studied with the American dance pioneer Martha Graham and danced with Alvin Ailey. She toured Europe with a production of *Porgy and Bess*, recorded an album, and was in an off-Broadway review, where she performed her own compositions. She was a member of the Harlem Writer's Guild and is a civil rights activist and feminist. For me she is a poet of life. In 1961 she moved to Cairo with her son

Guy to live with Vusumzi Make, a South African freedom fighter, and at the end of that relationship she moved to Ghana and taught at the University of Ghana in the music and drama department, where she met and befriended Malcolm X. She moved back to the United States in 1964 to help him build a new civil rights movement, the Organization for Afro-American Unity, but shortly after her return he was assassinated. Dr. Martin Luther King asked her to be the Northern Coordinator for the Southern Christian Leadership Conference that was founded after the arrest of Rosa Parks in 1955 and the subsequent Montgomery Bus Boycott. Maya was devastated when he too was assassinated on her fortieth birthday. She sent flowers to his widow Coretta King every year on that date until Mrs. King died in 2007.

With the help and encouragement of her good friend and mentor, the writer James Baldwin, whom she had met in Harlem Writer's Guild, she began to write an autobiography that helped her overcome her grief. The result was *I Know Why the Caged Bird Sings*, published in 1970 to international acclaim.

My first encounter with her was in the passages that told the story of her early life. At the age of three she and her brother were sent to live with their paternal grandmother in Stamps, Arkansas. At the age of eight when she went back to live with her mother in Saint Louis, Missouri, she was raped by her mother's boyfriend, who was later found murdered, probably by one of her uncles. Maya was so sure that she was responsible for his death—because she had accused him of rape—that she didn't speak another word for more than five years. After the murder she and her brother returned to Stamps but finally she went back to her mother, this time in San Francisco. Maya finished high school at the age of seventeen, a few months before her son Guy was born.

As a young girl I was a voracious reader and enjoyed novels such as *Little Women* and *Jane Eyre*. Maya Angelou's book was a revelation. For the first time in my life I read about a little Negro girl growing up in rural Arkansas who had similar experiences to my own. Even though she was twenty years older, her early years in Arkansas at her grandmother's home even seemed to be a mirror of mine. Little had changed in those twenty years. I recognized the racism and the fear as well as the humble and noble characters who struggled to maintain their dignity in a system where their lives had less value than the farm animals. I recognized the songs she sang, the simple joys, the solidarity, the rural church, and strict pious upbringing. She had a teacher, Mrs. Flowers, who helped her to speak again and who introduced her to great literature, just like my high school teacher, Mrs. Harper, would do for me; and we shared a great love of Shakespeare. I was reading her book during a break at an opera rehearsal and I started to laugh, cry, and laugh again uncontrollably. Everyone looked curiously at me. I started to tell the story and realized that what I found so funny they would not understand.

In 1987 French *Vogue* asked me to be the guest editor for their December–January issue. They had guest editors once a year and I was allowed to decide completely what the main section of the magazine would contain. I had a section on up-and-coming young classical musicians and I wanted to feature artists and other personalities whose work had been important to me. For my issue I invited guests to have a conversation with a journalist, a writer, or a colleague. I wanted to have a conversation between Bernard Kouchner and Mother Teresa. I tried on many occasions to reach her but without success. One day, just as I was about to give up, I called her office and she answered the phone herself. We chatted a while but she finally said that she regretted not to be able to do the conversation for the magazine. Instead I had an excellent article with Abbé Pierre, the French Catholic priest who started Emmaus, and that was the beginning of a close friendship that lasted until his death. The Italian conductor Riccardo Muti was interviewed by André Tubeuf; the Hungarian conductor Antal Dorati interviewed his close friend Torolf Engström, Martin's father, who was a well-known painter and sculptor in Sweden; the publisher of the Montreal daily *La Presse* interviewed the Canadian baritone Gino Quilico; and Francesca Comencini interviewed her father Luigi Comencini. However the great black American Maya Angelou I kept for myself.

I flew to New York and met her at the Algonquin Hotel. We did not have an interview but a fantastic conversation. We shared two of the most inspiring hours of my life, hours filled with howls of laughter and tears. I started off by telling her how much the first book of her autobiography had meant to me and she asked me, "Do you know the poem 'Sympathy' written by Paul Laurence Dunbar that begins 'I know what the caged bird feels, alas!' and ends 'I know why the caged bird sings'?" She did not wait for an answer but said, "A bird does not sing because it has an answer but because it has a song." We spoke about how important it is to keep close to your roots. She disagreed with the writer Thomas Wolfe, who wrote, "You can't go home again." She and I agreed that we carry everything, our home and experiences, with us wherever we go. I was curious to know more about how she wrote and the role that her readers play in her work. She described a ritual that she started when she wrote *I Know Why the Caged Bird Sings*. She rose at five in the morning, checked into a hotel, and went to a room where the walls were bare, cleared of any photos or pictures. She wrote on a yellow legal pad while lying on the bed with a deck of cards to play solitaire, a bottle of sherry, the Bible, and Roget's Thesaurus.

Maya Angelou said in a 1989 interview with the BBC that she goes through this process to "enchant" herself and to "relive the agony, the anguish, the Sturm und Drang." She places herself back in the time she is writing about, even traumatic experiences like her rape in *Caged Bird*, in order to "tell the human truth" about her life. She also stated that she played cards in order to get to that place of enchantment, in order to access her memories more effectively. "It may take an hour to get into it, but once I'm in it—ha! It's so delicious!" She does not find the process cathartic; rather, she has found relief in telling the truth.

When she spoke to me about her relationship to her readers and the vision of the task that she was born to accomplish, I felt as if I had found a true sister. She said, "If no one reads me I do not exist. I need to know that people laugh in rehearsal as you did or shed a tear on the subway while reading my words. I enjoy reading letters from people who write, 'You give me courage.' In my autobiography, I write *I* but I mean *We*."

We met again briefly during the presidential inaugural celebrations for Bill Clinton in 1993. The president had chosen her to write a poem for the ceremony. With her usual sense of history she kept us spellbound as she recited "On the Pulse of the

Morning." She also invited me to her seventieth birthday party, organized by her good friend Oprah Winfrey in Winston-Salem, North Carolina, in 1998.

"Courage is the most important of all the virtues," she once said, "because without courage you can't practice any other virtue consistently. You can practice any virtue erratically, but nothing consistently without courage."

Bill Clinton and Aretha Franklin

In the 1970s when I performed for junior and high school students in the Lincoln Center Student Program in the New York inner city schools, I always used the example of Aretha Franklin to explain to them the repertoire that I could not sing. At that time I never imagined that I might meet the great Aretha someday or that I would actually sing with her. The producer George Stevens Jr. invited me to sing at the annual Christmas concert in Washington in December 1990, which the presidents and their wives usually attended. I sang Gounod's "Ave Maria" and a medley of Christmas carols with some of the other artists, including Reba McIntyre, John Denver, and Aretha Franklin. Aretha and I sang a duet together. She was quite distant to me at first. I think that she expected an opera singer to behave like a capricious diva. During our first rehearsal I could not contain my enthusiasm and told her that I thought she had one of the greatest voices of all time and that I was honored to be on stage with her. She immediately warmed up to me.

President Bush was suffering from the flu and consequently Mrs. Bush came alone. The First Lady invited some of us back to the White House after the show. I was able to bring along my sister Ruthie and her husband, Dick, who lived not far from Washington. When Aretha sat down to play the piano, Mrs. Bush asked her to sing; she began to play "Amazing Grace" and we all joined in. Even though it was not a Christmas carol we left the White House that evening with a unique Christmas memory thanks to Aretha. The next time that we met was for the inaugural gala for President Clinton in 1993.

Although we grew up in Arkansas at the same time, William Jefferson Clinton was no more than a name to me when he decided to run for president of the United States. He had been governor of Arkansas and I knew that my mother did not like him because she was unhappy about some changes in the education system that he had made while he was in office. From the time that I became eligible to vote, my mother and I had never voted for the same person, so I decided that maybe I should check out Clinton. I had to educate myself completely about this young man from Arkansas who wanted to become the Democratic candidate for president. After he won the nomination for his party I stayed up until the wee hours of the morning to watch all of the televised debates between him and George H. W. Bush. I was impressed. He was intelligent and had a quick grasp of the issues. He did not seem as well versed or as interested in foreign affairs as was his opponent, and this lack of interest and curiosity bothered me. But I thought that all in all he was by far the better candidate for the job. It seems that Clinton sang in his high school choir. Although he is two years older than I, had we attended desegregated high schools, we might have sung together or been in some of the same classes. I had great hopes for his presidency, for someone from my generation had finally come of age and was ready to accept the responsibility to lead. He would have the opportunity to realize some of the dreams for our nation and the world that we had in our twenties in the 1960s.

It was truly an honor to be invited to participate in Clinton's pre-inauguration gala. On that day we arrived at the venue for rehearsals very early and for security reasons we were not allowed to leave until after the concert. We were given trailers to use as dressing rooms. Many of the artists had brought big entourages and staff with them. When I saw Aretha was there I went immediately to say hello to her. I could hardly get into her trailer; it was filled with her musicians and her makeup and dressing personnel. I knocked and peeked through the door; she said, "Hello, Barbara, it's good to see you again. Come in and join us." She then introduced me proudly as her opera-singing friend. Music was playing on a stereo and lively conversation was going on. When her makeup artist and her hairdresser heard that I was alone in my trailer, they offered to do my makeup and hair for me because they had lots of time to kill and couldn't leave the venue either.

I graciously declined because I always do my own makeup and hair and I wanted to be alone before the performance. I had told Martin, my sister Ruthie, and her husband, Dick, not to come backstage until the end of the show.

I met Quincy Jones there and we had time to speak about my upcoming concert at the next Montreux Jazz Festival. Quincy had performed earlier in the day at the Lincoln Memorial along with Bob Dylan, and although I did not get to meet Dylan, just knowing that we were a part of the same celebration seemed to enhance my idea that our generation was somehow coming of political age.

When I left Aretha's trailer I ran into Goldie Hawn, whom I had met briefly in Stockholm many years before with one of Martin's friends, and she invited me to her trailer with Sally Field. I went by to say hello and then wandered back to my trailer. Once the dress rehearsal was over we had to wait several hours before the concert would begin. I particularly enjoyed watching the spectacle of one of the singers who went in and out of the backstage door each time that a new television crew arrived so that she could be filmed arriving at the venue. A friend of mine in Switzerland had begged me to get an autograph from Barbra Streisand, who was a big Clinton donor and who was also singing in the gala; after the rehearsal of the finale I spoke to her and asked if I might come back to her dressing room and get an autograph for a friend. She reluctantly agreed but was so unpleasant about it that I decided against it.

I met President and Mrs. Clinton at the end of the concert. We all stood in a line backstage and they greeted each one of us and then proceeded to their waiting car. He knew that I was from Arkansas and thanked me for coming and I said that I worked for the UN and would like to contact him. He said, "Yes, please do."

The next day I had a wonderful view of the entire inauguration ceremonies of the forty-second president of the United States. In the evening Martin and I went to one of the balls. Arthur Porter, my high school choir director, was playing at the "Arkansas Ball," but I did not know this and was so sad that I had missed him there.

I wrote a letter to Clinton shortly after his inauguration about the dire situation in Bosnia because I was sure that it was not on his list of priorities. I was very disappointed that the Clinton administration did not show enough resolve in January 1993 to do what was needed to stop the killing and suffering there. I believe that Clinton considered the conflict a European problem and that the Europeans, not the United Nations—and certainly not the United States—should be the first ones to solve it. The UN Security Council is set up in a way that makes it impossible to act decisively against aggression without US support. I felt that without a concerted effort by the Security Council the Serbian forces would continue to commit the most egregious crimes against humanity right in front of our eyes, live on the nightly news, as we watched helplessly. I had put a great deal of hope in this new administration and I waited to see what they would do. A year after I sang in Washington, DC, for Clinton's inauguration and just after my return from Sarajevo I decided to write an open letter pleading for his help entitled "Hope in the First Hour, But the Faith Is Gone." It was published in the *International Herald Tribune* on January 12, 1994, but I received no response from the president.

Later in the year I had a concert in New York and wrote to ask for a meeting with him, and I did receive a polite reply offering me a photo opportunity that I summarily refused. I wanted to speak to him, not to have a photo taken with him. I wanted substance, not the appearance of substance. The situation in Bosnia was not getting any better and I felt that he might benefit from my limited but first-hand experience of the situation on behalf of the civilians and the United Nations Protection forces (UNPROFOR) under siege in Sarajevo. Later I was told that it was Hillary Clinton who had insisted that he respond to my request.

I wrote another open letter to him entitled "Stay Away from Moscow," published in the *International Herald Tribune* on May 5, 1995, when he was to go to Russia for the fiftieth anniversary of the end of World War II. I was asking him to please use the opportunity to bring up the problem in Chechnya with Russian president Boris Yeltsin. We know how that turned out.

Finally in 1995 he decided to confront the Serbs in a NATO intervention that began in August and lasted until the end of September. It led to the imperfect Dayton Accords that were signed in November 1995. This ended the fighting in Bosnia, but unfortunately only after the ethnic cleansing of ex-Yugoslavia had been successfully achieved.

Bill Clinton and I met in Dili, East Timor, for the independence ceremonies in 2002, and again in Stockholm in 2009. The Swedish Postcode Lottery has been an important donor to the UNHCR's fund raising foundation in Stockholm, of which I am president, and they invited me to a meeting that they had organized about the environment and climate change. The speakers were Bill Clinton; Tony Blair; and the Kenyan environmentalist, political activist, and Nobel Peace Prize winner Wangari Maathai. After the meeting I went back to meet Wangari, whom I knew—we have both participated several times in the yearly Spain-Africa Conferences of "Women for a Better World" that have been held both in Africa and in Spain since 2008. I also wanted to say hello to my fellow Arkansan Bill Clinton. He did remember me this time, from Timor, and we spoke briefly about how well his wife was doing as secretary of state.

Aretha still lives in Detroit, Michigan. She is the uncontested queen of soul and she also has a warm and generous soul. In 2000 I sang a recital at the University of Michigan and when I arrived for the concert there was a big beautiful bouquet of flowers with a card from her: "I am sad not to be able to come to hear you tonight and I send you my best wishes for a great concert."

Andrei Sakharov and Yelena Bonner

During a tour in the Soviet Union with Dmitri Alexeev in 1987 I had the good fortune to meet two of the great human rights activists of our time, Yelena Bonner and Andrei Sakharov. He was the father of the Soviet bomb and had the courage in the 1960s to oppose nuclear proliferation because he believed that an arms race could lead to a nuclear war. Sakharov was remarkable not only for his intelligence but also for his courage and commitment to human rights as one of the founders of the Committee on Human Rights in the USSR. He felt that human rights should be the basis for all politics and openly criticized the Soviet Union for the suppression of free expression and opinion of its citizens as well as for capital punishment and punitive psychiatry. Other members of the committee included Aleksandr Solzhenitsyn and the activist Yelena Bonner, whom Sakharov married in 1972. She was not just the wife of the great scientist but had been an ardent activist for the human rights movement many years before meeting him. He received the Nobel Peace Prize in 1975 and the Nobel Committee called him "the conscience of mankind."

My recital tour with Dmitri began in Leningrad, where I sang the first of many concerts in the legendary Philharmonic Hall near Nevsky Prospekt. I had come with a program that concluded with Rachmaninoff songs that I had studied with Jennie Tourel in New York. She had never sung in Russia so it was a very meaningful performance for me because I felt as if I had brought her home with the songs that she loved so much. The concert was filmed by French television. The legendary violinist and activist Yehudi Menuhin, who had just finished a tour in the Soviet Union the night before in the same hall, was seated in the audience with his wife Diana. The concert was a truly unforgettable and moving experience and was the beginning of a very strong relationship between the Russian audience and me.

The next day we took the night train to Moscow and it was ten below zero when we arrived. Martin and I went immediately to our rooms in the enormous Rossiya Hotel because I was longing to get some sleep. I knew not to expect luxury, but the room was very tiny—about 120 square feet—and there were two intersecting highways outside the window. The heating did not work at all and the room was like a freezer. I could have dealt with the noise of the traffic and the size of the room but not the cold because I risked getting sick.

I called our interpreter, alias KGB agent, and asked to change rooms. I was told that it was not possible because the hotel was full. "In that case, I will cancel the concert because I cannot stay two days in this freezer." Martin and I sat on our suitcases in our coats waiting for an answer for about two hours before we received a call from reception informing us that a retired general in the Russian military had given up his room for me. I was so relieved because this room was spacious and deliciously warm.

That evening the American ambassador had invited us to dinner at the American embassy. When we arrived I saw that the other guests were Yehudi and his wife and I could hardly believe my eyes because sitting next to them were Andrei Sakharov and Yelena Bonner. Although I would not have been able to have an in-depth conversation with Sakharov about his research in physics, I felt some kinship with him and an enormous admiration for his work simply because I had studied physics myself. In 1979 Sakharov had protested against the Soviet invasion of Afghanistan and was sent into internal exile in Gorky where he stayed until Gorbachev came to power. He was released in December 1986 and was allowed to return to Moscow. Now, one year later, in November 1987, I was seated next to this great man. I could hardly find the words to express my admiration for his work as a physicist searching for scientific answers about our universe and also as a humanist searching for the moral meaning of human existence. His wife spoke some French and she was able to interpret for me. During the dinner Yehudi told us that he and Diana had flown from Leningrad but when they arrived at the hotel in the afternoon they were put into a very tiny room that was extremely noisy and the heat did not work. I looked at Martin with a surprised look and then I told Yehudi about my experience with my cold room and that I had to threaten to cancel in order to change the room. And he said, "I have finished my tour and have no leverage so I have to stay in this room." I said, "Oh, Yehudi, if I did not have to sing tomorrow I would change rooms with you in a minute but I do need the warm room for tonight." I was relieved when he said, "I would not think of taking your room because you must be in top shape for your concert tomorrow so that you can give the Moscow audience the same wonderful experience that you gave us in Leningrad."

Yehudi and I met many times over the years at conferences on human rights at the Council of Europe and the European Parliament, and I performed with him often at UNESCO, including for Peter Ustinov's seventieth birthday celebration. The last time that we worked together was at his festival in Gstaad, Switzerland, with him conducting. Like the Sakharovs he also wanted to live his life based on moral criteria dictated by his conscience; he and Leonard Bernstein are among the few classical musicians I have met who have had an authentic commitment to human rights.

Danielle and François Mitterrand

The first time that I met President Mitterrand and his wife Danielle was in 1985 in Paris after the inauguration at the Trocadéro of the *parvis des droits de l'homme* (the Human Rights Plaza) on the place where the Universal Declaration of Human Rights was adopted in France on December 10, 1948. On this occasion I sang the first movement of Villa Lobos's Bachianas Brasileiras no. 5 with the Orchestre de Paris.

During the French bicentennial celebrations in July 1989 Danielle Mitterrand invited me to participate in a forum of female human rights activists from all over the world that was organized by her foundation France Libertés. The forum included, among others, Hortensia Allende, the widow of Salvador Allende, whose democratically elected government was overthrown in a military coup in Santiago, Chile on September 11, 1973; Ida Nudel, the Soviet refusenik; and the Mothers of Plaza de Mayo from Argentina, mothers and grandmothers who had become human rights activists in order to find their missing children who had been abducted by the military regime during Argentina's Dirty War (1976–1983). I also met Miriam Makeba, known as "Mother Africa." After giving a speech in 1963 at the UN against apartheid Miriam's South African citizenship was revoked and she was forced into exile. She received honorary citizenship from at least ten different countries and when we met again many years later in South Africa she told me that Danielle Mitterrand had been responsible for getting her a French passport that enabled her to travel. During two days I listened to these remarkable women and was moved and impressed with the stories of the struggle of each and every one and I realized that most were fighting alone or in a vacuum, unaware that others like themselves were also struggling at the same time. I was so grateful that Danielle Mitterrand had brought us all together because we need to fight together for ourselves and for one another. This was the beginning of a friendship, and she and I met on many occasions in the context of her foundation and my work for the UNHCR. Danielle brought Lauren Bacall and I together in Paris a year after the birthday gala for Lenny for a benefit gala for France Libertés. It was also a celebration of the hundred years of the Moulin Rouge, featuring Hollywood artists of the golden age, such as Jerry Lewis, Dorothy Lamour, Tony Curtis, Donald O'Connor, Jane Russell, and Esther Williams. Among the musicians were Ray Charles and Ella Fitzgerald, who performed an unforgettable duo.

When the program was being planned I proposed to sing an aria from Offenbach's *Barbe Bleue* that Jennie Tourel had often sung as an encore at the end of her recitals and Gershwin's "Summertime" from *Porgy and Bess*. I received word that Ella Fitzgerald also wanted to sing "Summertime," so I asked if she would not mind singing something else, since she had a much wider repertoire that coincided with what the orchestra, which was not a classical formation, could play. She was very graceful and replied very simply, "This is no problem." I met her after the concert and thanked her very humbly.

President Mitterrand's command of the French language was the first thing that attracted him to me. It was a joy to hear; I had always enjoyed listening to him whenever he spoke on television. In 1992 I received the Légion d'honneur de la Republique Française from his hands in a memorable ceremony. He was even more impressive in person than he was on television. He made personal presentations to each of the recipients who were honored on that day, and he spoke remarkably without any written notes about each person in great detail and in the most beautiful French.

I believe President Mitterrand invited me to be one of his guests on the first state visit of a French president to South Africa during President Nelson Mandela's first term because of the discussions that Danielle and I had in South Africa when we were together for Mandela's inauguration some months before. She and I had shared a common aversion to apartheid and she knew how much this new era in South Africa meant to me. In September 1994 I boarded an Airbus that carried President Mitterrand and other members of the French government. I settled in my place on the plane—I had been assigned a seat next to Hubert Védrine, Mitterrand's diplomatic advisor, with whom I became friends. I began my usual routine for an overnight flight; I changed into pajamas, put some night cream on my face, and waited for dinner to be served. I wanted to try to get as much sleep as possible. Even

though I had been invited as Mitterrand's guest with no obligation to sing or speak, I wanted to be rested for the long day ahead.
Just when I had finished my preparations one of the president's
secretaries came to me and informed me that I was to dine with
the president. I looked over at Hubert and said, "Hmm, I suppose
that one does not refuse this invitation." He laughed and said,
"No, because everyone on this plane except you knows that he
will invite only a few persons to dine with him, as is his custom,
and all would give their eye tooth to be the one to receive an invitation." So I changed back into my clothes but kept my slippers
on and went to dinner in the forward cabin. The other dinner
guests were Jack Lang, the minister of culture, whom I knew; a
female politician whom I did not know; and a mysterious young
man. I was very curious about him, and as I love to invent stories
about who people are and what they do, I decided that he had won
some kind of competition in political science and the first prize
was to go on this first state visit to postapartheid South Africa. As
it turned out he was Mitterrand's daughter's boyfriend. At that
time the existence of his daughter Mazarine was not common
knowledge except in certain circles in which I did not circulate.
President Mitterrand was quite ill then and ate only a little bul-
lion and was not very talkative. He was more curious to hear from
us. I spoke to him a little about how I saw the struggle against
apartheid in America and in South Africa as a common and universal cause for human rights. After our dessert I went back to my
seat and prepared again to get a little sleep. The next morning
we landed and were greeted on the tarmac of the airport by the
members of the South African government and President Nelson
Mandela. We went to the hotel, showered, changed our clothing,
and then were taken to Parliament where President Mitterrand
gave a speech. I was seated on the floor above the main chamber
and when I looked down it was filled with radiant black faces.
Tears ran down my face. I was very grateful for the special gift
that President Mitterrand had offered me. I was invited to a lunch
given by Jack Lang and the South African minister of culture; I
met many South African artists as well as my friends from the
previous visit, the singer Johnny Clegg and the 1991 Nobel Prize
winner in literature, Nadine Gordimer. Johnny Clegg was known

as the "white Zulu" and formed one of the first interracial bands during the apartheid era. One of the ministers asked me during the lunch if I would sing something for the two presidents during the state dinner, but I said that it would be too difficult to organize. I would need to plan it, to rehearse with musicians, do a sound check, and so forth. I am used to people asking out of the blue, "Can you sing something?" I gave it no more thought and went to the dinner. During the cocktail hour I was mingling with the other guests, speaking about the exciting day. Just as I was finishing a glass of champagne the minister from lunch came to me and said, "It is all arranged."

"What's all arranged?"

"I have spoken with both President Mandela and President Mitterrand and they would love for you to sing a song during the dinner. There is a pianist who will be playing, and I am told that he can play everything."

I put down my glass and went to speak with the pianist and asked him if he knew Gershwin's "Summertime." He said, "Of course."

"Great. I would like to do it in the key of A."

"I can play just about everything, but only in the key of C."

I spent the next half hour in the ladies room trying to warm up. I managed to make some adjustments with the key of C and somehow the performance worked. With Gershwin's simple lullaby I was able to lift my voice in celebration of the end of apartheid with President Mandela and President Mitterrand.

On January 8, 1996, I heard on my car radio that President Mitterrand had died and I stopped the car to call my friend Daniel Toscan du Plantier. Although we knew that Mitterrand was quite ill, it was still a shock for both of us. Later that evening Daniel called me and said, "Jack Lang and I have just spoken, and he and the Socialists would like for you to come and sing at the Bastille at the vigil in two days, the night before Mitterrand's funeral in Notre-Dame." I agreed in principle but everything depended on whether I could find something appropriate to sing on such an occasion. They chose "Le temps des cerises," a song associated with the Paris Commune, which ruled the city between March and May 1871 and was the first assumption of power by the working classes of the Industrial Revolution whose aim was a democratic and socialist republic. I had never heard the song before and did not know its significance for the Socialist movement. I received a fax of the song and learned it before arriving in Paris. That evening Daniel called me and asked if I would be willing to sing during the funeral services at Notre-Dame on January 11 as well. I agreed and suggested "Pie Jesu" from Fauré's Requiem.

Upon arrival in Paris I was fetched from the airport and driven directly to Mitterrand's home. Danielle greeted me at the door and thanked me for coming and agreeing to sing. She took me into his room to view his body, which was lying peacefully on the bed. I spent some time with her and then I went directly to my hotel where Daniel was waiting to go with me to rehearse for the commemoration at La Place de la Bastille.

Jack Lang guided me to the platform on the steps in front of the Opera de Bastille. The police had no precise estimate of how many were present on that cold and rainy 10th of January, and I could not make out how many were standing below me, but there were people for as far as I could see. They had come to say a last farewell to their president just as a million people had welcomed him when he was elected in 1981 as France's first Socialist president. Many were carrying roses and holding lit candles. As soon as the accordionist began to play the first notes of "Le temps des cerises" a hush descended over the whole area. My voice and the sound of the accordion filled the space for miles around La Place de la Bastille. I felt the emotion that this simple song invoked in those who were weeping silently in the crowd below, which included former prime ministers Pierre Mauroy, Michel Rocard, Lionel Jospin, and Laurent Fabius, and other prominent socialists—Elisabeth Guigou, Martine Aubry, Hubert Védrine, and the present French president, François Hollande.

Mitterrand's death marked the passing of an era. He was the last of the great leaders of his generation who had known the horrors of World War II. As a twenty-year-old I had looked to Europe for inspiration from leaders like Olof Palme in Sweden and Willy Brandt in Germany. Together with them Mitterrand was among those who have inspired people all over the world to believe in the merits of social justice and social democracy.

Wole Soyinka and Toni Morrison

In December 1993 I was the guest artist for the Nobel Prize concerts and the ceremony in Stockholm. I was doubly honored and thrilled when I found out that the literature prize was to be awarded to the black American author Toni Morrison. When her book *Beloved* was released she was completely unknown in France and her editor wanted to present her to the French public. He organized a reading. I had read her previous books *Sula* and *Song of Solomon* and had devoured *Beloved* when it was released in America. Dmitri Nabakov, Vladimir's son, who lived in Montreux, contacted me on behalf of her French editor and asked me if I would be willing to read portions of her book in French at that presentation. I jumped at the chance, not because I wanted to read aloud, but because I wanted to help in some small way to inspire the French people to want to know her work. During that presentation she read some passages in English and I followed with some passages in French. Reading aloud was much more difficult than I had imagined from my experience reading bedtime stories to Jennie and Sebastian. Morrison read her own words with such passion and I tried to read my passages with the same involvement, as if I were singing.

During the Nobel week I was fortunate to meet a previous Nobel Prize laureate in literature from 1986, Wole Soyinka, the Nigerian writer, poet, and playwright, with whom I became close friends. Wole had always been a brave and outspoken critic of military dictatorships everywhere, not just those in Nigeria. After our first meeting in 1993, Wole became a goodwill ambassador for UNESCO and we had the opportunity to meet often. He was a thorn in the side of the Sani Abacha regime in Nigeria because he chose to speak out at great risk to his life during its entire reign (1993–1998). He wrote about "the oppressive boot and the irrelevance of the colour of the foot that wears it."

In 1997 the Nigerian government charged Wole with treason and pronounced a death sentence on him in absentia. I was very afraid for him and I had to go through many different channels, using aliases, in order to contact him. We met in Switzerland and he told me how he had escaped Nigeria on foot and motorcycle to avoid certain death. A year later I ran into him by chance in a London restaurant, where he was calmly having dinner with a fellow Nigerian writer, Ben Okri. I walked over to their table and said, "Wole, I think that it is irresponsible for you to walk around London with that big head of white hair so visible that one sees you coming from a mile away. You are a perfect target—either cut your hair or wear a hat." He laughed heartily and the sound filled the room. "Dear Barbara, don't worry. I have made many sacrifices during my life to stay active and to stay alive but I am not giving up my hair. I will die with it just like this." I put him in contact with the Swedish organization IDEA, the International Institute for Democracy and Electoral Assistance in Stockholm, to ask for help for him and other Nigerian dissidents to meet and to better organize against the Abacha regime. Even after the end of that regime he still continues to speak his mind about political transgressions in his country and in the world.

Henning Mankell and Ingmar Bergman

During the many summers that I spent on Gotland I longed to run into Ingmar Bergman, who had a house on Fårö and was usually there during the summer months. This was a dream because I knew that the chances were nil for us to run into one another otherwise. However we nearly met because I had become friends with his son-in law, the writer Henning Mankell. Henning contacted me and invited me to participate in a long interview with him for German *Vogue* and we connected immediately. Shortly afterward he asked me for another interview, which we did together in a small boat on the waters surrounding Stockholm for the Franco-German TV network Arte, and this sealed our friendship. When I learned that he was married to one of Ingmar Bergman's daughters, Eva, I related a funny story about my only meeting with Bergman at the stage entrance of Dramaten, the Royal Dramatic Theater, where Bergman had been the boss and where my husband, Ulf, had learned his craft.

Ulf and I had been out shopping at the nearby market when I needed urgently to go to the toilet. As we were quite near the theater Ulf suggested that I pop in through the stage door because there was a toilet just inside. When I walked in I saw two people standing between the inner and outer doors of the entrance with their heads together engaged in what seemed like a very important discussion. One was the actress Gunnel Lindblom and the other was Bergman. I would have loved to speak to him but I did not dare interrupt them. I came back after about five minutes and this time he nodded to me and opened the door for me. Later in the car, Ulf said to me, "I feel so stupid, I should have introduced you to him," and I said, "But you saw that it would have been awkward to interrupt them; their conversation seemed so intense." When I related this to Henning he told me that Bergman had already mentioned this incident to him and had said "How silly that I did not stop and speak with her." Henning then told me that Bergman had insisted that he attend one of the many screenings of my filmed performance in *La bohème*, and that Bergman was a great admirer of mine.

During the summer of 2002 we were in Gotland for the festival, and Henning tried to arrange for Ulf and me to visit Bergman on Fårö. Unfortunately that summer he was not well and the visit did not happen. He had also seen our film of Stravinsky's *Rake's Progress* directed by Inger Åby and I knew that his production of the opera for Swedish television was a legend in the annals of the opera in Sweden. It would have been wonderful to speak to him about our film and the state of public service radio and television in Sweden and in Europe. Our production of *The Rake's Progress* was one of the last operas filmed for Swedish television.

After reading the French edition of this book in one sitting, Henning called me and asked to publish the Swedish edition for his publishing house, Leopard. The book was released in October 2012 with a preface written by Henning.

Human Rights 14

Lord, make me an instrument of thy peace. Where there is hatred, let me sow love.

—Francis of Assisi

Violence can only be concealed by a lie, and the lie can only be maintained by violence.

—Aleksandr Solzhenitsyn

The world is in greater peril from those who tolerate or encourage evil than from those who actually commit it.

—Albert Einstein

I was born with an intrinsic sense of justice and fairness. Even as a small child I reacted strongly against injustice, especially when the perpetrator was in a position of power over the victim. I could not stop myself from taking a stand. I often defended my brothers when I felt that my father was unfair to them, pleading their side of an argument like a little defense attorney. I usually did not win. This does not mean that I was a little angel—far from it! I was conscious of my own bad behavior and accepted my punishment when it was just and fair. In fifth grade I was very unhappy when a new girl came into my class and was better than I was at math. I was very rude to her and I persuaded my friends to ostracize her. After a while I was the one feeling bad and was so unhappy with myself that I did a complete turnaround. She eventually became my best friend and we studied math together.

In 1985, when Jennie was one year old and Sebastian was three, we moved from Paris to Switzerland, home to many international humanitarian institutions such as the International Red Cross, and also to many United Nations agencies, including the Human Rights Commission and the United Nations High Commissioner for Refugees, the UN refugee agency. Shortly after the beginning of 1986 I received a call from Leon Davicho, the spokesperson for the UNHCR, who asked to meet me and talk about the organization. I agreed and we met in a café in Montreux.

He said, "We at the UNHCR want to start a goodwill ambassador program similar to the one that UNICEF has with Danny Kaye and Sir Peter Ustinov, and I have been given the task to recruit you to become one of our first goodwill ambassadors." I do not remember if Leon told me why I was chosen. It could be because I was always quite outspoken about my political opinions in the media. Michel Béroff and I had performed a benefit recital for Amnesty International at the Opera-Comique in Paris and I was an ardent supporter of their work for human rights.

I answered, "I have heard the name UNHCR in numerous newscasts but I have no idea about the exact function of the organization."

Leon began by giving me a detailed history of the UNHCR, its mandate, its mission, and its goals. He gave me a lot of reading material too.

The organization emerged in the wake of World War II to help Europeans displaced by that conflict. On December 14, 1950, the United Nations General Assembly optimistically established the Office of the United Nations High Commissioner for Refugees with a three-year mandate to complete its work and then disband. The following year, on July 28, the United Nations Convention relating to the Status of Refugees—the legal foundation for helping refugees and the basic statute guiding UNHCR's work—was adopted.

By 1956 UNHCR was facing its first major emergency: the outpouring of refugees from Hungary when Soviet forces crushed the Hungarian Revolution. Any expectation that the UNHCR would become unnecessary has never resurfaced. In the 1960s, the decolonization of Africa produced the first of that continent's numerous refugee crises needing UNHCR intervention. Over the following two decades, UNHCR had to help with displacement crises in Asia and Latin America. By the end of the century there were fresh refugee problems in Africa and, turning full circle, new waves of refugees in Europe from the series of wars in the Balkans.

The start of the twenty-first century has seen UNHCR helping with major refugee crises in Africa—in the Democratic Republic of the Congo and Somalia—and in Asia, especially the more than thirty-year-old Afghan refugee problem. At the same time, UNHCR has also been asked to use its expertise to help many people internally displaced by conflict within their own country. Less visibly, it has expanded its role to helping the stateless, a largely overlooked group of millions of people in danger of being denied basic rights because they do not have any citizenship. In some parts of the world, such as Africa and Latin America, the original 1951 mandate has been strengthened by agreement on regional legal instruments.

In 1954, the new organization won the Nobel Peace Prize for its groundbreaking work helping refugees in Europe. Its mandate had just been extended until the end of the decade. More than a quarter century later, UNHCR received the Nobel Peace Prize again in 1981 for what had become worldwide assistance to refugees, with the citation noting the political obstacles facing the organization. From only 34 when UNHCR was founded, it now has 6,650 national and international staff members, including 740 in its Geneva headquarters. The agency works in 118 countries, with a staff based in 108 main locations, including regional and branch offices, and 151 often remote sub-offices and field offices.

Explaining the UNHCR was the easy part. Defining the budding ambassador program was more complicated.

In the early 1980s, just as the reach of the UNHCR had to be expanded to deal with new conflicts taking place all over the world, many international governments, the sole financial support for the work of the organization, began to reduce their contributions.

Some at the UNHCR wanted to follow the successful example of UNICEF and to call upon goodwill ambassadors to help spread the message to the general public about the functions and needs of the organization in order to solicit funds and engender more governmental support. However this proposal did not appeal to everyone in the UNHCR. Many thought the time and effort that such a program would demand could be better used directly in the field where the refugees are. Sergio Vieira de Mello was one of the latter. But the high commissioner at the time, Jean-Pierre Hocké, a Swiss, was very much in favor of the program.

After studying all of the literature about the UNHCR and after more in-depth discussion with Shannon Boyd, who was to be in charge of the program, I met with Mr. Hocké and agreed to become a goodwill ambassador for an initial two-year period. Shannon was my contact person and a most faithful colleague at headquarters until her retirement in 2004. Leon, who had become my godfather in this adventure, met with me often. The more I learned about the UNHCR and the work that it did, the more I came to understand that the promotion and defense of human rights and refugee problems and solutions are closely intertwined. I became very interested in working with the organization to find durable solutions for refugees. I said to Leon, "I understand that refugees are the victims of abuse of human rights; and I believe that by accepting this offer to work together with the UNHCR, I may be able to put into action in some small way my belief that the path to peace and harmony in our lives, and in the world, must be founded on respect for the human rights of those we encounter, from the most private to the most public relationships."

The fact that the program was new and not yet clearly defined meant that I was able to design my own role as its ambassador. I did not know much about how I should proceed but I did know some of the things that I would *not* do. I had recently seen a benefit classical concert on television dedicated to raising money for victims of the Ethiopian famine in 1985. It certainly was a well-intentioned endeavor, but the juxtaposition of bejeweled ladies and photos of hungry children with swollen stomachs really bothered me. The cherry on the cake of that concert was when a richly adorned retired actress introduced an adorned (to a lesser degree) soprano and announced that she would sing "the jewel aria" from *Faust* for the hungry children in Ethiopia! So gala concerts and gala dinners, I felt, could and would be better served by someone else. I informed Leon and Shannon that a classical artist, even a very well known one, could in no way earn the same sums of money for benefit concerts that a pop or rock performer could. Nevertheless, on the political front I would give my all to be the best advocate for the rights and dignity of the refugees and would try to be an asset to the cause. I insisted that I be able to go regularly to the field, where the refugees were, and that I be independent—to speak freely and openly about what I would see and experience, without censure. They accepted my conditions and I began to work.

I was given my first copy of the Universal Declaration of Human Rights and since then I always carry a copy with me in my purse.

As soon as I accepted the offer, Shannon set about organizing my first trip to visit refugees in the field. I was to go to Zambia. This was my first ever trip to Africa and I was very excited. I had been invited several times to sing in Rhodesia (today Zimbabwe) and South Africa, and had always refused. In the last invitation to South Africa, received just before the fall of the apartheid regime, I was assured that I would be able to give some concerts in the black townships as well as the concert halls for white South Africans. They insisted that it would be no problem for me to come with my white husband because I would be designated "honorary white" during my stay and therefore we could live together in the hotel that was normally reserved for whites only. I declined the offer, saying, "I want to come to South Africa and will only do so when I can come as just a human being." I was also afraid that once I was there they could manipulate my visit to fit their own scenario and I did not want to have anything to do with that. After my unforgettable visit for the inauguration of Nelson Mandela I did return to South Africa in 2002 to perform concerts with the great Miriam Makeba, Mother Africa, whom I had met while she was in exile in 1989 in Paris with Danielle Mitterrand. This time I came not as an "honorary white" but as an African to sing my classical repertoire and some South African songs that

Miriam taught me. We were working on a European tour together but it did not materialize because of her untimely death.

I arrived in Lusaka, Zambia, in the fall of 1987. I was to visit two different groups of refugees. The first were Namibians who were on the verge of departure for their homeland where they would prepare for an independent Namibia.

In 1884 the Germans colonized South-West Africa and between 1904 and 1907 nearly decimated the indigenous population in what was the first genocide of the twentieth century. They dispossessed the land of the survivors and installed a system of forced labor and racial segregation following the example of the Jim Crow laws in the American South. This would be the precursor of the apartheid system that came later to South Africa and Rhodesia. During World War I the British occupied the colony and administered it as a League of Nations mandate territory; they gave it to South Africa in 1946. The UN passed a resolution ending the mandate in 1966 and South-West Africa was renamed Namibia after the Namib Desert. South Africa refused to return the land to the UN and this provoked the Namibian War of Independence that extended to Angola and affected all of the neighboring countries in some way. These conflicts gave rise to an exodus of refugees into countries like Zambia.

After a UN peace plan was established for the region, South Africa agreed to give up the colony in 1988, and a transition to independence was underway when I arrived. I met with refugees of all ages but was most moved by the contagious enthusiasm of the teenagers and young adults who had been born outside of their homeland during the fight for independence and who had never set foot on their native soil. I will always have in my mind the sight of the open trucks packed with those singing youngsters bouncing with joy and anticipation as the trucks turned the corner out of sight toward Namibia.

This vision represents what we at the UNHCR consider our cherished outcome: refugees being able to return to their homeland to start their new lives with dignity and in peace. Many people predicted chaos and an eventual bloodbath because it was clear that the South African military was ready to fight the liberation forces and maybe go all the way to Angola. In 1968 the UN General Assembly had created the post of UN high commissioner for Namibia to assert the UN authority over the territory that was being illegally occupied by South Africa. On December 21, 1988 the high commissioner for Namibia, the Swede Bernt Carlsson, was killed on Pan Am flight 103, which was blown up over Lockerbie, Scotland. Carlsson had worked tirelessly to mediate the independence of Namibia from South Africa that the UN Security Council had agreed upon in its Resolution 435 in 1978. It took ten years to be implemented due to the resistance of the South African government and its sympathizers on the Security Council, such as the United States and Britain. It was finally implemented in June 1989, six months after the death of Bernt Carlsson, and in April one of the previous high commissioners, the Finn Martti Ahtisaari, was called in to oversee the transition from occupied country to independence.

I was not able to travel to the capital, Windhoek, for the Independence Day ceremonies that were attended by Secretary General Javier Perez de Cuellar, the president of South Africa, F. W. de Klerk, and the newly released political prisoner and future president of South Africa, Nelson Mandela. But during the early months after independence I followed with great interest the news about Namibia; despite the many difficult moments, the bloodbath that was predicted happily did not happen.

The second group of refugees that I visited in Zambia was in camps situated on its southeastern border with Mozambique. Shortly after the overthrow of Portugal's military dictator in 1974 in their Carnation Revolution led by leftist members of the military, the Portuguese colonies Angola, Mozambique, and Portuguese Guinea received their independence. For more than ten years FRELIMO, the Front for the Liberation of Mozambique, had been fighting the Portuguese for independence. Shortly after they won, an anti-communist political party was formed, RENAMO, the Mozambican National Resistance. FRELIMO supported the other liberation movements in the region, including the ANC in South Africa and ZANU in Zimbabwe. RENAMO was fostered and funded by the secret service of Rhodesia and later South Africa to fight against the government in Maputo, the capital of Mozambique. The civil war had begun in 1977 and only ended in 1992 when the Rome General Peace Accords were signed. In mid-1995 the last of the nearly two million refugees who had fled the civil war from Mozambique and who were dispersed throughout the bordering countries of Malawi, Tanzania, Swaziland, Zimbabwe, and Zambia finally returned home. Unlike the young Namibians, the Mozambican refugees that I visited in 1987 in Zambia would have to wait nearly eight more years before being able to finally return home, twenty years after their initial exodus.

Already during this first field mission I encountered the two different scenarios that I would most often come across during my subsequent trips: refugees who are able to return home in a peaceful and successful repatriation process, and the generations born and raised in exile whose desire to return is just as fierce. Neither case holds any interest for the mass media, the first because of the lack of bloodshed and drama, and the second because long, drawn-out follow-up stories do not sell.

The UNHCR did not give me any specific guidelines about what I should do during a field trip. The local representative organized my visit but I could also ask to meet with young women or with mothers and children. I was eager to know the story of each person with whom I met and spoke. Women and children comprise 80 percent of all refugees and I was immediately attracted to the children and to their mothers who were often alone with the total responsibility for their children and members of their extended families. Some even took care of orphans and the elderly who had no family. The dignity and courage with which these women assumed the responsibility, in spite of their own vulnerability within a refugee camp situation, moved me deeply and is still a source of inspiration to me.

I came away with many thoughts and images from this first mission and was impressed by the devotion of the humanitarian workers from the UNHCR as well as our indispensable partners from the UN, such as UNICEF, and the many nongovernmental organizations, such as Médicins sans Frontières, Handicap International, and the Red Cross, just to mention a few.

There were two very important elements involved in the situation on the ground in southern Africa. One, of course, was the intervention of apartheid South Africa, whose interests were to combat any resistance to their hegemony in the region; and the other was the Cold War, the war by proxy of the two monoliths, the United States and Russia. The human suffering inflicted on the peoples of Africa was collateral damage. Even today in Namibia, Angola, and Mozambique they still deal with anti-personnel landmines that were dispersed throughout the countryside during the conflicts and, of course, the victims are usually civilians.

The Cold War warriors were not content with fighting their proxy wars in Africa. They were also fighting in Asia and Latin America. One of the most well-known theaters of this cruel political play was Vietnam and, later, Laos and Cambodia. In the years following the end of the Vietnam War in 1975 nearly a million people fled these three countries. We have all heard about the plight of the boat people, which became an international humanitarian crisis. The refugees risked their lives fleeing in small fishing boats out into the South China Sea; some lucky ones were rescued by freighters, but many others suffered from hunger, thirst, and the notorious Thai pirates who robbed, raped, and murdered them. Officials from countries such as Thailand who did not want them to land on their shores had even shot at some of them. Governments who authorized pushing boat people back to the sea were in defiance of international law. In the fall of 1989 the UNHCR had planned for me to visit camps of Cambodian refugees in Thailand, but just before I could leave, the UNHCR canceled the trip and decided instead to send me to the famous camp of Pulau Bidong in Malaysia, which they were finally preparing to close.

This camp was one of the major refugee camps set up to receive the boat people. It was built to house about 14,000 persons but soon had as many as 42,000. Nearly 250,000 Vietnamese and many Cambodians passed through Pulau Bidong.

There were still many refugees there but it was not at its fullest. I arrived with a little more experience after my first field trip but I still did not have a specific plan except to be open: open eyes, open heart, and open mind. I was there not to give my ideas or opinions but to learn. I wanted to know about every aspect of the journey that had led them to Pulau Bidong. Most stories were heartbreaking because people hadn't wanted to leave their homeland, their culture, or their loved ones behind. Their courage and perseverance were incredibly inspiring to me. I sat through a screening process for those who were seeking asylum in the west. Refugees who had arrived after March 1989 had to prove that they were political and not economic refugees. There was so much paperwork involved in the process to be resettled in a third country.

A group of women and girls was housed separately from the other refugees. They were rape victims. Once the pirates had stolen everything that they could from the boat people they often raped some of the women and young girls. A boat could be besieged by many different groups of pirates along their way before arriving at a safe haven. Each time they had to find something to give up. Pirates even took the boat's engine when there was nothing else left to take, leaving the boat to drift helplessly. Some women and girls were taken away to the pirates' ship and those who were not kept or killed were later returned to the boat. Everyone knew that they had been raped and they were immediately ostracized. I spoke at great length to the young Vietnamese American psychologist who ran the center, a former refugee and rape victim. I asked her for advice about how to speak to the women. For cultural reasons it was almost impossible for a rape victim to speak out about her ordeal because of the overwhelming shame and guilt that she was made to feel. She was ostracized by all of those who had been on the boat with her, including members of her own family. I was reluctant to invade their private space with my questions but the director convinced me. "Their story must be told and you will speak only with those who want to talk with you." I was given most of the background information on each of the young women who had decided to speak with me. Two of the youngest were seventeen or eighteen but looked younger to me, like small, innocent children. They spoke to me about the fear they had felt back in Vietnam and during the trip, and about the unspeakable violence of their ordeal. Now they were isolated and still experiencing pain since their families and friends had rejected them and treated them like total strangers. They felt they might as well have been dead. As they told me what had happened to them their body language reflected the fear that they were feeling, the memories of the assaults, and their sadness. But when they started to speak about their dreams and wishes for their future there was a visible change. They opened up a little and occasionally a fleeting smile would light up their fragile faces. They wanted to leave Pulau Bidong and to start over and have a new and better life in France, the United States or Canada. They hoped that I could in some small way help make that happen.

The camp was about to be closed and most of the remaining refugees were among those that were considered harder to resettle. I became very attached to a little four-year-old, an adorable little boy, who was the youngest in the group of unaccompanied minors. He had somehow gotten separated from his mother just as they were about to board the boat. He did not know his full name and the only information that we had about him was that his mother was planning to join her husband who had arrived six months earlier in America. This child was the darling of the camp and everyone took care of him. I could have easily been tempted to adopt him and take him away from the camp, but I considered this a sentimental attitude that had no place in my task to work for the refugees. After I left Pulau Bidong, I kept in contact with the UNHCR representative there and was able to follow the child's story to its happy end. His mother was found safe and sound; in the pushing and shoving to get onto the small boat she had been pushed away from her son but she managed to get herself onto another boat and survived. They were eventually reunited and were granted asylum in the United States, where they joined his father in California. Pulau Bidong was finally closed in 1991.

I was beginning to formulate for myself what my task for the UNHCR—and above all for the refugees—should be. I would become exactly what the German word for *ambassador*—*Botschafter*—suggests: the refugees' *messenger*. I had to find the means to get the message right and to deliver it clearly and concisely so that it would be easily understood. I needed to be able to tell the true story that would have an impact on public opinion. Public opinion is the only way to move elected leaders and politicians to act when their actions do not directly affect their constituency. Many politicians seem to have an attention span that is only equal to the time passed between elections because they continue to campaign for their next election instead of having the conviction and courage to use their time in office to actually serve and govern the electorate. So influencing public opinion about unknown people in faraway places is necessary.

In 1990 I gave myself two tasks that I hoped to realize in a small way for the UNHCR's fortieth anniversary in 1991. One was to raise the recognition of the UNHCR so that people would not say, "UN what?" and to help the general public understand what the agency had done and was doing in the world since 1951. The other was to present the humanity that I saw in the faces of the refugees. I wanted citizens of the donor countries to understand that what refugees want most of all is to go back home to their own land, their own culture, and their own family. They want to have the opportunity to live with dignity and in peace, and to give their children the chance to grow and mature in a land where their human rights will be respected. I wanted to get past the preferred media images of the refugee as only a victim, asking for a handout.

After only two field missions it became clear to me how complex each refugee situation is and how different from one another they are, each having its own problems and each demanding its own solutions. As far as the work of the UNHCR is concerned the task is a humanitarian one. But the underlying solutions that can prevent the exodus of people from their homelands and those that will enable them to return home are definitely political. We need the political will from the international community at large, national governments, regional organizations such as the European Union, as well as the UN and in particular the UN Security Council. The five permanent members of the Council—the United States, China, Russia, France, and the United Kingdom—have veto power over any substantial action and, more often than not, vote solely in their own national interests.

They must give support to those of us who work in the humanitarian sphere for the work that they have mandated us to do. Moreover, they also need the will to deal with the roots of the problem and not allow humanitarian work to be the Band-Aid on the colossal open wound that is the abuse of human rights. This lack of will and action resulted in the fact that many of the refugees that I met from Mozambique, Vietnam, and Cambodia who were not eligible for resettlement to third countries had to wait in refugee camps for many more years than necessary before being able to return home.

It was not always easy to get access to the media and to be given the time needed to get this important message across. I decided to use the limited time that I was given on television, the radio, and in other interviews to talk about refugee issues instead of talking about my own concerts. Once, when I had reached the height of my career, a journalist asked me, "Why have you stopped singing to devote your time to working for refugees?" He was surprised when I informed him of my full schedule. I assumed that since my career was going full blast and I was singing for full halls in Europe, North and South America, and Asia that I did not need the publicity for myself. I decided that I should find a better balance between promoting my own singing career and the cause for refugees by mentioning my performances and recordings but giving most of my time to promote my humanitarian engagement. I prefer that my career serves this important cause and not vice-versa.

The UNHCR remained ambivalent about its goodwill ambassador program. Many of the representatives in the field felt that the time and energy needed to take care of an untrained and inexperienced "personality" would be a distraction and would take away from the limited time and resources that they had to do their work. Shannon told me that the ones that I had met had changed their minds after my visits. I did not demand or expect special treatment—I went to work from dawn to dusk living and eating just like the rest of the staff in the camp.

UNICEF has had a goodwill ambassador program since the 1950s that has been a great success. Audrey Hepburn, like me, lived in the Canton de Vaud and became a goodwill ambassador for UNICEF in 1988, shortly after I began to work for the UNHCR. We often ran into each other at the Swissair lounge at the Geneva airport and exchanged our different experiences from the field. She was a wonderful example for me, using her own professional image at the service of the cause that she defended so well. She brought the same gracious understated manner that we have seen in her film work to her devotion to alleviating the suffering of children in the world. She was great at getting her message across. Never letting her personality or the noise about her personal life get louder than the message that she had to share allowed her to be extremely effective. We encouraged one another during the difficult times. When I appeared as the evening's guest on the French television program *Sept sur sept* with Anne Sinclair she wrote me a lovely note a few days later, congratulating me for my advocacy for the refugees and human rights. I never hesitated whenever she called on me to support something that she was doing for UNICEF. I was on tour in Japan when she died, and I was sad to lose a friend and a colleague and even sadder that I could not accept her son's invitation to sing for her at her funeral in Switzerland.

Another UNICEF ambassador whom I saw as an example to follow was Peter Ustinov, who also lived in the Canton de Vaud, in Bursins, Switzerland. Sir Peter had been a goodwill ambassador since 1969 and had proved to be perfect at it, fulfilling his function with joy and his unmatchable humor. We were on a plane together from Geneva to Frankfurt and he had just returned from Washington, DC, where he had attended a state dinner hosted by President Reagan for Prince Charles and Lady Diana. His imitation of Reagan was so funny that I was howling with laughter, tears running down my face from take-off in Geneva until landing in Frankfurt. I laughed so much that I began to fear for my performance the following day. I will never forget that plane ride and for the sake of my voice it is good that we were not traveling to Sydney together. Like Audrey, Sir Peter's devotion and clarity of purpose was an inspiration to me. The UNHCR is the ambulance of the UN: new conflicts and natural disasters are popping up without pause and they take up all of our attention. Therefore we rarely have the luxury of being able to plan projects and campaigns like UNICEF can.

After the early departure of High Commissioner Jean Pierre Hocké in 1989, the Norwegian diplomat Thorvald Stoltenberg replaced him in 1990. Stoltenberg was very enthusiastic about the goodwill ambassador program and we met often to speak about how it could become a really effective asset. I was devastated when after only one year on the job he called me at home to say, "My dear Barbara, you are the first person that I am calling to say that I must leave the UNHCR because I have been called back by my prime minister, Gro Harlem Brundtland, to become the foreign minister of Norway. It makes me so sad to leave before my work is done here and to leave so many of those who are as dedicated to the refugee cause as you are, but I feel that it is my duty to return to my country and answer her call." I, like many, was distraught because the premature departure of Mr. Hocké had been very difficult for the organization and now another departure made it virtually impossible to make the important decisions that were necessary to ensure that the organization could continue to function at its maximum capacity. The goodwill ambassador program was virtually put on hold.

While we waited for the nomination of a new high commissioner there was no one to make certain decisions, and some of the projects that were planned for the fortieth anniversary were canceled altogether. I did manage to get a video made; I found all of the funding myself and even had to take the money first myself and then give it to the UNHCR because no one had the authority to receive the money from the donor. I had tried to put together "UNHCR Awareness" concerts around the fortieth anniversary but all but one of those had to be canceled. It took place in October 1991 in Ferrara, Italy, with the European Youth Orchestra, with Claudio Abbado conducting an all-Mozart program. Sergio Vieira de Mello, who had been on the side of the argument against the goodwill ambassador program, came to represent headquarters. He probably decided to attend the concert because he truly loved Mozart but I do believe that it was my speech in support of the UNHCR's forty years of work for refugees that turned him around. This was the beginning of a great collaboration and friendship.

As much as I was sad when Stoltenberg left the UNHCR, I was just as thrilled that the new high commissioner was to be a woman, Sadako Ogata. She served from 1991 to 2000 and did not show the same enthusiasm for the ambassador program as her predecessors. Nor did the American journalist Sylvana Foa, whom she brought in as her press coordinator. Immediately after Sylvana's arrival Shannon received mixed signals from her about the program. It had already suffered due to the two abrupt changes of high commissioners, but the arrival of Sylvana Foa nearly signaled its death knell.

Although Mrs. Ogata showed little interest in the program, during our periodic meetings she always expressed her appreciation and gratitude to me for my work. I had built up a strong relationship with the representatives and staff that I had met in the field and in my travels for my own work. I was also in contact with the regional offices throughout Europe, North America, and Asia. They asked me to participate in their local refugee projects or to speak with the press during stops on my own concert tours. I had acquired two very strong supporters who appreciated the positive impact of my work, Søren Jessen-Petersen, who between 1990 and 1993 served as chef de cabinet of the high commissioner for refugees in Geneva while also serving as director of external relations (1992–1994), and Sergio Vieira de Mello, who had changed from a doubter about the necessity of the program to my loudest cheerleader. But he had been sent to Cambodia in 1991 soon after our meeting in Ferrara to administer the repatriation of the refugees and displaced persons as well as to act as the interim director of the Cambodian Mines Center, so I could rarely call upon him in Geneva.

Shortly after Sylvana's arrival I noticed that the communication from headquarters was not the same. Shannon Boyd had been moved to another office and was no longer directly in charge of the GWA program. Sylvana's intentions at that time were not very clear: Shannon did not know if she wanted to scrap the entire program or if she just wanted to get rid of me. The program began to die a slow death of starvation for lack of vision, commitment, and means. Søren, knowing more about what was happening behind the scenes, asked me to come to Geneva to meet with him and Sylvana. In this meeting, and in subsequent ones, she showed that she was skeptical about the goodwill ambassador program in general but pretended to want me to stay and to continue to be active. Her actions, however, indicated the opposite.

I did not know what to expect when I disembarked in Dubrovnik on December 31, 1991. We had arrived on a chartered plane from Paris to the Italian coastal city of Bari late in the afternoon the previous day and then boarded an old Polish cruise ship that evening for the nearly nine-hour crossing from Italy to Croatia. I had not been able to sleep during the night and sat in the miniscule bathroom so as not to wake Martin, writing a speech inspired by Martin Luther King's "I Have a Dream" that I planned to read at the end of the concert. I was relieved that the military guns that were stationed on the hilltops of Dubrovnik had not fired on us on our way over from Italy, and it was calm when we left the ship the next morning. I had seen the images of the city under siege on television, but the sights of the bombed out shops in the streets brought the conflict home to all of us. There was indeed a war going on in Europe, a conflict complete with ethnic cleansing. Had we not vowed "Never again" after learning about the atrocities of World War II?

We were a group of about sixty persons who had come to show our solidarity with the people under a brutal siege in Dubrovnik that was taking place before our eyes less than a few hours' flight from Paris. Martin, my friend Rachel Zahn, Peter Brook, Simone and Antoine Veil, Peter Townsend, Michel Piccoli, Christine Ockrent, and the Toulouse Chamber Orchestra were among those who volunteered to accompany us. It was very cold and I could not believe that this was the same town that I visited during a musical cruise some years before. The conflict had already caused much damage to the town. Most of the shops had been bombed and were closed. I was touched to see impromptu Nativity scenes that had been placed in some of the display windows as a sign of resistance. We walked along the small streets until we came to the church of the Franciscan Monastery where the concert was to take place and it seemed to be even colder inside than outside. I checked out the room that would be my dressing room and I was happy that it was heated. As soon as the orchestra arrived we began our rehearsal of Bach's Cantata no. 51 and Mozart's Exultate Jubilate. This was not the original plan. The program should have been Mozart's Requiem with orchestra and choir.

What had led me to Dubrovnik, Croatia on December 31, 1991?

In October, shortly after the beginning of the siege of Dubrovnik, I was invited to participate in one of my favorite public affairs programs on French television, *La Marche du Siècle*, hosted by Jean-Marie Cavada. The program was in honor of Javier Perez de Cuellar, who was just about to finish his term as secretary general of the UN, and was broadcast live from the Sorbonne. The secretary had requested that I be one of his guests. The program was about the many activities that the UN undertakes each day, the evolution of the UN during his tenure, and the future of the UN in a "new world order" after the end of the Cold War. With the fall of the Berlin Wall and the dissolution of the Soviet Union in 1991, we in the international humanitarian community were starting to get very excited about the positive possibilities of working for the first time since the inception of the UN in 1945 in a world free of the bipolar tensions of the Cold War. How wrong we were to be so naïve! Already by October of 1991 the beginning of the new European nightmare had begun in Yugoslavia. The Yugoslav Peoples Army attacked Dubrovnik. The press provided images of the conflict and we watched the destruction of Croatia and the siege of Dubrovnik every night in our living rooms. There was immediate condemnation of the shelling of Dubrovnik, a UNESCO World Heritage Site. This designation should have saved it from destruction but it did not stop the bombardment that left more than 68 percent of the old town damaged when the bombing ceased in June 1992. The international community expressed its indignation, put pressure on the Serbs, and tried to broker countless ceasefires, all to no avail. Federico Mayor, the director general of UNESCO, called and asked if I would be willing to come to Paris to participate in a concert and demonstration against the destruction of the city. While I was living in Paris I had been invited on many occasions to UNESCO where I met Federico, and we became close friends. He had asked me many times to be a goodwill ambassador for UNESCO but I wanted to honor my commitment to the UNHCR, and I already had enough trouble trying to stop the confusion when I spoke to the press. In the middle of an interview I often had to diplomatically correct the journalist and say, "It is the UNHCR, the UN agency for refugees, not UNICEF or UNESCO." However I did later agree to be a nonpaid special advisor for intercultural affairs at UNESCO for a two-year period. I participated in and gave my input to Federico's "Culture of Peace Program," whose objectives revolved around four main themes: education for peace, human rights, and democracy; the fight against isolation and poverty; the defense of cultural diversity and intercultural dialogue; and conflict prevention and the consolidation of peace. On September 13, 1999, the UN General Assembly adopted the Declaration and Programme of Action on a Culture of Peace, which embodies Mayor's greatest aspirations from both a conceptual and practical standpoint.

When Federico called me about the concert in Paris, Martin suggested that if we really wanted to bring more attention to the plight of the people in Dubrovnik and the displaced persons who had taken refuge in the city, we should go there. Federico thought that this was a great idea and we began to try to organize a concert of Mozart's Requiem. The day that I came to Paris for *La Marche du Siècle* Federico informed me that the project was too complicated for UNESCO to organize and he was going to have to give up this great idea.

That same evening I was sitting in a small room that had been reserved for makeup before the television show with SG Perez de Cuellar. Seated next to me was Bernard Kouchner, who was at that time a junior minister in the Mitterrand government as secretary of state for humanitarian action. We started to speak about Dubrovnik and I told him about the concert that had just been canceled and he offered to take over the project.

Martin and I contacted our friends who were singers, conductors, and musicians to put the concert together. At least three English orchestras agreed to come and then canceled because they were told in no uncertain terms by their foreign office not to do it. We were not able to find three other singers to make up the vocal quartet so finally I was left with no choice and had to simplify my artistic ambitions. I decided to go it alone and to sing Mozart's Exultate, jubilate and the Bach Cantata Jauchzet Gott in allen Landen. A British conductor who had agreed to conduct the concert sent a fax on December 27 canceling his participation and even suggesting that the concert was "not a neutral gesture but was essentially pro-Croatian." I saw our project as pro–human rights and anti–ethnic cleansing and antimassacre. With only a few days before the departure it was impossible to find a replacement. The Toulouse Chamber Orchestra who finally agreed to come with us were used to playing with the first violin leading their ensemble, so we decided to do the concert without a conductor. The concert was to be shown live on French and Croatian television. Just before the performance, we had intense discussions about who should be allowed to speak before and afterward. I noted that it is sometimes very difficult to avoid being manipulated and co-opted by the leaders of the people that we have come to help. They have their own agendas and sometimes theirs might not coincide with ours. In these circumstances it is important and necessary to be very clear about our own humanitarian intentions, to be sure that our actions are based neither on a condescending nor a sentimental attitude about the victims of conflict. And at the same time we must also be very vigilant that we are not manipulated or portrayed as taking any side other than that of the defense and respect for human rights. At the end of the concert I read:

I have a dream . . .

. . . A Dream that there will exist in the very near future a new world order based on the defence and protection of human rights, the one common struggle that unites us all and excludes no one.

. . . A Dream that we will work together to solve the many global problems with which we are confronted on this planet in order not to perish together.

. . . A Dream that we will be able to sit down together and resolve our differences without resorting to violence, barbarism, and destruction.

. . . A Dream that each child will be able to grow up with dignity and realize his own potential.

. . . A Dream that we will assume our responsibility and duty as citizens of the global community to cry out against injustice and suffering and to dare to interfere.

. . . A Dream that this very near future will begin in the first hour of the first day of 1992 here in Dubrovnik.

In spite of Sylvana's resistance I received the OK from Mrs. Ogata to prepare for another visit to the field in the spring of 1992, my first since she had become high commissioner. The relations between Thailand and the UNHCR had improved because in 1991 the Paris Accords paved the way for the UNHCR to repatriate 360,000 refugees and displaced persons from Thailand who had fled from the Khmer Rouge in Cambodia. I visited first the famous "Site B," situated four kilometers from the Cambodian border. This was the largest camp on the Thai border and covered seven square kilometers. It housed mostly refugees from neighboring Cambodia but there was also a small Vietnamese population. I arrived just before the beginning of the repatriation of refugees who were being prepared for their return home after nearly fourteen years in exile. The countryside in Cambodia was riddled with mines, and the refugees, especially the children, had to be taught to recognize and to look out for the dangerous small items that could kill them or handicap them for life.

We left Site B to go to Khao I Dang Holding Center some fifty kilometers away from Site 2, a smaller camp covering less than three square kilometers. The camp was opened in 1979 as a holding camp for refugees that were to be repatriated or resettled. The Thai government's open-door policy that began in October 1979 ended in January 1980 and more than 100,000 persons arrived from Cambodia during a three-month period. The population of Khao I Dang (known as KID in the aid community) reached 160,000 in March 1980. KID was administered by the Thai government and the UNHCR. The ICRC (the Red Cross) had set up a surgical hospital at first to tend to war casualties and later to the increasing numbers of victims of land mines. I visited with some of the doctors and the land mine victims there and then went across the street to the facilities of an NGO from Lyon, France, Handicap International, who had been in Thailand since 1982. They explained to me that their first activities had been to provide assistive devices to amputees in refugee camps along the Thai-Cambodian border but they had to broaden their activities to prosthetic services and local rehabilitation projects for refugees with disabilities, including land mine victims, training for local prosthetic technicians, and mine risk education projects.

After a visit to the premises I was invited to go outside in the courtyard where a basketball game was underway; all of the players had prosthetics that had been made for them at KID. Some of the prosthetics had even been made by the refugees themselves. I watched the game for a while and was very moved by the vitality of the young boys transcending their handicaps. They would be able to return home with hope to start a new life in spite of them, all thanks to the work of Handicap International.

The following fall I was in Lyon rehearsing the opera *Don Pasquale* with Gabriel Bacquier, Luca Canonici, and Gino Quilico. The opera house was being renovated so the rehearsal took place an old warehouse that the opera had rented. After the first rehearsal I walked outside on my way to eat lunch and to my surprise found myself face to face with the main headquarters of Handicap International, in a modest building just opposite the entrance to our rehearsal room. Some days later before returning to rehearsal after my lunch break I went to the door, knocked, and was met by one of the founders, Jean-Baptiste Richardier. He had already heard about my visit to KID and was very happy to speak to me at length about what HI was doing and the plans for projects within Cambodia after the repatriation. This was the beginning of a long-lasting friendship and a close collaboration with HI.

Jean-Baptiste is one of the true humanitarians. He comes under the category of the "the real deal" and is not one of the impostors who speak about humanitarian values but do not live them. I was already goodwill ambassador to UNHCR so I could not be officially associated with HI as an ambassador but I wanted to work with them as a concerned citizen who believed in what they were doing. I found funding for a joint project with the UNHCR and Handicap International that started in Cambodia shortly after the beginning of the repatriation of the refugees from Thailand and lasted from 1992 to 1995. During this time HI taught returning Cambodians who were mine victims to build prostheses and trained them to assist the rehabilitation of others. HI was a founding member of the International Committee to Ban Landmines and I joined Jean-Baptiste and his colleagues on many occasions during their campaign to outlaw the fabrication and use of land mines. I continue to support this struggle today. Land mines have been one of the major obstacles to peaceful and safe repatriation in nearly every major refugee camp and repatriation situation that I have encountered since Namibia—in Mozambique, in Cambodia, and in the former Yugoslavia. On December 3, 1997, the Mine Ban Treaty was signed in Ottawa, Canada. The following week, Handicap International was cowinner of the Nobel Peace Prize, which was awarded to the six founding organizations of the International Campaign to Ban Landmines. The treaty has passed but the work goes on because there are indecent sums of money to be made selling the death and destruction of innocent victims. The treaty has yet to be signed by the United States, Russia, India, Israel, and China.

In October 1991, at the same time that the offensive in Dubrovnik was under way, the Paris Agreements on the Comprehensive Political Settlement of the Cambodia Conflict was signed—a peace treaty to end the conflict and prepare the country for elections. The agreements assigned to the United Nations an unprecedented role and they set up an operation, the United Nations Transitional Authority in Cambodia (UNTAC), which would supervise the ceasefire, the end of foreign military assistance, and the withdrawal of foreign forces; disarm all armed forces of the Cambodian parties; control and supervise the activities of the administrative structures, including the police; ensure the respect of human rights; and organize and conduct free and fair elections.

In May 1992 UNTAC set up office in Phnom Penh and the UNHCR began the successful repatriation and resettlement of 360,000 refugees and displaced persons in Cambodia that would eventually lead to the first democratic elections in the country in May 1993. I came to Phnom Penh to follow up on my previous visit to Thailand and to see the repatriation in action. It was early spring and Sergio Vieira de Mello and his staff were making the preparations for the last of the refugees to return from some of the camps that I had visited the year before in Thailand. He was very busy and every minute of my trip was organized to give me a complete picture of the situation with which the UNHCR and the refugees were confronted. From the first day of my visit I was aware of the frustration that Sergio and his staff felt working under the weak UN head of mission, Yusushi Akashi, who they felt was jeopardizing their mission by refusing to enforce the Paris Accord. If the warring factions did not disarm and fulfill their end of the bargain, then the UNHCR could be preparing the refugees to return to a land that they thought was at peace only to be caught up in a certain bloodbath. Sergio explained to me that the landmine clearing was difficult and slow because there was neither enough manpower nor enough funds provided to do a better job. I visited my friends at Handicap International and was happy to see that they had already begun our joint project. I insisted on going to Siem Reap, where the famous Angkor Wat was located, hoping that there might be some time left to visit it. But most of all I wanted to see how Sergio's unorthodox decision to allow refugees who had chosen to return home to a province that was still largely controlled by the Khmer Rouge had worked out. I knew that the region was still dangerous, and I was learning that sometimes one has to bend the rules and take risks in order to help the refugees; but I was a little uneasy that maybe he had gone too far and given up some of his principles by allowing them to return and live among the monsters that we knew the Khmer Rouge to be. I met a few of the returnees whose land had been cleared of mines and who had already been able to use their UNHCR household kits to build houses. They could hardly believe that they were actually home after so many years in exile. There were still some sporadic skirmishes in the area between the government forces and some remnants of the Khmer regime, but we did not have any problems and I was treated with a 4 AM sunrise over Angkor Wat. Just as we were leaving, a group of French soldiers and peacekeepers passed us, and Sergio said, "You must have fans in the French military because I just heard one of them say to the others, 'Hey, that was Barbara Hendricks we just passed.'"

Before leaving Phnom Penh I gave a press conference and exercised the independence that I had demanded when I started with the UNHCR. I gave my honest opinion about what I had seen during my visit, and I was much harder on the UN head of mission than Sergio could be. "A successful repatriation cannot happen if the necessary groundwork for a durable and lasting peace is not laid and maintained by those who have the responsibility for peacekeeping and policing tasks. This is not the UNHCR's responsibility, nor is it a part of our mandate." Sergio did have to do a bit of cleanup after my visit but no one disputed the veracity of what I had said.

On my last night Sergio and I went to a local restaurant for dinner. I had heard that Cambodians ate dogs, so I silently counted the ones lying around in front of the restaurant as we went in and counted them again on my departure. I do not know if I ate dog meat at the meal but I was sure that it was not one of the four that were lying in front of the restaurant.

After the repatriation and resettlement, the camps, Site B and KID, were closed. Sergio went to the closing ceremony in KID and accompanied the last convoy from that camp to Cambodia. The successful repatriation paved the way for elections in May 1993. Nearly 90 percent of the population voted for twenty parties and this led to a constitution being written. The UNHCR had done its job, despite all of the naysayers predicting failure and maybe even massacres. But the peace was neither lasting nor secure. In 1994, refugees returned to the Thai border and in 1997 a coup d'état undid some of the good work that Sergio and his courageous staff had done. The overwhelming corruption of the government even made the Khmer Rouge seem attractive to some of the people. During that short visit Sergio and I became close friends and allies in the cause of refugees in the world. The next time that we would meet out in the field was a year later, in 1993, in Sarajevo.

During the preparations for the concert in Dubrovnik in 1991 we had seriously considered moving the concert to Sarajevo if the bombardment of Dubrovnik made it too dangerous for us to land there. It was common knowledge that Bosnia was likely to be Milosevic's next target in his campaign for a Greater Serbia, and the JNA, the Yugoslav People's Army, had already attacked a Croatian village in Bosnia on its way to attack Dubrovnik in 1991. Sarajevo had always been a symbol of religious diversity in Yugoslavia because the major religions—Islam, Orthodoxy, Judaism, and Catholicism—coexisted peacefully there until the Bosnian War.

After Slovenia and Croatia had declared independence from Yugoslavia, Bosnia-Herzegovina followed suit with a referendum of its people in March 1992. This did not at all coincide with Serbian president Slobodan Milosevic's plans. From May 1992 and during the first half of 1993 Sarajevo saw the heaviest fighting in the city during its four-year-long siege by the Serbian forces. For the concert in Dubrovnik we had founded an association that we called "Première heure du premier jour" (The first hour of the first day of each New Year), with the idea that we would organize a concert somewhere in the world on December 31 every year in order to bring attention to the civilian victims of conflicts whom the international community was ignoring. It seemed to be a great idea at the time but it became clear that a concert was not necessarily the most effective way to highlight the majority of the ongoing conflicts in the world, especially those in the developing world, where a classical concert would just be ridiculous and superfluous. So I did not do another concert in 1992.

In 1993 my dear friend Leon Davicho called me. "The orchestra in Sarajevo wants to invite you to come there and perform with them on December 31 this year in solidarity with the people of Sarajevo like you did on New Year's Eve 1991 in Dubrovnik." Leon, who was Serbian, was also a member of our association, and his devotion to the project and his expertise had made possible the 1991 Dubrovnik concert. The members of the orchestra in Sarajevo had decided to resist the war the only way that they knew how: by continuing to play together even though they did not always have the opportunity to give concerts. The lack of will and courage of European and American leaders during this conflict was actually contributing to the rising violence and brutality. I could not refuse this invitation. I knew that Sergio had taken leave from the UNHCR to join the UNPROFOR (UN Protection Force) in Bosnia and he was stationed in Sarajevo. He also thought that it was a good idea to accept the invitation and it would give us another chance to see each other, albeit under more dangerous circumstances. This was not a UNHCR mission but I was under their auspices.

The fighting in Sarajevo was very fierce in December 1993 compared to the lull in fighting that we encountered in Dubrovnik. I had little to organize since I had been invited as a soloist so I did not have to convince an orchestra and other soloists to join me. I sent my program to the orchestra and again Leon took care of most of the organization with some logistical help from the UNHCR, who were responsible for my safety. It was not possible to go with a large group of civilians as we had done in Dubrovnik. We did not even have our own television crew. Martin and I decided that he should stay home this time with Sebastian and Jennie, who were old enough to understand the danger for me. I gave a lot of thought to the dangerous situation that I was about to enter but I felt very serene and my intuition told me that I would return home safe and sound.

I boarded a plane from Geneva to Zagreb with Leon Davicho and we met Bernard Kouchner and four other members of the association in Zagreb. From Zagreb to Sarajevo we were allowed to travel in the limited space available on a military plane with some Norwegian peacekeepers. The military plane was more like a cargo plane than a passenger plane; I was given one of the few seats. We sat crouched together for the flight into the Sarajevo airport.

The UNHCR representative who met me in Zagreb had given me valuable equipment: a helmet and a bulletproof vest that weighed over forty pounds. I was given strict instructions never to go outside unless I was wearing the vest and helmet, and never to leave the vest outside my room. It was worth a lot of money on the black market and they had already been forced to replace too much stolen equipment.

I was happy to get out of the cramped position on the plane, but I was a little frightened to go out onto the tarmac of the infamous Sarajevo airport that I had seen under siege on the nightly newscasts. We were escorted to a bunker where our papers were approved; I was traveling with my UNHCR passport. Foreign dignitaries such as Hillary Clinton were going in and out of Sarajevo but the suffering of the people continued. While I was waiting for my papers to be processed Valery Giscard D'Estaing, the former president of France, greeted me on his way to the departure area.

Once the paperwork was finished the UNHCR representative escorted me to a waiting car. I will never forget the ride from the airport to the Holiday Inn. I had seen this road many times on the nightly news but those shocking images had in no way prepared me for the actual sight of the destruction of this modern city. I was still in Europe in a city situated no more than an hour and half flight away from the peaceful surroundings of Switzerland, from where Leon and I had just come. I began to feel as if I had stepped inside of a Kafka novel. Yes, indeed, the only word that can describe the situation I saw is *absurd*.

We arrived at the Holiday Inn, home to Sarajevo's foreign visitors and, of course, the foreign press. There was no electricity and no heating in the hotel. The water sometimes came on for a few minutes a day. It was freezing cold in my room. I slept in a sleeping bag that I had brought with me, with all of my clothes on top of me to stay warm. I often reflect that had I been in an unheated hotel room on tour in a country that was not a war zone, I would have certainly caught a cold and had other vocal problems. So many of the must dos and must haves that we think are necessary to function are often crutches that our mind fools us into believing we need in order to walk.

I was so happy to meet Sergio that evening for dinner. He introduced me to Lieutenant General Francis Briquemont from Belgium who had just taken over from the Frenchman Philippe Morillon as the commander of UNPROFOR.

The next day I went to the first rehearsal with the orchestra. I was still in my Kafka novel. During one piece the horn player was missing and the conductor, Michel Tabachnik—who had at the last minute replaced the Bosnian conductor who had fallen ill—asked, with a bit of annoyance in his voice, "Where is the first horn player?" Out of a cold silence came a voice that said in a very matter of fact manner, "Oh, he was killed by a sniper two days ago." I always face an orchestra during our first rehearsal as a means to establish a musical dialogue with them, hopefully inspiring them to participate with me in the musical process. Out of habit and without thinking about it I turned to face them and the chorus as they started to play the first notes of Mozart's Laudate Dominum. Their pale faces, broken spirits, and emaciated bodies were almost too much for me to bear. Most of them had lost as much as forty pounds of their normal weight due to the scarcity of food and the hardship and stress of living under siege. Their sunken eyes were mirrors of their suffering and grief. They had invited me to come to them but I felt a weariness and even some distrust emanating from their sad, half-shut eyes. It was too late to turn around because they would have understood why. I had to close my eyes from time to time as the rehearsal progressed, but when I began the last verse of Schubert's "Ave Maria" I kept them closed because I wanted to cry and I knew that I could not let a single tear drop from my eyes for fear that they would interpret it as pity. The last thing that they needed from me was pity and pity was the last thing I wanted to show them. I had come to support their courage and wanted to resist this war with them. Although I was a very minor character I now had a part to play in this war, this absurd nightmare. When I reopened my eyes at the end of the Schubert song it seemed to me that the orchestra of cadavers that had begun the rehearsal had been slightly transformed into more warm-blooded human beings. I could see the colors of their eyes, and their skin seemed less ashen. Schubert's music had warmed us all.

At the end of the rehearsal the entire atmosphere had changed. Everyone gathered around me. In spite of the cold I felt great warmth from the orchestra, the members of the choir, and especially the children's choir and their conductor, with whom I had sung two Bosnian songs that I had learned just for this concert. I was told later by one of the musicians, "It was unbelievable for us that you should come and sing with us, the people of Sarajevo, and we artists in particular have grown distrustful of the politicians as well as the 'artists' who have come and gone with their empty promises. We feel that some have used us and our desperate situation as a backdrop for some self-aggrandizing publicity stunt."

The rehearsal had been held in the Radio House, which was where the Bosnian authorities wanted the concert to take place, with invited guests only. We had hoped for a more open venue and when we met with President Alija Izetbegovic and his staff we suggested the National Theater or a local cinema that we had visited after the rehearsal. His staff said that they were afraid for our safety and that the Serbs would love to have an excuse to destroy the National Theater. General Briquemont's sources had indicated that the Serbs had said they would not attack the concert. As far as the cinema was concerned we were told that the television equipment could not be safely transferred and installed there. We did not know whom or what to believe. There seemed to be two camps: those authorities who wanted to keep the city's "victim status" in order to get more help—and maybe arms— from the international community; and those who believed an open concert would show that the civilians in Sarajevo were strong and capable of resisting the Serbs' barbaric treatment. Every one of the solutions that Leon suggested was met with resistance and excuses about technical difficulties and other such things. We finally gave up and the concert took place in the Radio House. Again, as I had experienced in Dubrovnik, there is a very fine line that one must walk when doing a humanitarian project. And even today I do not know if we were manipulated, and, if so, by whom.

I returned to the hotel and lingered at the bottom of the staircase hoping that some gallant journalist would offer to help me carry my bulletproof vest up the seven flights of stairs to my room. I tried to rest in the cold room as I usually do on the day of a concert, but I could not come to terms with the mixture of my feelings of fear, defiance, and excitement about the evening's concert. I decided to go out—we had been invited to visit the French troops who were stationed in the post office across the street. I put on my vest and helmet and we crossed "sniper alley" running in a zigzag pattern so as to make it more difficult to be targeted. I arrived safely and had to do the same dance on my return to the hotel.

In the evening I went to the Radio House for the concert that was being broadcast live on French television. I was happy that Sebastian and Jennie would be able to see me on TV and to know that I was safe. The first person I saw in the audience was Sergio, beaming like a proud brother. General Briquemont had gone to the front lines to be with his troops for New Year's Eve. When the concert was nearly finished there was a blackout in the studio—or perhaps in the entire city. It lasted less than five minutes; then the lights came back on and we were able to finish the concert as planned. When I was told that France 3 had not resumed the concert after the blackout I was horrified to think that Sebastian, Jennie, and Martin did not know that I was all right. I was told that the BBC had a satellite telephone in the building and that I could use it for a quick call home to Switzerland. My family was so relieved to hear my voice. Jennie said, "Mom, are you all right? Have you been hurt?" I said, "No Jennie, we were not bombed; it was only a short electricity outage." Sebastian took the phone and said, "Mom, you sang really well. We are proud of you but you must come home now!" I was so happy to speak with them and to hear their voices. I could not stay long on the phone but I said, "I will be home day after tomorrow, I promise." It was already January 1, 1994.

Before leaving the Radio House, we heard a very loud explosion just outside the building and when we came outside we saw the large hole where the bomb had hit. There was no further damage and luckily no injuries from the blast. We left to join Sergio at General Briquemont's headquarters. I had, as usual, brought some food for the New Year's Eve meal and Sergio had invited some young Bosnian musicians who played selections from the musical *Hair*. Sergio and I sang along and he tried to teach me to dance the samba. I followed along as best I could but did not really get it. It was so good to let off the pressure of the last few days with some laughter, song, and dance.

The next morning I went down to eat breakfast and was told that one of the children from the choir was waiting to see me. The night before, a young girl about ten years old had come at the end of concert and asked if she could see me at the hotel before I left, and I had said yes. Her name was Isabella and she was a pretty little blonde angel. I invited her to come to the breakfast room with me. Isabella told me that she and her family lived on the twenty-second floor of their apartment building and that they had to walk up and down with water and food. The elevators no longer worked because there was no electricity. I offered her some breakfast. She answered me very proudly, "Oh, no thank you. I did not come to get something from you. I wanted to give you a present from me." She reached into her pocket and gave me a child's necklace. I wanted to cry; her simplicity and earnestness moved me deeply. I hugged her and told her that my prayers would be with her and her family and that I knew this nightmare would come to an end soon.

Isabella haunted me during the next two years as the people of Sarajevo continued to suffer and to be killed. In December 1994 I wrote an open letter to Isabella to ask her to forgive me for letting her down and for allowing her to still be in the hell that was Sarajevo. After the war I returned to Sarajevo in 1999 for the UNHCR and in 2007 for a concert. I tried hard to find her or to find out what happened to her and her family but without any success.

After breakfast I prepared my bag and went to meet General Briquemont who had invited us for lunch before taking our flight back to Zagreb. We discussed the frustration that we all felt with the lack of will to confront the ethnic cleansing, fascism, and genocide. The international community, Europe, the United States, and the United Nations were failing miserably to stand up and fight this aberration and affront to international law. He said that the Security Council and European Community should spend less time passing resolutions on the former Yugoslav republic and concentrate instead on sending enough peacekeeping troops. "I don't read the Security Council resolutions any more because they don't help me. There is a fantastic gap between the resolutions of the Security Council, the will to execute those resolutions, and the means available to commanders in the field. The resolution contains beautiful words, but it was a little bit of hypocrisy." He criticized a European Community initiative, sponsored jointly by France and Germany, to open new corridors for humanitarian aid in Bosnia and an airport in the center of the country. "We asked for four thousand men, four battalions, to do the job. At the end of the meeting, we were offered zero. The key to international success in dealing with any future Bosnia is to be pragmatic and to focus on what is achievable rather than what is desirable. To manage a crisis you must have clear political objectives and a military strategy supported by the contributing nations. When we study the case of Yugoslavia, we see all the errors we shouldn't make."

Just after lunch, Sergio said to me, "Barbara, the general was so sad to miss the concert last night. Couldn't you sing just one song for him before going?" I thought, "Great, Sergio, I have just finished eating, have drunk a glass of wine, and am certainly not warmed up." Instead I said, "Sergio, of course I will sing for you and the general." I stood up and began to sing a Negro spiritual, "Sometimes I Feel Like a Motherless Child." In the middle of my singing there was a terrific blast. It was repeated, but I kept singing. I thought to myself, "If I must die here there is no better way to go than in song." When I finished, General Briquemont looked at me astonished and said, "Thank you so much, you did not stop singing, you did not even flinch, incredible." Sergio gave me a big hug. I knew that he was proud of me for my activism and devotion, but now he saw me as a true warrior and this experience sealed our friendship forever.

"Hello, do you remember me?" One of the violinists from the orchestra was approaching me as I was coming out of a rehearsal for Strauss's *Vier letze Lieder* with the Cincinnati Orchestra conducted by Paavo Järvi. I did vaguely recognize his face but I could not remember where I had met him, so I said, "Help me." He said "Of course it is difficult because I weighed many kilos less when we worked together in Sarajevo in December 1993." I could not believe my eyes. He was unrecognizable from the pale, bony person that had sat in front of me during that first rehearsal in the cold hall of the Radio House. He said, "I wanted to thank you for accepting our invitation to come to Sarajevo when we were under siege. You do so many concerts all over the world so maybe you cannot imagine how much it meant to everyone in Sarajevo and especially to us in the orchestra and choir. You gave us the energy to continue to resist those last two horrible years until the fighting stopped. Our concert was broadcast on television so many times that in spite of the fact that there were so many people in Sarajevo who could not come out for it, and despite the many electrical outages, just about everyone eventually saw the concert or heard it on the radio. We were all uplifted and encouraged by your musical and spiritual gift to us. I can never thank you enough." We hugged each other and I was grateful to get his feedback and to know that the concert had truly mattered to them. I knew that a concert would not stop the conflict but I could not sit idly by and just shrug my shoulders helplessly. His words and those of others that I have met when I returned to Sarajevo counterbalanced the cynicism that I have encountered about my humanitarian activism from the classical music media. A journalist once asked me during an interview, "How do you feel about the fact that in the world of classical music, some consider your activities to be indecent and think that you go to Dubrovnik or Sarajevo to sell your records?" I looked at her in disbelief and answered, "Madame, first of all I will not bother to answer to 'some' and do not care one bit about what 'some' say about me. As far as increasing my record sales, I could easily get myself invited to some popular television show and do a strip tease; it would certainly embarrass my children to death but it would not risk making them orphans."

Artists like myself who are activists for humanitarian action have to walk a thin line and be extra careful that nothing in our comportment will cause the slightest suspicion that our engagement for our humanitarian work is in any way a tool for advancing our careers. The UNHCR did not impose ethical rules on me but I have imposed very strict rules on myself. For example, I refused to be the face of a luxury product even though I could have earned quite a bit of money doing so. I believe that one can be a true human rights activist and have a high standard of living, including owning luxury items. But I thought that my message could be misunderstood if images of me promoting a luxury product were seen side by side with images of me in a refugee camp asking for funding for the UNHCR. I must honor my commitment to not let the important and complex refugee message be overshadowed, even if I must slight my own professional message.

Just before going on stage to begin the concert in Sarajevo I was interviewed live via satellite by Patrick Poivre D'Arvor, the anchor of the news on TF1. He had obviously received a copy of my latest CD from my record company and just as he was about to pick it up to show it at the end of the interview I let out a little groan, "nooooooo," that he heard in his earphone. He understood and put it gently back down. I was not expecting the criticism that would come my way after the Sarajevo concert but it would have certainly given them ammunition against me if he would have said, "Barbara Hendricks is in Sarajevo, under siege, and also just happens to have a new CD coming out today."

On October 21, 1993, Burundi's first democratically elected president, Melchior Ndadaye, was killed by renegade soldiers. Revenge killings swept the countryside and seven hundred thousand Hutus streamed into Rwanda, Tanzania, and Zaire to escape army reprisals.

Then, on April 6, 1994, the presidents of Rwanda and Burundi were killed in mysterious circumstances when their aircraft crashed approaching Kigali airport. Rwandan soldiers and Interahamwe began house-to-house searches and instigated a genocide in which between five hundred thousand and one million people were slaughtered.

On April 28, 1994, nearly a quarter million Rwandans fled across the Rusumo bridge into Ngara, Tanzania, in just twenty-four hours. This first flight of Hutu refugees was the largest and fastest movement of refugees in modern history. Worse followed. More than one million Rwandans flooded into the eastern Zaire town of Goma in four days in July. Cholera broke out and as many as fifty-thousand people died within a matter of weeks in squalid camps. A huge international aid effort, costing two billion dollars in the first two weeks alone, was launched.

Even in August 1994, the office in Geneva was still reeling from the fallout of the debacle of the visit that Sylvana had organized for Sophia Loren to the Kenyan-Somali border two years earlier. The refugee camp had been overrun by Italian paparazzi who were completely insensitive to and disinterested in the refugees' plight. They were only concerned about getting photos of the star, Sophia Loren, with the poor refugees as a backdrop for their gossip press. This put the sincere Ms. Loren in a very difficult situation and made it very hard for her to establish her own credibility. Now Shannon was trying hard to organize a much-needed trip for me to visit refugees that had fled from the Rwandan genocide into Tanzania. The UNHCR was strained everywhere. The media gave full coverage to the cholera epidemic when it was at its worst but as soon as the death toll started to come down they packed up and left, no longer interested in the rest of the story. Shannon called me and said, "We have enough backing to organize a trip to Ngara, Tanzania, on the Rwandan border. Can you go now?"

I was free to go and the plans began without Sylvana's knowledge. When she did hear about it I was already in the air between Nairobi and Ngara. Corinne Pertuis from the UNHCR office in France joined me and had brought her camera with her so that she could be our photographer. The budget for this field mission was so tight there was no money for extra journalists and camera crews.

We had arrived in Nairobi the evening before and were met by the UNHCR representative, who gave us a detailed briefing on the situation. After dinner I went straight to bed because I wanted to get a good night's sleep, knowing that I would have a very long day ahead. Early in the morning we boarded the small plane that was to take us to the Tanzanian border with Rwanda, not far from Lake Victoria. In the hotel elevator I met some journalists from Antenne 2 in France who had been covering the cholera epidemic in Zaire. They were on their way back to France. I said, "Why are you leaving now? There is still so much to tell; refugees are still arriving in the camps. I am going to visit a camp tomorrow that has so many problems—we need this to be covered." One of them looked at me with some understanding but said, "I know, but these camps are not big news, sorry." I said, "Not enough deaths?" He shrugged his shoulders and said, "Yes, perhaps."

We were supposed to stop to refuel halfway to Ngara but after some hours in flight the pilot informed us that we would have to make a detour because that station was out of gas and we had just enough gas to get to another location a bit further away.

Corinne and I sighed with relief when the plane finally landed in a small field in the middle of nowhere—we were soon to run out of gas and we also needed desperately to go to the toilet. This was no service station; there was neither a building nor toilets, just a gas pump and a small hut. We had landed in the late afternoon just before the sun was about to set. The sheer beauty of nature around me, especially the colors of the earth and sky, were breathtaking. We could not linger because we absolutely had to land in Ngara before it was completely dark. Our "airport" there was a just a dirt landing strip, short and very narrow without any lighting. I reboarded the plane and carried with me the rich smell of the soil in my nostrils. It is a smell that I always associate with Africa.

When we were airborne again the African land and sky offered us a wonderful spectacle as the sun performed a colorful dance with myriad veils as it moved westward. When there was only a sliver of light left I assumed that we had to land soon, but we continued another thirty minutes flying by the light of the stars. I did not worry too much because when I looked down below I saw fires that had been lit, and I assumed that they were there to show the way for the landing. But we continued past them and only after another ten minutes did the pilot land the little Cessna. When we took off on our trip home some days later I saw how very, very small and narrow the landing strip was. And when we flew over the land where the fires had been burning we saw that they had been lit by the local farmers to clear the lands for planting, not to show us the way. The pilot had landed on a wing and a prayer.

Corinne and I were greeted by members of the UNHCR staff and then driven to the K9 Compound. The UNHCR and the NGO agencies lived together at K9, the compound located halfway between the town (Ngara) and the Benaco camp. The camp was set up on a hill that looked down on an artificial lake from which a million liters of water was pumped and treated in order to provide drinking water for the refugees. One of the members of the UNHCR staff who was away had lent me his tent. I put away the few belongings that I had brought and went to take a shower in the outdoor shower, a bucket of warm water suspended overhead that was regulated by a string that I pulled. I had to be careful to use just enough water so that I could wash myself and have enough left for rinsing away the soap. We then met everyone working for the UNHCR and their many partners from the UN and NGOs. During dinner we ate local food with the staff, and Jacques Franquin, the coordinator for UNHCR activities in Ngara, briefed me again about the sudden influx of refugees who had come there on just one day at the end of April.

"The Rusumo road was just one compact mass of people, like a flow of lava descending inexorably toward the Tanzanian border," Franquin told us. "I rushed to my radio and called Médecins sans Frontières to quickly send us reinforcements, supplies and, above all, a water provision specialist. Joel Boulanger of MSF jumped into a car and arrived at Benaco together with David Trevino, also of MSF. They worked all night to provide a minimum of drinking water to the refugees."

Thanks to constant cooperation from nongovernmental organizations, UNHCR managed to cope with the arrival of this human tide and save many lives. Franquin described this in *Refugees* magazine, September 1, 1994:

> "The cooperation between UNHCR and the NGOs in this emergency situation was almost perfect," said Franquin. "We had an enormous advantage. We were already here and waiting. So were the NGOs. We had been working together on a project for Burundi refugees and knew each other well. So it was very easy to get organized and deal with the exodus of Rwandese. Because of this, we gained a lot of time." "You can't set up a town of 250,000 inhabitants like the camp at Benaco without a lot of help," Maureen Connelly, head of the UNHCR Emergency Unit in Tanzania added. "And I think what was done was beyond what one could ever have imagined. The task accomplished by a rather reduced number of aid workers was a miracle."

After dinner I went back to my tent, took out my mosquito net, hung it over my bed, and went to sleep. I woke early the next morning eager to get on my way. The sun was already burning on the roof of my small tent. I climbed out of my mosquito net and began to prepare myself for the day ahead. After breakfast I listened to one of the many daily meetings of the UNHCR and its partners. This good coordination of the task especially in the early days of the camp contributed to the success of the operation. The fact that the UNHCR was already on the ground when the first refugees arrived meant that they did not have to deal with the usual two- to three-month wait for funds to be allotted and approved.

I was not prepared for the enormous size of the camp. For as far as I could see in every direction there was only blue, the color of UNHCR tents. I went to speak to refugees in the schools and medical centers. The first wave that had arrived in the spring was in basically good physical condition and they had even brought along some food and supplies. However, the latest wave had arrived empty-handed, and some of the smaller children were suffering from differing degrees of malnutrition.

There were at least five or six children in the feeding center when I arrived and I was told that the weakest and frailest ones are not necessarily the ones that will not survive. "Everything is in the eyes: if there is no flicker of light or movement in the eyes the chances for recovery are slim because the child has given up and has lost all interest in eating." There were no facilities in the camp to feed the children intravenously. I witnessed an unforgettable scene there. I will always carry with me an image of a young mother who was breast-feeding her young baby while trying to persuade an older boy of about four years old to eat. I looked into the eyes of this little boy huddled next to his mother. Although he was breathing, I could not detect the slightest flicker of life in his gaze. He had lost the will to live. His mother looked slowly back and forth between him and the baby that was feeding at her breast, and she seemed to accept that she was going to lose him. She knew that she had to maintain her strength so that she could continue to take care of her other children who still had a chance to survive. The lack of expression in the boys' eyes was heartbreaking but it is the mother's look that I will never forget.

I interviewed some of the latest arrivals in order to find out why they had fled Rwanda. I wanted to know if they had feared for their lives, if they personally had experienced violence before fleeing. The majority of the refugees were Hutus who feared reprisals and imprisonment for genocide. There were also a few Tutsis in the camp who had fled during the genocide; they were hidden from the others for their own safety, and I had to meet with them in a secret location.

The more information and input that I could get from my trip, the greater the chance to get my story out, so I decided that I wanted to retrace the path of the refugees' exodus from the border to the camp. Over lunch I spoke with a soldier who was on loan from the Norwegian military who knew the area very well; he was traveling daily to the border on the lookout for new arrivals. He offered to accompany me so that I could see for myself what the refugees had to go through in order to travel on foot to the camp. The route was extremely bumpy and what would have taken forty-five minutes on decent roads took us about four hours there and back. After dark it was a dangerous area because of smugglers and other criminals. We went to Lake Victoria, where so many refugees had tried to cross, knowing that not all had survived the trip. I could sense the dangers that people were subjected to when they felt that they had no other choice but to flee their homeland. The trip took longer than we had planned and needless to say Jacques was a little nervous and annoyed with my Norwegian chauffeur when we arrived back at the camp after dark. It was an exhausting trip but very informative. Red dust had covered everything and everyone so I went straight to my tent and lined up for a shower. I apologized to the representative for worrying him because I knew that one of the main objections that the representatives in the field have against the goodwill ambassador program is that they are afraid they will have to devote precious time to babysitting some squeamish opera diva or princess instead of dealing with the enormous problems at hand. He said, "I was only worried for your safety but am happy that you fit so easily into the work that we are doing."

After dinner I was lucky that the satellite phone was working so I made a quick call home to say that all was well. I joined some of the UNHCR staff and doctors from MSF at Hard Rock Benaco, a bar that was the meeting place for the social gatherings and late-night discussions that cemented the unusually close-knit humanitarian community there. Even though the collaboration between the UNHCR, other UN agencies, and the NGOs is essential for the success of any refugee operation, too often they are in competition for recognition and the eventual funding that can be engendered by media attention. It is a very thin line to travel between being there to help the victims and using the plight of the victims to raise money. The late-night discussion that I took part in was about the duty to aid refugees who most certainly were guilty of the most egregious crimes against humanity. One of the young doctors said, "In previous situations, when I looked at the patient that I was treating I never judged him or her, but with some of the Hutus who are here it is very difficult not to think that I could be saving the life of a killer!"

An independent television crew was in Ngara, and Corinne managed to get some footage from our trip so that I could present it to television on my return. Corinne called the major channels and offered the footage, and I spoke directly with the anchor of the nightly news at TF1 but was told, "Rwanda is no longer in the news, the cholera epidemic is over, and besides we are going with Haitian refugees this weekend; I will try to fit you in on Monday." I got lucky and was able to speak on Monday about the ongoing problems for the Rwandan refugees. I wanted the public to know that the problems were still there and we still needed funding for the bare essentials. What we did not know was that the worst was yet to come in Goma, Zaire.

In November 1994 I called Secretary General Boutros Boutros-Ghali on many occasions and asked for help. I said, "I know that you are aware of the dire situation in the camps in Goma. The UNHCR cannot do its work unless the camps are demilitarized. We need help now!" "I know. I am working hard to get the Security Council to agree to send soldiers to help." A few days before Christmas his secretary called me at home, and Sebastian answered the phone. "Hello, the Secretary General Boutros Boutros-Ghali wants to speak to Mme. Hendricks." Sebastian thought that it was a prank call and answered, "Yes, of course, and I'm the Queen of England." He handed me the phone and said, "It's someone pretending to be the secretary general," and I said, "It *is* the secretary general—I am waiting for a call from him." Boutros-Ghali said, "I have great news: the Security

Council has agreed to send soldiers to the camps." I was delighted but it turned out to be a cruel Christmas present because nothing actually happened.

Shortly after the first of January I called again and asked him, "Where is the peacekeeping force?" The situation had worsened. The militias were holding those refugees who wanted to return hostages with our help because we were caring for their sick and feeding them. They used threats of violence to pressure the refugees and when that did not work they resorted to beating and killing those who resisted. The UN and the International Community had not had the will to prevent the genocide in Rwanda, and now we were all turning a blind eye to the tragedy unfolding before us and in which we were complicit. This time he was very despondent. "In spite of the resolution passed in December the members have neither been forthcoming with the funding, nor the peacekeepers that are needed." Many of the UNHCR's NGO partners left Goma because of the ethical uneasiness of their inherent complicity with those guilty of genocide who were using the camps to plot military action against the Tutsis in Rwanda.

During this time I was in regular contact with Emma Bonino, the European commissioner for the European Commission Humanitarian Aid Office (ECHO), who was as exasperated as I was at the lack of interest in helping the civilians in the camps. As a commissioner for the EU she had more leverage than I did, but it did not seem to help.

Sergio came home to Geneva from Bosnia and at Christmastime he joined a few of our UNHCR colleagues—Søren Jessen-Pettersen; Omar Bakhet, a Swede who had come to Sweden as a refugee from Eritrea; his wife, Munira, and daughters, Huda and Aida; and Sergio and his wife, Anny, and his sons, Laurent and Adrien—at our annual family glögg party at home in Clarens. Of course we spoke about the desperate situation in Zaire and our helplessness in light of the international community's refusal to commit themselves to do anything but give the minimum humanitarian aid in the place of political will and action. But we also enjoyed the rare moments of being together with our families.

In the fall of 1995 I was president of La Fondation pour l'Action Humanitaire in France and went to Rwanda and Burundi. The foundation had supported a school for orphans outside Kigali, and I went to see how it was working. I was amazed by the natural beauty of the country. It is very green with tranquil rolling hills; Rwanda is called the country of a thousand hills. Who could imagine that the horror of genocide could take place in such an idyllic setting? Upon arrival I made immediate contact with the UNHCR representative to say that I was in town. I then called on my friend Omar Bakhet who had left the UNHCR and was working for the UN Development Program in Kigali. Both were able to bring me up to date about the current situation in the country. I visited the orphanage run by a lovely lady named Immaculée. She had lost her husband and children during the genocide and decided to help the many orphans that were living in her village.

Although I was not officially on UNHCR business I had contacted Mrs. Ogata in Geneva at UNHCR headquarters before leaving and asked her if she had a message for President Kagame in case I was successful in getting a meeting with him. The Rwandan government had been giving mixed signals about the repatriation of the refugees and Mrs. Ogata wanted to know if the president was willing to guarantee the safety of all refugees who wanted to return. Kagame wanted the UN to dismantle the camps because he was aware of the military threat that they posed since many in the camps still wanted to overthrow his government and return to power; but he did not want to see an immediate influx of a million people. He agreed to meet with me and he told me to assure Mrs. Ogata that the refugees were all free to return home and need not fear for their safety. In reality, things were not so simple. The UN was in an intractable quagmire in the Great Lakes region that would soon deteriorate even further and turn into a broader humanitarian disaster. The aftermath of the refugee situation in Goma still haunts those of us at the UNHCR and the NGOs who were involved. The UNHCR is still trying to better define our new purpose in the post–Cold War world disorder.

I visited two overcrowded prisons filled with suspected war criminals and listened to a description of pure horror. Within a three-month period nearly one million Tutsis and moderate Hutus were violently massacred. But it was the stories of survivors like Immaculée that left the deepest impression on me. Omar had arranged for me to meet with a group of widows who had survived, and one story stood out and just made my blood run cold. One of the widows told me that her neighbor, a Hutu, had been married to a Tutsi and they had had four children. In order to exterminate the "bad Tutsi blood" in his family he killed his wife and two of his children. I was nearly fainting when I returned to the famous Hotel des Milles Collines, and I had trouble getting to sleep. All through the night I had nightmares. The horror was inconceivable: neighbors killing neighbors in churches, in their homes. And then there was the complicity of the church. I imagined hearing the voices of hatred that were broadcast nonstop on the radio station "Milles Collines" that demonized the Tutsis and encouraged the barbarism.

My experiences in Bosnia and Rwanda made me wonder what it takes to transform a sane person into a monster capable of murdering his neighbor up close with a machete, hacking away at his body until he dies. How could the killer continue? Was he deaf to the screams of his victim whose blood splattered his murderous hands and body? What does it take to go so mad? I am afraid that the answer is, "Much too little." How far must one go down the road from sanity to commit acts of barbarism? Not nearly as far as I had imagined before being in Sarajevo and Kigali. Before arriving in Rwanda I had pondered a long time about what I could bring to the survivors in Kigali or how I could support them to get back on the road to a better life. I assumed that it would take at least another generation for that to happen. I had prepared in my mind lofty words about forgiveness and reconciliation as tools toward finding inner peace and serenity. Instead of talking I listened to the widows as they spoke to me in quiet tones, sometimes nearly whispering their stories of horror, and I was overcome with sadness and great humility. One of them said to me, "It is too early for us to talk about forgiveness and reconciliation; maybe that will come, maybe not. But what we ask for now, what we ask you to help us with, is to get justice—not to get revenge, but justice—to insure that this will never happen again."

When I left Kigali I knew I had to become an advocate for their justice, not only for them but also for all of the innocent victims of crimes against humanity. I started to speak about this to whomever would listen—Sergio, Kofi Annan, and my friend Emma Bonino in Brussels. In 1993 Emma had founded "No Peace without Justice" (NPWJ) and her party, the Transnational Radical Party, campaigned for the creation of the International Criminal Tribunal for the Former Yugoslavia (ICTY). After its establishment they then focused on raising public awareness worldwide for the creation of an International Criminal Court resulting in the convening of the Diplomatic Conference of Plenipotentiaries in Rome that took place between June 15 and July 17, 1998. I, along with more than eighty human rights activists, heads of state, Nobel laureates, and world leaders, signed the appeal they launched that contributed significantly to the successful ICC Statute at the Rome Conference.

NPWJ and the mayor of Rome, Francesco Rutelli, invited me to participate in the opening ceremony of the conference that established the International Criminal Court, together with Kofi Annan, who was UN secretary general, and Mary Robinson, the UN commissioner for human rights. On July 17, 1998, the Rome Statute was adopted by a vote of 120 to 7, with twenty-one countries abstaining. The seven countries that voted against the treaty were Iraq, Israel, Libya, the People's Republic of China, Qatar, the United States, and Yemen.

Emma returned to the tormented Great Lakes region in November 1996 and January 1997, while an offensive was going on in Zaire, piloted from Rwanda and Uganda, to knock out Mobutu's regime. Among the military objectives was the removal of the refugee camps. A huge Hutu hunt took place in the tropical forests. Emma defended these refugees' rights to humanitarian aid, searched for signs of them, and found about two hundred thousand in the improvised Tingi-Tingi camp. She said, "It is a people who don't exist."

The lack of will to deal with the refugees in the camp in Goma would lead to what has been called the African World War that began in 1998. The war killed 5.4 million people, mostly civilians, and the use of sexual violence and rape as a weapon of war was the worst in the world. Although peace accords were signed in 2003, the region remains unstable today.

In spite of the support that I had at the UNHCR headquarters, Sylvana was furious that my mission to Ngara had been successful and organized without her knowledge. I began to feel her resistance more and more and thought that maybe it was time for me to quit as a goodwill ambassador and move on to something else. I had amassed a wealth of knowledge and had become very adept at understanding and disseminating the message. Without directly soliciting money the UNHCR received quite a few small donations from people who had seen me on TV, heard me on the radio, or read an interview where I spoke about refugees. Søren told me once that those contributions added up to more than what some governments gave annually to the UNHCR. This made me happy, but as I had said to Leon Davicho in 1986, fundraising abilities would not be the greatest asset that I could offer to the cause. I wanted to influence the decisions that could prevent people from being forced to leave their homes in the first place, but if that failed those decisions that could ensure them a climate of lasting peace in a landscape free of mines upon their return. With each mission and each encounter with the refugees themselves I became more and more attached to the refugee cause. I rarely went to headquarters in Geneva until Sergio returned in 1995 to work as Mrs. Ogata's right-hand man. I passed by as often as possible when he was in to have a chat and exchange ideas about matters in the world, but also about our families. He had immediate access to Mrs. Ogata and added his support to Søren's for my work as a goodwill ambassador. The devotion of the many UNHCR staffers whom I met during my visits to the field fostered my attachment to the organization; but it was indeed the refugees themselves, especially the women and the children, who gave me the inspiration and strength to continue. Because of the lack of commitment from the top for the ambassador program, I had entertained the idea after the untimely death of my friend and fellow goodwill ambassador Audrey Hepburn of following her to UNICEF, an organization that knew how to run a goodwill ambassador program. But I kept coming back to the fact that it was indeed the difficulty and the complexity of the refugees, their problems and their solutions, that I found so compelling. Whenever I doubted or was frustrated, the eyes of a refugee mother would seem to jump out of my memory and look me straight in my eyes, asking me to be her voice, tell her story. This was an appeal that I could not refuse, and Sergio and Søren asked me not to abandon the cause. I decided to stay and was for a long time the solitary international goodwill ambassador.

Obviously Sylvana had wanted to organize her own goodwill ambassador program. After inviting Sophia Loren to be a goodwill ambassador in 1992 she was also rumored to be behind the invitation to Fergie, the ex-wife of Prince Andrew, an invitation that was never fulfilled. In 1996 she went to New York City to become the UN spokesperson for the secretary general, Boutros Boutros-Ghali, and to help him in his unsuccessful re-election bid.

Since my first mission for the UNHCR in Zambia in 1987, I studied in depth the history of each refugee situation that I visited and tried to understand the complex geopolitical background against which tragic exodus takes place. Neither refugee problems nor their eventual solutions can be painted in simple colors, or in black and white. Nor can the protagonists be characterized as all good or all evil. The truth on the ground is usually more complex than it might appear on the surface. It is that very intricacy, inherent in our human condition, that attracts me to this work. I want to help find the solutions that will ensure a lasting peace for the victims of cruel conflicts. I believe that those solutions must be rooted in the principles of the Universal Declaration of Human Rights. The active promotion and defense of human rights are absolutely vital; without this, the efforts and sacrifices of inspiring and devoted humanitarian aid workers in the field will be reduced to a cruel joke as the vicious circle of horror and injustice persists. Too often the political actors sitting safely in their offices in Paris, Brussels, New York, and Washington, far away from the actual battlefields, are content to use the work of these brave and dedicated individuals as a humanitarian alibi, a substitute for the courage and political will to make the necessary decisions that can prevent or stop conflicts.The governments of the UN member states owe them gratitude and should not waver in giving them their full support. It is enormously frustrating for me when I see that sometimes the efforts on the ground of the UNHCR, other UN agencies, and our indispensable NGO partners during an emergency, are performed within a political vacuum. We are like a fire truck that arrives when the house is nearly burned down, administers some emergency aid, and then is forced to run off to a new emergency before the house is rebuilt on a solid foundation. Our work is squeezed in between the missed opportunity to predict and prevent conflicts and the sorely lacking long-term vision and means needed to rebuild in the aftermath of an emergency.

While I have remained faithful to my personal commitment to the refugee cause, I have always been open to work with other organizations such as UNESCO and the Council of Europe because the problem of refugees cannot be solved by the UNHCR alone.

In the mid-1980s I stood on a hill at the Prague Castle overlooking the rooftops of the city with two members of the Amadeus String Quartet, Peter Schidlof and Norbert Brainin. I listened to them describe the Prague that they had known as young men before World War II. When they were students in Vienna they had looked to this vibrant, avant-garde, and progressive city for cultural and political inspiration. As they reminisced we all agreed that we would never live to see the city free from the yoke of the Soviet Union. Peter died in 1987 and the quartet disbanded. The Berlin Wall fell November 9, 1989, and Norbert and I did live to see what we thought then was impossible. We could never have dreamed that the Eastern Bloc would break apart piece by piece and that by 1991 the Soviet Union would be dissolved.

I certainly could not have imagined that I would be in East Berlin on the 9th of December and would be a first-hand witness to the key event of this political shift. Nor could we have fathomed that most of the countries that formed the Warsaw Pact would become members of the European Union. While we in the humanitarian community were basking in the positive vibrations and expectations of these incredible events, our hope was that we would finally be able to contribute to the forming of a new world order based on respect for human rights.

However we did not expect that the ugly multiheaded monster of racism, xenophobia, anti-Semitism, and intolerance that lurks in all of us would be so quickly awakened and rear its ugly head in Europe. At the end of the Second World War, Europe had sworn with so much conviction, "Never again." The older politicians in Europe who remembered the war should have recognized the symptoms immediately! But they were very slow to acknowledge what was happening and to take a stand against the rise of far-right-wing, neo-fascist parties on the European continent. I was concerned about this and wanted to prevent this from infecting the youth of Europe. In 1993 I voiced my concerns to Catherine Lalumière, the secretary general of the Council of Europe, whom I had met after a concert in Strasbourg. I was frustrated that the leaders in Europe seemed to be ignoring this issue. Instead of addressing the real problems of immigration and integration head-on, they tried for electoral purposes to appease the fearmongers with their own populist ideas. Some could have been in denial but others, I believe, agreed with the far right that the problems facing Europe were brought on by too many immigrants being accepted there. The UNHCR has to deal more and more with stricter and sometimes very unjust and immoral rules against asylum seekers that have made it harder for us to help those who are most in need of protection.

I did not see this generation of leaders showing the necessary political will to find the solutions. I felt that Europe's youth were not ignorant of their violent past but were less laden with its baggage and were open-minded and forward-looking. I hoped not only to be able to challenge and inspire them but that they would in turn inspire and challenge me.

The ideals of the European Union and the Council of Europe were both forged from the ashes of World War II out of the strong desire to find ways for all Europeans to live together in peace on this continent after centuries of strife and destruction. The Council of Europe now comprises forty-seven countries in Europe and states as its objective, "to create a common democratic and legal area throughout the whole of the continent, ensuring respect for its fundamental values: human rights, democracy, and the rule of law." When I spoke to Catherine about the danger of leaving even the smallest hole for the ideas of hatred and rejection to enter and eventually destroy the fabric of the COE, she said to me, "You must be reading my mind because we have been discussing this problem too, and we at the Council of Europe want to organize a campaign based on tolerance for the youth of Europe. We would love to have you working alongside us—would you be one of our patrons?"

She told me that in October 1993 the heads of government of the then thirty-two members of the COE had met at a summit in Vienna and made this statement: "The end of the division of Europe offers an historic opportunity to consolidate peace and stability on the continent. All our countries are committed to pluralist and parliamentary democracy, the indivisibility and universality of human rights, the rule of law, and a common cultural heritage enriched by its diversity. Europe can thus become a vast area of democratic security." Their plan of action was to launch a broad European Youth Campaign to mobilize the public in favor of a tolerant society based on the equal dignity of all its members and against manifestations of racism, xenophobia, anti-Semitism, and intolerance.

Catherine invited me to participate in a conference in Strasbourg in March 1994 with Yehudi Menuhin and Elie Wiesel entitled "Europe against Intolerance." I chaired a roundtable about the experiences of intolerance in Europe entitled "Racism, Xenophobia and Runaway Nationalism." I became a patron for this great project along with other Europeans such as Bronislaw Geremek. Earlier that year Federico Mayor had appointed me his special advisor on inter-cultural relations at UNESCO. I was able to bring along support from UNESCO for this campaign for the youth of Europe. I worked closely with Mireille Paulus, who was in charge. The campaign was launched in December 1994.

The European Youth Campaign against Racism, Xenophobia, Anti-Semitism and Intolerance—All Different–All Equal—came out of that Vienna Summit. Between 1994 and 1996 enthusiastic young people in every European country organized their own campaigns with concerts, theater projects, art exhibitions, and open forums in schools and universities. The aim was to foster understanding between people of different cultural backgrounds and to teach them to embrace the very things that made them different. The campaign reached its high point during European

Youth Week in Strasbourg in June 1995. Young people arrived on trains from the four corners of Europe and there were also several events in the twenty-four countries through which they passed on their way there. That week of stimulating discussions and exchanges still inspires me today. At the end of the campaign Catherine's successor, Daniel Tarschys, as secretary general of the Council of Europe, lacked her vision and commitment to this project; it did not receive further funding and was sadly allowed to end. In 2006 the campaign was revived until 2008, but I would like to see it as a permanent fixture in the European landscape because I sincerely believe that we have not begun to tap the most powerful resources that we have: our youth's energy, sense of justice, and hope. I still keep a close relationship with the COE and my friend Mireille who is still working there. In 2010 the Council of Europe's secretary general, the Norwegian Thorbjørn Jagland, invited the UN secretary general Ban Ki-Moon and me to speak to the organization's General Assembly in celebration of the sixtieth anniversary of the European Convention on Human Rights.

When I marked my ballot for Bill Clinton in the 1992 presidential election I felt I had only partially performed my civic duty. Although I tried to make as intelligent and informed a choice that I could, I was completely unable to fill out the rest of the ballot. Neither the senator nor the governor for whom I had voted in previous elections was on this ballot. Although I lived in Europe I tried to keep up with the political scene in America, but before the arrival of the Internet and nonstop 24/7 news this was not so easy. I knew nothing about the new candidates from either party. I also had to leave blank the different propositions and other items on the ballot. It was a great source of frustration to me that I was neither able to participate fully as a citizen by voting nor able to affect the political discussion taking place in the United States. I had been living in Europe since 1977 and my family, my work, and most of my friends are all based there.

Leading up to the vote in France on the Maastricht Treaty in 1992 I was asked to participate in a nationally televised debate.

I hesitated because I felt that a non-European should not try to influence the debate, but after some thought I accepted on behalf of my children, Jennie and Sebastian, who are European citizens in the true sense—Swedish and American citizens, born in Paris, raised in Switzerland, speaking three languages fluently (Swedish, English, and French), and managing well in at least two others (German and Spanish). They represented the diversity of the new EU.

This debate awakened my curiosity about the EU, and I became very interested to know more about the ideals and visions of Robert Schuman and Jean Monnet, the founders of what is today the European Union. They wanted to go even further than the Council of Europe. In April 1951, six nations—France, Germany, Luxembourg, the Netherlands, Belgium, and Italy—signed the Schuman Plan that evolved into the European Union and today has twenty-seven member states: "Unity in diversity." For Jennie and Sebastian's sake I wanted to be able to take part in what Robert Schuman called "this great experiment" of diverse peoples with distinct and rich cultures actively working to live together in peace.

In 1994 I became a European citizen, a Swedish citizen. At that time a Swede could not have two nationalities so I had to give up my American citizenship. Even though I do not travel with an American passport, I still feel very American; I can never lose—nor do I have a desire to turn my back on—something that makes me who I am. It is a privilege to carry two cultures within me. But my desire to participate politically in Europe is stronger than just being able to vote. Although I didn't know it at the time, becoming a Swedish citizen did not automatically give me the right to vote in Sweden. In 1998 I was in Beijing to sing Liu in the first production of Puccini's *Turandot* to be staged in the real Forbidden City. I went to the Swedish embassy in Beijing where the ambassador and his staff greeted me warmly, and I was allowed to vote. I had been having lunch at a garden restaurant where we often ate near our hotel, and I met a Swedish lady who was a friend of a friend. We chatted for a while, then I excused myself, saying, "I have to leave you now because I have to get to the embassy so that I can vote before going to rehearsal tonight."

When I returned to Switzerland I received a note from her: "Dear Mrs. Hendricks, I have never voted in my life before but I was so moved that you, a new Swedish citizen felt so strongly about voting that I have now voted for the very first time, and this will not be the last. Thank you for inspiring me to take my civic duty seriously." But when I asked for my ballot for a subsequent election the authorities told me that I could not vote, according to an addition to the Swedish Constitution, because I had never been a resident in Sweden. Martin has not lived in Sweden since he was twenty-two but he still has the right to vote in all Swedish elections. The law makes sense to me but neither the Swedish ambassador in Switzerland, who gave a dinner in my honor when I became a Swedish citizen, nor the ambassador in Beijing were aware of the clause. Had I known about it I would not have given up my US citizenship at that time because since 2000 a Swede can have multiple citizenships.

I am now able to vote in local elections in Switzerland, and I do so because it is my duty to let my voice be heard. Not having the right to vote in Sweden, however, has made me even more active and vocal about world affairs, and especially European affairs. My experience in the former Yugoslavia taught me that Europe has a responsibility and a necessary role to play in international affairs. It needs desperately to add its own political voice to the conversation in the world and more importantly to find the will to fulfill its own political vision. We are still at the beginning of this "great experiment" and I feel that in spite of difficulties and setbacks it is an experiment worth defending. I will continue to make my small contribution.

In 1993 I was a founding member of La Fondation pour l'Action Humanitaire in Paris with Bernard Kouchner and in 1995 was elected its president, a post that I held until 1997. It was an unpaid position and I covered all of my own expenses. I would have liked to go into the field to work on all of the foundation's projects, but due to my own active singing career it was impossible to do so. I have had to keep a balance between my professional commitments and my humanitarian work. If I had canceled concerts in order to run off to the field for the HCR or the foundation during an emergency, no matter how dire, I would have lost all my credibility within my profession. I have always been strict with myself about respecting my professional commitments even when something very interesting comes along.

I was expected to accept the reports of the foundation's projects coming from the field without being able to personally verify them, and I gradually began to feel that I was really nothing more than a figurehead. I realized that I was not going to be able to accomplish my goals of working for human rights and justice within this organization. When I was in agreement with Bernard, things went well. But when I refused to rubber-stamp actions with which I disagreed, or when I actually tried to exert my authority by demanding accountability from everyone, including Bernard, it became clear that he and I did not share the same values. It also became difficult to work with those in the organization who were more than willing to follow him blindly without question. I had worked with enough true humanitarians at the UNHCR and elsewhere—Corinne, Sergio, and Omar, among others; Jean-Baptiste at Handicap International; Staffan de Mistura at UNICEF—to know that I was simply wasting my time in an unserious organization.

I then worked with another foundation in Switzerland, but I was again expected to just be the front figure, without the power to make the real decisions. It was time for me to become my own boss. I felt a real need to extend my humble activities in support of the refugee cause. I wanted to work for the prevention of conflicts so that exodus and exile might be avoided, as well as to work for reconciliation and durable peace when refugees have been successfully repatriated.

The Barbara Hendricks Foundation for Peace and Reconciliation was born in 1998. It gives me a framework to accomplish small, modest projects concerning refugees with reliable partners like Handicap International, the Refugee Education Trust, the Martin Ennals Award for Human Rights Defenders, and the Human Rights Film Network. I do not solicit money from the public. I put fees from some of my concerts as well as prize money that I have received, such as from the Lions Clubs International, into the foundation.

From my own personal experience, I know the importance of education for every child, and one of the first projects of my foundation was in collaboration with the Refugee Education Trust. In 2000, before leaving the UNHCR, Mrs. Ogata founded the RET to fill a gap in the UNHCR budget for the education of adolescent refugees. When the funding for education exists in the UNHCR emergency budget, it is only for primary education, never for secondary education. When she asked me to be a member of the board I accepted because I had seen too many young people in the camps who were wasting their most formative years doing nothing. Education and vocational training could be an important tool for them to rebuild their lives and their country and to foster peace and reconciliation when they return home, instead of reigniting old conflicts. Without education and vocational training the opportunities that await them are very limited and the prospects for their future are dire. Their only options would be to become laborers, exploited at home or in some distant land; petty criminals; or maybe even members of lawless militias. Having an education and skills gives one choices in life, and the very essence of being free is to be able to choose. Beginning in 2000, I was on the board of RET, and am now a member of the strategic leadership council. My foundation (BHFPR) gave the RET financial support during its beginning and its most difficult moments.

So many ethnic conflicts have been perpetuated by the use of the "cultural alibi"—that is to say, "my culture versus your culture." This is a powerful excuse, a driving force that justifies war, barbarism, and destruction. I believe that intercultural interaction can, on the contrary, be an even more powerful force for bringing people together. Cultural exchange and interaction means going beyond eating food from a foreign country and watching performances of folkloric song and dance. I proposed to Federico Mayor at UNESCO and to the UNHCR representative in Sarajevo to set up, in partnership with my foundation, small cultural centers in Bosnia Herzegovina that would be like safe islands, cultural demilitarized zones, where children from the ages of nine to sixteen, from every ethnic group in Bosnia Herzegovina, would feel free to sing, dance, participate in amateur theater productions together, or just read in the library. I wanted to start the first children's cultural center in a small town before trying it out in a large metropolis like Sarajevo. The municipality of each town would provide for the space in as neutral a setting as possible and UNESCO would help to provide a library that would be the meeting point around which the other activities would revolve. The representative from the UNHCR was also on board to help me with coordinating with the local authorities on the ground. I felt that it would be necessary to establish a volunteer staff. I did not have the means to employ the adults who would serve as the rector and the directors of the choir, musical ensembles, and theater. It was necessary that they should be local and come from the different communities. We had thought that a school would be a good location, but the ethnic cleansing had been so successful in Bosnia Herzegovina that most children lived in segregated neighborhoods and went to segregated schools. Because I had grown up in a segregated society it was very difficult for me to come to terms with the disastrous results of our lack of courage and to see this kind of segregation in the year 1999 in modern Europe.

I came to Sarajevo from Geneva with Sebastian, who was making the trip as a school assignment, and some days before leaving he admitted to me that he was a bit nervous about the tragedies that he might see. I assured him that the war was over, but I too was very curious to see what had happened to the city since that first day of 1994. We landed at the same Sarajevo airport with a SwissAir flight from Zurich. I could hardly believe my eyes—it was already functioning as a flourishing shopping center just like most modern airports. The UNHCR representative met us at the airport and I marveled at the changes that had taken place on the route to the same Holiday Inn where I had stayed five years before. I did not recognize the hotel at all with no holes outside from exploded bombs; all of the usual facilities were functioning—running water, even the elevator. I walked out with Sebastian to "sniper alley" and we strolled across the same street to the post office. Sebastian was quite impressed and relieved; he knew that the fighting had stopped but he still carried the images from the televised nightly newscasts in his mind. Two days before our arrival a plane carrying UN and NGO passengers had crashed in the mountains, killing everyone aboard. Just before leaving Switzerland I received a call from the Geneva office asking if I would agree to sing at the memorial service that was to take place on the morning after our arrival. I agreed and they found a young organ student to accompany me singing Schubert's "Ave Maria." I went to the church in the morning and practiced with him. Sebastian sat behind me while I sang for a despondent UN and NGO community who had lost very good friends and colleagues. We left the church and were driven to a small town about an hour from Sarajevo. The young mayor of the town was very enthusiastic about my idea and personally gave us a tour of his city. Unusually, there were Serbs, Bosnians, and Croatians holding offices in his government, although not in equal numbers. The UNHCR was overseeing the returnees in different communities. We spoke to some who had settled into homes that had belonged to people who had fled. It was a complex problem to solve; returnees wanted to repossess their homes and squatters were afraid to return to their original homes that were also occupied by others. One of the solutions was to help returnees as well as displaced persons from other regions to build new homes. Sebastian and I visited some of the new homeowners who had returned to a Croatian neighborhood. The ubiquitous problem of mines was another obstacle that had to be solved before people could return. In the afternoon I had a meeting with the Bosnian president Alija Izetbegović. A funny thing happened as we were going up the stairs to the presidential office. One of his aides, a young woman, asked the UNHCR representative, "While Mrs. Hendricks is in with the president what shall we do with the child?" I overheard and I interjected, "The child stays with me." So we went in together and I introduced Sebastian to the president, who remembered me from our concert in 1993 and welcomed me back to Sarajevo. We talked about what his government was doing to facilitate the return of the non-Bosnian population who had fled the fighting, and he assured me of his full support of the UNHCR's efforts. Sebastian had sat quietly, but at the end of the meeting asked permission to ask the president a question. He wanted to know if the president believed that Sarajevo would again be the open city for all ethnic groups that it had been before the war. Of course the president's answer was yes.

Before leaving Sarajevo I wanted to go up to the hills surrounding the city with Sebastian. It was hard to imagine that in these same hills the Serbs had stationed eighteen thousand troops and rained down terror, death, and destruction on a civilian population during four years. I had felt that terror for only three days—the vibrations of the bombs that were too close for comfort—and seen the death and terror in the eyes of the city's inhabitants. When I stood in that same place with Sebastian I could not fight back the tears that welled up in my eyes, tears of indignation at the futility of it all and tears of shame for our indifference.

We left Sarajevo on March 21. On the plane back to Zurich, Sebastian said to me, "Mom, I was really afraid to come here because I did not know if I could stand to see suffering like I have seen on television; but it was the best way for me to learn about what you are doing and I understand why you are so passionate. So thank you."

On March 22 the airport of Sarajevo was closed. After the breakdown in talks about Kosovo with the Federal Republic of Yugoslavia, NATO started its bombing campaign that continued for more than two months before Serbia surrendered in June. This ended the Serbian aggression in Kosovo, but it also disrupted the project that I had just begun to put into place in Bosnia. When the summer was over I tried to piece together the project again but in September the UNHCR representative in Bosnia was rotated to another post and I had to start to reorganize from scratch. In December, when Federico Mayor's final term at UNESCO ended, his successor promptly canceled all of his pending projects, including mine, without even consulting me.

The Portuguese colonized Timor in the sixteenth century, and when the country declared its independence in 1975, Indonesia began a brutal and violent occupation that lasted until 1999. After a referendum that same year sponsored by the UN, Timor declared its independence again.

I had been aware of the conflict in East Timor for some time before I met José Ramos-Horta in the 1990s in Prague. President Havel hosted a human rights conference for Nobel Peace Prize laureates and I was invited to speak. At that time José was the spokesman for the East Timorese resistance in exile. I was very moved by his devotion to his cause and we shared a common support of his fellow laureate Aung San Suu Kyi.

In May 1999 Sergio was sent to Kosovo to assess the situation, including the collateral damage of the NATO bombing and Serbian aggression. In June he was appointed the interim special representative of Secretary General Kofi Annan, but the permanent post had to go to a European, so after preparing the groundwork Sergio moved on and was appointed the UN transitional administrator for East Timor's independence.

Sergio had a daunting task before him because armed clashes were still taking place, and as usual he was expected to complete his mission in a short amount of time with limited means. I talked to him whenever we could by phone and he always asked, "Can't you stop by when you are out in the wider world on tour?" I said, "Sergio, Dili is not on the way to anywhere. I promise that when and if the opportunity presents itself I will be there." When we spoke at the beginning of 2002, he said, "My job here will be finished in about five months and the Timorese are planning for their independence in May. Would you consider coming to sing on that occasion? I know that José and the Timorese people would be honored by your presence. We do not even have funds to pay for your travel from Europe, but if you can get to Bali you can travel to and from Dili on a UN plane that will be coming here."

I marked the date in my calendar and was determined to be with Sergio and the people of the UN's youngest member on that day. On May 16, 2002, Ulf and I landed in Bali and boarded a UN plane the next day to Dili. Sergio met us at the airport and later showed us around a little. He was exuberant for two reasons. First, he had managed, in just two years, a very complicated transition of a land that had gone through a twenty-five-year civil war into an independent, democratic new nation. As we drove through the streets of Dili he said, "Look around you—when I arrived here two years ago there was nothing but ruins and it was too dangerous to walk in the streets. I have no official role in the independence ceremonies because my job finishes tomorrow night when you sing. I do not want to receive awards or applause; my reward will be on Independence Day when I will take Carolina, the love of my life, by the hand and walk through the streets of Dili like any normal lovers out for a stroll." Carolina was the second cause of his exuberance. For the first time since I had known Sergio he spoke to me about another woman in his life. I guessed that there had been others, and I knew that he had not been happy in his marriage. I remember a discussion that we had in his office in Geneva when I told him that I was getting divorced. I confided in him about how difficult and painful the decision was for me. I then asked him, "I know that you are unhappy; when are you going to fix that?" He agreed that he should take care of it, and he expressed his concern for his sons for they were very important to him. When he was in New York as UN undersecretary general for humanitarian affairs we met for dinner and I told him that I had met Ulf. Sergio was very happy for me and we touched on the subject of his marriage again but he was not ready to act. Finally when he met and fell in love with Carolina in East Timor he was anxious to begin the long and painful process to leave his wife. After so many years he had finally decided to live honestly because he planned to marry Carolina as soon as his divorce became final. In Dili I met Carolina for the first time and he met Ulf for the first time. I saw that his relationship with Carolina was serious and I was so pleased to see him so happy.

Sergio knew that the peace and the new democracy were fragile and that the road ahead would not be easy because as usual the international community always wants quick, cheap fixes to deeply rooted, serious problems. But he said, "I have given my all and I believe that the people here, their new President Gusmao, and our old friend José will also give their all to make it succeed. Let's hope and pray that they will." José became the first minister of foreign affairs and the second president of his country. Sergio would have been heartbroken about the violence that broke out in 2006 and the attempts in 2007 on the lives of both Gusmao and José, but he would not have been surprised.

I met Bill Clinton again in Dili for the first time since his inauguration; he did not seem to remember me until he heard me sing. He came up to me the following day and said, "When I heard you sing last night I was very moved and remembered that I had a recording of your Negro Spirituals that I played so much that I nearly wore out the CD." Kofi and Nane Annan were there, as well as UNHCR's high commissioner, Ruud Lubbers. Kofi was very proud to welcome Timor as the newest member of the UN.

There was a bit of musical chairs going on for rooms on the old cruise ship that was used as a hotel for the guests; the room that Ulf and I had on our first night had been given to one of the members of the large Clinton delegation, and Ulf and I moved to Sergio's assistant Jonathan Price's home, while Kofi and Nane slept in Sergio's apartment. I think that when things settled down Sergio and Carolina ended up on the ship somewhere. I was happy to have been able to keep my promise to Sergio to come to Dili and to see José free at home and to sing the songs of my people—"Oh, Freedom" and "We Shall Overcome"—for him and the East Timorese. Ulf and I boarded the plane back to Bali together with Nane and Kofi, and as we spoke of our hopes for this new nation, we immediately began to talk about the threat on the horizon—the American-led invasion of Iraq. I was also fishing on Sergio's behalf to know where the secretary general planned to send him next.

In September 2002 Sergio was appointed high commissioner for human rights in Geneva. I was very happy that he was going to be nearer. Sergio and Carolina came home and he was going to try to get the troubled Human Rights Commission and finally his own personal life in order. One of the first projects that we did together was to become the patrons of the International Film Festival and Forum on Human Rights that we inaugurated in March 2003 during the Human Rights Council.

Everyone now knows that the invasion of Afghanistan was in retaliation for the attacks on the World Trade Center in New York on September 11, 2001. We are still bogged down in Afghanistan today with waning public support around the world for what was seen and accepted as a justifiable war at the beginning. But once the invasion of Afghanistan had succeeded, the Bush government and Tony Blair shifted all of their attention to the prize: Iraq and the overthrow of Saddam Hussein. Afghanistan was put on the back burner and left to smolder into a potential quagmire for years to come. In the meantime, the civilian population, especially girls and women, continue to suffer.

We are now beginning to learn the truth about the lead-up to the March 2003 invasion in Iraq —Tony Blair and George Bush's illegal and immoral war.

I was among the millions all over the world who protested against the invasion of Iraq because I agreed with Joschka Fischer, the German minister of foreign affairs, who said in a passionate speech, "After looking at the American and British arguments, I am not at all convinced." Before the invasion the architects of the debacle treated the UN with disdain and dismissed the organization, but once the irreversible mess had taken place they called the UN in to help clean up. I had been sickened and saddened that this unjustifiable war was taking place under the helpless watch of the UN. I was even sicker that the UN, the Security Council, and the weapons inspectors had all been manipulated with lies and false evidence for the ends of those who wanted to invade Iraq at all costs. I could not in good conscience pray for the defeat of British and American forces because that would mean that I would pray for innocent young men and women to die needlessly. So I prayed for the truth. I knew that the truth has enormous power and cannot be kept down for long. I often rang Kofi to talk about the state of the world and boost his morale. I reminded him that in spite of the enormous pressure that he and the UN were under, he was the secretary general of all of the nations of the United Nations, not of any one country or one faction. He also encouraged me when I was feeling down. We knew that his phones and maybe the entire house were wiretapped so before hanging up I said, "I suppose we should say good night to whomever is listening."

In September 2004 Kofi Annan said, "From our [the UN's] point of view and from the Charter's point of view the war was illegal." Just recently the new British deputy prime minister Clegg has said the same thing. We have seen the images provided by the embedded media at the beginning of the war. But we have also seen the images of the suffering of the civilian population and later of the disgrace and shame of Abu Ghraib and Guantanamo Bay. We've learned about extraordinary rendition, closed prisons, and torture. Now we know that Tony Blair's justifications to the British Parliament for the invasion have all proven to be completely false. There were no Weapons of Mass Destruction.

The millions of people all over the world who demonstrated against this invasion had, of course, doubted it all along. In July 2003 I was a *sommarpratare* (summer speaker) on Swedish Radio. This is a fifty-year-old tradition in which every day of the summer, a well-known personality does a seventy-five-minute program about whatever interests her, interspersed with music that she has chosen. Another *sommarpratare* that summer was Hans Blix, the former UN chief weapons inspector in Iraq, and I met him at the dinner given for all of the participants in September. I found myself seated next to him and of course could not contain my curiosity. I asked him to tell me his side of the story about the weapons inspections in Iraq and the lead-up to the invasion. He was very candid about the refusal of the American and British to allow the inspections to continue. WMDs were only a false alibi for the invasion, because they were determined to invade Iraq. He was pretty sure that his offices had been wiretapped.

It is a matter of record that on January 30, 2003, Britain's then–attorney general, Lord Goldsmith, informed Prime Minister Blair that the use of military force against Iraq was illegal without the sanction of the United Nations Security Council and when that sanction failed to materialize Lord Goldsmith changed his mind.

As the Nuremberg verdict stated, "War is essentially an evil thing. Its consequences are not confined to the belligerent states alone, but affect the whole world. To initiate a war of aggression, therefore, is not only an international crime, it is the supreme international crime, differing from other war crimes in that it contains within itself the accumulated evil of the whole." Eliza Manningham-Buller, director-general of MI5 (English military intelligence) from October 2002 until April 2007, testifying at

the Chilcot inquiry, offered blunt and withering criticism of the
Blair government's decision to go to war in Iraq. During the run-
up to the invasion, it turns out, this highly experienced expert
on counter-terrorism held views not at all different from those
held by the rank amateurs of the British public. She believed, for
example, that another war against a Muslim country, and one not
implicated in the September 2001 attacks on the United States,
would assist in radicalizing young British Muslims, persuading
them to become involved in mounting terrorist attacks in their
home country. Some had, after all, made the extraordinary decision to go off to fight in Afghanistan already. Tony Blair ignored
the MI5 director-general's advice, as he did the public's protests,
but history has proved her fears to be uncannily accurate.

The last straw was to come on August 19, 2003. In May, Ulf
and I were having lunch at an outdoor restaurant in beautifully
restored Beirut. I had sung a concert the evening before and was
enjoying some time off with my friend Staffan de Mistura, the
UN representative there, whom I had met when he was working
for UNICEF in Dubrovnik. Ulf and I had accompanied him to
the border with Israel for a meeting with his staff and an award
ceremony. When Staffan arrived for lunch he said, "I have heard
that Kofi is going to ask Sergio to go to Baghdad." I said, "He
can't do that—Sergio has worked so hard to straighten out the
mess at the UNHRC in Geneva and he is just starting to see some
progress. He has no time to take off from that demanding task,
and besides, why should the UN send in its best people to clean
up the mess that they had tried to prevent? First we are bypassed
and then they ask us for help. They naively thought that there
would be democracy and peace in Iraq in time for the summer
vacations." I thought that Sergio might take the direct flight the
next day to New York City. I did not want to call him at the office;
I preferred to reach him at home. I tried all evening but there was
no answer. Carolina later told me that they had just moved into
a new apartment and had not yet installed the phone. I did not
expect to convince Sergio not to go to Iraq but I just wanted to
hear his voice and his point of view about the matter. We had discussed at length our frustration with the constant undermining of

the UN by politicians who use the organization with impunity as a scapegoat during their national election campaigns.

I knew that Sergio was a man with a strong sense of duty and loyalty and that if he was called upon to serve, he would answer that call. The next time I saw him was on the news; he was standing next to Kofi at a press conference at the UN in New York City announcing his departure for Baghdad. Sometime after he arrived there we spoke and he assured me that he was going to do all that he could to be at my wedding to Ulf in August. When I asked about the Human Rights Commission, he said, "I will stay here only until the fall because I am committed to my work in Geneva, and by then my divorce will be final too."

As the date of the wedding approached, the chances were slim that he might be in Sweden on the sixteenth.

On July 18, 2003, Sergio wrote:

Dear Barbara,

Thank you for your invitation. It has arrived here in Baghdad, a little late, but Cecilia, my secretary in Geneva, had immediately informed me of its arrival at the office.

However, it is not probable that Carolina (she is here too) and I can be with you in Sweden on August 16. Believe me, we regret it.

We said to each other, thinking about you and Ulf and this missed opportunity, that it's enough now with all the sacrifices that we have made, particularly when it means missing an exceptional moment like your wedding. We have promised to put our private lives and our friends before everything else in 2004. But we will meet again, I am sure before the end of the year, in Switzerland. Carolina and I send you both a big hug.

Sergio

Sergio had one last-minute plan up his sleeve. He was to travel to New York to meet with Kofi around the time of the wedding and was hoping to somehow go via Stockholm. When he told me this plan I feared that it was a very long shot and would not work, but I held out hope.

On August 16, 2003, Ulf and I were married in the Swedish Archipelago surrounded by family and friends, but a few of my closest friends were not there. Daniel had died of heart failure in February and Sergio was in Baghdad. Because of the crisis in Iraq and the new involvement of the UN, Kofi and Nane were also stuck in New York City. Kofi suggested that he and Nane would celebrate our marriage with us when they would come to Stockholm on August 25. Kofi sent us a letter that was read by Staffan de Mistura, who had come from Beirut.

On August 19 we waved good-bye to Sebastian, Jennie, their friends from Switzerland, and the last wedding guests. I went back into the house and put on the radio. Then I heard the unbelievable news that the UN headquarters in Baghdad had been bombed, many were killed, and Sergio was trapped under the rubble. Ulf and I were glued to the radio for the rest of the day, as we have no TV. I could not accept the possibility that Sergio would not make it out alive. I kept saying to myself, "Sergio always manages; no matter how difficult the situation, he always walks away." But not this time. Sergio was under the rubble for hours before he died. Carolina had left the meeting in Sergio's office and had been in her office only a few minutes when the blast occurred. Injured and distraught, she tried to pull away some of the rubble with her bare hands, to no avail.

Sebastian was working as an unpaid intern at the UNHCR that summer with Shannon Boyd, who was just about to retire. As soon as he arrived at the airport in Geneva he immediately contacted the UNHCR, and when the news came into headquarters he called me to say that Sergio and twenty-one members of his staff had not survived the attack. Sergio and those staff members were the very best that the UN had to offer. They were among that small group of dedicated servants that always answered the call to go into the most difficult situations, jeopardizing their well-being and even their personal lives (the UN has a very high divorce rate) because they believed in the principles of the UN—for which they eventually died. They always held out hope that by working together under a set of just and moral rules the world could become a better place for all, not just for a privileged few.

I was still on a high from my wedding, one of the happiest days in my life, and the news of this attack at the heart of the UN brought me down—now I had to face yet another personal loss so soon after Daniel's sudden death.

Daniel and I had not even had the chance to discuss the invasion of Iraq and he did not get to tell some embarrassing and funny story at my wedding. The loss of Sergio was almost too much for me to bear. I was so grateful that Ulf was such a wonderful support and understood my strong attachments to two extraordinary men.

I went to Geneva for Sergio's funeral and tried in some way to comfort his sons, Adrien and Laurent. I realized that they had hardly known him. They vaguely remembered accompanying him to my home for the Christmas party. I told them that Sergio and I had often spoken about them and that they were his pride and joy. I understood his widow's grief, and I felt doubly sad because Sergio had waited so long to deal with his failed marriage that there was a cloud hanging over his wife and sons' farewell to him. I knew that it would have turned Sergio's stomach to see how unjustly Carolina was treated—the UN excluded and almost discarded her. Luckily she had formed a very close relationship with his mother, Gilda Vieira de Mello, and they have been a very important support for one another.

I greeted José Ramos-Horta at the funeral. We were both in shock; we could not believe that Sergio was dead. When he asked where Carolina was I had to explain to him that she had been flown directly from Baghdad to Buenos Aires and had not been allowed to be in Geneva for the funeral. I had brought two red roses that I lay in his grave, one from me and one from Carolina and Gilda.

In the memorial service at the UN headquarters in Geneva I spoke about the good times and the fun times with Sergio because I needed to help myself gather the strength to sing "Oh Freedom," just for him. I said, "Sergio, you always asked me to sing a song in the most difficult and sometimes dangerous moments, whether I had warmed up my voice or not. You knew that if you asked me I would never say no, but tonight, Sergio, is certainly the hardest time for me." And I sang in spite of my trembling voice and my tears.

In October 2003 I was on tour in Brazil and had a concert in Rio de Janeiro. Gilda invited Ulf and me to come visit her. A small, strong woman opened the door and hugged me for a long moment; neither of us was able to hold back our tears. She invited us in and we greeted Carolina, who was standing behind her. We had not met since we were in Dili. I had met Gilda many times before because I had always invited her to my concerts whenever I had come to Rio to sing. She usually came backstage afterward to thank me shyly for the concert and the invitation and then quietly left. This was the first time she had invited me to her home. She and Carolina showed us the apartment where Sergio had grown up. Gilda showed us the picture of him on the beach where he always wanted to go for a swim as soon as he arrived back in Rio. We looked through all the family albums and I saw that the man who had become my brother had always been the same smiling, hopeful little boy who looked back at me from the photos in their albums.

In 2007, when Staffan called me to say that he was to become the special representative for the secretary general to Iraq, a chill went up my spine. Luckily he survived that post, and his last assignment for the UN was as the special representative for the secretary general in Afghanistan. He is now the undersecretary of state in the Italian government.

———

Mrs. Ogata left the UNHCR at the end of her second term in 2000, after eight years as a tireless HC; the Dutchman Ruud Lubbers succeeded her. Shortly after his arrival he asked for a meeting with me to discuss my thoughts on the organization, its evolving mandate in the quickly changing world, and to give my views on the goodwill ambassador program. As the UNHCR's longest-serving goodwill ambassador I stated my firm conviction that GWAs can play a very positive role for the UN and that they should be public figures, but most of all they should be capable of passing on our complicated and difficult message to the media.

I believe that if your private life is displayed on the front covers of gossip magazines, then your message gets diluted because the tabloid headlines will always scream louder than the humanitarian message. I spoke with Nane Annan about this matter over breakfast one morning in New York City. I tried to explain why I could not share her enthusiasm about two well-known personalities who had just agreed to become GWAs for the secretary general's office. I did not in any way question their sincerity, but at that time they were both in the tabloids almost weekly, and the subject was their personal problems and not the UN. I am by nature a discrete person but I have also felt an extra, self-imposed obligation to the UNHCR: to keep my private life out of the press so as not to compete with the UNHCR's message. I actually had to announce my divorce two years after the fact so that when I came to Cannes Festival with Ulf there would not be any speculation about us. In spite of the fact that many of the Hollywood stars that are active for the UN and NGOs are truly sincere and do very good work, many others just want to have a charity or UN logo on their résumés. It is obvious that they only want their humanitarian action to serve their ambitions and careers. I read in the bio of a classical singer that she was a GWA for Perez de Cuellar at a time when the secretary general's office did not even have GWAs! This kind of opportunism makes it difficult for those who are sincere and dedicated to be taken seriously.

When the anti-personnel mines ban treaty passed in Ottawa in 1997 shortly after the tragic death of Princess Diana, I was asked by a journalist in New York City on the Bloomberg News channel, "Is it frustrating for you that Princess Diana posthumously received the credit for the passage of the treaty even though she had been a Red Cross VIP volunteer for a little more than a half a year, while you and others such as your friends at Handicap International have been working in the field for nearly a decade to make it happen? And do you think that her engagement was sincere?"

I replied, "First of all I would never attempt to judge the sincerity of another person in these matters but I can say that if her tragic death and her support for the ban, no matter how short, has made this treaty possible, not only am I not frustrated but I am

thrilled that we have arrived. I do not need to own it because neither the victory nor the Nobel Prize that the campaign received
for that matter belong to any of us. They both belong to the innocent victims of these horrible weapons and to those that we hope
will be spared in the future."

In 2001, I had already worked fourteen inspiring years for the
UNHCR and felt that I belonged to another generation of GWAs
like Audrey Hepburn and Peter Ustinov. During the meeting with
Shannon and High Commissioner Lubbers I welcomed him to
the UNHCR and said that it was time for me to move on and
leave the work to a new generation. Some time later I tendered my
resignation, but he refused to accept it and asked me to stay on
in the capacity of honorary goodwill ambassador for life as a kind
of senior diplomat for the cause of refugees. Since the cause of
refugees and the promotion of human rights is part and parcel of
who I am, I accepted because I knew that I would have continued
to advocate for the cause even without the title.

The UNHCR calls on me when they need me for special
projects and campaigns, and I am usually present at the Nansen
Refugee Award ceremony in Geneva every year. In October 2009
the prize was given in a posthumous ceremony in Washington,
DC, to the late Senator Ted Kennedy who had been a tireless
advocate for refugees during his long career as a senator in the US
Congress. The high commissioner could not be present so I went
and participated in a very moving ceremony in the presence of his
widow and other members of his family and his staff.

Since 2008 I have worked very actively with the Regional
UNHCR office for the Nordic and Baltic Countries in Stockholm
and am chairman of the board of the UNHCR Fund-raising
Foundation. My own foundation supports them with a yearly
donation and fees from some of my concerts I have sent directly
to the foundation.

I continue to go into the field; in October 2010 I went to Ethiopia for the UNHCR to visit refugees from Somalia and Eritrea.
Usually I can see some light at the end of the tunnel for some if
not all of the refugees I visit, but the possibility of finding suitable
solutions for them is remote because of the different yet extremely
difficult political situations in both countries. The camps in the

region are all are shamefully underfunded. My colleagues on the ground in partnership with the local authorities are making some positive progress in the domain of education for both the refugees and the local population. But we desperately need lasting political solutions for the near future, not in fifteen or twenty years; the international community is completely deaf to our cries and do not seem committed to finding the answers that will put an end to the suffering and injustice.

In the spring of 2012 Salafist forces invaded northern Mali and thousands fled across the borders into neighboring countries, including Burkina Faso. In July 2012 Ulf and I went to Burkina Faso to give the Gilda Vieira de Mello prize at the human rights film festival, Ciné Droit Libre. The UNHCR and I decided that I should also visit some of the camps while I was there. I met with refugees, and on my return I wrote an appeal that was published in *Le Monde*, asking for help for the emergency and for a longer-term political solution in the Sahel region of Africa. It will be an important challenge for the region and the world for years to come. I hope that we do not make the same mistakes as were made in Afghanistan.

On October 31, 2012, I went to the Geneva headquarters of the UNHCR for the first part of a day of celebration of twenty-five enriching and inspiring years with the organization. When High Commissioner Antonio Guterres and I came out the elevator on the ground floor of the atrium I saw my colleagues standing on every floor of the building surrounding me, beaming with pride. So many precious memories of those twenty-five years flooded through my mind—meetings with Leon, Shannon, and Søren; vaccinations that I did not want to take; and discussions in Sergio's office over a glass of wine for me and a whiskey for him. Before presenting me with a bronze sculpture, Antonio Guterres said, "You are really the princess of the humanitarian and human rights world; the authority of your voice is a precious instrument for our fight." I was moved and felt appreciated and loved.

THERE IS NO CONCLUSION, ONLY CONTINUATION

The sage lives openly with apparent duality and paradoxical
   unity...
Nurturing things without possessing them,
he works, but not for rewards;
he competes, but not for results.
When the work is done, it is forgotten.
That is why it lasts forever.

—from Tao Te Ching

M other Nature has been a source of wonder, meditation, and strength for me since I was a little girl in rural
Arkansas. I was able to let my imagination soar in the
surrounding nature that was my kingdom. I have always needed
to live in her embrace and she has helped me hear my inner voice
and stay true to myself. As the seasons change year after year
I observe in amazement the simple leaf that perfectly fulfills its
destiny throughout each of the changing seasons. I know that I
too have a destiny to fulfill; yet unlike the leaf I have the possibility to affect the outcome because I have been endowed with
reason and the ability to choose. And that is where the problems
begin, because we human beings arrogantly believe that we are
so superior to that leaf and other beings in nature. Yet it is we

who have introduced disharmony in the perfection of Creation. Neither the leaf nor the wind that pushes it decides the moment when it will fall from the tree in the autumn. Nor can I know what will lie around the next corner. I have been presented with fantastic opportunities during my life's journey and I felt prepared to assume the directions that I have chosen to take. Sometimes I envy the simplicity of the leaf's existence but I am more attached to the essential consciousness that I have needed to face the challenges that life has presented to me.

Since my birth many extraordinary beings have accompanied me on my journey from Stephens, Arkansas, to being the world citizen that I am today. I have shared many peak emotional experiences with them, full of love, joy, and pain, laughter and sorrow. They helped me to realize that Art is an expression of the human condition unique to human beings, and I believe that it is as essential to human existence as the water that we drink and the air that we breathe. My "angels" have inspired me to strive to serve my art and to live my life as an art. I am eternally grateful to those who have helped me to live a poetic life in an epoch that has little time for poetry.

The mathematician in me is very attracted to string theory, sometimes called the theory of everything. It implies that all matter can be reduced down to a string that oscillates. I like to think that there was one original chord that was dispersed by a big bang into a multitude of smaller chords that are continually searching for their source, for their truth.

The musician in me believes that by humbly serving my art I may merit the privilege of being an instrument that can vibrate in tune with that original chord.

There are moments during a concert when I feel that the audience is hearing collectively, as if with one ear, the divine music of the great geniuses. The music actually circumvents our small, self-important, controlling minds and goes directly to the source with such power that for just a spilt second we are reunited with the original vibration and reminded that we all belong to the family of humanity. I believe the place that the original chord vibrates in each one of us is the same place from which the Universal Declaration of Human Rights has sprung.

I become closer to little Barbara Ann with each passing day. I maintain and enhance her joy and curiosity to learn, to understand. I am fulfilling my need to make a humble contribution to humanity, though it amounts to just a few drops into that vast ocean. I give thanks every day for the blessings in my life and look forward to the wonders and miracles that await me.

For now, there is no conclusion to make of my journey, only continuation—and full speed ahead.

MUSICAL PORTRAIT

Barbara Hendricks is one of most beloved musicians in the world and during forty years of an outstanding international career, her vast repertoire has ranged from opera, lieder, and orchestral repertoire, to jazz and blues and the Negro spirituals that she has sung since her childhood. "My repertoire has no borders and the different musical styles that I sing nurture and enhance one another," she says.

She has recorded nearly one hundred albums and sold more than fourteen million. In 2006 she created Arte Verum, her own record label, to freely record the music she loves. In this *Musical Portrait*, she has chosen some of the most beautiful songs of her repertoire.

Arte Verum is offering to you this *Musical Portrait*. You can chose to either receive a free CD or download the sampler with high-definition MP3 files.

To receive your *Musical Portrait* of Barbara Hendricks:
1. Visit http://liftingmyvoice.barbarahendricks.com
2. Enter the code below
3. Register
Download code: BS14-1UE0-260J-03HV
Expiration date: June 1, 2019

If you have any questions, please contact: info@arteverum.com.

OFF THE RECORDS sprl | Rue d'Albanie, 69 | B-1060 Brussels Belgium | Tel. +32 2 524 49 24

COMPLETE DISCOGRAPHY
OF BARBARA HENDRICKS

Arte Verum

SONGS, LIEDER, AND CHAMBER MUSIC

Canciones Españolas — Spanish Songs
Songs by Enrique Granados, Fernando J. Obradors, Xavier
    Montsalvatge and Manuel de Falla
Barbara Hendricks (soprano), Love Derwinger (piano)

Ludwig van Beethoven — *Lieder & Volkslieder*
Barbara Hendricks (soprano), Love Derwinger (piano), Christian
    Bergqvist (violin), Leo Winland (cello)

Johannes Brahms — *Lieder*
Barbara Hendricks (soprano), Love Derwinger (piano)

Gabriel Fauré — *Songs & La Bonne Chanson*
Maurice Ravel — *Trois Poèmes de Mallarmé, Chansons
    madécasses*
Barbara Hendricks (soprano), Love Derwinger (piano), Swedish
    Chamber Ensemble

Gustav Mahler — *Lieder eines fahrenden Gesellen, Der
    Abschied, Rückert-Lieder*
Barbara Hendricks (soprano), Love Derwinger (piano), Swedish
    Chamber Ensemble
(release 2015)

Francis Poulenc — *Tel jour telle nuit* (songs)
Barbara Hendricks (soprano), Love Derwinger (piano)

Franz Schubert — *Ave Maria*
Barbara Hendricks (soprano), Roland Pöntinen (piano)
(maxi CD, 5 Lieder, 20' min.)

Franz Schubert — *Die schöne Müllerin D 795*
Barbara Hendricks (soprano), Roland Pöntinen (piano)

Franz Schubert — *Winterreise D 911*
Barbara Hendricks (soprano), Love Derwinger (piano)

Robert Schumann — *Lieder*
Barbara Hendricks (soprano), Roland Pöntinen (piano)

Dmitri Shostakovich — *Seven Poems of Alexander Blok Op. 127 & Trio for piano, violin and cello Op. 67*
Barbara Hendricks (soprano), Love Derwinger (piano), Christian Bergqvist (violin), Leo Winland & Claes Gunnarsson (cello)

OPERA, ORATORIO, AND ORCHESTRA

Endless Pleasure
Opera arias & songs by Henry Purcell and Georg Friedrich Handel
Barbara Hendricks (soprano), Drottningholms Barockensemble

Giovanni Battista Pergolesi — *Stabat Mater & Cantate Orfeo*
Barbara Hendricks (soprano), Ulrika Tenstam (mezzo-soprano), Drottningholms Barockensemble

***Shout for Joy* — Spiritual Christmas**
Barbara Hendricks (soprano), Ulrika Tenstam (mezzo-soprano), Harald Pettersson (hurdy-gurdy) Agneta Hellström (pipes), Björn Gäfvert (organ), Mats Bergström (guitar), Georg Riedel (double bass), Drottningholms Barockensemble

PORTRAIT

Barbara Hendricks — *A Musical Portrait* (2CD)
Opera arias, oratorio, songs, spirituals, jazz
with Love Derwinger, Roland Pöntinen, the Magnus Lindgren Quartet, the Berliner Philharmoniker, the Los Angeles Philharmonic Orchestra, the Orchestre National de France, Herbert von Karajan, Esa-Pekka Salonen, Sir Colin Davis, Carlo Maria Giulini

JAZZ AND BLUES

Barbara Sings the Blues
Billie Holiday — Bessie Smith — Duke Ellington
Barbara Hendricks, Magnus Lindgren Quartet
(also available in vinyl disc 180 gr., audiophile quality)

EMI

SONGS, LIEDER, AND CHAMBER MUSIC

Johann Sebastian Bach — *Cantates*
With Hakan Hardenberger (trumpet), Kammerorchester Carl Philipp
    Emanuel Bach
Conductor: Peter Shreier
Recorded in 1989

Johann Sebastian Bach — *Magnificat*
Antonio Vivaldi — *Gloria*
With Ann Murray, Jean Rigby, Uwe Heilmann, Jorma Hynninen
Academy Chorus of St. Martin-in-the-Fields
Conductor: Neville Marriner
Recorded in 1990

Hector Berlioz — *Les Nuits d'été*
Benjamin Britten — *Les Illuminations*
Chœurs de Radio France, English Chamber Orchestra
Conductor: Sir Colin Davis
Recorded in 1994

Georges Bizet — *Les Pêcheurs de perles*
With John Aller, Gino Quilico, Chœurs et Orchestre du Capitole de
    Toulouse (choir master: Marcel Seminara; singing master: Jeff
    Cohen)
Conductor: Michel Plasson
Recorded in 1989

Emmanuel Chabrier — *Messe* and *Air Gwendolyn*
Chœurs de Toulouse Midi-Pyrénées (choir master: José Aquino),
    Orchestre du Capitole de Toulouse
Conductor: Michel Plasson
Recorded in 1990

Claude Debussy — *Mélodies*
With Michel Béroff (piano)
Recorded in 1985

Gabriel Fauré — *Mélodies*
With Michel Dalberto, piano
Recorded in 1989

Charles Gounod — *Messe solennelle de Sainte-Cécile*
With Laurence Dale, Jean-Philippe Lafont, Chœurs de Radio France,
    Nouvel Orchestre Philharmonique
Conductor: Georges Prêtre
Recorded in 1984

Charles Gounod — *Mors et Vita*
With Nadine Denize, John Aller, José Van Dam, Orféon Donostiarra
    (choir master: José Antonio Sainz), Orchestre du Capitole de
    Toulouse
Conductor: Michel Plasson
Recorded in 1992

Joseph Haydn — *Schöpfungsmesse – Creation Mass*
With Ann Murray, Hans Peter Blochwitz, Mathias Holle, Leipzig
    Radio Choir (choir master: Gert Frischmuth), Staatskapelle
    Dresde
Conductor: Neville Marriner
Recorded in 1989

Wolfgang Amadeus Mozart — *Sacred Arias*
Academy of St. Martin-in-the-Fields and Academy Chorus
Conductor: Neville Marriner
Recorded in 1987

Wolfgang Amadeus Mozart — *Lieder et Mélodies*
With Maria Joao Pires (piano), Göran Söllscher (guitar), Orchestre de
    Chambre de Lausanne
Conductor: Mika Eichenholz
Recorded in 1990

Francis Poulenc — *Stabat mater & Gloria*
Chœurs de Radio France, Orchestre National de France
Conductor: Georges Prêtre
Recorded in 1984 (Stabat) & 1988 (Gloria)

Maurice Ravel & Henri Duparc — *Mélodies - Songs*
Orchestre de l'Opéra de Lyon
Conductor: John Eliot Gardiner
Recorded in 1988

Franz Schubert — *Lieder* Vol. I
With Radu Lupu (piano)
Recorded in 1986

Franz Schubert — *Lieder* Vol. 2
With Radu Lupu (piano), Sabine Meyer (clarinet), Bruno Schneider
   (horn)
Recorded in 1993

Richard Strauss — *Lieder*
With Ralf Gothoni (piano)
Recorded in 1991

Richard Strauss — *Vier Letzte Lieder*
Philadelphia Orchestra
Conductor: Wolfgang Sawallisch
Recorded in 1996

Heitor Villa-Lobos — *Bachianas Brasileiras 1, 5, 7*
With Eldon Fox (cello), Royal Philharmonic Orchestra
Conductor: Enrique Batiz
Recorded in 1986

Hugo Wolf — *Mörike et Goethe Lieder*
With Roland Pöntinen, piano
Recorded in 1999

Hommage à Jennie Tourel
With Staffan Scheja, piano
Recorded in 1997

Mélodies françaises – French Songs
With Michel Dalberto, piano - Cherubini Quartet
Recorded in 1992

Sacred Songs — Chants Sacrés
Eric Ericson Chamber Choir, Orphei Dranger, Stockholm Chamber
   Orchestra and members of the Swedish Radio Symphony
   Orchestra
Conductor: Eric Ericson
Recorded in 1990

OPERA, ORATORIO, AND ORCHESTRA

Georges Enesco — *Œdipe*
With Gino Quilico, José Van Dam, Gabriel Bacquier, Marjana
    Lipovsek, Brigitte Fassbaender, John Aler, Nicolai Gedda, Marcel
    Vanaud, Jocelyne Taillon, Cornelius Hauptmann, Laurence
    Albert, Jean-Philippe Courtis, Orfeon Donostiarra, Orchestre
    Philharmonique de Monte-Carlo
Conductor: Lawrence Foster
Recorded in 1989

Gabriel Fauré — *Requiem Orchestral Music*
With José Van Dam, Orfeon Donostiarra, Orchestre du Capitole de
    Toulouse
Conductor: Michel Plasson
Released 1985

Christoph Willibald Gluck — *Orphée et Eurydice*
With Anne Sofie von Otter, Brigitte Fournier, Monteverdi Choir,
    Orchestre de l'Opéra de Lyon
Conductor: John Eliot Gardiner
Recorded in 1989

Engelbert Humperdinck — *Hänsel und Gretel*
With Anne Sotie von Otter, Barbara Bonney, Andreas Schmidt,
    Hanna Schwarz, Marjana Liposek, Eva Lind, Bavarian Radio
    Symphony Orchestra
Conductor: Jeffrey Tate
Released in 1990

Wolfgang Amadeus Mozart — *Opera & Concert Arias*
With José-Luis Garcia (violin), Leslie Pearson (harpsichord), English
    Chamber Orchestra
Conductor: Jeffrey Tate
Recorded in 1984

Wolfgang Amadeus Mozart — *Opera & Concert Arias*
English Chamber Orchestra
Conductor: Ion Marin
Recorded in 1998

Carl Orff — *Carmina Burana*
With Michael Chance, Jeffrey Black, London Philharmonic
    Orchestra, Saint Albans Catherdral Choir
Conductor: Franz Welser-Möst
Recorded in 1989

Richard Strauss — *Der Rosenkavalier*
With Anne Sofie von Otter, Kurt Rydl, Richard Leech, Franz
    Grundheber, Staatskapelle Dresden
Conductor: Bernard Haitink
Recorded in 1990

Giuseppe Verdi — *Don Carlo*
With José Carreras, Mirella Freni, Nicolai Ghiaurov, Agnes Baltsa,
    Piero Cappuccilli, Ruggero Raimondi, José Van Dam, Edita
    Gruberova, Berlin State Opera Chorus, Berlin Philharmonie
    Orchestra
Conductor: Herbert von Karajan
Recorded in 1978

Au Cœur de l'Opéra – At the Heart of the Opera
Orchestre Philharmonique de Radio France
Conductor: Paavo Järvi
Recorded in 2003

Operetta Arias & Duets
With Gino Quilico, Ambrosian Singers, Philharmonia Orchestra,
    Orchestre de l'Opéra de Lyon
Conductor: Lawrence Foster
Recorded in 1992 and 1994

Operetta Duets
With Gino Quilico, Orchestre de l'Opéra de Lyon
Conductor: Lawrence Foster
Recorded in 1994

COMPILATIONS

Aaron Copland — *Quiet City*
Samuel Barber — *Knoxville: Summer of 1915*
London Symphony Orchestra
Conductor: Michael Tilson Thomas
Recorded in 1994

Barbara Hendricks Sings Christmas Favourites
Stockholm Chamber Orchestra, Eric Ericson Chamber Choir,
    Children Choir of the Adolf Fredriks Musikklasser
Conductors: Eric Ericson and Alain Lanceron
Recorded in 1995

Barbara Hendricks Sings Disney
London Voices (choir master: Terry Edwards), Abbey Road Ensemble
Conductor: Jonathan Tunick

Negro Spirituals
With Dmitri Alexeev (piano)
Recorded in 1983

Nordic Songs
With Roland Pöntinen (piano)
Recorded in 1998 & 2002

Spirituals, Give me Jesus
Moses Hogan Singers
Recorded in 1998

Tribute to Duke Ellington
Monty Alexander Trio
Recorded in 1994

A Tribute to George Gershwin: It's Wonderful
With Ira Coleman and Ed Thigpen, Guildhall String Ensemble
Conductor: Paul Bateman, arranged by Geoffrey Keezer
Released in 2001

La Voix du Ciel/ The Voice of Heaven
Compilation
Released in 1995

Other Recording Companies

Ludwig van Beethoven — Symphony No. 9
With Heljä Angervo, Hermann Winkler, Hans Sotin, Berliner
    Philharmoniker, Tokyo University of the Arts Chorus
Conductor: Herbert von Karajan
Recorded in 1977
Tokyo FM / King Records (Japan)

Johannes Brahms — Requiem
With José Van Dam, Wiener Singverein (Vienna Choir), Wiener
    Philharmoniker
Conductor: Herbert von Karajan
Recorded in 1985
DGG

Emmanuel Chabrier — *Le Roi malgré lui*
With Isabel Garcisanz, Gino Quilico, Peter Jeffes, Jean-Philippe
    Lafont, Bernadette Gardet (violon solo), Chœurs de Radio
    France (choir master: Jacques Jouineau), Nouvel Orchestre
    Philharmonique de Radio France
Conductor: Charles Dutoit
Recorded in 1985
ERATO

Claude Debussy — *La Damoiselle élue*
With Jocelyn Taillon, Chœur de l'Orchestre de Paris, Orchestre de
    Paris
Conductor: Daniel Barenboïm
Recorded in 1979
DGG

David Del Tredici — *Final Alice*
The Chicago Symphony Orchesta
Conductor: Sir Georg Solti
Recorded in 1981
DECCA

Gaetano Donizetti — *Don Pasquale*
With Gabriel Bacquier, Luca Canonici, Gino Quilico, René Schirrer,
    Chœurs de l'Opéra de Lyon (choir master: Donald Palumbo),
    Orchestre de l'Opéra de Lyon
Conductor: Gabriele Ferro
Released in 1990
ERATO

George Gershwin — *Barbara Hendricks Sings Gershwin*
With Katia and Marielle Labèque (piano)
Recorded in 1981
PHILIPS

George Gershwin — *Porgy and Bess*
With Willard White, McHenry Boatwright, François Clemmons,
    Arthur Thompson, Leona Mitchell, Florence Quivar, Barbara
    Conrad, Cleveland Orchestra and Chorus
Conductor: Lorin Maazel
Recorded in 1975
DECCA

Edvard Grieg — *Peer Gynt*
Oslo Philharmonic Chorus, Oslo Philharmonic Orchestra
Conductor: Esa-Pekka Salonen
Recorded in 1987
CBS

George Frideric Handel — *Salomon*
With Nancy Argenta, Joan Rodgers, Della Jones, Anthony Rolfe
    Johnson, Stephen Varcoe, Monteverdi Choir, English Baroque
    Soloists
Conductor: John Eliot Gardiner
Recorded in 1984
PHILIPS

George Frideric Handel — *Xerxes*
With Carolyn Watkinson, Paul Esswood, Ortrun Wenkel, AnneMarie
    Rodde, Ulrik Cold, Ulrich Studer, Ensemble vocal Jean Bridier,
    La Grande Écurie et la Chambre du Roy
Conductor: JeanClaude Malgoire
Recorded in 1979
CBS

Joseph Haydn — *Il Ritorno di Tobia*
With Benjamin Luxon, Linda Zoghby, Della Jones, Brighton Festival
    Chorus, Royal Philharmonie Orchestra
Conductor: Antal Dorati
Recorded in 1979
DECCA

Joseph Haydn — *L'Infedeltà Delusa*
With Claes H. Ahnsjo, Aldo Baldin, Michael Devlin - Orchestre de
    Chambre de Lausanne
Conductor: Antal Doráti
Recorded in 1980
PHILIPS

Joseph Haydn — *Nelson-Messe (Mass for Lord Nelson)*
With Marjana Lipovsek, Francisco Araiza, Peter Meven, Bavarian
    Radio Symphony Orchestra and Choir
Conductor: Sir Colin Davis
Recorded in 1985
PHILIPS

Edouard Lalo — *Le Roi d'Ys*
With Jean-Philippe Courtis, Dolores Ziegler, Eduardo Villa,
  Marcel Vanaud, Michel Piquemal, Philippe Boheen, Chœurs
  de Radio France (choir master: Michel Tranchant), Orchestre
  Philharmonique de Radio France
Conductor: Armin Jordan
Released in 1990
ERATO

Gustav Mahler — *Symphony no. 2*
With Christa Ludwig, The Westminster Choir, New York
  Philharmonic
Conductor: Leonard Bernstein
Recorded in 1987
DGG

Gustav Mahler — *Symphony no. 4*
Chaim Taub (violon), The Israel Philharmonie Orchestra
Conductor: Zubin Mehta
Recorded in 1979
DECCA

Gustav Mahler — *Symphony no. 4*
Los Angeles Philharmonic
Conductor: Esa Pekka Salonen
Recorded in 1992
SONY

Wolfgang Amadeus Mozart — *Die Zauberflöte*
With June Anderson, Ulrike Steinsky, Jerry Hadley, Robert Lloyd,
  Thomas Allen, Gottfried Hornik, Scottish Chamber Orchestra
  and Chorus
Conductor: Sir Charles Mackerras
Recorded in 1991
TELARC

Wolfgang Amadeus Mozart — Idomeneo
With Francisco Araiza, Susanne Mentzer, Roberta Alexander,
  Uwe Heilmann, Werner Hollweg, Harry Peeters, Chor- und
  SymphonieOrchester des Bayerischen Rundfunks
Conductor: Sir Colin Davis
Recorded in 1991
PHILIPS

Wolfgang Amadeus Mozart — *La Finta semplice*
With Siegfried Lorenz, Douglas Johnson, Ann Murray, Eva Lind,
    Hans Peter Blochwitz, Andreas Schmidt, Christine Schornsheim
    (harpsichord), Kammerorchester Carl Philipp Emanuel Bach
Conductor: Peter Schreier
Recorded in 1991
PHILIPS

Wolfgang Amadeus Mozart — *Le Nozze di Figaro*
With José Van Dam, Ruggero Raimondi, Academy of Saint
    Martinin-the-Fields
Conductor: Neville Marriner
Recorded in 1985
PHILIPS

Wolfgang Amadeus Mozart — *Mass in C minor*
With Janet Perry, Peter Schreier, Benjamin Luxon, David Bell (organ),
    Wiener Singverein (Vienna Choir), Berliner Philharmoniker
Conductor: Herbert von Karajan
Recorded in 1981
DGG

Wolfgang Amadeus Mozart — *Mass in C minor*
With Pamela Coburn, Hans-Peter Blochwitz, Andreas Schmidt,
    Rundfunkchor Leipzig (Leipzig Radio Choir), Staatskapelle
    Dresden
Conductor: Peter Schreier
PHILIPS

Carl Orff — *Carmina Burana*
With John Aller, Hakan Hagegard, London Symphony Chorus
    (choir master: Richard Cooke), The Boy's Choir of Saint Paul's
    Cathedral (choir master: Barry Rose), London Symphony
    Orchestra
Conductor: Eduardo Mata
Recorded in 1981
RCA

Giacomo Puccini — *La bohème*
With José Carreras, Gino Quilico, Angela Maria Blasi, Orchestre
    National de Radio France
Conductor: James Conlon
Recorded in 1987
ERATO

Giacomo Puccini — *Turandot*
With Placido Domingo, Ruggero Raimondi, Siegmund Nimsgern,
    Wiener Saengerknaben (Vienna Boys' Choir), Wiener
    Staatsopernchor (Vienna State Choir), Wiener Philharmoniker
Conductor: Herbert von Karajan
Recorded in 1981
DGG

Richard Strauss — *Die Ägyptische Helena*
With Gwyneth Jones, Matti Katsu, Dinah Bryant, Kenneth Jewell
    Chorale, Detroit Symphony Orchestra
Conductor: Antal Dorati
Recorded in 1979
DECCA

Giuseppe Verdi — *Falstaff*
With Renato Bruson, Katia Ricciarelli, Leo Nucci, Dalmacio
    Gonzalez, Lucia Valentini Terrani, Los Angeles Master Chorale
    (choir master: Roger Wagner), Los Angeles Philharmonic
    Orchestra
Conductor: Carlo Maria Giulini
Recorded in 1982
DGG

Antonio Vivaldi — *Motets*
Conductor: Jean-Claude Malgoire
Recorded in 1979
CBS

Richard Wagner — *Parsifal*
With José Van Dam, Victor von Halem, Kurt Moll, Peter Hofmann,
    Siegmund Nimsgern, Dunja Vejzovic, Chor der Deutschen
    Oper Berlin (choir master: Walter Hagen-Groll), Berliner
    Philharmoniker
Conductor: Herbert von Karajan
Recorded in 1980
DGG

Airs d'Opéra Français – French Opera Arias
Orchestre Philharmonique de Monte-Carlo
Conductor: Jeffrey Tate
Recorded in 1983
PHILIPS

A LIFE—AND HISTORY

1939   Marian Anderson sings to a crowd of seventy-five thousand
        at the Lincoln Memorial after being barred by the Daughters
        of the American Revolution from singing in Constitution
        Hall in Washington, DC

1948   **November 20, Barbara Hendricks is born in Stephens,
        Arkansas**

        Richard Strauss composes the last of his *Vier letzte Lieder* in
        Clarens, Switzerland

        December 10, the United Nations proclaim the Universal
        Declaration of Human Rights

1949   Death of Richard Strauss

1950   Beginning of the Korean War

1952   According to the Tuskegee Institute, for the first time since
        1881 no Negroes are lynched in the United States

1954   The Supreme Court rules in the decision of *Brown v. Board
        of Education* that school segregation is unconstitutional

1955   August 28, Emmett Till, aged fourteen, is beaten, shot, and
        killed in Money, Mississippi

        December 1, Rosa Parks refuses to give up her bus seat to a
        white man; the beginning of the Montgomery Bus Boycott
        led by Martin Luther King

1956   The home of Martin Luther King is bombed

        November 13, Montgomery Bus Boycott ends in victory after
        the Supreme Court declares segregation on public buses
        illegal.

Hungarian Revolution is crushed by the USSR

1957   March 25, Treaty of Rome creates the European Economic Community

The Little Rock Nine are met with violence and the Arkansas National Guard when they try to integrate Little Rock Central High School.

1960   Lunch counter sit-ins started at a Woolworth by four college students in Greensboro, North Carolina, spread throughout the South.

The Student Nonviolent Coordinating Committee (SNCC) is founded

John F. Kennedy is elected president of the United States

1961   August 13, Berlin Wall is built

Freedom Rides into the South

1962   Cuban Missile Crisis

James Meredith is the first Negro to be admitted to the University of Mississippi

1963   August 28, more than 250,000 people participate in the March on Washington and hear Martin Luther King deliver his "I Have a Dream" speech

November 22, President John F. Kennedy is assassinated in Dallas, Texas

1964   **BH elected "Miss Horace Mann" Homecoming Queen**

Mississippi Freedom Summer, a voter registration project. Two white students, Andrew Goodman and Michael Schwerner, and one Negro civil rights worker, James Chaney, are murdered.

Civil Rights Act of 1964 enacted in July

Martin Luther King Jr. receives the Nobel Peace Prize

1965   Selma to Montgomery March

BH graduates from Horace Mann High School and enters Lane College, Jackson, Tennessee

The Voting Rights Act passes and President Lyndon B. Johnson signs it into law, ending literacy tests and other obstacles used to prevent minorities from voting.

Malcolm X is assassinated

1966   Founding of the National Organization for Women (NOW) to fight for equality for women

SNCC head Stokely Carmichael uses the term "black power" for the first time

1967   Race riots erupt throughout the country

Thurgood Marshall becomes the first Negro justice of the Supreme Court

BH attends Nebraska Wesleyan University in Lincoln, Nebraska as an exchange student

1968   January 5, Alexander Dubček is elected first secretary of Czechoslovakia and the Prague Spring begins, only to be squashed by Soviet troops soon after

February 24, the Tet offensive ends in Vietnam

March 16, American soldiers massacre civilians in the town of My Lai

April 4, Martin Luther King is assassinated

May 3, Four hundred students occupy La Sorbonne in Paris

June 6, Robert Kennedy is assassinated

BH attends Aspen Music Festival and meets Jennie Tourel

1969   **BH transfers to the University of Nebraska and receives bachelor of science in chemistry and mathematics**

BH begins studies with Jennie Tourel at the Juilliard School New York City

Olof Palme becomes prime minister of Sweden

Willy Brandt becomes chancellor of West Germany

Stonewall Riots mark the beginning of the gay rights movement

1970   **BH wins first prize at the Liederkranz Competition in New York City**

Four students at Kent State University are shot dead by the Ohio National Guard

1971   **BH wins special prize at Concours de Genève**

1972   **BH wins first prize and Mozart Prize at Concours International de Paris**

1973   **BH graduates from the Juilliard School with a bachelor of music in voice**

BH wins National Opera Award

BH wins second prize at Naumburg Competition

BH has Paris recital debut

September 11, Military coup led by General Pinochet overthrows Chile's democratically elected government, and president Salvador Allende is assassinated

Jennie Tourel dies

Paris Peace Accords establish the end of the Vietnam War

BH tours in Israel with Berlin Chamber Choir and Israel Chamber Orchestra

1974   **BH has United States opera debut at San Francisco Opera in Cavalli's *L'Ormindo***

BH has European opera debut at Glyndebourne in Cavalli's *La Calisto*

American premiere of Gilbert Amy's *D'un espace déployé*, Chicago Symphony Orchestra, Sir Georg Solti and Amy conductors

BH has recital debut in Scandinavia in Stockholm's Konserthus with Staffan Scheja, piano

1975   Khmer Rouge seize power in Cambodia

American premiere of Janáček's *The Cunning Little Vixen*, Santa Fe Opera, Colin Graham directing

Recording debut, Clara in *Porgy and Bess*, Cleveland Symphony Orchestra, Lorin Maazel, conducting

Debut Holland Festival of Gluck's *Orfeo*, Hans Vonk conducting

1976   **New York City recital debut in Town Hall with Lawrence Skrobacs, piano, and Richard Stoltzman, clarinet**

Jimmy Carter is elected president of the United States

World premiere of David Del Tredici's *Final Alice*

1977   **Debut in Salzburg Festival, Mahler Second Symphony, Vienna Philharmonic, James Levine, conductor**

Asian debut in Japan, Beethoven's Ninth Symphony, Berlin Philharmonic, Herbert von Karajan, conductor

Orchestra debut, Radio France, Pergolesi's *Stabat Mater*

Antiapartheid activist Steve Biko dies in police custody in South Africa

Amnesty International receives the Nobel Peace Prize

1978   **Debut with Deutsche Oper Berlin as Susanna in Mozart's *Le nozze di Figaro*, Götz Friedrich, director; Daniel Barenboim, conductor**

Aix-en-Provence Festival, Susanna in Mozart's *Le nozze di Figaro*, Neville Marriner, conductor

Marries Martin T:son Engström, Menton, France

The body of Aldo Moro is found in a parked car in Rome

1979   Americans are taken hostage at the US embassy in Tehran, Iran

The USSR invades Afghanistan

1980   **Salzburg Easter Festival, Das Erste Blumenmädchen in Wagner's *Parsifal*, Herbert von Karajan, director and conductor**

John Lennon is murdered in New York City

1981   **Sebastian Amadeus is born**

Chorégies d'Orange, Pamina in Mozart's *Zauberflöte*

François Mitterrand is elected president of France

Martial law is introduced in Poland after Solidarity protests

1982 **Debut at Covent Garden in London and Teatro Comunale in Florence, Nanetta in Verdi's *Falstaff*; Ronald Eyre, director; Carlo Maria Giulini, conductor**

Debut with Paris Opera in Gounod's *Romeo et Juliette*; Georges Lavaudant director; Alain Lombard, conductor

La Scala Milano recital debut, Ralf Gothoni, piano

1983 **Salzburg Festival, Brahms's Requiem, Herbert von Karajan, conductor**

1984 **Jennie Victoria is born**

Chorégies d'Orange, Micaëla in *Carmen* with José Carreras

Death toll reaches one million from the famine in Ethiopia

Winter Olympics are held in Sarajevo

1985 Gorbachev introduces glasnost and perestroika in the USSR

1986 **Receives Commandeur des Arts et des Lettres from the French Minister of Culture**

Debut at Metropolitan Opera as Sophie in Strauss's *Der Rosenkavlier* with Elisabeth Söderström and Brigitte Fassbaender; Jeffrey Tate and James Levine, conductors

Olof Palme is assassinated in Stockholm, Sweden

1987 **Becomes UNHCR goodwill ambassador and travels to Zambia to visit refugee camps**

Opera debut at La Scala, Milan, as Susanna in Mozart's *Le nozze di Figaro*; Giorgio Strehler, director; Riccardo Muti, conductor

Film debut as Mimì in Puccini's *La bohème*, with José Carreras; Luigi Comencini, director; James Conlon, conductor

1988 **Receives doctorate degree from Nebraska Wesleyan University**

Prix Grand Siècle Laurent-Perrier for her service to French culture and society

Sings Susanna in Mozart's *Le nozze di Figaro* at the Metropolitan Opera

Lockerbie bombing of Pan Am Flight 103

1989   Protests in Tiananmen Square, Beijing

November 9, Records Mozart's C-minor Mass in East Berlin, Peter Schreier, conductor

November 9, Fall of Berlin Wall

1990   **Honorary Member of the International Institute of Humanitarian Law, Sanremo, Italy**

Honorary Doctor Université Catholique, Louvain

Member of Swedish Academy of Music

1991   First Gulf War begins

Peace Concert in Dubrovnik

1992   Maastricht Treaty marks the founding of the European Union

Bosnia Herzegovina declares independence

President de l'Association "á la première heure du premier jour"

Honorary Doctor of Law, University of Dundee, Scotland

1993   **Inauguration gala for Bill Clinton**

World premiere of Tobias Picker's *The Rain in the Trees*, Pittsburgh Symphony; Lorin Maazel conductor

Chevalier du Legion d'Honneur from François Mitterrand

Peace concert Sarajevo

1994   Nelson Mandela is elected president of South Africa

Ten thousand French and Swiss schoolchildren invite BH to sing with them a song for peace in Bosnia at the foot of the Eiffel Tower in Paris

Guest of President Mitterrand on the first state visit of a French president to South Africa

Genocide in Rwanda

Debut at Montreux Jazz Festival with Monty Alexander, Ira Coleman, Ed Thigpen

1995   **At the invitation of Johannes Rau (later German president) sings for fifth anniversary of German reunification**

Films *The Rakes Progress* with Inger Åby, director; Esa Pekka Salonen, conductor. Film receives Prix Italia

Students in Orange, France (sixth through ninth grades), vote to name their school Collège Barbara Hendricks

Srebrenica Massacre, in which eight thousand Muslim men are murdered and women raped by Serbian forces

Dayton Accords end war in Bosnia Herzegovina

1996   Kofi Annan becomes seventh secretary general of the UN

Death of François Mitterrand

Sings "Le temps des cerises" at the Place de la Bastille in memory of President François Mitterrand

Sings Fauré's "Pie Jesu" for Mitterrand's funeral

1997   **Secret meeting with Aung San Suu Kyi, who is under house arrest in Burma**

Mine Ban Treaty

Nobel Peace Prize awarded to International Campaign to Ban Landmines (Handicap International)

1998   **Starts Barbara Hendricks Foundation for Peace and Reconciliation**

Barbara Hendricks's Rose bred by François Dorieux II

Sings Liu in Puccini's *Turandot* in décor of the Forbidden City in Beijing, Zhang Yimou director, Zubin Mehta conductor

Rome Statute of International Criminal Court is adopted

1999   **Honorary Doctor, Université de Paris VIII**

       Member of the jury at Cannes Film Festival

       NATO bombing of Serbia leads to Serbian withdrawal from Kosovo

2000   **Sings Tatiana in Tchaikovsky's *Eugene Onegin* at the Nice Opera; Ivo Lipanovic, conductor**

       Honorary Doctor of Music, Juilliard School; gives the commencement speech

       World premiere of Sven-David Sandström's *Mölna Elegy*, Gotland Chamber Music

2001   Attack on the World Trade Center in New York City

       Sings at the Nobel Peace Prize Ceremony and Gala for Kofi Annan and the United Nations

       Lions Clubs International Prize for humanitarian engagements, Indianapolis

       Humanitarian crisis of epic proportions in Democratic Republic of the Congo

2002   **Sings for East Timor's first Independence Day celebrations**

       East Timor becomes a member of the United Nations

       World premiere of Bruno Mantovani's *Das erschafft der Dichter nicht;* Ensemble Intercontemporain, Paris

       UNHCR Lifetime Goodwill Ambassador

2003   **Patron with Sergio Vieira de Mello for International Film Festival and Forum on Human Rights (FIFDH), Genève**

       Invasion of Iraq

       Marries Sven Ulf Erik Englund; Sweden

       UN Baghdad office is attacked and twenty-two staff members are killed, including the UN representative, Sergio Vieira de Mello

       Anna Lindh, Swedish foreign minister, is assassinated in Stockholm

       War in Darfur begins

2004   The CIA admits that there was no imminent threat from
       WMD before the invasion of Iraq

       Abu Ghraib prison torture revealed

       World premiere of Arvo Pärt's *L'Abbé Agathon*

       **World premiere of Peter Eötvös's *Angels in America*,
       Theater du Chatelet, Philippe Calvario, director; Peter
       Eötvös, conductor**

       **Premio Internacional Xifra Heras, Girona University,
       Spain**

       **Médaille de la Ville de Paris from Maire Bertrand
       Delanoë**

2005   Hurricane Katrina devastates US Gulf Coast

       BH starts own record label, Arte Verum

       Member of Jury Premi Internacional Catalunya

2006   Ellen Johnson Sirleaf took office as president of Liberia and is
       the first female head of state in Africa

       **Catalonia highest civil distinction, Creu de Sant Jordi,
       from the President Pasqual Maragall**

       **World premiere of Johan Hammerth's *Fyra
       kàrlekssånger*, Jönköpingings Sinfonietta, Jan Stigmer,
       conductor**

2007   Buddhist monks lead protests in Burma

       **Inauguration of Barbara Hendricks Salle du Concert,
       Laval, France**

       Receives medal of city of Sarajevo

2008   East Timor President José Ramos Horta is seriously injured
       in an assassination attempt

       Crash of world economy

       Barack Hussein Obama is elected president of the United
       States

       Artist in residence, Piteå, Sweden

       **BH Foundation gives Sergio Vieira de Mello Prize
       FIFDH**

2009   **President of UNHCR's Fundraising Foundation, Stockholm**

          Receives Save the Children Award in Madrid

          Performs at the UNHCR's Nansen Award given posthumously to Senator Edward Kennedy

2010   American troops withdraw from Iraq

          Beginning of Arab Spring

          Fourth jazz concert at Olympia, Paris, France

          Release memoirs, *Ma Voie,* in France

          Aung San Suu Kyi is released from house arrest

          Visits refugees from Somalia and Eritrea in Ethiopia

2011   Osama bin Laden is killed in Pakistan

          "Promenade Barbara Hendricks" inaugurated in Saint-Avertin, France

2012   **BH Foundation gives Gilda Vieira de Mello prize in memory of her son Sergio at FIFDH in Geneva and Ouagadougou, Burkina Faso**

          Visits Malian refugees in Burkina Faso

          Birth of first grandchild

          UNHCR celebrates BH's twenty-five years service to the refugee cause

          Re-election of President Barack Obama

2013   Ceasefire agreement is signed in Darfur, Sudan

          Aung San Suu Kyi's first visit to Europe began in Bern, Switzerland, where she and BH meet again

          Release of memoirs in Spain, *En Propia Voz*

          Received HM the King's Medal from Swedish King Carl Gustaf for her artistic achievements

          Advisory Council for Women for Africa Foundation

2014   **Arte Verum's fourteenth CD is released**

INDEX